The New
BEACHCOMBER'S GUIDE
to the Pacific Northwest

The New Beachcomber's Guide to the Pacific Northwest

Completely Revised and
Expanded 2019

J. Duane Sept

HARBOUR
PUBLISHING

HARBOUR PUBLISHING CO. LTD.
P.O. Box 219, Madeira Park, BC, VON 2H0
www.harbourpublishing.com

All photographs copyright © the author, except the following: Robin Agarwal (Taylor's seahare, Japanese bubble snail, frost-spot nudibranch); Minette Layne (jelly-dwelling anemone); Jerry Kirkhart (surfgrass limpet); Linda Schroeder (opalescent squid).

Edited by Patricia Wolfe
Indexed by Michelle Chiang
Cover design by Setareh Ashrafologhalai

Text design by Shed Simas / Onça Design
Printed and bound in Canada

Harbour Publishing acknowledges the support of the Canada Council for the Arts, which last year invested $153 million to bring the arts to Canadians throughout the country.

Nous remercions le Conseil des arts du Canada de son soutien. L'an dernier, le Conseil a investi 153 millions de dollars pour mettre de l'art dans la vie des Canadiennes et des Canadiens de tout le pays.

We also gratefully acknowledge financial support from the Government of Canada and from the Province of British Columbia through the BC Arts Council and the Book Publishing Tax Credit.

LIBRARY AND ARCHIVES CANADA CATALOGUING IN PUBLICATION

Title: The new beachcomber's guide to the Pacific Northwest : completely revised and expanded 2019 / J. Duane Sept.
Other titles: Beachcomber's guide to seashore life in the Pacific Northwest
Names: Sept, J. Duane, 1950- author.
Description: 2019 edition. | Previously published under title: The beachcomber's guide to seashore life in the Pacific Northwest. | Includes bibliographical references and index.
Identifiers: Canadiana (print) 20190051310 | Canadiana (ebook) 20190051337 | ISBN 9781550178371 (softcover) | ISBN 9781550178579 (HTML)
Subjects: LCSH: Seashore animals—Pacific Coast (North America)—Identification. | LCSH: Seashore plants—Pacific Coast (North America)—Identification. | LCSH: Seashore biology—Northwest, Pacific. | LCGFT: Field guides.
Classification: LCC QH104.5.N6 S46 2019 | DDC 578.769/909795—dc23

Table of Contents

Introduction

The Pacific Northwest Coast is one of the world's richest, most diverse habitats for intertidal marine life. Hundreds of species and subspecies of animals and plants live along these shores, and each of them has developed a unique niche in which it lives, coexisting with its neighbors. To learn what these species are and how they are interrelated is a step toward learning how all the parts of the world work together in the giant puzzle we call life.

The intertidal zone—that part of the shoreline that is submerged in water at high tide and exposed at low tide—is a particularly gratifying place to observe wildlife and plant life alike. Species are diverse, abundant and endlessly interesting, and many of them can be observed easily without any special knowledge or equipment. Some are animals that are found both intertidally and subtidally, but whose appearance is completely transformed out of water. Anemones, for instance, are often seen on the beach with their tentacles closed, and some marine worms close their tentacles or leave distinctive signs on a beach when the tide recedes. Other species, such as the moonglow anemone or Merten's chiton, occur in several color forms.

This guide is designed to enhance your experience of observing and identifying animal and plant species in the many fascinating intertidal sites of the Pacific Northwest. Many of these areas are so rugged they seem indestructible, but in fact they are fragile ecosystems, affected by every visit from humans. Please tread carefully, exercise caution and let your eyes, camera and magnifying glass be your main tools for exploring the seashore.

Understanding Tides

Tides are caused primarily by the gravitational forces of both the moon and the sun upon the earth. These gravitational forces override the centrifugal forces of the earth's rotation. They create a high tide, or "bulge" (see figure on next page) of water on the earth near the moon, which has a stronger gravitational effect than the sun because it is so much closer to the earth. A similar "bulge" is created on the opposite side of the earth. When the tide is high in one area, the displacement of water

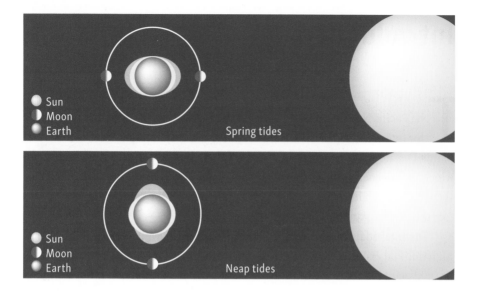

Sun
Moon
Earth
Spring tides

Sun
Moon
Earth
Neap tides

causes a low tide in another area. The earth makes one complete revolution under the "bulges" during one tide cycle, so there are two high tides and two low tides during each tide cycle. Tides have the greatest range when the moon is closest to Earth.

During the new moon, the combined gravitational pull of the sun and the moon generate even higher tides and correspondingly lower tides. During the full moon, however, the moon's and sun's gravitational pull oppose each other, which dampens the tidal effect. The lunar cycle is completed every 27⅓ days, thus the moon orbits earth 13 times each year. On each day of the year there are two high tides and two lows. The best time to view intertidal creatures is close to the lowest tide, so plan to arrive an hour or two before low tide. You can find this time—as well as the predicted height of the tide—by checking tide tables, available from tourist, sporting goods and marine supply stores and often published in local newspapers. (Keep in mind that these tables are usually based on standard time and on a particular geographical reference point, so daylight savings time and your actual location may have to be factored in.)

Tidal heights are measured from different reference points in the USA and Canada. For the most accurate information, use the reference point closest to the area you plan to visit. In the USA, tides of 0.0′ are the average of the lower low tides for that year. Tides lower than this value are referred to as minus tides in the USA. In Canada, the published tide tables are 2.5′ (0.8 m) lower than equivalent values in the USA. Times when tide levels are lower than 0.0′ in the USA and 2.5′ (0.8 m) in

Low and high tide from the same location.

Canada are excellent for observing animal and plant life at intertidal sites. Any visit will be rewarding, but these are the optimal times to see intertidal life.

Understanding Intertidal Habitats

The rich marine life found "at the edge" of the Pacific Ocean is due in part to the wide variety of habitats in this range. Some creatures occupy quite a limited habitat, hardly venturing from a small area throughout most of their adult lives, because they can tolerate a very narrow range of conditions. Other more adaptable species can be seen in several intertidal zones and into the ocean depths.

The intertidal region comprises several different habitats and zones. Each combination provides a unique set of physical conditions in which many creatures survive and coexist.

These two very different shorelines (rocky and sandy) illustrate the bands of marine life at various intertidal levels.

An intertidal zone is characterized by several "key" species of marine flora and fauna—species typically found within that zone. The zone may be only a favored location; the species may occur in other zones as well.

SAND BEACHES AND MUDFLATS

We often picture the Pacific coast as a vast sandy beach with gentle waves rolling toward shore, but this is only one of the many environments where seashore creatures have survived for millennia.

Thousands of years have passed since the last glaciers left their enormous deposits of sand and clay. Through time, the movement of land and sea have shifted huge volumes of these materials, which have provided numerous intertidal creatures with a place to burrow. The presence of many of these animals can be detected only by a slight dimple or irregularity in the surface of the sand or mud.

Sand Beaches

Sand beaches are commonly found in both exposed and protected sites. Exposed sandy areas occur as sandspits or sand beaches. Creatures commonly seen on such beaches include the Pacific razor-clam and purple olive. These and other species are well adapted to survive the surf-pounded beach. Protected beaches or sand flats,

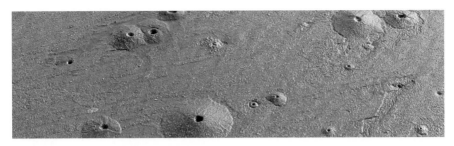
This sandy beach is home to the bay ghost shrimp.

away from the pounding surf, are a significantly different habitat, often occupied by Dungeness crab, Nuttall's cockle and other species that are not adapted to the pounding waves of the outer coast. Some species occur in both exposed and protected sand beach habitats.

This mud beach is home to several worms and clams.

Mudflats

Mudflats are situated in sheltered locations such as bays and estuaries. Like sandy shores, they support a smaller variety of obvious intertidal life than rocky shorelines. The yellow shore crab and Pacific gaper are species to look for in these areas. Several species are characteristic of both mudflats and sand beaches. These include Lewis's moonsnail, Pacific geoduck and softshell-clam.

ROCKY SHORES

Creatures have evolved special adaptations to live in certain habitats, so different species are found on exposed rocky shores than on sheltered ones. The California

Rocky shores occur in a number of different forms. These rocks move little from year to year.

This boulder area provides a habitat for a wide variety of life forms.

mussel and black Katy chiton occur in exposed areas, whereas more sheltered rocky sites harbor such creatures as the painted anemone and hairy hermit.

Marine biologists divide rocky shores, as all shorelines, into several distinct intertidal zones: the splash zone and the high, middle and low intertidal zones. On rocky shores these zones are especially evident. The placement of these creatures in the various zones is likely a complex combination of adaptations and environmental factors, including heat tolerance, food availability, shelter and suitable substrate availability. The presence of predators may also limit the range of intertidal zones an animal can inhabit. Purple stars, for example, prey upon the California mussel, which pushes the mussel into a higher intertidal habitat.

Splash Zone

This zone can be easily overlooked as an intertidal zone, and the few small species present here seem to occur haphazardly. But these creatures are actually out of the water more than they are in it, so they must be quite hardy to tolerate salt, heat and extended dry periods. The acorn barnacle and ribbed limpet are two of these species.

High Intertidal Zone

This zone is characterized by such species as the mask limpet, aggregating anemone and California mussel. Nail brush seaweed is one plant species that occurs in this zone, typically on top of rocks. (Seaweed species, like invertebrates, live in specific areas of the intertidal habitat.)

Middle Intertidal Zone

This zone, also called the mid-intertidal zone, is home to the Vosnesensky's isopod and plate limpet, as well as feather boa kelp and rockweed. Most creatures in the mid-intertidal zone are normally not found in subtidal waters.

Low Intertidal Zone

The sunflower star and purple sea urchin are among the many creatures to be found in the low intertidal zone, site of the most diverse and abundant marine life in the entire intertidal area. Creatures here often are found in subtidal waters too. In the low intertidal zone there is more food, shelter and probably a greater chance that the animal will be caught in a very low tide, as low tides affect this zone only rarely during the year compared with the high and mid-intertidal zones. The time marine life is exposed to the heat of the sun is also reduced; as a result heat is not a major limiting factor on the creatures of the low intertidal zone. There are also more species to be found in subtidal waters.

MICRO HABITATS

Under Rocks

This environment is an important one. Whether the shore is rock, gravel, sand or mud, many species such as the daisy brittle star, purple shore crab and black prickleback require this micro habitat for survival.

Tidepools

The grainyhand hermit, aggregating anemone, mossy chiton, stout shrimp, umbrella crab and many other species are often found in tidepools but are not restricted to them. These creatures live in a somewhat sheltered environment that may be different from the zone in which the pool is located.

Floating Docks and Pilings

These man-made sites attract a wide range of marine plants and invertebrates. Like rocky shores, they provide solid places for settling. The short plumose anemone, giant barnacle and shield-backed kelp crab commonly invade this habitat. Some are often attached to or living on the floating dock, so viewing is not restricted to low tides.

Harvesting Shellfish

One of the great pleasures of beachwalking can be gathering shellfish for a fresh dinner of seafood. Be aware that you need a license to harvest seashore life such as clams, oysters and (in some areas) seaweeds, and there are harvesting seasons and bag limits. Before you take any shellfish, check with local officials for current restrictions. Shellfish harvest areas may also be closed due to pollution, or to harmful algal blooms such as red tides (see next page). Check with local authorities to make sure the area you wish to harvest is safe. Then let the fun begin!

RED TIDE

At certain times of the year, tiny algae reproduce rapidly in what is referred to as an algal bloom. Each of these algae can contain minute amounts of toxins, which are then concentrated in the body tissues of filter-feeding animals such as oysters, clams, mussels, scallops and other shellfish. Once the algae die, the animals' bodies begin to cleanse themselves of the toxins naturally, a process that takes time—as little as four to six weeks, but as long as two years for species such as butter clams.

Some experts believe that harmful algal blooms can produce a poison (saxitoxin) that is 10,000 times more toxic than cyanide. So if you eat even a tiny amount of shellfish that have ingested these toxins, you can become seriously or even fatally ill with paralytic shellfish poisoning (PSP). Symptoms include difficulty in breathing, numbness of tongue and lips, tingling in fingertips and extremities, diarrhea, nausea, vomiting, abdominal pain, cramps and chills. Reports of this ailment go as far back as human occupation along the Pacific Northwest Coast. Authorities regularly monitor shellfish for toxin levels, and affected areas are closed to shellfish harvesting. Watch for local postings of closures on public beaches and marinas, but to make sure, check with a PSP hotline or ask fisheries officials before harvesting any shellfish.

PSP (RED TIDE) HOTLINES

To obtain current marine toxin information contact the following:
BC: Fisheries and Oceans Canada, contact your local DFO office.
WASHINGTON: Washington Department of Health, PSP Hotline, (800) 562-5632.
OREGON: Oregon Department of Agriculture, Shellfish Harvest Hotline, (800) 448-2474.

Protecting Our Marine Resource

Today more than ever it is essential for us to take responsibility for protecting our natural surroundings, including our marine environments. At many coastal sites human presence is becoming greater—sometimes too great. Habitat destruction, mostly from trampling, has been severe enough to cause authorities to close some intertidal areas to the public. In most cases this is not willful damage but people's unawareness of how harmful it can be simply to move around a seashore habitat.

To walk safely through an intertidal area, choose carefully where to step and where not to step. Sand and rock are always the best surfaces to walk on, when they are available. Mussels have strong shells, which can often withstand the weight of a person without difficulty. Barnacles can also provide a secure, rough walking surface and can quickly recolonize an area if they become dislodged.

Please return all rocks carefully to their original positions, taking care not to leave the underside of any rock exposed. Take all containers back with you when you leave, as well as any debris from your visit. And please leave your dog at home when you visit intertidal sites.

Observing Intertidal Life

A magnifying glass is a must for any visit to the seashore, and a camera is the best way to take souvenirs. Another excellent item to take along is a clear plastic jar or plastic pail. Fill it with cool salt water and replace the water frequently. This will enable you to observe your finds for a short time with minimal injury to them. Make sure to return them to the exact spot where you found them. And if you must handle sea creatures, do so with damp hands so their protective slime coatings will not be harmed.

A NOTE OF CAUTION

Before you visit an intertidal site, be aware of tide times and plan accordingly. During any visit to the beach it is important to stay out of low-lying areas that have no exit, and to keep a close watch on the water at all times. Many an unsuspecting beachcomber has become stranded on temporary islands formed by the incoming tide.

Strong wave action can take you by surprise. Dangerous waves come by a number of different names—sneaker waves, rogue waves, etc.—all of which indicate the nature of waves in exposed situations. Unexpected and powerful waves can and do take beach visitors from the shore. If you do get caught off guard by a wave, the best defense is to lie flat, grabbing onto any available rocks that may provide a handhold. This will make it possible for the wave to roll over you rather than taking you out to sea. A vigorous surf can also toss logs up on shore unexpectedly. Please be careful!

Seaweeds can present a slippery obstacle to those venturing into intertidal areas. In order to provide food and protection for the many creatures found along the shore, these plants cover just about everything. In some areas a two-footed and two-handed approach is necessary to move around safely. Rubber boots with a good tread will help you observe intertidal life without slipping or getting soaked. It's a good idea to exercise caution around barnacles and such creatures, as their shells are hard and sharp-edged.

Even for a short visit, take along a backpack, some drinking water and a small first-aid kit.

Visiting the intertidal sites of the Pacific Northwest is one of the most rewarding pastimes on Earth. A little bit of preparation and a healthy dose of caution will help make every trip to the seashore a wonderful adventure.

Getting the Most out of This Guide

The field guide section of this book includes color photographs of the common animals and plants to be seen along the Pacific Northwest seashore, and concise information that will help you identify species.

❶ INTRODUCED SPECIES: Introduced species are noted with a symbol that indicates that this species is not native to this area. This alien species has been introduced by accident or for a specific purpose by humans.

NAME: The current or most useful common name for the species; also the scientific name, a Latin name by which the species is known all over the world. This scientific name has two parts: the genus (a grouping of species with common characteristics) and the species. The Latin name is followed by the authority. The authority is the name of the first scientist and author who officially described that species in scientific literature and it is followed by the year of its publication. If the authority is in brackets then the original genus of the species has changed and the new name is now recognized.

OTHER NAMES: Any other common or scientific names known for the species.

DESCRIPTION: Distinguishing physical features, behavior and/or habitat to aid in identifying the species.

SIZE: Dimension(s) of the largest individuals commonly seen.

HABITAT: The type of area where the species lives.

RANGE: The area of the Pacific Northwest where the species is found.

NOTES: Other information of interest, usually relating to the natural history of the species or ways in which it differs from a similar species.

PLATE 1. Limpets. **A:** Whitecap Limpet, *Acmaea mitra*; **B:** Ringed Blind Limpet, *Cryptobranchia concentrica*; **C:** Giant Owl Limpet, *Lottia gigantea*; **D:** Shield Limpet, *Lottia pelta*, rock form. SHELLS NOT TO SCALE.

PLATE 2. Limpets. **A–D:** Shield Limpet, *Lottia pelta*; **A:** rock form; **B:** mussel form; **C:** feather boa kelp form; **D:** eelgrass form (formerly eelgrass limpet). SHELLS NOT TO SCALE.

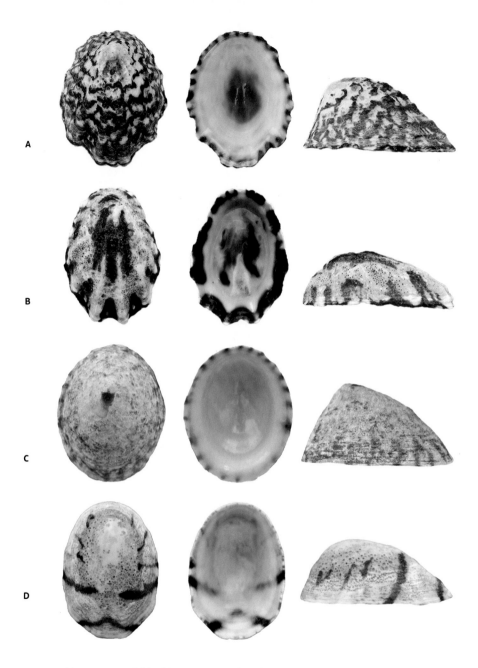

PLATE 3. Limpets. **A–B:** Ribbed Limpet, *Lottia digitalis*; **A:** rock form; **B:** goose barnacle form; **C–D:** Dwarf Ribbed Limpet, *Lottia paradigitalis*; **C:** rock form; **D:** goose barnacle form. SHELLS NOT TO SCALE.

PLATE 4. Limpets. **A:** Rough Limpet, *Lottia scabra*; **B:** Black Limpet, *Lottia asmi*; **C:** Fenestrate Limpet, *Lottia fenestrata*; **D:** Mask Limpet, *Lottia persona*. SHELLS NOT TO SCALE.

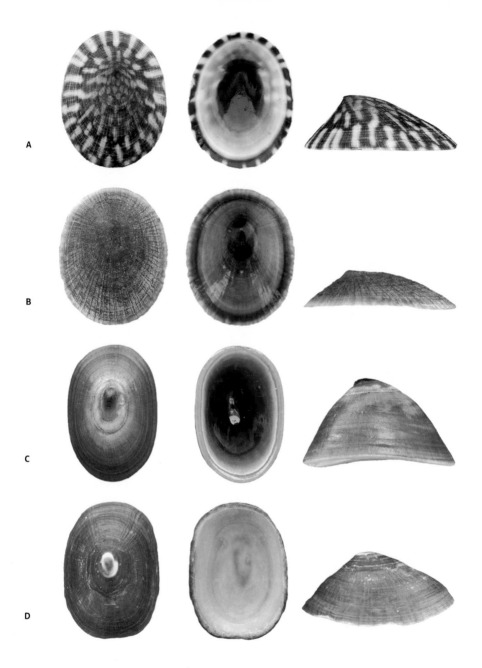

PLATE 5. Limpets. **A–B:** Pacific Plate Limpet, *Lottia scutum*; **C:** Seaweed Limpet, *Discurria insessa*; **D:** Unstable Limpet, *Lottia instabilis*, kelp form. SHELLS NOT TO SCALE.

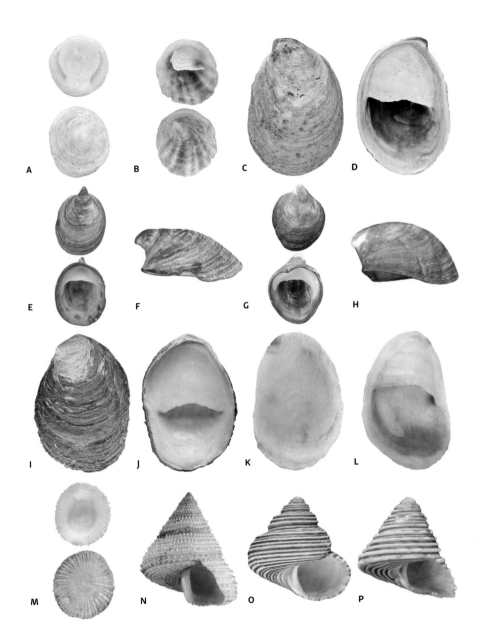

PLATE 6. Slippersnails & snails. **A:** Flat Hoofsnail, *Antisabia panamensis*; **B:** Pacific Half-slippersnail, *Crepipatella lingulata*; **C–D:** Onyx Slippersnail, *Crepidula onyx*; **E–F:** Hooked Slippersnail, *Garnotia adunca*; **G–H:** Atlantic Convex Slippersnail, *Crepidula convexa*; **I–J:** Northern White Slippersnail, *Crepidula nummaria*; **L:** Western White Slippersnail, *Crepidula perforans*; **M:** Reticulate Button Snail, *Trimusculus reticulatus*; **N:** Purple-ring Topsnail, *Calliostoma annulatum*; **O:** Blue Topsnail, *Calliostoma ligatum*; **P:** Channelled Topsnail, *Calliostoma canaliculatum*. SHELLS NOT TO SCALE.

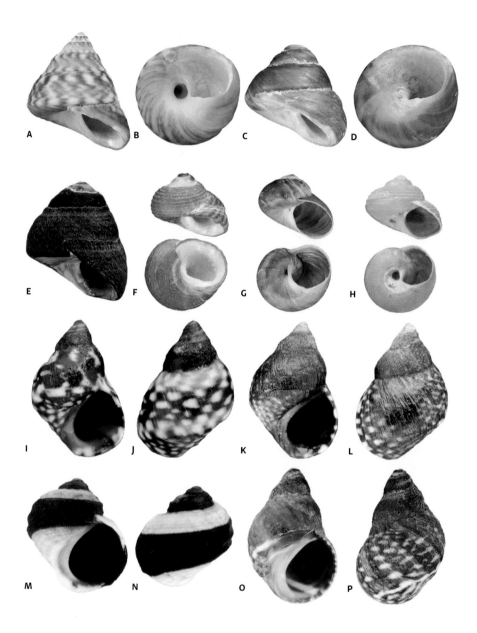

PLATE 7. Snails. A–B: Dusky Turban, *Promartynia pulligo*; **C–D:** Brown Turban, *Chlorostoma brunnea*; **E:** Black Turban, *Chlorostoma funebralis*; **F:** Dark Dwarf-turban, *Homalopoma luridum*; **G:** Spiral Margarite, *Margarites helicinus*; **H:** Puppet Margarite, *Margarites pupillus*; **I–J:** Checkered Periwinkle, *Littorina scutulata*; **K–L:** Little Checkered Periwinkle, *Littorina plena*; **M–N:** Sitka Periwinkle, *Littorina sitkana*; **O–P:** Flat-bottomed Periwinkle, *Littorina keenae*. SHELLS NOT TO SCALE.

PLATE 8. Snails. **A–B:** Salt Marsh Periwinkle, *Littorina subrotundata*; **C:** Variable Lacuna, *Lacuna variegata*; **D:** Wide Lacuna, *Lacuna vincta*; **E:** Mudflat Snail, *Batillaria attramentaria*; **F:** Threaded Bittium, *Neostylidium eschrichtii*; **G:** Common Purple Sea-snail, *Janthina janthina*; **H:** Boreal Wentletrap, *Opalia wroblewskyi*; **I:** Tinted Wentletrap, *Epitonium tinctum*; **J:** Money Wentletrap, *Epitonium indianorum*; **K:** British Columbia Balcis, *Vitreolina columbiana*; **L:** Lewis's Moonsnail, *Neverita lewisi*; **M:** Aleutian Moonsnail, *Cryptonatica aleutica*; **N:** Oregon Triton, *Fusitriton oregonensis*; **O:** Checkered Hairysnail, *Trichotropsis cancellata*; **P:** Angular Unicorn, *Acanthinucella spirata*. SHELLS NOT TO SCALE.

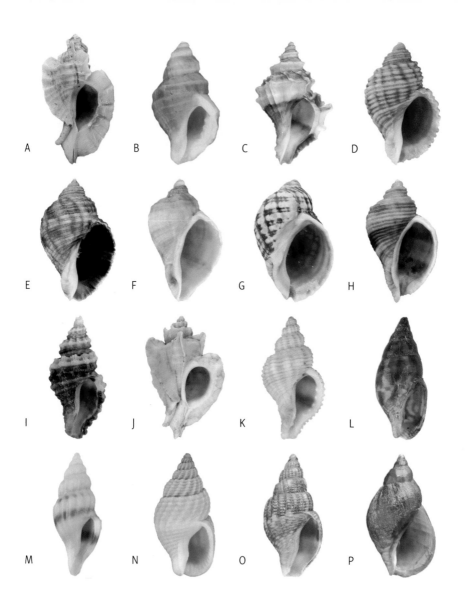

PLATE 9. Snails. **A:** Leafy Hornmouth, *Ceratostoma foliatum*; **B–C:** Frilled Dogwinkle, *Nucella lamellosa*; **B:** smooth form; **C:** frilled form; **D:** Northern Channelled Dogwinkle, *Nucella canaliculata*; **E:** Lined Dogwinkle, *Nucella analoga*; **F:** Northern Striped Dogwinkle, *Nucella ostrina*; **G:** Emarginate Dogwinkle, *Nucella emarginata*; **H:** File Dogwinkle, *Nucella lima*; **I:** Sculpured Rocksnail, *Ocinebrina interfossa*; **J:** Japanese Oyster Drill, *Ocenebra inornata*; **K:** Atlantic Oyster Drill, *Urosalpinx cinerea*; **L:** Carinate Dovesnail, *Alia carinata*; **M:** Violet-band Mangelia, *Mangelia crebricostata*; **N:** Variegated Amphissa, *Amphissa versicolor*; **O:** Wrinkled Amphissa, *Amphissa columbiana*; **P:** Baer's Buccinum, *Buccinum baeri*. SHELLS NOT TO SCALE.

PLATE 10. Snails and Bivalves. **A:** Big-mouth Whelk, *Volutharpa ampullacea*; **B:** Dire Whelk, *Lirabuccinum dirum*; **C:** Western Lean Nassa, *Hima mendica*; **D:** Japanese Nassa, *Hima fratercula*; **E:** Giant Western Nassa, *Nassarius fossatus*; **F:** Western Fat Nassa, *Caesia perpinguis*; **G:** Eastern Mud Snail, *Tritia obsoleta*; **H:** Purple Olive, *Callianax biplicata*; **I:** Baetic Olive, *Callianax baetica*; **J:** Zigzag Olive, *Callianax pycna*; **K:** White Bubble Snail, *Haminoea vesicula*; **L:** Japanese Bubble Snail, *Haminoea japonica*; **M:** Green Bubble Snail, *Haminoea virescens*; **N:** Pleatless Barrel-bubble, *Acteocina eximia*; **O:** California Mussel, *Mytilus californianus*; **P:** Pacific Blue Mussel, *Mytilus trossulus*. SHELLS NOT TO SCALE.

PLATE 11. Bivalves. **A:** Mediterranean Mussel, *Mytilus galloprovincialis*; **B:** Blue Mussel, *Mytilus edulis*; **C:** California Datemussel, *Adula californiensis*; **D:** Northern Horsemussel, *Modiolus modiolus*; **E:** Straight Horsemussel, *Modiolus rectus*; **F:** Olympia Oyster, *Ostrea conchaphila*; **G:** Pacific Oyster, *Magallana gigas*; **H:** Eastern Oyster, *Crassostrea virginica*; **I:** Smooth Pink Scallop, *Chlamys rubida*; **J:** Spiny Pink Scallop, *Chlamys hastata*; **K:** Giant Rock Scallop, *Crassadoma gigantea*; **L:** Weathervane Scallop, *Patinopecten caurinus*; **M:** Western Bittersweet, *Glycymeris septentrionalis*; **N:** Green False-jingle, *Pododesmus macrochisma*. SHELLS NOT TO SCALE.

PLATE 12. Bivalves. **A:** Western Ringed Lucine, *Lucinoma annulatum*; **B:** Kellyclam, *Kellia suborbicularis*; **C:** Mud Shrimp Clam, *Neaeromya rugifera*; **D:** Little Heart Clam, *Glans carpenteri*; **E:** Boreal Astarte, *Astarte borealis*; **F:** Nuttall's Cockle, *Clinocardium nuttallii*; **G:** Low-rib Cockle, *Keenocardium blandum*; **H:** Fat Gaper, *Tresus capax*; **I:** Pacific Gaper, *Tresus nuttallii*; **J:** Hooked Surfclam, *Simomactra falcata*; **K:** Arctic Surfclam, *Mactromeris polynyma*; **L:** Pacific Razor-clam, *Siliqua patula*; **M:** Sickle Jackknife-clam, *Solen sicarius*; **N:** Rough Diplodon, *Diplodonta impolita*; **O:** Northern Baltic Clam, *Limecola balthica*. SHELLS NOT TO SCALE.

PLATE 13. Bivalves. **A:** Oval Macoma, *Macoma golikovi*; **B:** Bent-nose Macoma, *Macoma nasuta*; **C:** Pointed Macoma, *Macoma inquinata*; **D:** Sleek Macoma, *Macoma lipara*; **E:** Expanded Macoma, *Rexithaerus expansa*; **F:** White-sand Clam, *Rexithaerus secta*; **G:** Bodega Tellin, *Megangulus bodegensis*; **H:** Plain Tellin, *Tellina modesta*; **I:** Purple Mahogany-clam, *Nuttallia obscurata*; **J:** California Sunset Clam, *Gari californica*; **K:** Rose-painted Clam, *Semele rubropicta*; **L:** Rock Venus, *Irusella lamellifera*; **M:** Pacific Littleneck, *Leukoma staminea*; **N:** Japanese Littleneck, *Ruditapes philippinarum*; **O:** Thin-shelled Littleneck, *Callithaca tenerrima*. SHELLS NOT TO SCALE.

PLATE 14. Bivalves. **A**: Washington Butter Clam, *Saxidomus gigantea*; **B**: Softshell-clam, *Mya arenaria*; **C**: Truncated Softshell-clam, *Mya truncata*; **D**: California Softshell-clam, *Cryptomya californica*; **E**: Boring Softshell-clam, *Platyodon cancellatus*; **F**: Arctic Hiatella, *Hiatella arctica*; **G**: Ample Roughmya, *Panomya ampla*; **H**: Pacific Geoduck, *Panopea generosa*; **I**: Rough Piddock, *Zirfaea pilsbryi*; **J**: Flat-tip Piddock, *Penitella penita*; **K**: Beaked Piddock, *Netastoma rostratum*; **L**: Punctate Pandora, *Heteroclidus punctatus*; **M**: Rock Entodesma, *Entodesma navicula*; **N**: California Lyonsia, *Lyonsia californica*. SHELLS NOT TO SCALE.

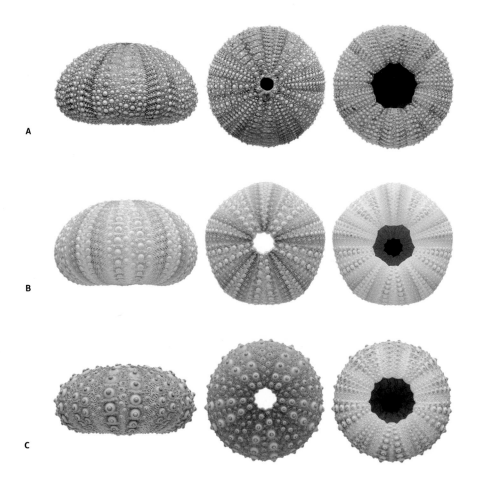

PLATE 15. Sea Urchin Tests. **A:** Green Sea Urchin, *Strongylocentrotus droebachiensis*; **B:** Purple Sea Urchin, *Strongylocentrotus purpuratus*; **C:** Giant Red Sea Urchin, *Mesocentrotus franciscanus*. TESTS NOT TO SCALE.

Field Guide

Orange finger sponge,
Ilsodictya rigida

Sponges

PHYLUM PORIFERA

Sponges are filter-feeding, colonial animals that live together as a larger unit. They appear to be plants, but are in fact invertebrate animals. Unique to the animal world, sponges have canals throughout their bodies that open to the surrounding water, allowing both oxygen and food particles to reach each individual.

Yellow Boring Sponge

Cliona celata Grant, 1826

OTHER NAMES: Boring sponge, sulfur sponge.
DESCRIPTION: The color ranges from **yellow to bright lemon-yellow.** The hidden portion of sponge is located inside holes and tunnels.
SIZE: Diameter normally to 0.1″ (3 mm); height to 0.1″ (3 mm).
HABITAT: On mollusc shells, barnacles and limestone rocks; low intertidal zone to depths of 400′ (120 m).
RANGE: Prince William Sound, Alaska, to Baja California, México; Gulf of St. Lawrence to Gulf of México.
NOTES: The boring sponge lives in the calcareous shells of a wide variety of sea life including large barnacles, some clams, moonsnails, oysters and others such as the giant rock scallop. This remarkable sponge bores holes in shells that are either living or dead. It secretes sulfuric acid to dissolve a small portion or pit in a calcareous shell. Under favorable conditions this sponge will overgrow its host completely.

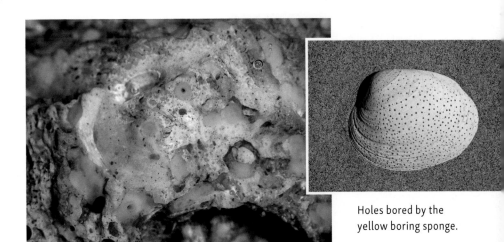

Holes bored by the yellow boring sponge.

Yellow-green Encrusting Sponge

Halichondria panicea (Pallas, 1766)

OTHER NAMES: Bread crumb sponge, crumb of bread sponge, crumb-of-bread sponge.
DESCRIPTION: Color varies from dirty yellow to **yellow-green**. This **encrusting** species displays **regularly spaced oscula (pores) on the tops of volcano-like protuberances**. The texture is firm, compressible and easily torn.
SIZE: To 24″ (60 cm) across and larger; height to 2″ (5 cm).
HABITAT: On rocks of exposed coast and more protected shores; mid-intertidal zone to depths of 328′ (100 m).
RANGE: Bering Sea to Baja California, México; Arctic to Cape Cod; Mediterranean; North Sea; western Baltic; widespread.
NOTES: This species gets one of its common names from its bread crumb-like texture. If broken, it is said to smell like gunpowder after being ignited. Various nudibranchs feed on this sponge, including the Monterey sea lemon, which can often be found on the sponge once the tide has receded. Interestingly, this species is dioecious (males and females are separate).

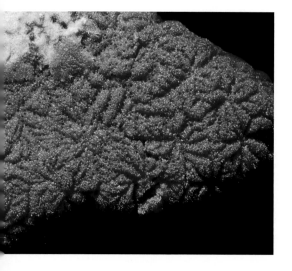

Red Encrusting Sponge

Clathria pennata and others
(Lambe, 1895)

OTHER NAMES: Velvety red sponge; formerly classified as *Desmacella pennata*, *Ophlitaspongia pennata*.
DESCRIPTION: Color ranges from bright red to red-orange. **The oscula (pores) are tiny, closely spaced and star-like**, and the surface is velvety to touch.
SIZE: To 39″ (1 m) across; 0.25″ (6 mm) thick.

HABITAT: On rocks; high intertidal zone to depths of 295′ (90 m).

RANGE: Alaska to Baja California, México.

NOTES: This species is the most common of several species of sponges that look very similar to it. A microscope is required to tell them apart. Check specimen closely to find the red sponge nudibranch feeding, which perfectly matches the sponge in color. The nudibranch also lays its red eggs on this sponge, its main food source.

Purple Encrusting Sponge

Haliclona cinerea (Grant, 1826)

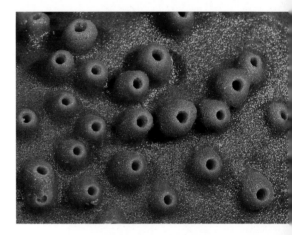

OTHER NAMES: Encrusting sponge, purple sponge, purple intertidal sponge, violet encrusting sponge, violet volcano sponge; formerly classified as *Haliclona permollis*.

DESCRIPTION: The color is normally **purple** but can also be lavender or gray. This **encrusting** species is somewhat **soft with scattered oscula** that can reach up to 0.2″ (5 mm) in diameter **on volcano-shaped protuberances**.

SIZE: To 39″ (1 m) across but normally much smaller.

HABITAT: On the sides and undersides of rocks in relatively exposed shores; mid-intertidal zone to depths of 146′ (50 m).

RANGE: Southeast Alaska to southern California.

NOTES: The purple encrusting sponge is often found on the lower, shaded sides of large rocks and boulders. Several nudibranchs feed on this beautiful sponge. The ringed nudibranch is able to find this sponge by the chemicals the sponge releases into the water.

Cobalt Sponge

Acanthancora cyanocrypta (de Laubenfels, 1930)

OTHER NAMES: Cobalt blue sponge, deep blue sponge; formerly classified as *Hymenamphiastra cyanocrypta*.

DESCRIPTION: Color is **normally cobalt blue** but there is also another color form that is

light orange (which is more difficult to identify). This sponge is a **thin, encrusting** species.

SIZE: To 39″ (1 m) across but normally much smaller; thickness to 0.1″ (3 mm).

HABITAT: On sides and undersides of rocks that are shaded; low intertidal zone to depths of 121′ (37 m).

RANGE: British Columbia to northern México.

NOTES: The cobalt sponge is an uncommon species that contains a symbiotic blue-green alga, which gives it its distinctive color. If this symbiotic blue-green alga is not present, the sponge color is light orange.

....

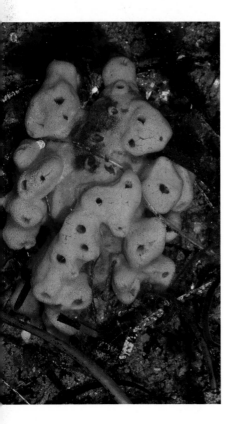

Orange Finger Sponge

Isodictya rigida (Lambe, 1893)

OTHER NAMES: Branched apically perforated finger sponge; formerly classified as *Esperiopsis rigida, Neoesperiopsis rigida*

DESCRIPTION: Color ranges from yellow to orange. The finger-like branches are normally erect with **terminal ossicles**. The "fingers" are quite variable in shape.

SIZE: Height to 8″ (20 cm).

HABITAT: On rocks of the outer coast; very low intertidal zone to depths of 100′ (30 m).

RANGE: Southern Alaska to northern California.

NOTES: The intertidal shores of the Pacific Northwest do not normally host many erect sponges. The orange finger sponge is one that does occasionally reveal itself at the lowest of tides. This sponge provides food for nudibranchs including the spotted leopard dorid.

Aggregating anemone,
Anthopleura elegantissima

Sea Anemones, Hydroids & Jellies
PHYLUM CNIDARIA

Members of the phylum Cnidaria occur in two body types: the polyp or the medusa. The medusa body type is normally free-floating while the polyp is attached to a solid base such as a rock. Some species include both body types in their life cycle.

This group is characterized by the presence of nematocysts or stinging capsules in the tentacles around the mouth. These capsules are used to obtain food and for defense. Individuals use their nematocysts to sting their prey when contacted. If a person's hand touches the tentacles of an amemone they only feel sticky, since the skin on our hands is too thick to allow penetration, but a stinging sensation was definitely felt by an individual who licked the tentacles of one species, using his much more sensitive tongue. (This technique, however, is not recommended!) Most anemones feed upon fishes, crabs, sea urchins, shrimps and similar prey. Habitat varies from the high intertidal zone to as deep as 30,000′ (9,000 m) for some species in the Philippines.

The size of the species included in this phylum ranges from a couple of millimeters to greater than 40 meters long.

Sea Anemones & Cup Corals
CLASS ANTHOZOA

The class Anthozoa includes both sea anemones and cup corals, anemone-like organisms with hard, cup-shaped skeletons.

Orange Cup Coral
Balanophyllia elegans Verrill, 1864

OTHER NAMES: Cup coral, orange-red coral, orange coral, solitary orange cup coral, solitary coral, vivid orange-red solitary coral.
DESCRIPTION: Overall **bright orange**, cup-shaped organism with **hard, seat-like shape** surrounded by many small tentacles. Resembles a small anemone; its hard seat helps

in identifying it correctly as a hard coral.

SIZE: Diameter of skeleton to 0.4″ (10 mm); height to 0.4″ (10 mm).
HABITAT: On rocks; low intertidal zone to depths of 160′ (48 m).
RANGE: Northern Southeast Alaska to Baja California, México.
NOTES: Identification of this species is easily made since no other orange hard or "stony" coral is found intertidally in the Pacific Northwest. Its vivid orange color comes from a fluorescent pigment. Feeding is accomplished with small,

transparent-like tentacles and a mouth that opens to trap food. Although this species is small, its presence is always a welcome splash of color.

....

Aggregating Soft Coral

Discophyton rudyi
(Versewveldt & van Ofwegen, 1992)

OTHER NAMES: White disc soft coral; formerly classified as *Alcyonium rudyi*.
DESCRIPTION: The overall color varies from white or cream-colored to orange or pinkish. Individuals form aggregations that are **disc-shaped and soft with numerous polyps**—each of which has 8 tentacles and very delicate side branches. The colonies are **spaced regularly in aggregations**.
SIZE: Colony to 0.6″ (15 mm) in diameter.
HABITAT: On rocks and shell rubble of the outer coast in areas with currents; low intertidal zone to depths of 65′ (20 m).
RANGE: Botanical Beach, Vancouver Island, British Columbia, to Point Lobos, California.
NOTES: The aggregating soft coral reproduces both sexually and asexually. Individuals reproduce asexually by fission and as a result produce distinctive clones that are fairly easy to identify in their aggregations.

Jelly-dwelling Anemone

Peachia quinquecapitata

McMurrich, 1913

OTHER NAME: Formerly classified as *Bicidium aequoreae*.

DESCRIPTION: The tentacles are pinkish-brown or yellowish. **Twelve tentacles are present** but the remainder of the organism is hidden.

SIZE: Diameter of tentacular crown to 0.8″ (20 mm); height to 1.2″ (30 mm).

HABITAT: Juveniles are pelagic; adults in sand or mud; low intertidal zone to depths of 531′ (161 m).

RANGE: Nanoose Bay, Vancouver Island, British Columbia, to Santa Maria Basin, California; Japan.

NOTES: This remarkable sea anemone is a parasite in its larval stage on jellies. The jelly-dwelling anemone spawns in the spring and the larvae attach to adult jellies. Each larva begins to feed on its mobile host's gonads, remaining on the jelly while increasing in size. When the larva runs out of food on one jelly, it is able to hitch onto another jelly to repeat the procedure. This insatiable appetite continues until it reaches a length of 1 cm and its weight pulls it to the ocean floor where it simply drops into the sand or mud and begins its life as a sedentary sea anemone.

....

Ten-tentacled Anemone

Halcampa decemtentaculata Hand, 1955

OTHER NAME: Ten-tentacled burrowing anemone.

DESCRIPTION: Overall color ranges widely from cream-colored to pink or purple or brown and may also be marked with V-shaped bands. This anemone is conical in shape with **10 tentacles** at the anterior end. A small portion of the column may also be visible above the surface of the substrate.

SIZE: Diameter of tentacular crown to 1″ (2.5 cm); height to 3.1″ (8 cm).

HABITAT: Buried in sand, gravel, debris or in algae holdfasts or surfgrass roots; low intertidal zone to depths of 1,313′ (398 m).

RANGE: British Columbia to California.

NOTES: Due to its small size, this burrowing anemone can easily go unnoticed. Its column is buried and can sometimes reach 3″ (8 cm) long when fully extended. Tentacles and column can become somewhat translucent when extended. Little is known about the biology of this species.

....

Moonglow Anemone

Anthopleura artemisia

(Pickering in Dana, 1848)

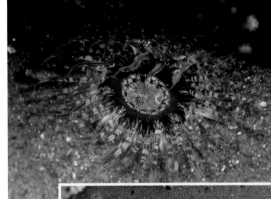

OTHER NAMES: Beach sand anemone, buried green anemone, burrowing green anemone, buried moonglow anemone.

DESCRIPTION: Color of tentacles and oral disc vary widely from green to blue, bright pink, orange or brown **with transverse white bands.** The upper third of column gray, black or green and remainder white or pink. The numerous tentacles are long and slender. No acontia or defensive stinging cells are present.

SIZE: Diameter of tentacular crown to 4″ (10 cm); height to 10″ (25 cm).

HABITAT: Anchored to rocks in sandy sites along open coast and in tidepools; mid-intertidal zone to depths of 100′ (30 m).

RANGE: Alaska to southern California.

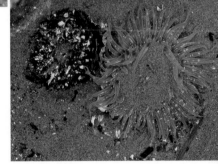

The tentacles are closed on the left individual.

NOTES: The species gets its name from the luminous quality often exhibited by the tentacles. The moonglow anemone is usually found in sandy areas, where it is attached to a large shell or rock, buried up to 12″ (30 cm) beneath the surface. The aggregating anemone can look similar when living in sand, but it lacks the white bands on its tentacles.

Aggregating Anemone

Anthopleura elegantissima

(Brandt, 1835)

OTHER NAMES: Aggregate anemone, aggregated anemone, pink-tipped green anemone.

DESCRIPTION: The oral disk and tentacles are **green and often tinged with pink** or purplish-pink. Thin brown lines radiate from the center of the disk to the outer edge. The tentacles are **short, numerous with several whorls and if aggregating are all the same coloration**.

SIZE: Diameter of tentacular crown (aggregating individuals) to 3.1″ (8 cm), (solitary individuals) to 10″ (25 cm); height to 6″ (15 cm).

HABITAT: On rocks of exposed shores; mid-intertidal zone to depths of 60′ (18 m).

RANGE: Alaska to Baja California, México.

NOTES: Aggregating anemones are well known for their ability to multiply asexually by dividing into two identical individuals. As a result, they are capable of colonizing large rock surfaces as genetic clones. At some locations, their clones completely carpet entire rocks. Sexual reproduction is also possible. By necessity, this species must be very tolerant of harsh conditions including exposure to the sun, wind and waves. They are often observed in a closed position, out of water, which prevents them from drying out. However, this changes their appearance dramatically. This anemone's predators include the leather star.

Closing disc in tidepool.

Giant Green Anemone

Anthopleura xanthogrammica
(Brandt, 1835)

OTHER NAMES: Giant green anemone, giant green sea anemone, giant tidepool anemone, green sea anemone, green anemone, green surf anemone, solitary green anemone.

DESCRIPTION: Color of the oral disc and tentacles ranges from **pale blue to pale green.** In caves and similar locations, the green color may not be present. The **large disc is armed with short tentacles that are uniform in color** without visible rows of tentacles.

SIZE: Diameter of tentacular crown to 10″ (25 cm); height to 12″ (30 cm).

HABITAT: On rocks, in surge channels on the exposed surf-swept shores and in tidepools; mid-intertidal zone to depths of 100′ (30 m).

RANGE: Sitka, Alaska, to Panama; uncommon from southern California to Panama.

NOTES: This sea anemone is found in both a solitary existence and in groups, often in tidepools. Microscopic green algae live inside the tentacles, giving the animal its green color. This species attains adult size at age 14 or 15 months and has been known to live longer than 30 years in captivity. Humans have utilized the giant green anemone in different ways. The Haida historically cooked it carefully over a fire before eating it. More recently, this species has been used as the source of a heart stimulant for humans.

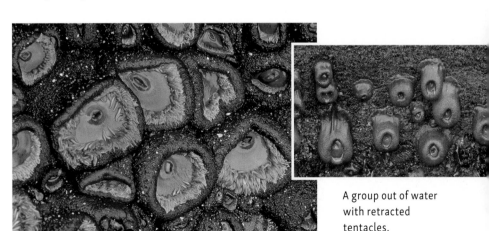

A group out of water with retracted tentacles.

Incubating Anemone

Aulactinia incubans

Dunn, Chia, and Levine, 1980

OTHER NAME: Warty-columned anemone.
DESCRIPTION: Overall color varies widely from dark gray or greenish to red, orange, or cream-colored. **Bright white stripes radiate from the center** of the oral disk. The **column bears vertical rows of tubercles (warts)** and several slender elongated tentacles grace its upper end.
SIZE: Diameter of tentacular crown to 1.4″ (35 mm); height to 0.6″ (15 mm).
HABITAT: Attached to rocks, buried in sand of sheltered habitats on exposed shores and in tidepools; low intertidal zone.
RANGE: Vancouver Island, British Columbia, to near Santa Cruz, California.
NOTES: The incubating anemone broods its young internally and, remarkably, releases its young to the outside world through the pores located at the tips of its slender tentacles. This species is normally found with several individuals present at one location.

Brooding Anemone

Epiactis lisbethae Fautin and Chia, 1986

OTHER NAME: Giant brooding anemone.
DESCRIPTION: Color varies widely from red to purple or green with **fine white pinstriping over entire animal, including middle portion of column. As many as 300 small young are often found on the column**, arranged in as many as 5 rows—all the same size. The column is adorned with up to 96 tentacles on its oral disc.

SIZE: Diameter of tentacular crown to 3.2″ (8 cm); height to 1.6″ (4 cm).

HABITAT: On rocks in areas of rough water such as surge channels; low intertidal zone to depths of 100′ (30 m).

RANGE: Southern Alaska to southern California; rare in Oregon and California.

NOTES: For years this anemone was thought to be the same species as the similar proliferating anemone (below). Young brooding anemones are all female; however, once they begin to grow, they develop testes and change to hermaphrodites. This causes some problems as they often fertilize themselves and significant inbreeding results.

SIMILAR SPECIES: Proliferating anemone.

Proliferating Anemone

Epiactis prolifera Verrill, 1869

OTHER NAME: Small green anemone.

DESCRIPTION: Color varies greatly from brown or green to red, pink, blue or gray. **White vertical pinstriping is also present on the base but does not extend to top of the column. Young of various sizes are usually present** on the column, up to 30 at one time crowded into a single row.

SIZE: Diameter of tentacular crown to 3.2″ (8 cm); height to 4″ (10 cm).

HABITAT: On rocks of the outer coast and in bays; low intertidal zone to depths of 60′ (18 m).

RANGE: Southern Alaska to southern California.

NOTES: This anemone has a sex life similar to that of orchids, referred to as gynodioecy. Young adults are usually female. As mothers, they grow in size and they also grow testes. Upon full maturity they are hermaphrodites, having both testes and ovaries. The eggs develop within the digestive cavity of the parent, exit through the mouth and eventually attach themselves to the middle of the parent's column. Later the young move away from the parent to venture forth on their own.

SIMILAR SPECIES: Ritter's Brooding Anemone *Epiactis ritter* Torrey, 1902 is similar, except no vertical stripes are present on the column, radiating white lines are present on its broad oral disk and it broods its young internally.

Stubby Rose Anemone

Urticina coriacea (Cuvier, 1798)

OTHER NAMES: Beaded anemone, leathery anemone, red-beaded anemone; formerly classified as *Tealia coriacea*.

DESCRIPTION: Overall color varies from **gray to brick red with bands of white**. The column has adhesive warts that are not in distinct rows but normally buried and hidden from view. The **tentacles are noticeably short and blunt**.

SIZE: Diameter of tentacular crown to 6″ (15 cm); height to 6″ (15 cm).

HABITAT: Buried in sand or gravel between large rocks; low intertidal zone to depths of 150′ (45 m).

RANGE: Alaska to Monterey, California; Europe.

NOTES: This anemone attaches itself to rocks or other solid objects beneath the surface, leaving only its crown visible. It is commonly found in shallow, rocky intertidal areas. Its chief enemy is the leather star, a sea star that specializes in eating anemones. Little else is known about this anemone's biology.

Warty Painted Anemone

Urticina grebelnyi Sanamyan & Sanamyan, 2006

OTHER NAMES: Christmas anemone, northern red anemone, painted anemone; in the past erroneously identified as *Urticina crassicornis*.

DESCRIPTION: Oral disk is yellowish-green, lilac or brownish, and the **column is red or green often with patches of green or red**. The **column of this large species is covered with numerous, non-adhesive verrucae or warts** that can be inconspicuous. The oral disk is flat and circular with tentacles that are short, thin and may number to 200.

SIZE: Diameter of tentacular crown to 10″ (25 cm); height to 8″ (20 cm).

HABITAT: On rocks or shells of protected sites; low intertidal zone to depths of 10′ (25 m).

RANGE: Pribilof Islands, Alaska, to south of Monterey, California.

NOTES: The scientific name for this species has recently changed with the realization that the sea anemone found in the Pacific Northwest is not the same as *Urticina crassicornis*, a species that is found in the north Atlantic. The true *Urticina crassicornis* features a column that is completely smooth and lacks any verrucae or warts. The warty painted anemone has been known to live to 80 years in captivity. Young individuals are normally found higher intertidally, while occasionally the tidepooler can view older, larger specimens at the lowest of tides.

Fish-eating Anemone

Urticina piscivora (Sebens & Laakso, 1977)

OTHER NAMES: Fish-eating urticina, rose anemone, velvety red anemone.

DESCRIPTION: The **column is maroon, normally without any markings**; however, red lines are occasionally present on the oral disc. The **smooth** column is protected with an oral disc that has numerous short tentacles.

SIZE: Diameter of tentacular crown to 8″ (20 cm); height to 10″ (25 cm).

HABITAT: On rocks, especially on prominences; very low intertidal zone to depths of 160′ (48 m).

RANGE: Polar seas to La Jolla, California.

NOTES: As the common and scientific names of this species indicate, it feeds upon small fish. It also dines on shrimp and a variety of other invertebrates. The tentacles are known to cause some **severe stings** to uncovered skin. Although this species is believed to be strictly subtidal, it is found intertidally occasionally at the lowest of tides. Research in Bamfield, BC, showed a remarkable response of this sea anemone toward the leather star. If small specimens of the fish-eating anemone are attacked they simply release their attachment to the substrate and float away in the water.

SIMILAR SPECIES: Warty painted anemone.

White-spotted Anemone

Urticina lofotensis (Danielssen, 1890)

OTHER NAMES: Strawberry anemone; formerly classified as *Tealla lofotensls*.

DESCRIPTION: Column is **scarlet or crimson with white verrucae or warts arranged in longitudinal rows.** The **column is smooth** without any sand or debris attached.

SIZE: Diameter of tentacular crown to 4″ (10 cm); height to 6″ (15 cm).

HABITAT: On rocks; low intertidal zone to depths of 75′ (23 m).

RANGE: Southeast Alaska to San Diego, California; both sides of North Atlantic.

NOTES: This species is truly beautiful to view, but unfortunately, not much is known about its biology. It is sometimes found hanging from the side of a rock or boulder and in some cases hidden from view under seaweed. Smaller individuals are normally found intertidally.

This individual is out of the water.

Short Plumose Anemone

Metridium dianthus (Ellis, 1768)

OTHER NAMES: Frilled anemone, sun anemone, fluffy anemone, white plume anemone; formerly classified as *Metridium senile*.

DESCRIPTION: Color ranges widely from white to tan, gray, orange or brown. The elongated column terminates with a crown of tentacles and mouth at one end and a pedal disc at the base. **Fewer than 200 slender tentacles are normally present** on a lobed oral disk. This species **typically forms "dense colonial groups" of similarly colored individuals from asexual reproduction. Catch tentacles (used for defense) are often present.**

SIZE: Diameter of tentacular crown to 2″ (5 cm);

Two color phases of short plumose anemones, dockside. The right individual has catch tentacles visible.

Tentacles retracted (left) and extended (right) underwater.

height to 4″ (10 cm). The **pedal disc diameter (base)** is normally 1″ (2.5 cm) **to a maximum of 1.6″ (4 cm)** across.

HABITAT: On rocks, jetties and floats of bays and harbors; low intertidal zone to depths of 100′ (30 m).

RANGE: Southern Alaska to southern California; Mediterranean; North Atlantic; North Sea.

NOTES: This anemone is easily found as it is commonly attached to floating docks and similar sites throughout its range. It feeds on copepods and various invertebrate larvae. Unlike its relative, the giant plumose anemone, this anemone reproduces asexually. In fact, a new anemone can arise from tissue left behind when it moves along to a new site. The new individual is a clone of the original. It is truly amazing that this species and the giant plumose anemone fooled biologists for many years into believing that only the one species existed.

SIMILAR SPECIES: Giant plumose anemone.

Giant Plumose Anemone

Metridium farcimen (Brandt, 1835)

OTHER NAMES: Frilled anemone, frilled plumose anemone, gigantic anemone, tall plumose anemone, powder puff anemone, sun anemone, white-plumed anemone; formerly classified as *Metridium giganteum*.

DESCRIPTION: Color normally white but also occasionally salmon, brown or speckled.

The elongated column terminates with a crown of tentacles and mouth at one end and a pedal disc at the base. **Normally more than 200 slender tentacles are present** with numerous large lobes on the oral disk. **Catch tentacles are absent.**

SIZE: Diameter of tentacular crown to 12″ (30 cm); height to 39″ (1 m). The **pedal disc diameter (base)** is normally to 5″ (12.5 cm) **to a maximum of 8″ (20 cm)** across.

HABITAT: On rocks, piers and pilings in protected sites; low intertidal zone to depths of 1,000′ (300 m).

RANGE: Alaska to northern México.

NOTES: This large species is found on piers and pilings in areas of low salinity. At low tide it can sometimes be seen hanging from ledges assuming surreal-looking postures. Until a few years ago, this anemone was thought to be a form of the short plumose anemone. Biologists now know that the two forms are two separate species. The giant plumose anemone grows much larger, which is often the easiest method to identify it when seen out of water.

SIMILAR SPECIES: Short plumose anemone.

Orange-striped Anemone ⓘ

Diadumene lineata (Verrill, 1871)

OTHER NAMES: Japanese anemone; formerly classified as *Haliplanella luciae*.

DESCRIPTION: Column is olive-green, gray or brown with **distinctive orange, yellow or white vertical stripes.** The cylindrical column has up to 100 slender tentacles.

SIZE: Diameter of tentacular crown to 1.5″ (4 cm); height to 1.25″ (3 cm).

HABITAT: On rocks and in tidepools; high to mid-intertidal zone.

RANGE: Alaska to southern California; Bay of Fundy to Texas; Japan.

NOTES: This anemone is thought to have been introduced accidentally in the late nineteenth century, when the Pacific oyster was brought to North America for commercial purposes. Its small size makes it an easy species to overlook. Wentletrap snails are known to prey upon this species.

Hydroids & Allies
CLASS HYDROZOA

Hydroids often appear stick-like or bush-like and attached to a firm substrate. Many hydroids alternate between an attached stage and a tiny hydromedusa or jelly-like form. Hydroids possess polyps that hold numerous nematocysts, which are used for protection. Most hydroids require a microscope for identification of species.

Purple Encrusting Hydrocoral

Stylantheca papillosa (Dall, 1884)

OTHER NAMES: Purple carpet; formerly classified as *Allopora papillosa, Allopora petrograpta, Stylantheca petrograpta, Stylantheca porphyra.*

DESCRIPTION: Color always a vivid purple. This encrusting colony is covered in minute pits. Touching the surface reveals its **hard texture.**

SIZE: To 6″ (15 cm) across, 0.1″ (3 mm) thick.

HABITAT: Low intertidal zone and below in exposed areas, often on faces of shaded rocks. Found at the lowest of tides in areas of extreme tidal fluctuations.

RANGE: Alaska to California.

NOTES: This species is somewhat of an uncommon hydrocoral. Although there are several species of similar-looking hydrocorals, recent studies have shown that this is the only species that is found at intertidal levels. Purple encrusting sponge is similar looking, with a noticeably soft texture and large openings rather than tiny pores.

Turgid Garland Hydroid

Symplectoscyphus turgidus (Trask, 1857)

OTHER NAME: Formerly classified as *Sertularella turgida.*

DESCRIPTION: Displays elongated yellow stalks with a **distinctive wavy pattern and tooth-like lobes.**

SIZE: To 2″ (5 cm) high, 1.5″ (4 cm) wide.

HABITAT: On rocks and similar hard objects; low intertidal zone to water 656′ (200 m) deep.

RANGE: Alaska to Baja California, México.

NOTES: Very little is known about the biology of this distinctive hydroid. We do know that to reproduce, it retains its eggs while sperm are released to the sea for fertilization.

Ostrich-plume Hydroid

Aglaophenia spp. (Lamouroux, 1812)

DESCRIPTION: Color varies from yellow to light red or black. The **elongated feather-like plumes have polyps on only one side.** Egg capsules are elongated.

SIZE: To 5″ (13 cm) high.

HABITAT: Attached to rock in surf-swept rock clefts on exposed shores, low intertidal to water 528′ (160 m) deep.

RANGE: Alaska to Central America.

NOTES: This species is easily confused with a plant, but hydroids start out as a larva called planula, and adults are composed of tiny filter-feeding polyps. The elongated yellow eggs are often found attached to the plumes.

Solitary Pink-mouth Hydroid

Ectopleura marina (Torrey, 1902)

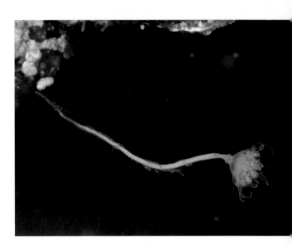

OTHER NAMES: Pink mouth hydroid, solitary hydroid, solitary pink mouth hydroid; formerly classified as *Tubularia marina.*

DESCRIPTION: Feeding polyp is **pink**. A **single, slender stalk** arises and holds the single polyp. May also be found in association with other single individuals.

SIZE: Stalk to 3″ (7.5 cm) long.

HABITAT: On sheltered sides of rocks and similar sites on exposed shores; low intertidal zone to subtidal waters of 121′ (37 m).

RANGE: British Columbia to Monterey, California.

NOTES: This beautifully slender species is occasionally found in intertidal situations. The medusa has tentacles that resemble those of miniature jellies.

By-the-wind Sailor

Velella velella (Linnaeus, 1758)

By-the-wind sailor stranded on the beach.

OTHER NAMES: By-the-wind-sailor, purple sailing jellyfish, purple sail jellyfish, sail jellyfish, sail jelly fish; formerly classified as *Velella lata.*

DESCRIPTION: A bright **blue to purple float** is accompanied **by a transparent triangular sail** that is held above the water surface.

SIZE: To 2.5″ (6 cm) long.

HABITAT: Pelagic; on the surface of the water.

RANGE: Temperate and tropical oceans worldwide.

NOTES: This remarkable species is a floating hydroid that relies upon the wind to move on the ocean's surface. Its colorful base is made up of gas-filled pockets that enable it to float. It occasionally washes ashore by the thousands in late spring and early summer. This species feeds upon the eggs of fish and a variety of microscopic invertebrates.

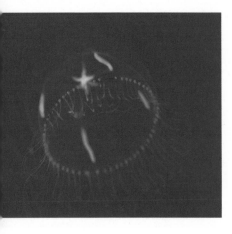

Cross Jelly

Mitrocoma cellularia (Agassiz, 1862)

OTHER NAMES: Cross jelly fish, cross jellyfish; formerly classified as *Halistaura cellularia*.
DESCRIPTION: The overall color is transparent. Four thin canals radiate out from the central stomach creating **a white cross**; long, thin gonads are present; up to 350 short tentacles are present along the outer margin.
SIZE: Medusa to 3.5″ (9 cm) in diameter.
HABITAT: Pelagic.
RANGE: Bering Sea to southern California.
NOTES: The cross jelly is a species that exhibits strong bioluminescence, found only in a narrow band around its margin.

Many-ribbed Hydromedusa

Aequorea spp. Péron & Lesueur, 1810

OTHER NAMES: Water jelly; formerly classified as *Aequorea aequorea*, *Aequorea victoria*.
DESCRIPTION: A small, transparent bell-shaped **jelly with 100 or more distinctive fine, rib-like radial canals**. Numerous trailing tentacles are also present along the rim of the bell.
SIZE: Bell to 10″ (25 cm) in diameter.
HABITAT: Pelagic, near shore.
RANGE: Bering Sea to southern California.
NOTES: Many-ribbed hydromedusa is likely several different species. Large individuals are present in Alaska, which probably represent one northern species or a larger variety of the southern Pacific species. There is also an Atlantic species that may be the same or a completely different species. More research is needed on this genus. Many-ribbed hydromedusa is bioluminescent on the outer rim of its bell. This organism is known to eat other jellies and on occasion to cannibalize its own species.

Red-eye Medusa

Polyorchis penicillatus (Eschscholtz, 1829)

OTHER NAMES: Bell jelly, bell medusa, bell-shaped jellyfish, penicillate jellyfish, redeye jellyfish, red-eye jellyfish, red-eye jelly fish, red-eyed jellyfish; formerly classified as *Polyorchis minuta, Polyorchis montereyensis.*
DESCRIPTION: Color overall is translucent **white with minute red spots at the bases of the tentacles.** Approximately 100 tentacles are normally found attached but there may be as many as 160 on large individuals.
SIZE: Height to 2.4″ (6 cm).
HABITAT: Pelagic; often found in bays and harbors.
RANGE: The Aleutian Islands, Alaska, to Sea of Cortez, México.
NOTES: The red-eye medusa possesses light-sensitive eye-spots positioned at its red "eyes." Research has shown that these receptors are used to avoid light. This species uses increasing light intensity to initiate a dawn sinking in order to avoid daylight. The specimen used to illustrate this species was found in a small tidepool that held the organism at low tide, thus preventing it from descending into the depths.

Aggregating Jelly

Eutonina indicans (Romanes, 1876)

OTHER NAME: Umbrella jelly.
DESCRIPTION: Transparent umbrella with short tentacles; 4 radial canals are visible in the umbrella. The central peduncle hangs below the umbrella edge.
SIZE: Bell to 1.4″ (3.5 cm) in diameter.
HABITAT: Pelagic; near shore and near the surface.
RANGE: Aleutian Islands, Alaska, to Santa Barbara, California; Hokkaido, Japan.
NOTES: The aggregating jelly likely obtained its common name from its habit of forming dense congregations near Vancouver Island and the San Juan Islands. At other locations it is not found in these large numbers. It feeds on a variety of small invertebrate eggs, larvae and other small hydromedusae.

Large True Jellies & Stalked Jellies
CLASS SCYPHOZOA

The rhythmic pulses of jellies are intriguing to observe—indeed, their fluid movements have a near-hypnotic effect. The purpose of this movement is probably to keep the animal near the surface of the water. Its seemingly random wanderings are influenced and aided by currents.

Jellies date back to Precambrian times: one Australian fossil has been aged at 750 million years. There are a thousand known species of these primitive carnivores, which feed primarily on zooplankton. The life cycle of a jelly has two distinct stages: the polyp (a tube-like organism with a mouth and tentacles to capture prey) stage followed by the medusa (umbrella-shaped organism) stage. The jelly captures its food and lifts it to its mouth to eat.

Jellies are composed of up to 96 percent water. Several species are consumed as food in various Pacific cultures. They are eaten boiled, dried or raw. The giant sunfish *Mola mola*, which has been known to grow to 2,700 lb. (1,215 kg), attains its huge size by feeding on jellies and similar coelenterates with nibbling and sucking techniques. This fish has been seen as far north as Haida Gwaii (Queen Charlotte Islands), British Columbia.

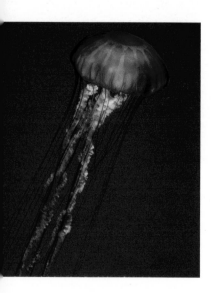

Pacific Sea Nettle

Chrysaora fuscescens Brandt, 1835

OTHER NAMES: Sea nettle; formerly classified as *Chrysaora helvola*, *Chrysaora gilberti*; often referred to incorrectly as *Chrysaora melanaster* (another species).
DESCRIPTION: The exumbrella is dark amber. **Bell has 24 tentacles positioned along the edge** in groups of 3. The 4 oral arms are long, strongly spiraled and screw-like.
SIZE: Bell to 17.7″ (45 cm) in diameter; with oral arms to 15′ (4.6 m) long.

The Pacific sea nettle on display in a public aquarium.

HABITAT: Near the surface, just offshore and stranded on beaches.

RANGE: Gulf of Alaska to México, most common Oregon to California; Japan, Siberia.

NOTES: This jelly is known to have a very unpleasant sting. It feeds upon a wide range of organisms including pelagic ascidians, pelagic molluscs, planktonic crustaceans, comb jellies, fish eggs and other jellies. The Pacific sea nettle swims continuously with its tentacles and oral arms extended.

SIMILAR SPECIES: Lion's mane jelly.

Lion's Mane Jelly

Cyanea capillata

Linnaeus, 1758

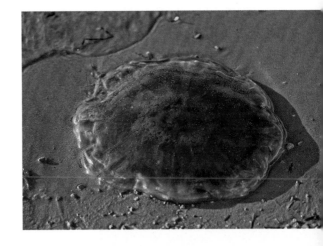

OTHER NAMES: Lion's mane jellyfish, lion's mane medusa, red medusa, sea blubber, sea nettle.

DESCRIPTION: The **flat-topped bell is yellowish, reddish-brown** or **pink**. Trailing tentacles are in 8 clusters located between the 16 lobes of the bell's margin. There are **70–150 tentacles in each cluster.** Suspended beneath the bell lies a shaggy mass containing the feeding tube, lips and ribbon-like gonads.

SIZE: Bell normally to 20″ (50 cm) in diameter, with tentacles to 10′ (3 m) long; rarely to 8′ (2.5 m) in diameter and tentacles to 119′ (36 m) long.

HABITAT: Usually found floating near the surface of the water and occasionally stranded on the beach.

RANGE: Alaska to southern California, Arctic to Florida and México.

NOTES: The lion's mane jelly is the largest jelly in the world. Its tentacles deliver a burning sensation and rash to those who touch it. **Exercise caution**, even if you find a jelly stranded on the beach. All jellies are poisonous to some degree.

Fried Egg Jelly

Phacellophora camtschatica Brandt, 1835

OTHER NAMES: Fried egg jellyfish; formerly classified as *Callinema ornate, Haccaedecomma ambiguum, Phacellophora ornate, Phacellophora sicula.*
DESCRIPTION: The **gonad mass is bright yellow.** The margin made up of 16 large lobes that alternate with small lobes creating a scalloped margin. A cluster of up to 25 tentacles hangs from each lobe.
SIZE: Bell to 24" (60 cm) in diameter, tentacles to 20' (6 m) long and longer.
HABITAT: Pelagic in coastal waters.
RANGE: Kamchatka, Alaska to Chile; Japan in the Pacific, North and South Atlantic and the Mediterranean.
NOTES: This jelly obtained its common name from the striking similarity in appearance to a fried egg. Its tentacles are known to cause a mild sting. A variety of amphipods and juvenile crabs often live symbiotically within its large bell.

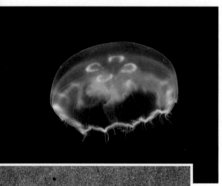

Pacific Moon Jelly

Aurelia labiata Chamisso and Eysenhardt, 1821

OTHER NAMES: Moon jelly; formerly and incorrectly classified as *Aurelia aurita.*
DESCRIPTION: Overall color is white, often mixed with pink, lavender or yellow (color does not indicate gender as is sometimes believed). The bell margin is scalloped into 8 large lobes, each of which have a slight notch and seem to appear like 16 lobes. Translucent, bell-shaped, with many, short trailing tentacles and **4 round or horseshoe-shaped gonads or reproductive organs.** The oral arms extend only to the edge of the bell.
SIZE: Bell to 16" (40 cm) in diameter, 3" (7.5 cm) high.
HABITAT: Pelagic, usually found floating near surface.
RANGE: SE Alaska to Newport Beach, California, and Honolulu, Hawaii.

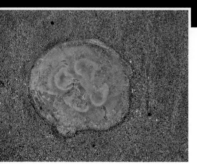

A stranded Pacific moon jelly.

NOTES: Sometimes collects in quiet waters such as harbors when plankton blooms in the spring. In these large aggregations, spawning also occurs. Tentacles cause a slight rash when handled. This jelly is often misidentified as the Atlantic Moon Jelly, *Aurelia aurita*, which is now also found in California. The Atlantic moon jelly has 4 tapering oral arms that extend beyond the bell.

SIMILAR SPECIES: Boreal moon jelly *Aurelia limbata* (Brandt, 1835) is another species found in Alaskan waters with brown pigment on the bell's outer margin.

Oval-anchored Stalked Jelly

Haliclystus stejnegeri

Kishinouye, 1899

OTHER NAMES: Stalked jellyfish; formerly classified as *Haliclystus auricula, Haliclystus sanjuanensis*.

DESCRIPTION: Color is extremely variable and includes yellowish, orange, olive green and reddish-brown. Eight separate clusters of tentacles are present equally spaced at the feeding end of the organism.

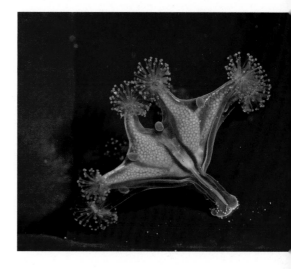

Between each cluster of tentacles an egg-shaped structure that lacks a stalk **is present along on the margin.**

SIZE: To 1″ (2.5 cm) in diameter, 1″ (2.5 cm) high.

HABITAT: On rocks, algae or eelgrass at exposed sites; extreme low intertidal zone to depths of 33′ (10 m).

RANGE: Alaska to Puget Sound, Washington; Northern Japan.

NOTES: Stalked jellies resemble sea anemones and have a relatively sedentary lifestyle. Although they can move from one location to another, they tend to remain at a favorable location that provides a readily available food source. The oval-anchored stalked jelly is one of several species that may be encountered in the Pacific Northwest. None are common in an intertidal environment. This predator uses its clusters of knobbed tentacles to capture small crustaceans. Once captured the marginal lobe bends slowly inwards to enable the transfer of prey from its tentacles to the mouth. The color of this organism normally matches the color of its substrate.

SIMILAR SPECIES: Trumpet stalked jelly *Haliclystus salpinx* James-Clark, 1863, is distinctive with trumpet-shaped anchors with conspicuous stalks on the margin.

Sea gooseberry,
Pleurobrachia bachei

Comb Jellies
PHYLUM CTENOPHORA

Comb jellies are characterized by tiny cilia (hair-like appendages) that make up eight rows of comb plates called ctenes. These tiny cilia are responsible for the comb jellies' wave-like movements. As a result comb jellies do not move great distances using this technique. Water currents likely have a much greater impact on their movements. Some comb jellies are found on the water's surface while others live in deeper waters. Their best defense against predators is their transparency. They are also known to "show" rainbow-like colors when they move. This is simply sunlight diffracted off their beating cilia.

With extended tentacles.

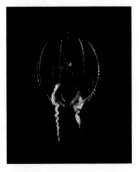

With retracted tentacles.

Sea Gooseberry

Pleurobrachia bachei A. Agassiz, 1860

OTHER NAMES: Cat's eye, cat's eye comb jelly, comb jelly, combjelly, ctenophore, sea walnut, sea walnut comb jelly.
DESCRIPTION: Transparent in color. The small organism is **egg-shaped with 2 long tentacles**.
SIZE: Diameter to 0.8″ (20 mm); tentacles to 6″ (15 cm) long.
HABITAT: Found near shore, often in large numbers.
RANGE: Alaska to Baja California, México.
NOTES: This is the only common species of comb jelly likely to be found in Pacific Northwest waters. Comb jellies use sticky cells on the tentacles, rather than stinging cells, to capture food. They are often found in spring and summer swimming in large swarms. Occasionally they wash up on the beach. Each individual is both male and female. Eggs and sperm are released from the mouth to be fertilized in open water. This species has been called a voracious carnivore, as swarms can severely reduce schools of young fish. Most comb jellies are bioluminescent, but this species cannot produce its own light.

Two-spotted ribbon worm,
Amphiporus bimaculatus

Marine Worms

PHYLA PLATYHELMINTHES, NEMERTEA, ANNELIDA, SIPUNCULA, ECHIUROIDEA

Marine worms are a collection of unrelated yet similar animal groups. These worms are classified in several phyla, including flatworms, ribbon worms, segmented worms, peanut worms and spoonworms.

Flatworms
PHYLUM PLATYHELMINTHES

Marine flatworms are members of the class Turbellaria. These organisms are thin, oval and compressed. Many species are predators, feeding on a variety of organisms depending upon the species. They move slowly with the use of thousands of cilia or hair-like structures on their lower surface. They feed with a mouth on their underside, which is also where they release wastes. There are about 3,000 species found in the world.

Large Leaf Worm
Kaburakia excelsa Bock, 1925

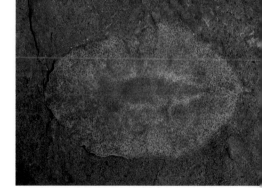

OTHER NAMES: Giant leaf worm, leaf worm.
DESCRIPTION: Color varies from orange to brown marked with dark brown dashes or spots. Tough, firm, large, oval body. 2 short retractable tentacles, each with an eyespot, near the brain.
SIZE: Length to 4″ (10 cm); width to 2.75″ (7 cm); thickness to 0.1″ (3 mm).
HABITAT: Under rocks, inside holes, on pilings, on boat bottoms and among mussels; sometimes in large numbers; mid- to low intertidal zone.
RANGE: Sitka, Alaska, to Newport Harbor, California.
NOTES: This giant species responds negatively to sunlight. Approximately 50 minute, light-sensitive eyespots are located along the entire margin of this flatworm. This worm glides over the substrate by using thousands of tiny cilia, blending in to its environment so well

that it is often difficult to detect. There is a mouth on the lower or ventral side but no anus, thus wastes pass back through the worm's mouth to be expelled. It is believed that this species feeds on animals such as limpets.

....

Red Saddled Flatworm

Notocomplana sanguinea (Freeman, 1933)

OTHER NAMES: Saddleback flatworm; formerly classified as *Notoplana sanguinea*.
DESCRIPTION: Color of the body is gray with a distinctive **red saddle-like band running across the central part** of its dorsal surface.
SIZE: Length to 1″ (2.5 cm) long.
HABITAT: On and under rocks of protected shorelines; low intertidal zone to shallow subtidal depths.
RANGE: Alaska to Central California; common in Puget Sound, Washington.
NOTES: This is one of very few flatworm species that is easily identified in the field due to its distinctive coloration.

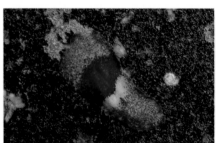 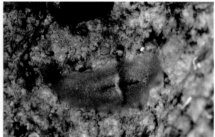

Ribbon Worms
PHYLUM NEMERTEA

The worms in this group are more advanced than flatworms, with blood or circulatory systems. The ribbon worm has a retractable proboscis (snout) with either sticky glands or poisonous hooks to capture its prey. Most break or constrict into several pieces when they are picked up. This is believed to be a way in which they multiply: each worm piece regenerates its missing parts to form a whole new identical worm.

Six-lined Ribbon Worm

Tubulanus sexlineatus (Griffin, 1898)

OTHER NAMES: Six-lined nemertean, lined ribbon worm; formerly classified as *Carinella sexlineata, Carinella dinema.*
DESCRIPTION: Chocolate brown or black in color, with **5–6 white longitudinal stripes and up to 150 cross-bands.** The body is relatively thick and elastic.
SIZE: Length normally to 8″ (20 cm) but occasionally to more than 39″ (1 m) long.
HABITAT: Among rocks, mussels, algae and pilings, from the low intertidal zone to water 26′ (8 m) deep.
RANGE: Sitka, Alaska, to southern California.
NOTES: The six-lined ribbon worm builds a transparent, parchment-like tube in which it then lives. A variety of worms make up the diet of this distinctive and beautiful nemertean.

Orange Ribbon Worm

Tubulanus polymorphus Renier, 1804

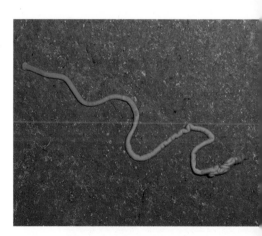

OTHER NAMES: Orange nemertean, red ribbon worm; formerly *Carinella rubra.*
DESCRIPTION: Color a vivid, uniform red or orange. Body is thin, elastic, round, soft with no distinct markings on the head.
SIZE: Length normally to 3′ (90 cm) long, and to an amazing 10′ (3 m) in large specimens, but often somewhat contracted due to its elastic nature; to 0.2″ (5 mm) wide.
HABITAT: Among mussels, in gravel or under rocks in quiet areas, sometimes in higher numbers; low intertidal zone to 165′ (50 m) deep.
RANGE: Aleutian Islands, Alaska, to San Luis Obispo County, California; northern Europe; Mediterranean Sea.
NOTES: This highly visible worm can often be observed moving slowly along in intertidal pools, hunting for prey. Its slow movement and rounded shape are characteristic. Often common in spring and summer.

Rose Ribbon Worm

Cerebratulus montgomeryi Coe, 1901

OTHER NAME: Incorrectly *Cerebratulus montgomeri.*
DESCRIPTION: Overall color is **dark rosy pink, with a white, mouth-like mark across the tip of the head**. The body is thick and elongated.
SIZE: Length normally to 80″ (2 m) long; occasionally to 120″ (3 m).
HABITAT: Under rocks in mud, from the low intertidal zone to water 1,320′ (400 m) deep.
RANGE: Unalaska Island, Alaska, to Monterey Bay, California; Japan; Siberia.
NOTES: The rose ribbon worm is a large species that, unlike other ribbon worms, does not break easily when handled.

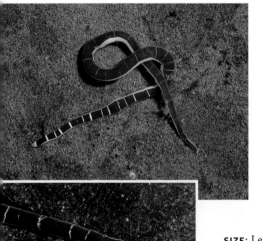

Lavender and White Ribbon Worm

Micrura verrilli Coe, 1901

OTHER NAMES: Purple ribbon worm, Verrill's ribbon worm; formerly classified as *Lineus striatus.*
DESCRIPTION: Color of the dorsal surface is a **rich reddish-purple to dark brown with numerous white transverse bands**. Its head is white with a **bright orange triangular tip**.
SIZE: Length to 20″ (50 cm).
HABITAT: Beneath rocks, among algae and in tidepools; low intertidal zone to shallow subtidal depths.
RANGE: Prince William Sound, Alaska, to Monterey Bay, California.
NOTES: The lavender and white ribbon worm is perhaps the most striking of our ribbon worms! It produces a transparent tube-like structure that it uses for protection. A caudal cirrus, or small tail-like extension at the posterior end of its body, may be present but it breaks off easily and may be missing.

Two-spotted Ribbon Worm

Nipponnemertes bimaculata
(Coe, 1901)

OTHER NAMES: Chevron amphiporus, chevron ribbon worm, two-spotted ribbonworm, thick amphiporus, twisted brown ribbon worm, two-eyed ribbon worm; formerly classified as *Amphiporus bimaculatus.*

DESCRIPTION: Color on the dorsal side ranges from orange to brownish-red. The **body is short and stocky** with a lighter-colored **head, which has a pair of dark triangular markings.**

SIZE: Length to 5″ (13 cm).

HABITAT: Usually in rocky areas, low intertidal zone to water 450′ (137 m) deep.

RANGE: Sitka, Alaska, to Baja California, México.

NOTES: This common species, which resembles a leech, can sometimes be seen swimming after it has been disturbed. It breeds in July in the southern portion of its range. Like many worms, this one shuns light. The 2 eye-like markings in the head region are not eyes; tiny light-detecting organs located near these markings help the worm detect light and find its way to darkness.

....

V-Neck Ribbon Worm

Amphiporus angulatus (Müller, 1774)

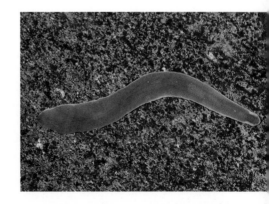

OTHER NAMES: Chevron amphiporus, many-eyed ribbon worm; formerly classified as *Cosmocephala beringiana, Fasciola angulata, Omatoplea stimpsonii.*

DESCRIPTION: Color ranges from brick red to pink or purple on the dorsal side and lighter ventrally. This rather **thick-bodied** species displays **2 triangular white patches behind the head along the margins.**

SIZE: Length to 8″ (20 cm).

HABITAT: Beneath stones in sand and cobble; mid-intertidal zone to depths of 492′ (150 m).

RANGE: Bering Strait and Unalaska Island, Alaska, to Point Conception, California; uncommon south of Puget Sound, Washington; circumpolar; Japan; Greenland to Massachusetts.

NOTES: This ribbon worm appears leech-like with its thick body shape. The distinctive whitish areas of the head region bear 12 small eyespots and 20 larger eyespots on each side. These eyespots are the reason this species is sometimes referred to as the many-eyed ribbon worm.

SIMILAR SPECIES: Two-spotted ribbon worm.

....

Pink-fronted Ribbon Worm

Amphiporus imparispinosus Griffin, 1898

OTHER NAMES: Thin amphiporus, white nemertean.

DESCRIPTION: Color is white overall, often with a **pinkish or orange tinge toward its anterior end**. The body of this small worm is flattened, elongated and elastic in appearance.

SIZE: Length to 2″ (5 cm).

HABITAT: On the open coast in rocky areas of the intertidal zone.

RANGE: Bering Sea to Ensenada, Baja California, México; Siberia.

NOTES: It is believed that the pink-fronted ribbon worm feeds on amphipods while it moves between mussels or barnacles, or around seaweed holdfasts. It uses its retractable proboscis (snout) for feeding. A microscope is needed to observe additional differences in the proboscis, between similar-looking species.

SIMILAR SPECIES: White intertidal ribbon worm *Amphiporus formidabilis* Griffin, 1898 is a similar species that lacks the pink or orange coloration and reaches a larger size.

Many-eyed Ribbon Worm

Amphiporus cruentatus Verrill, 1879

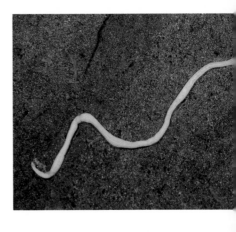

OTHER NAME: Formerly classified as
Amphiporus leptacanthus.
DESCRIPTION: Color of body ranges from
yellow to flesh-color. The body of this species
is small, slender and flat with **5–10 eyespots on
both sides of the slender head.**
SIZE: Length to 1″ (2.5 cm).
HABITAT: On and among various growths in
rocky sites; low intertidal zone to depths of
65′ (20 m).
RANGE: Southern British Columbia to San Diego, California; Atlantic coast.
NOTES: The many-eyed ribbon worm is a small species that is easy to miss. The minute
eyespots are best viewed with a good quality 10x hand lens or a quality digital camera.

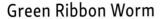

Green Ribbon Worm

Emplectonema gracile (Johnson, 1837)

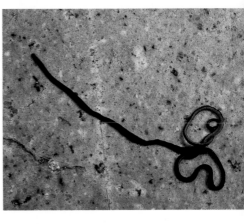

OTHER NAMES: Green and yellow
ribbon worm; formerly classified as
Nemertes gracilis.
DESCRIPTION: The body is **dark green
above** and yellowish-green below,
flattened, long and elastic in appearance.
SIZE: Length to 20″ (50 cm).
HABITAT: Rocky shores and among
barnacles and mussels in the
mid-intertidal zone.
RANGE: Aleutian Islands, Alaska, to Baja California, México; northern Europe; Chile.
NOTES: The green ribbon worm is a small, distinctive species with many eyespots on the
sides of its head. A group of 8 to 10 eyespots can be seen on the front of each side; these
are best viewed from below. Another cluster of 10–20 smaller eyespots can be found above
the brain, but these are more difficult to see. This nemertean is most often active at night
feeding on barnacles, including the acorn barnacle. It is a specialist that uses its proboscis
(snout) to suck out the flesh of its prey. There are also reports of this worm feeding on
segmented worms and limpets.

Purple-backed Ribbon Worm

Paranemertes peregrina Coe, 1901

OTHER NAMES: Mud nemertean, purple ribbon worm, restless worm, wandering ribbon worm, wandering nemertean.

DESCRIPTION: **Purple-brown varying to bluish-purple above** and cream-colored below. The body is flattened, long and elastic in appearance.

SIZE: Length normally to 5″ (13 cm); occasionally to 10″ (25 cm).

HABITAT: In rocky and muddy areas from the mid- to low intertidal zone.

RANGE: Aleutian Islands, Alaska, to Ensenada, Baja California, México; Japan; Siberia.

NOTES: The purple-backed ribbon worm feeds on a variety of segmented worms, including

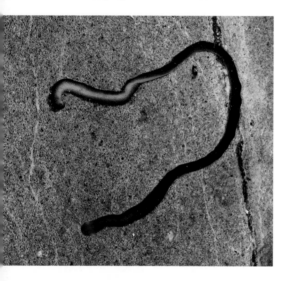

the pile worm. This species cannot detect its prey until it actually bumps into it, at which time it immediately coils its proboscis (snout) around its unlucky prey. This extendable feeding apparatus is armed with a stylet, a nail-like weapon on the tip of the worm's proboscis that is used to stab its prey, after which a nerve poison called anabaseine is released to paralyze the prey. The worm then briefly lets go, allowing the neurotoxin to work before eating the prey whole. The purple-backed ribbon worm is known to live as long as 1.5 years.

Segmented Worms
PHYLUM ANNELIDA

Segmented worms are easily identified by the many visible rings that make up their bodies. Over 9,000 species have been identified in this phylum. Many marine species are found on the sea bottom but are not restricted to it.

American Proboscis Worm

Glycera americana Leidy, 1855

Note the extended proboscis, used to capture prey.

OTHER NAMES: American bloodworm, beakthrower, blood worm, corrugated worm, proboscis worm.

DESCRIPTION: Color is iridescent and pinkish. The **body resembles an earthworm** and consists of a number of crowded segments and a pointed head segment. It bears **numerous parapodia** and an enormous evertable proboscis with 4 hooks on the tip. Gills are finger-like and branched (requires a microscope to view).

SIZE: Length to 14″ (35 cm).

HABITAT: In mud or sandy mud on protected shores; low intertidal zone to depths of 1,040′ (315 m).

RANGE: British Columbia to Chile; Atlantic coast; Japan; Australia; New Zealand.

NOTES: Four black jaws grace this worm's proboscis, which it can evert rapidly to almost a third of its body length. The worm uses its proboscis to capture prey. It also extends its proboscis into the sand, where its end swells to act as an anchor in bringing the body forward. **Exercise caution** if you handle this worm. Its remarkable proboscis can inflict quite a bite. Several species of proboscis worms, *Glycera* spp., are found in the Pacific Northwest but they require a microscope to identify.

Bat Star Worm

Oxydromus pugettensis (Johnson, 1901)

OTHER NAMES: Bat star commensal worm; formerly classified as *Ophiodromus pugettensis*, *Podarke pugettensis*.

DESCRIPTION: Color varies from **reddish-brown to purple** or black. Head bears **6 pairs of tentacles on a single segment**.

SIZE: Length to 1.5″ (3.8 cm); width to 0.1″ (3 mm).

HABITAT: Lives in the grooves of sea stars,

primarily the bat star, on floats and pilings and in muddy bottoms; low intertidal zone to shallow subtidal depths.

RANGE: Alaska to Gulf of California; Peru; Japan.

NOTES: This worm lives among the tube feet of the bat star and other sea stars as a commensal worm. The bat star worm locates its host by scent, and studies show that nearly half of them leave their host each day and return later to another. There have been instances where up to 20 worms have been found living on one bat star at a time. This number is much higher during winter months. The bat star worm can also be found free-living on silty bottoms, floats and pilings.

Pile Worm

Nereis vexillosa Grube, 1851

OTHER NAMES: Banner sea-nymph, clam worm, clamworm, large mussel worm, mussel worm, piling worm, sand worm.

DESCRIPTION: Color is dark green, often with a bluish tint, and in bright sunlight it may appear iridescent. The segmented body features **elongated parapodia** of certain segments. There are also 4 black eyes and a pair of black jaws.

SIZE: Length to 12″ (30 cm); width to 0.4″ (10 mm).

HABITAT: In sand and mud beaches, beneath rocks, on wharf pilings and in mussel beds; mid-intertidal zone to shallow subtidal depths.

RANGE: Alaska to Santa Barbara, California; Russia.

NOTES: The breeding season of this common worm is linked to the full moons of summer, at which time huge congregations can be observed at night. They use their flattened parapodia or leg-like appendages for swimming. The males release their sperm, then the females release eggs. Once the breeding sequence is completed, both sexes perish. One of its major predators is the purple ribbon worm. **Exercise caution** when handling the pile worm. Large individuals have been known to deliver the occasional nasty bite!

Giant Clam Bed Worm

Alitta brandti Malmgren, 1865

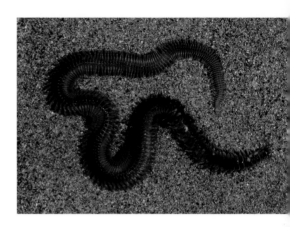

OTHER NAMES: Giant clam worm, giant piling sea-nymph, giant pile worm, giant piling worm, giant mussel worm; formerly classified as *Nereis brandti, Neanthes brandti*.
DESCRIPTION: Color varies from **dark iridescent greenish-blue to reddish-brown**. The body of this **extremely large segmented worm** is adorned with leaf-like dorsal lobes on its posterior appendages. Numerous toothlike projections are present on the everted proboscis.
SIZE: Length normally to 3.3′ (1 m), occasionally to 5′ (1.5 m); width to 1.2″ (3 cm) in diameter.
HABITAT: Buried in mud or sand bars and in eelgrass beds; low intertidal zone to subtidal waters.
RANGE: British Columbia to California; Siberia.
NOTES: This worm is known to swarm while spawning—a truly extraordinary sight for worms of this size! This behavior has been observed in spring and early summer in the southern part of the species' range.
SIMILAR SPECIES: Common clam bed worm *Alitta virens* (M. Sars, 1835) is very similar looking but only reaches 12″ (30 cm) in length. A microscope is required to identify this species.

Leafy Shimmyworm

Nephtys caeca (Fabricius, 1780)

OTHER NAMES: Red-lined worm, sand worm; occasionally misspelled as *Nephthys caeca*.
DESCRIPTION: Color is light tan to bronze with beautiful **iridescent** tones. The body is cylindrical at the anterior section and near rectangular at the posterior in cross-section, with up to 150 segments. Long cirri or hair-like structures are curved

inwards between segments. **Leaf-like extensions are present behind the parapodia** or pairs of projections from the body.

SIZE: Length to 10″ (25 cm); width to 0.6″ (15 mm).

HABITAT: In sand; low intertidal zone to depths of 3,300′ (1,000 m).

RANGE: Arctic Ocean and Bering Sea; Alaska to California; circumboreal; Japan; Arctic to Rhode Island; North Sea; western Baltic.

NOTES: The leafy shimmyworm is one of several species of shimmyworms that may be found in the Pacific Northwest. However, a microscope is necessary to identify them to species. There is a possibility that it may have been introduced from the East Coast.

....

Copper-haired Sea Mouse

Aphrodita japonica Marenzeller, 1879

OTHER NAMES: Sea mouse; formerly classified as *Aphrodita cryptommata*.

DESCRIPTION: Color of body is light brown overall. In sunlight the hair-like **setae have** an impressive **copper or gold-colored metallic sheen**. The body is oval with about 40 segments that are completely covered with felt-like setae, which hide the elytra.

SIZE: Length to 9″ (22 cm), but normally much smaller.

HABITAT: Buried in soft sand and mud; subtidal depths to 300′ (90 m).

RANGE: Alaska to Ecuador; Japan.

NOTES: This large, plump, unusual-looking worm is sometimes found washed up on the sand after a storm. Its scientific name *Aphrodita* is appropriate: Aphrodite was a Greek goddess of love and beauty who was tossed onto the shore after a storm. The hair-like setae are very sharp and have been known to deliver painful wounds. Two pairs of minute eyes are present but difficult to see. There are other species of *Aphrodita* in the Pacific Northwest but they do not have the copper or gold metallic sheen visible in direct sunlight.

....

Painted Fifteen-paired Scaleworm

Harmothoe imbricata (Linnaeus, 1767)

OTHER NAME: Fifteen-scaled worm.

DESCRIPTION: The overall **color is variable and includes red, orange, brown, green, gray**

and black—speckled or mottled. Some individuals may also have a black stripe down the back. **It has a total of fifteen pairs of scales.** Although two pairs of eyes are present on the frontal lobe, only one pair can be seen from above; the other pair can only be seen from below.

SIZE: Length to 2.5″ (6 cm), width to 0.75″ (19 mm).

HABITAT: Under rocks, in tidepools, on mussels, holdfasts and similar locations, and estuaries; low intertidal zone to depths of 12,172′ (3,710 m).

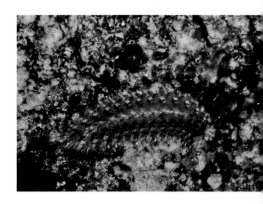

RANGE: Point Barrow, Alaska, to southern California; Arctic to New Jersey; Europe; Indian Ocean; Arctic Ocean.

NOTES: The painted fifteen-paired scaleworm is a species that has been found in many areas around the globe. In some regions, females are known to brood their eggs beneath their scales. Females of various sizes are known to lay from fewer than 5,000 up to 40,000 or more eggs. This species is able to live quite happily in brackish water. Opportunistic, it also lives commensally with tubeworms or inside the shells occupied by hermit crabs.

....

White-banded Scaleworm

Gaudichaudius iphionelloides

(Johnson, 1901)

OTHER NAME: Formerly classified as *Gattyana iphionelloides*.

DESCRIPTION: Color of the elytra are brown with **a white band often present** on an anterior pair of elytra. The body is short and rather broad with 36 segments that are covered with **large scales that have near polygonal-shaped sections** within.

SIZE: Length to 1.4″ (3.5 cm).

HABITAT: On or beneath rocks, shells and similar hard objects in muddy environments and eelgrass beds; low intertidal zone to shallow subtidal depths.

RANGE: Alaska to California; Siberia.

NOTES: This beautiful scaleworm is not as common as the other scaleworm species found in the Pacific Northwest. Only diligent searching in the correct habitat will help to locate it.

Depressed Scaleworm

Eunoe depressa Moore, 1908

DESCRIPTION: The elytra are **cream-colored** with elevated brown spots. The flattened body is covered with large elytra and many rows of long spines with slightly hooked tips. The margins of **elytra are smooth without any papillae** or nipple-like projections (a hand lens is needed to view).

SIZE: Length to 1.1″ (2.9 cm).

HABITAT: In rocky areas; low intertidal zone to depths of 900′ (270 m).

RANGE: Bering Sea, Alaska, to San Juan Islands, Washington; northwestern Atlantic; Sea of Japan.

NOTES: The depressed scaleworm is a delicate species that has been found to be both free-living and also to live commensally with hermit crabs and the king crab, *Paralithodes camtschatica*, in Alaska.

Eighteen-paired Scaleworm

Halosydna brevisetosa Kinberg, 1856

OTHER NAME: Eighteen-scaled worm.

DESCRIPTION: Color ranges widely from yellow, orange, gray or brown; white or black spots are often present. The body includes 37 segments that are covered by **18 pairs of elytra** on the dorsal side—the only species in the Pacific Northwest to have this.

SIZE: Length to 3″ (8 cm); width to 0.5″ (13 mm).

HABITAT: In rocky areas; low intertidal zone to depths of 1,788′ (545 m).

RANGE: Kodiak Island, Alaska, to Baja California, México.

NOTES: This worm can release 1 or more scales if it feels threatened and generate a replacement in a mere 5 days. Like several other scaleworms, it can live independently or commensally on a host. Those that choose a host often grow to twice the length of free-living individuals, perhaps because more food is available to the commensal worms. This worm has even been found attached to the body, hood and cerata of the hooded nudibranch.

Frilled Commensal Scaleworm

Arctonoe fragilis (Baird, 1863)

OTHER NAMES: Fragile ruffled scaleworm, ruffled scale-worm, fragile scaleworm, fragile commensal worm, scale worm.
DESCRIPTION: Color is overall light and can be cream-colored, yellowish-orange, reddish-brown or pale green. The body made up of up to 70 segments and 34 pairs of elytra. **The elytra are very frilled or folded at the margin**.
SIZE: Length to 3.4″ (8.5 cm).
HABITAT: Commensal on the underside of several sea stars; on rocky shores; low intertidal zone to depths of 910′ (275 m).
RANGE: Alaska Peninsula, Alaska, to Baja California, México.
NOTES: The frilled commensal scaleworm feeds on detritus. It is often found living on the underside of several species of sea stars including mottled star, painted star and morning sunstar. Normally only one scaleworm is found on a host at a time, but there have been reports of up to 4 at a time.

Red Commensal Scaleworm

Arctonoe pulchra (Johnson, 1897)

OTHER NAMES: Dark-spotted scale worm, scale worm.
DESCRIPTION: Color varies with host but **often red with a black spot**. This commensal worm bears up to 33 pairs of **elytra that have smooth to slightly undulating margins**.
SIZE: Length to 2.8″ (7 cm).
HABITAT: Commensal on several marine organisms on rocky shores; low intertidal zone to depths of 910′ (275 m).
RANGE: Gulf of Alaska to Baja California, México.
NOTES: The coloration of the red commensal scaleworm usually matches the coloration of its host. This species, like several other scaleworms, feeds on detritus. It is found on the underside of a variety of organisms, including the rough keyhole limpet, giant Pacific chiton, leather star and California sea cucumber.

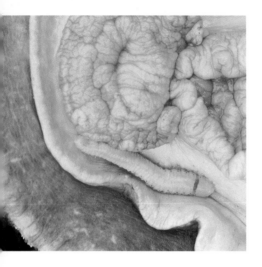

Red-banded Commensal Scaleworm

Arctonoe vittata (Grube, 1855)

OTHER NAMES: Pacific scale worm, yellow scale worm; formerly classified as *Polynoe vittata*.

DESCRIPTION: Color overall yellow or tan often **with a reddish-brown band across the dorsal side** of segments 7 and 8. The coloration often matches the host's coloration. The body is covered with more than 30 pairs of scales.

SIZE: Length to 4″ (10 cm).

HABITAT: Free-living or commensally on the undersides of various hosts; mid-intertidal zone to depths of 902′ (275 m).

RANGE: Bering Strait to Ecuador; Japan.

NOTES: Some individuals are free-living, some live commensally. Hosts vary from the rough keyhole limpet and giant Pacific chiton to 9 species of sea stars, including the leather star and Pacific blood star. The host attracts the worm by releasing a chemical scent. This species actually helps protect its host from predators such as the purple star by biting at the predator's tube feet when it attacks. It is definitely in this worm's best interest to ensure its host continues to live!

Porcupine Worm

Euphrosine spp. Lamarck, 1818

DESCRIPTION: Colors of this group vary with the individuals. All species are **covered with long notochaetae.**

SIZE: Length to 1.2″ (3 cm).

HABITAT: Under rocks, while others are pelagic; low intertidal zone to subtidal depths.

RANGE: Alaska to México.

NOTES: The coloration of some species in this genus is quite striking!

Fringed Filament-worm

Dodecaceria fewkesi

Berkeley & Berkeley, 1954

OTHER NAMES: Black tube-building cirratulid worm, cemented tube worm, colonial tubeworm, fringed tubeworm, Fewke's fringed worm, honeycomb worm; occasionally misspelled *Dodecaceria feweksi*.

DESCRIPTION: This species lives in a colony of numerous individual worms. Body is **dark green to black overall**. The elongated body is hidden from view in the colony, leaving only the crown of 12 tentacles visible. The **colony forms a solid calcareous mass** with tiny holes in which each worm lives.

SIZE: Length of worm to 1.6″ (4 cm); colony to 39″ (1 m).

HABITAT: On rocky shores of protected coasts; mid-intertidal zone to shallow subtidal depths.

RANGE: British Columbia to southern California.

NOTES: The fringed filament-worm is a colonial species that originates from a single worm that reproduces by asexual fission. As a result, the colony made up of identical organisms living in a large reef-like structure that resembles concrete.

....

Sheathed Bristle-cage Worm

Flabelligera affinis M. Sars, 1829

OTHER NAME: Flabby bristle-worm.

DESCRIPTION: The body is **covered in a transparent outer layer** that reveals the inner organs. The body is elongated with many **papillae and setae that protrude** outward.

SIZE: Length to 5.1″ (13 cm).

HABITAT: Under rocks at muddy sites; low intertidal zone to depths of 8,202′ (2,500 m).

RANGE: Alaska to southern California; Japan; Atlantic Ocean; Arctic Ocean.

NOTES: The sheathed bristle-cage worm is a distinctive annelid that creates its own cage from two very long fan-like chaetae, or bristles, originating from either side of its head. The resulting "cage" remains over the worm if it crawls to a new location. This species is a surface deposit feeder. Females ready for reproduction produce a pheromone that signals males to release sperm. Once sperm is released into the water the female is stimulated to release her eggs. The eggs are thus fertilized in the ocean.

Utility-worm

Thoracophelia spp. Ehlers, 1897

OTHER NAMES: Blood worm; formerly classified as *Euzonus* spp.
DESCRIPTION: Color is **bright red** due to the presence of hemoglobin in the blood. The **body is very slender, elastic and made up of 3 distinct regions**. It is also very difficult to collect intact specimens
SIZE: Length to 1.5″ (4 cm).
HABITAT: On clean sand beaches; mid-intertidal zone, burrowing to a depth of 4–12″ (10–30 cm) below the surface.
RANGE: Vancouver Island, British Columbia, to Baja California, México.
NOTES: Utility-worms are often found in very high numbers, frequently in a band less than 3′ (1 m) wide along the shore. They burrow deeper into the sand as the water slowly recedes and the sand dries out. These worms are very important food for a wide variety of migrating shorebirds.

Pacific Lugworm

Abarenicola pacifica Healy & Wells, 1959

OTHER NAMES: Lugworm, lug worm, Pacific neapolitan lugworm, Pacific green lugworm.
DESCRIPTION: **Body color yellow to yellowish-green, head and abdomen light orange** (color is best viewed underwater). Stout, with branched gills along the body that expand underwater.
SIZE: Length to 6″ (15 cm).
HABITAT: In muddy sand; high intertidal zone.

Casting.

RANGE: Alaska to Humboldt Bay, California.

NOTES: Telltale castings of mud and sand often indicate the presence of this species. Beneath the slender fecal casting lies a J-shaped burrow harboring the lugworm, which extracts bacteria and organic debris from the sand. When this worm is first uncovered, its long body is greenish in color, but once immersed in water this seemingly unattractive creature contracts and quickly changes to a pleasant-looking worm with the hemoglobin of its body becoming visible. If left long enough, the gills eventually expand and become bright red. Lugworms have been used as bait by fishermen in Europe and elsewhere.

SIMILAR SPECIES: Rough-skinned lugworm *Abarenicola claparedi* (Levinsen, 1884) is a larger, dark species that lives in deeper levels on sandy seashores.

Red-banded Bamboo-Worm

Axiothella rubrocincta (Johnson, 1901)

OTHER NAMES: Bamboo-worm, jointworm, red-banded tube worm.

DESCRIPTION: Overall color is **green with red banding on segments 4–8**. The **body is bamboo-like** and made up of 22 segments in total, with a funnel-shaped end segment and finger-like projections that are unequal.

SIZE: Length of worm to 8″ (20 cm).

Worm and its tube.

Tube as observed on the beach.

HABITAT: In sand or muddy sand of bays and estuaries; low intertidal zone.
RANGE: Southern Alaska to México; Japan.
NOTES: Bamboo-worms get their name from their elongated segments, which bear a striking resemblance to bamboo cane. The red-banded bamboo-worm lives in a U-shaped tube that extends into the sand to 12″ (30 cm) deep. This species is known to share its tube with the commensal bamboo worm pea crab *Pinnixa longipes*. This is a very tiny crab to be able to live inside this very slender tube!

California Trumpetworm

Pectinaria californiensis
Hartman, 1941

OTHER NAMES: Ice cream cone worm; occasionally misspelled *Pectinaria califoriensis*.
DESCRIPTION: Body is pink overall with golden bristles that are visible when the worm moves at the open end of its tube. The worm has a flattened head and 2 sets of 14 long golden bristles. Its **remarkable, straight, cone-shaped tube** is created by cementing fine, red-brown grains of sand together.
SIZE: Length of worm to 2.4″ (6 cm); length of tube to 3.1″ (8 cm).
HABITAT: On sand and mud bottoms; the low intertidal zone to subtidal waters.
RANGE: Alaska to Baja California, México.
NOTES: This worm positions itself in the sand, usually with its narrow end up, and uses its beautiful golden bristles to dig so that its feeding tentacles can find food lower down in the sandy or muddy substrate. The worm's cone-shaped body fits tightly inside its distinctive cone.
SIMILAR SPECIES: Pacific trumpetworm *Pectinaria granulate* (Linnaeus, 1767) is easily identified by its curved cone.

Fringe-hooded Tube Worm

Pista pacifica Berkeley & Berkeley, 1942

OTHER NAMES: Fringed-hood spaghetti-worm, Pacific terebellid worm, tentacle-feeding worm.

DESCRIPTION: Color of the worm is gray overall and variously colored with white tentacles that are stiped in gray and brown. The **distinctive tube** is this worm's best identification—the exposed portion **resembles a hood that is parchment-like and bears numerous frills and droops.** The remainder of the tube is buried deep in the substrate.

SIZE: Length of worm to 15″ (37 cm); length of tube to 39″ (1 m).

HABITAT: In mud and sand of protected areas and in dense eelgrass; low intertidal zone to shallow subtidal depths.

RANGE: Vancouver Island, British Columbia, to California.

NOTES: This worm feeds with its long ciliated tentacles that scour the substrate's surface when the tide is in. When the tide is out the tentacles are retracted inside the hood. The eighteen-paired scaleworm possibly shares the tubes of this species commensally.

Basket-top Tube Worm

Pista elongata Moore, 1909

OTHER NAMES: Fibre-tube worm, fibre tube worm, elongate terebellid worm.

DESCRIPTION: This pinkish-colored worm produces a **distinctive tube with a unique, greatly enlarged end made up of a sponge-like fibrous network**.

SIZE: Length of worm to 8″ (20 cm); length of tube to 3″ (7.5 cm).

HABITAT: Inhabits a tube that is attached on or under rocks, in crevices and in the roots of surfgrass; mid-intertidal zone to depths of 207′ (63 m).

RANGE: British Columbia to San Diego, California; Panama; Japan.

NOTES: This worm produces an ornate, fibrous, spongy basket-like structure at the end of its tube. Feeding is accomplished by extending the long tentacles to capture tiny food particles in the water, then moving the particles to the mouth of the tube with tiny cilia.

Coarse-tubed Pink Spaghetti-worm

Thelepus crispus Johnson, 1901

OTHER NAMES: Curly-head spaghetti-worm, curly terebellid worm, curly terebellid, hairy gilled worm, hairy-headed terebellid worm, shell binder worm, shell-binder worm, spaghetti worm, terebellid worm.

DESCRIPTION: The overall color of the **worm is reddish-pink**. The head has many tentacles attached as well as **3 pairs of gills with unbranched filiments that are "curly." It builds a tube from coarse debris.**

SIZE: Length to 11.25″ (28 cm).

HABITAT: Tubes are attached to the undersides of rocks on outer rocky shorelines; mid- to low intertidal zone.

RANGE: Alaska to southern California; India.

NOTES: This is one of the most common species of spaghetti-worms and very similar to the brown intertidal spaghetti-worm, except for its color. Both species (like all spaghetti-worms) live inside permanent burrows and feed with their tentacles, moving minute particles of food to their mouth. Water is also circulated through their burrow for respiration.

SIMILAR SPECIES: Fine-tubed pink spaghetti-worm *Thelepus setosus* (Quatrefages, 1866) builds a sandy tube with a triangular hood that includes numerous fine threads of cemented particles.

....

Worm and its tube.

Brown Intertidal Spaghetti-worm

Eupolymnia heterobranchia (Johnson, 1901)

OTHER NAMES: Formerly classified as *Eupolymnia crescentis, Lanice heterobranchia.*

DESCRIPTION: Overall color is **dark brown to greenish-brown** with many small dark eyespots. The head of the worm has many extensible tentacles and lives inside a parchment-like tube covered with sand granules.

SIZE: Length to 5.1″ (13 cm).

HABITAT: In mixtures of sand, pebbles and mud in the intertidal zone.

RANGE: Alaska to México.

NOTES: Like all spaghetti-worms this species feeds with its tentacles, each of which is grooved and covered with tiny cilia to bring food to the mouth. Foods include detritus, diatoms, dead and dying crustaceans, and both living and dead segmented worms.

SIMILAR SPECIES: Coarse-tubed pink spaghetti-worm.

Robust Spaghetti-worm

Neoamphitrite robusta (Johnson, 1901)

OTHER NAME: Formerly classified as *Amphitrite robusta*.

DESCRIPTION: Color is brown overall with abundant white tentacles and red gills. The front of the body bears **hook-like setae in which the first 4 sets are arranged in single rows**. Its **tubes are made of mud**.

SIZE: Length of worm to 6″ (15 cm).

HABITAT: Tubes -found under rocks on muddy shores; low intertidal zone to depths of 6,496′ (1,980 m).

RANGE: Alaska to California.

NOTES: The robust spaghetti-worm builds its thick-walled tube from mud from which it feeds. Its feeding is much like most spaghetti-worms with a net of feeding tentacles spread out in fan fashion to gather its food.

Split-plume Feather-duster Worm

Schizobranchia insignis Bush, 1904

OTHER NAMES: Fan worm, feather-duster, feather duster worm, plume worm, split-branch feather-duster.

DESCRIPTION: Color of the crown of tentacles varies widely from tan or orange to mauve, green or brown with **a crown of transverse bands**. The body is comprised of two regions—the thorax and abdomen—with a **crown of tentacles that divide up to 5 times**.

SIZE: To 6.2″ (15.8 cm) long; tube to 8″ (20 cm) long.
HABITAT: On floats, wharves, wedged between rocks or boulders and in sandy mudflats; low intertidal zone to depths of 150′ (46 m).
RANGE: Alaska to central California.
NOTES: The tubes of this colorful worm are made of thick solidified mucus covered with grains of sand. It is normally gregarious and often intermixes with the larger northern feather-duster worm.

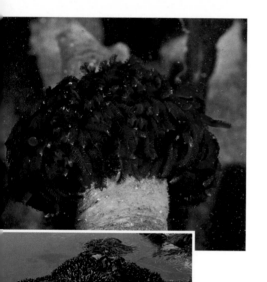

Northern Feather-duster Worm

Eudistylia vancouveri (Kinberg, 1866)

OTHER NAMES: Feather duster worm, parchment tube worm, plume worm, Vancouver feather-duster.
DESCRIPTION: The feathery tentacles are colored with alternating bands of green and maroon when expanded and submerged in water. The **large worms** are found in colonies. Each is **covered by a thick and rubbery parchment tube**.
SIZE: Length of worm to 10″ (25 cm); tube to 26.8″ (68 cm) long.
HABITAT: On rocky shores; low intertidal zone to depths of 100′ (30 m).
RANGE: Alaska to central California.
NOTES: This species is sometimes found in areas of heavy surf. The large parchment-like tube is so tough that it is difficult or impossible to remove it by hand from its supporting rock. If the tube breaks, the worm repairs it rather than building a new one. This worm's feathery tentacles, which draw both food and oxygen from the water, have light-sensitive eyespots that close with the slightest shadow.

Shell-binding Colonial Worm

Chone minuta Hartman, 1944

OTHER NAMES: Minute feather-duster, sand-binding colonial worm; formerly believed to be the same as *Chone ecaudata*.

DESCRIPTION: This species lives in a colony of numerous individual worms. The tiny dark bodies of the worms are not visible, however, the **tan-colored plumes** are exposed above the colony's carpet. This species **uses sand and shell fragments to build a protective "reef-like" environment** for their colony.

SIZE: Length of worm to 0.6″ (15 mm).

HABITAT: Among surfgrass, algal holdfasts and compound ascidians on exposed rocky shores; low intertidal zone to shallow subtidal depths.

RANGE: Alaska to southern California.

NOTES: The plume of this worm, which takes up a quarter of its length, is only visible while the worm feeds underwater. This species lives in a tube with a colony of hundreds of individuals. From shore, a reef-like colony of sand-binding colonial worms somewhat resembles white, textured cement-like mounds.

 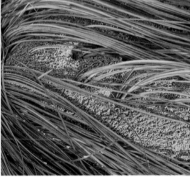

Worms feeding underwater.   Colony.

Red-trumpet Calcareous Tubeworm

Serpula columbiana Johnson, 1901

OTHER NAMES: Calcareous tube worm, red tube worm; mistakenly *Serpula vermicularis*.

DESCRIPTION: The tube is white; the worm is yellowish; the color of tentacles ranges widely from red to orange, pink and other colors, all with white banding. The **operculum (trap door) is red and trumpet-shaped**. The worm's tentacles are arranged in 2 separate spirals.

The tube is smooth, cylindrical and may be coiled.

SIZE: Length of worm to 3.1″ (8 cm); length of tube to 4″ (10 cm).

HABITAT: On and under rocks, and in tidepools; low intertidal zone to depths of 328′ (100 m).

RANGE: Alaska to California.

NOTES: The red-trumpet calcareous tubeworm is a very common species with a visible red operculum when its tentacles are retracted in the tube. The frilly circular tentacles filter tiny microorganisms from the water but disappear instantly with the slightest disturbance. This species is often incorrectly identified as *Serpula vermicularis*—a similar species found in the north Atlantic.

Peanut Worms

PHYLUM SIPUNCULA

Peanut worms are marine worms that are non-segmented and lack setae (hair-like structures). They are comprised of two body parts, one of which is much larger and more globular than the other. Only 320 species in this small group have been identified worldwide.

Pacific Peanut Worm

Phascolosoma agassizii Keferstein, 1866

OTHER NAMES: Agassiz's peanut worm; formerly classified as *Physcosoma agassizii*.

DESCRIPTION: Color overall ranges from light to dark brown, often with purple or brown spots. Narrow, extendable **neck-like portion of body has**

dark bands, followed by a wider, rough body section. A series of **25 rings of tiny tooth-like spines** are present at the anterior end and a ring of **slender tentacles surround the mouth.**
SIZE: Length to 4.75″ (12.1 cm) long; width to 0.5″ (13 mm) wide.
HABITAT: Beneath rocks, in gravel or crevices; mid- to low intertidal zone to shallow subtidal depths.
RANGE: Kodiak Island, Alaska, to Bahía de San Quintin, Baja California, México.
NOTES: This species is the most commonly encountered peanut worm living along the Pacific coast. A few short tentacles, located near the mouth, are used to feed on detritus. This species is also known to live in burrows abandoned by rock borers such as the rough paddock.

Bushy-headed Peanut Worm

Themiste pyroides (Chamberlin, 1919)

OTHER NAMES: Burrowing peanut worm, common peanut worm, flowering peanut worm, tan peanut worm, rich brown peanut worm; formerly classified as *Dendrostoma patraeum*, *Dendrostoma pyroides*.
DESCRIPTION: Color overall is medium brown with a light brown neck-like extendable portion. This is a plump worm with a tip of **bushy tentacles** on the feeding end of the worm. Many **small brown spines are found along the** "neck" region.
SIZE: Length to 8″ (20 cm); width to 2″ (5 cm).
HABITAT: Beneath rocks, in cracks; low intertidal zone to shallow subtidal depths.
RANGE: Vancouver Island, British Columbia, to Bahía de San Quintin, Baja California, México.
NOTES: This large species extends its tentacles when submerged in order to feed on minute organic particles while under the protection of a rock or similar situation. These tentacles are highly branched and covered with mucus, which aids the worm in collecting food. This species is also known to inhabit abandoned burrows made by rock-boring clams.

Feeding tentacles extended.

Spoonworms
PHYLUM ECHIURA (ALSO KNOWN AS ECHIURIDA OR ECHIUROIDEA)

The echiuran worms or spoonworms are a small group of worms that are closely related to segmented worms, but spoonworms' bodies lack segments. These worms include a sausage-like body, called the trunk, and an extendable organ used for feeding called the proboscis (snout) that can be shortened and lengthened but not retracted. It is often grooved and spoon-shaped—the reason for their common name. The proboscis also contains the brain. Echiura means "spiny tail" in Greek, a reference to the ring or rings of bristles that encircle the end of the worm.

Alaska Spoonworm
Echiurus echiurus alaskanus
Fisher, 1946

OTHER NAME: Fat innkeeper.
DESCRIPTION: Color of body or trunk is a pinkish-tan and its proboscis is orange. **The trunk is sausage-like and unsegmented, and its proboscis is trough-shaped.**
SIZE: To 10″ (25 cm) long, 1″ (2.5 cm) wide.
HABITAT: Under rocks lying in mud; mid- to low intertidal zone and subtidal depths.
RANGE: Point Barrow, Alaska, to Haida Gwaii (Queen Charlotte Islands), British Columbia.
NOTES: This species is closely related to the Arctic spoonworm *Echiurus echiurus*, a resident of the Atlantic and Arctic Oceans. The Alaska spoonworm uses its very sticky proboscis to feed, likely on detritus. The biology of this large species has not been studied in detail. Two large, curved, golden setae are located near the anterior end of the trunk. These are believed to be used in digging and possibly for anchoring the front part of the trunk when the worm's proboscis is extended.

Purple olive, *Callianax biplicata*

Molluscs

PHYLUM MOLLUSCA

Molluscs (or mollusks) are soft-bodied organisms that are normally protected by one or more valves (shells). This large phylum includes the chitons, abalone, limpets, snails, nudibranchs, clams, mussels and octopus. Molluscs have inhabited salt water, fresh water, land and even the air for short distances. They are highly diverse, having only a few characteristics in common. All molluscs possess a fold of soft flesh (mantle) that encloses several glands, such as the stomach and the shell-producing glands. Many molluscs also have a toothed or rasping tongue (radula) and a shell covering. Scientists estimate there are some 50,000 to 130,000 species of molluscs living in the world.

Chitons

CLASS POLYPLACOPHORA

Chitons, sometimes referred to as sea cradles and coat-of-mail shells, range in color from bright to well camouflaged. They have a series of 8 plates or valves held together by an outer girdle. Individuals in this group can be difficult to identify, as they are very similar in appearance.

Dwarf Chiton

Leptochiton rugatus complex
(Pilsbry, 1892)

OTHER NAME: Tan chiton.
DESCRIPTION: Color overall is **white or buff. The species' profile is rather high.**
SIZE: Length to 0.6″ (15 mm).
HABITAT: On muddy shores; low intertidal zone to shallow subtidal depths.

RANGE: Northern Alaska to northern México.
NOTES: This tiny chiton is common but its size makes it go unnoticed. This species is part of a complex of similar species and is currently under study. Little is known about the natural history of this species complex.

....

Lined Chiton

Tonicella lineata (Wood, 1815)

OTHER NAME: Lined red chiton.
DESCRIPTION: The valve colors are striking, varying from pink to orange-red. This chiton is named for the alternating light and dark zigzag lines on the plates. The first or **head plate** has dark brown or red-brown lines that border **concentric lines shaped in a simple arch without zigzags**. Outer girdle is dark, often with light blotches.
SIZE: To 2″ (5 cm) long.
HABITAT: On rocks, often with encrusting coralline algae; low intertidal to shallow subtidal zones.
RANGE: Adak Island, Aleutian Islands, Alaska, to Monterey, California.

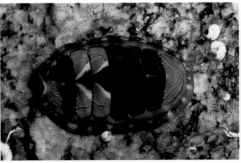

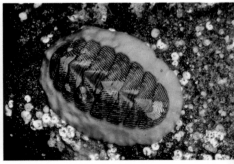

NOTES: This is one of the most beautiful chitons found in the Pacific Northwest, with brilliant colors that are not easily forgotten. Its color often closely matches the pink coralline algae on which it is most commonly found feeding. This chiton's main enemies are the purple star and the multi-lined six-rayed star.

SIMILAR SPECIES: White-line chiton; blue-line chiton.

White-line Chiton

Tonicella insignis (Reeve, 1847)

OTHER NAME: Red chiton.
DESCRIPTION: The valves are normally maroon or reddish-brown overall with rows of **white to yellowish fine wavy lines in pleural (central triangular) section.** The girdle is dark, often with spots.
SIZE: To 2.4″ (6 cm) long.
HABITAT: Low intertidal zone to subtidal depths of 170′ (52 m).
RANGE: Unalaska Island, Alaska, to northern Oregon.
NOTES: The distinctive markings of the white-line chiton make it one of the easier species of chitons to identify. The northern clingfish has been found to feed on this species in some areas.
SIMILAR SPECIES: Lined chiton; blue-line chiton.

Blue-line Chiton

Tonicella undocaerulea
Sirenko, 1973

OTHER NAME: Formerly included with *Tonicella lineata*.
DESCRIPTION: Color of the valves varies from pink to light orange. The **head valve features vivid blue zigzag lines without dark brown or black highlights.** Short dark maroon

streaks often extend into the pleural (central triangular) area of each valve. The girdle is light colored with a yellow outer ring and dark transverse bands.

SIZE: To 1.5″ (3.8 cm) long.

HABITAT: On boulders and rock covered with encrusting coralline algae in the low intertidal zone to waters 125′ (38 m) deep.

RANGE: Kodiak Island, Alaska, to Point Conception, California; Russia; Japan.

NOTES: This chiton is very similar to but smaller than the lined chiton. An important identifying feature is the zigzag pattern on the head valve. Appropriately, a portion of this chiton's scientific name is derived from *caeruleus* ("sky blue"). This chiton has narrow, bright blue, zigzag lines located longitudinally on all valves.

SIMILAR SPECIES: Lined chiton.

Northern Red Chiton

Boreochiton beringensis

(Jakovleva, 1952)

OTHER NAMES: Formerly classified as *Tonicella beringensis*, *Tonicella rubra*.

DESCRIPTION: The **valves** are normally pink or **reddish mottled with reddish-brown or purple**. The **girdle** is mottled reddish or reddish-brown and covered with minute **oval granules**. The valves have a noticeable beak.

SIZE: Length to 1.4″ (3.5 cm).

HABITAT: On rocks; very low intertidal zone to depths of 984′ (300 m).

RANGE: Circumboreal; Bering Sea and Aleutian Islands, Alaska, to at least Haida Gwaii (Queen Charlotte Islands), British Columbia; Arctic to Connecticut; Europe.

NOTES: The northern red chiton is only encountered with the lowest of tides. It feeds upon crustose coralline algae, other microalgae and diatoms.

Gould's Baby Chiton

Cyanoplax dentiens (Gould, 1846)

OTHER NAME: Formerly classified as *Lepidochitona dentiens*.

DESCRIPTION: Color of valves varies greatly, **often reddish-brown or green with various**

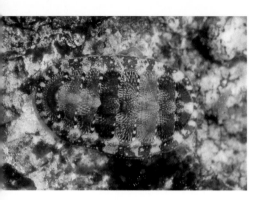

spots or flecks of blue. Dense granules are also present in the valves' lateral areas. The **girdle is usually light colored with dark banding, often with many small white dots.** Lateral areas of shells covered with dense granules; girdle medium width and rough-looking along the edge.
SIZE: Normally to 0.6″ (15 mm) long; occasionally to 0.8″ (20 mm) long.
HABITAT: On the top and sides of rocks and in tidepools; high intertidal zone to depths of 3.3′ (1 m).
RANGE: Auke Bay, Alaska, to La Jolla, California.
NOTES: Gould's baby chiton is a very common species, but because of its size and cryptic coloration it is often missed. True to its common name, this is a small species—much smaller than many other chitons found intertidally.
SIMILAR SPECIES: Fernald's baby chiton.

Fernald's Baby Chiton

Cyanoplax fernaldi (Eernisse, 1986)

OTHER NAMES: Hermaphroditic chiton; formerly classified as *Lepidochitona fernaldi*.
DESCRIPTION: The **valves are normally dark brown overall with no markings,** but there are often white markings, especially on the fifth valve. Valves are often eroded. **The girdle is overall dark, wide and slightly spiny looking.** The foot is slightly orange and the central valves are beaked.
SIZE: Normally to 0.5″ (13 mm) long; occasionally to 0.7″ (18 mm) long.
HABITAT: On the edge of tidepools next to aggregating anemones; high intertidal zone.
RANGE: Southeastern Alaska, to Brookings, Oregon.
NOTES: Fernald's baby chiton is found only in high intertidal tidepools among the aggregating anemones and the thatched barnacles. In fact, it often retreats between the crevices of the barnacle, making it exceeding difficult to find. A second chiton that may also be found in these tidepools is Gould's baby chiton. Fernald's baby chiton is a simultaneous hermaphrodite that broods its embryos, primarily in the winter and spring. The brood is located on either side of the foot.
SIMILAR SPECIES: Gould's baby chiton.

Smooth Lepidozona

Lepidozona interstincta (Gould, 1852)

OTHER NAMES: Formerly classified as
*Ischnochiton interstinctus, Lepidozona
interstinctus*; formerly believed to include
Lepidozona radians.
DESCRIPTION: The valves vary from yellowish-
brown to tan in coloration. The body is oval
with a narrow girdle. The **valves appear smooth
to the naked eye**; however, upon magnification
tiny tubercles are present in the central areas. The girdle is **covered with minute shining,
overlapping scales**.
SIZE: Length to 1″ (2.5 cm).
HABITAT: Under rocks; low intertidal zone to depths of 36′ (120 m).
RANGE: Alaska to at least San Juan Islands, Washington.
NOTES: The smooth lepidozona is not one of the more common intertidal chiton species,
but it is found at some sites.
SIMILAR SPECIES: Radiating chiton.

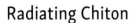

Radiating Chiton

Lepidozona radians (Carpenter in Pilsbry, 1892)

OTHER NAMES: Formerly classified as *Ischnochiton
radians*; formerly believed to include *Lepidozona
interstincta.*
DESCRIPTION: Valve colors are variable including
brown, orange, yellow or, rarely, white. The valves of
this **small species** are **smooth to the naked eye**. The
girdle is covered with nearly rectangular scales.
SIZE: Length to 0.4″ (10 mm).
HABITAT: On rocks; low intertidal zone to depths of 492′ (150 m).
RANGE: Port Hardy, Vancouver Island, British Columbia, to near Punta Colonet, México.
NOTES: The radiating chiton was formerly considered to be included with the smooth
lepidozona. They were recently found to be totally different but similar-looking species.
The radiating chiton is a much smaller species that is found intertidally in the northern
portion of its range.
SIMILAR SPECIES: Smooth lepidozona.

Cooper's Chiton

Lepidozona cooperi (Pilsbry, 1892)

OTHER NAME: Formerly classified as
Ischnochiton cooperi.
DESCRIPTION: Valve and girdle color is **gray or
gray-green** and occasionally orange. The valve
sculpture includes **bead-like pustules that are
situated on slightly raised ribs.** This species is
ovate with a **very high-peaked profile.**
SIZE: To 1.5″ (4 cm) long.
HABITAT: Under rocks and sediment deposits
on rocky sites; low intertidal zone to depths of 26′ (8 m).
RANGE: Northern British Columbia to México.
NOTES: This chiton, like most of its relatives, is usually found under rocks away from
sunlight, which ensures that it will not be easily seen by predators and will not dry out in
the heat of the sun.
SIMILAR SPECIES: Merten's chiton.

Merten's Chiton

Lepidozona mertensii (Middendorff, 1847)

OTHER NAMES: Mottled red chiton, red chiton.
DESCRIPTION: Valves range from **brown to brick-red or vivid purple in color,** with
intermittent white lines, giving this species a mottled look. **Bead-like pustules are found
on the valves in rows without raised ribs.** The **girdle is patterned with light-colored
bands and the girdle appears granulated** as it is made up of small scales. This ovate
species is **low in profile.**

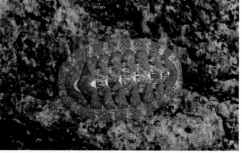

SIZE: To 2″ (5 cm) long.

HABITAT: Under rocks; low intertidal zone to 300′ (90 m).

RANGE: Auke Bay, Alaska, to Isla Guadalupe, México; Japan.

NOTES: Merten's Chiton is a common intertidal species, especially in the northern part of its range. Its colors help to identify it. Light-sensitive organs called aesthetes are found on the plates of this species, as in all chitons. These specialized organs help chitons retreat from light, since these creatures do not have eyes.

SIMILAR SPECIES: Cooper's chiton.

Three-rib Chiton

Tripoplax trifida (Carpenter, 1864)

OTHER NAME: Formerly classified as *Ischnochiton trifidus.*

DESCRIPTION: The valves are normally reddish-brown to orange. The girdle varies in color and is moderate in width. **On valves 2–7, the lateral areas are divided into 3 areas that are separated by 2 radiating grooves.** Approximately 20 grooves are found on the head valve.

SIZE: To 2.3″ (6 cm) long.

HABITAT: On rocks; low intertidal zone to depths of 365′ (110 m).

RANGE: Aleutian Islands, Gulf of Alaska, south to Puget Sound, Washington.

NOTES: A hand lens is a handy tool for looking at the minute granules covering the valves of this species. Although most chitons feed upon algae, the three-rib chiton dines on bryozoans.

SIMILAR SPECIES: Merten's chiton.

Split-plate Chiton

Schizoplax brandtii (Middendorff, 1847)

DESCRIPTION: The valves are normally a dark coloration, often olive green. The girdle is often dark, mottled with light patches, narrow and without bristles. **Valves 2–7 are split with a hairline crack down the mid-line.**

SIZE: To 1″ (2.5 cm) long.
HABITAT: On rocks of protected shorelines; mid- to low intertidal zone and possibly lower.
RANGE: Aleutian Islands, Alaska, to British Columbia.
NOTES: The split down the center of this chiton's plates 2–7 is not easy to view with the naked eye. These slits are filled by a narrow wedge of horny cartilage. A 10x loup will aid in viewing.

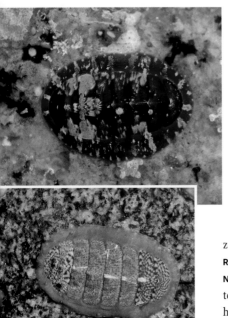

Painted Dendrochiton

Dendrochiton flectens (Carpenter, 1864)

OTHER NAME: Formerly classified as *Leptochitona flectens.*
DESCRIPTION: Color of valves ranges widely from red to orange, or green, speckled with blue, pale green and gray. **Girdle has a few long and curved hairs, especially around the last two valves.** Bristles are present on the hairs but these are not visible to the naked eye.
SIZE: To 1.2″ (3 cm) long.
HABITAT: In rocky areas; very low intertidal zone to water 80′ (24 m) deep.
RANGE: Sitka, Alaska, to San Pedro, California.
NOTES: This uncommon intertidal chiton is easy to identify in the field because of the distinctive hairs found on the girdle. Like several other marine species, this species has a long history of different scientific names.

Gem Chiton

Chaetopleura gemma Dalt, 1879

OTHER NAME: Formerly *Ischnochiton marmortus.*
DESCRIPTION: Color of valves varies from olive to red or yellow overall, and the **tail valve is dark brown to black often with a centered white mark.** The girdle is variable in its coloration. Longitudinal rows of granules are found in the central areas of valves and lateral areas with prominent bumps. The girdle is narrow and leathery.

SIZE: To 0.75″ (18 mm) long.

HABITAT: On rocks from the mid-intertidal zone to depths of 165′ (50 m).

RANGE: Vancouver Island, British Columbia, to Bahía Magdalena, Baja California Sur, México.

NOTES: The gem chiton is a tiny species with variable coloration. In California, this chiton spawns in June. Short transparent spicules are found on the girdle. A 10x loup will greatly aid the beachcomber in observing the details of this small species and others.

Northern Hairy Chiton

Mopalia kennerleyi Carpenter, 1864

OTHER NAMES: Hairy chiton, hairy mopalia; formerly included with *Mopalia ciliata*.

DESCRIPTION: Valves vary greatly in color and are often very colorful. **Wide outer girdle covered in short, soft setae** each with 3 or 4 rows of minute spicules on each seta. (A hand lens is required to view these). To help identify this species, gently touch the girdle to determine its texture. The animal's body shape is elongate-oval and a distinct cleft or notch is present at the rear.

SIZE: To 2.4″ (6 cm) long.

HABITAT: On protected sites, such as under rocks, mid- to low intertidal zone.

RANGE: Alaska to Bodega, Sonoma County, California.

NOTES: This chiton feeds at night and on cloudy days, grazing on tiny animals and diatoms, which it finds attached to rock. Its rasping tongue (radula) contains magnetite, a hard oxide of iron that aids the animal greatly while feeding.

SIMILAR SPECIES: Mossy chiton with stiff hairs.

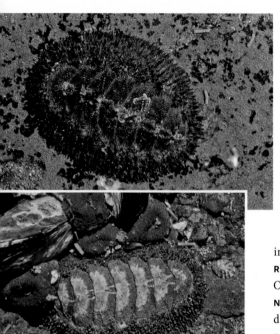

Mossy Chiton

Mopalia muscosa (Gould, 1846)

DESCRIPTION: The valves are brown, gray or black, occasionally tinted with red, orange, green or with white stripes. **Girdle is covered in stout stiff hairs**, making it look somewhat fuzzy. The oval body shape displays a shallow notch at the rear of the wide girdle.

SIZE: To 3.1″ (8 cm) long.

HABITAT: Often on top of rocks and in tidepools; high to low intertidal zone.

RANGE: Alaska to Isla Cedros, Baja California, México.

NOTES: This species is often observed in daylight since it does not hide under rocks as most chitons do. Instead, it stays in one place until darkness falls, when it begins feeding on algae. Mossy chiton can be distinguished from the similar-looking northern hairy chiton by gently touching its girdle. (The northern hairy chiton has soft hairs, while the mossy chiton has stiff hairs.) Individuals have been found to have a home range of 20″ (51 cm) in a tidepool, which forms their permanent home. The mossy chiton is often found with a variety of other intertidal life forms growing on its back. Accumulations of silt do not affect this species.

SIMILAR SPECIES: Northern hairy chiton has soft hairs.

Woody Chiton

Mopalia lignosa (Gould, 1846)

OTHER NAME: Hooked-bristled chiton.

DESCRIPTION: Valves can vary widely in color from brown, blue or green to gray, **often with radiating stripes in brown.** The **girdle is adorned with stiff hairs that stem from tiny light-colored spots.** The valves appear smooth to the naked eye and there is a prominent beak on only the posterior valve. The oval body does not display a rear notch on the wide girdle.

SIZE: To 3.1" (8 cm) long.

HABITAT: From the mid-intertidal zone to depths of 33′ (10 m).

RANGE: Prince William Sound, Alaska, to Point Conception, California.

NOTES: This common species is often found under or on the sides of large rocks. It feeds on a variety of food, including diatoms and more than two dozen species of other algae, chiefly sea lettuce. The woody chiton has been observed reproducing in captivity. Females release their eggs in single file and this cluster of eggs bunches up behind them. Males release their sperm into the water in spurts, fertilizing the eggs.

SIMILAR SPECIES: Northern hairy chiton.

Hind's Mopalia

Mopalia hindsii (Sowerby MS, Reeve, 1847)

OTHER NAME: Encrusted hairy chiton.

DESCRIPTION: Valves are variable from light to dark brown in color. Rows of fine **beaded sculpture cover the valves. Numerous fine slender hairs are found scattered over the entire wide girdle.** A **prominent notch** is present at the posterior end of the girdle.

SIZE: To 4" (10 cm) long.

HABITAT: On rocks and pilings on exposed shores; mid-intertidal zone to depths of 6.5′ (2 m).

RANGE: Kodiak, Alaska, south to Ventura County, California.

NOTES: This large chiton is commonly found on the open coast. In some individuals a white spot is found at the top of each valve. Unlike most other chitons, Hind's mopalia is able to live in areas with high concentrations of silt. It feeds on bryozoans, filamentous algae, amphipods and barnacles.

SIMILAR SPECIES: Swan's mopalia.

Swan's Mopalia

Mopalia swanii Carpenter, 1864

DESCRIPTION: Valves are highly variable in color, ranging from yellow, orange, red, green to brown. Rows of fine **beaded sculpture cover the valves. Girdle is wide**, mottled with various shades of brown and **sparsely scattered, short, very fine setae.**
SIZE: To 2.3″ (6 cm) long.
HABITAT: On undersides of rocks and under ledges; low intertidal zone to depths of at least 59′ (18 m).
RANGE: Unalaska Island, Alaska, to Malibu, California; rare south of Oregon.
NOTES: This mopalia has been observed feeding as it moves along its substrate, cleaning everything off as it goes and apparently having few food preferences. Its valves can include patterns, speckles and stripes, as well as combinations of these.
SIMILAR SPECIES: Hind's mopalia.

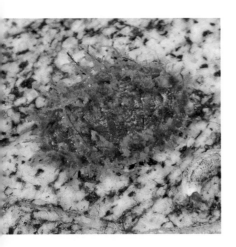

Sinuate Mopalia

Mopalia sinuata Carpenter, 1864

OTHER NAME: Dwarf hairy mopalia.
DESCRIPTION: The valves are whitish or greenish, mottled with brown or red. Lateral area is well defined by radial ribs; deep pitting in central areas. The **girdle hairs are long** (1–1.5 times the valve length). **Girdle hairs appear feather-like due to 2 or 3 rows of fine branches** (bristles).
SIZE: To 0.8″ (20 mm) long.
HABITAT: On the upper surfaces of rocks; low intertidal zone to depths of 164′ (50 m).
RANGE: Kachemak Bay, Alaska, to Monterey, California.
NOTES: This is an uncommon intertidal chiton that is very distinctive with its long, feathery hairs.
SIMILAR SPECIES: Long-haired mopalia *Mopalia cirrata* Berry, 1919. The girdle hairs are longer up to half the length of the chiton and not feathery.

Red-flecked Mopalia

Mopalia spectabilis
Cowan and Cowan, 1977

DESCRIPTION: Valves light green or olive, normally **with flecks of red and dazzling turquoise zigzag lines**; occasionally valves are suffused with orange. Longitudinal rows of pits are found on the central area of all valves except the head and tail valves. Girdle broad and hairy with a posterior notch.

SIZE: To 2.75″ (7 cm) long.

HABITAT: Under ledges and on bottoms of rocks; low intertidal zone to depths of 39′ (12 m).

RANGE: Kodiak Island, Alaska, to San Luis Obispo County, California.

NOTES: The red-flecked mopalia feeds on a variety of invertebrates, including sponges, hydroids, bryozoans and sea squirts. A species of scaleworm is sometimes found in the mantle cavity. This species often carries hitchhikers attached to its plates, including encrusting bryozoans and the shells of small tube worms.

Red Veiled-chiton

Placiphorella rufa Berry, 1917

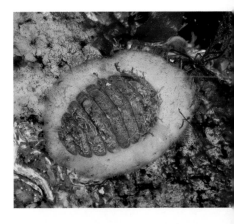

OTHER NAMES: Red hooded-chiton, red veiled chiton.

DESCRIPTION: Valves are normally red or orange with a white girdle. The girdle is occasionally mottled with green. The **fleshy, wide girdle is widest at the anterior end** and holds **sparse long and slender bristles**.

SIZE: To 2″ (5 cm) long.

HABITAT: On rocks along the outer coast; low intertidal zone to depths of 150′ (45 m).

RANGE: Prince William Sound, Alaska, to southern Oregon.

NOTES: The red veiled-chiton is a common subtidal species that occasionally is found on lower tides on outer, exposed coasts. It is often wider than it is long. It uses its large fleshy anterior end to trap invertebrates that happen to be swept there by an ocean current.

SIMILAR SPECIES: Veiled-chiton.

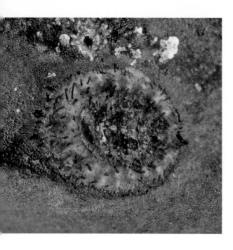

Veiled-chiton

Placiphorella velata (Carpenter MS, Dall, 1897)

OTHER NAMES: Veiled Pacific chiton, hooded-chiton.

DESCRIPTION: **Valves with multiple colors, especially olive-green.** The girdle is cream-colored to beige on the dorsal side. The **fleshy, wide girdle is widest at the anterior** end and normally displays **numerous thick bristles**.

SIZE: To 2.5″ (6 cm) long.

HABITAT: On rocks and under ledges, in more exposed areas; very low intertidal zone to water 65′ (20 m) deep.

RANGE: Prince William Sound, Alaska, to Isla Cedros, Baja California, México.

NOTES: Both the veiled-chiton and the red veiled-chiton are able to capture their prey in a remarkable way: by using the front portion of its girdle as a flap to seize its food. Small crustaceans and worms amble beneath this upraised hood, which is quickly lowered to trap the prey. Like many other chitons, this species also grazes on encrusting microalgae.

SIMILAR SPECIES: Red veiled-chiton.

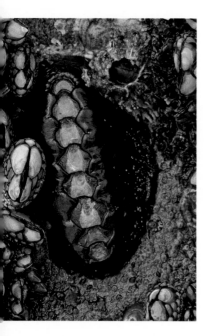

Black Katy Chiton

Katharina tunicata (Wood, 1815)

OTHER NAMES: Leather chiton, black chiton, black leather chiton, Katy chiton, black Katy, sea prune, small Chinese slippers.

DESCRIPTION: A brown to **black girdle covers most of this chiton. A white triangular shape is left uncovered on the top of each valve.** The tough, smooth, leathery girdle is distinctive.

SIZE: To 6″ (15 cm) long.

HABITAT: Rocks on exposed, rocky shorelines; mid-intertidal zone to shallow subtidal levels.

RANGE: Aleutian Islands, Alaska, to southern California; Siberia.

NOTES: This species is often found exposed during the heat of the day, feeding on algae growing on wave-washed rocks. It is large enough to have been used as food by coastal Indigenous people at one time. This chiton has a life span of only 3 years.

....

Giant Pacific Chiton

Cryptochiton stelleri (Middendorff, 1847)

OTHER NAMES: Gumboot chiton, giant red chiton, moccasin chiton, Chinese slipper.
DESCRIPTION: The **red-brown girdle completely covers the valves on the dorsal side**. Juveniles, which are less than 0.5″ (13 mm) long, are yellowish and a small portion of their valves are normally exposed (see photo).
SIZE: To 13″ (33 cm) long.
HABITAT: Rocks on exposed shorelines; low intertidal zone to subtidal waters 65′ (20 m) deep.
RANGE: Aleutian Islands, Alaska, to southern California; Japan.
NOTES: This species is often called the gumboot chiton, probably because of its rubbery appearance. It feeds on red algae and is known to live longer than 20 years. It is acclaimed as the largest chiton in the world. Small individuals were once considered edible by coastal

Juvenile.

Indigenous people. The giant Pacific chiton hosts a worm, the red-banded commensal scaleworm, which can live in the grooves on the underside of the chiton's body. The lurid rocksnail, which grows to only 1.5″ (4 cm) long, has been known to attack this chiton, but the snail merely eats a shallow pit in the chiton's back.

Abalone, Limpets & Snails
CLASS GASTROPODA

The gastropods are a diverse group of invertebrates with few features in common besides the muscular "foot" running along the underside of the body for locomotion (gastropod means "stomach foot"). Grazers, herbivores, scavengers and predators of many kinds all have a specialized tooth-bearing tongue (radula) for feeding. Another specialized organ—the otocyst, similar to our hearing apparatus—can also be found in the foot of many molluscs but is used to maintain balance.

Rough Keyhole Limpet

Diodora aspera (Rathke, 1833)

OTHER NAMES: Keyhole limpet, rough keyhole, rough key-hole limpet; formerly *Fissurella aspera*.
DESCRIPTION: Shell color varies from light brown to gray, often with banding. Shell is heavy with a high profile and an off-center opening at the shell apex. **The opening is about one-tenth the length of the shell.** Ribs radiate from top of the shell with every fourth rib larger. Numerous concentric lines cross the ribs at right angles.
SIZE: Shell length to 3″ (7.6 cm).
HABITAT: On rocky beaches, low intertidal to 130′ (40 m).
RANGE: Alaska to Nicaragua.
NOTES: The rough keyhole limpet has a large number of teeth on its radula for grazing on seaweed attached to rock. To protect itself from predators such as the purple star, this limpet erects a thin, soft mantle to cover its shell and prevent the star from attaching to it with its tube feet. The red-banded commensal scaleworm is sometimes found on the underside of this limpet.
SIMILAR SPECIES: Two-spotted keyhole limpet.

Two-spotted Keyhole Limpet

Fissurellidea bimaculata Dall, 1871

OTHER NAMES: Two-spot keyhole limpet; formerly *Megatebennus bimaculatus*, *Fissurellidea bimaculatus*
DESCRIPTION: The fleshy body varies widely in color from red, orange or brown to white mottled with brown. The shell has a **broadly elongated opening that is approximately**

one-third the shell length. When the shell is placed
on a flat surface the ends are noticeably upturned.
SIZE: Shell length to 0.75″ (19 mm); animal to 2″
(5 cm) long.
HABITAT: On kelp holdfasts and under rocks; low
intertidal zone to water 100′ (30 m) deep.
RANGE: Sitka, Alaska, to southern Baja
California, México.
NOTES: The two-spotted keyhole limpet feeds on

colonial tunicates and sponges. Its large, fleshy tissue
nearly dwarfs its tiny shell, which sits on the top of
its body. Harlequin ducks are known to feed occasionally on this species.

Hooded Puncturella

Cranopsis cucullata (Gould, 1846)

OTHER NAMES: Helmet puncturella, ribbed
keyhole limpet, hooded keyhole limpet;
formerly *Puncturella cucullata*.
DESCRIPTION: The shell is white with
13–23 strong, raised ribs radiating from apex,
and **elongated slit behind apex**. The top can be
noticeably hooked at the tip.
SIZE: Shell length to 1.5″ (4 cm).
HABITAT: On rocks, low intertidal zone to water 660′ (200 m) deep; more common
subtidally.
RANGE: Alaska to Baja California, México.
NOTES: The shell is oval in shape, nearly as high as it is long. The elongated slit in the
shell reveals it to be one of the keyhole limpets. Its shell is sometimes washed ashore
after a storm.

Many-ribbed Puncturella

Cranopsis multistriata (Dall, 1914)

OTHER NAMES: Also known as many ribbed keyhole limpet; formerly classified as
Puncturella multistriata.

DESCRIPTION: Shell color is white overall. Near the apex approximately 30 primary ribs are present along with 1–3 secondary ribs that radiate toward the outer margin. The opening forms a semi circle when viewed from the inside.

SIZE: Length to 1.4″ (3.5 cm).

HABITAT: On rocks, clamshells and similar hard objects; low intertidal zone to depths of 298′ (91 m).

RANGE: Northern Alaska to México.

NOTES: This species is found more often at intertidal sites in the northern portion of its range. Its empty shells may also be found washed up on the beach after winter storms.

SIMILAR SPECIES: Hooded puncturella.

Whitecap Limpet

Acmaea mitra Rathke, 1833

OTHER NAMES: Bishop's cap limpet, Chinaman's hat, Chinaman's hat limpet, dunce cap limpet, dunce-cap limpet, white cap, white-cap limpet, white cap limpet, whitecapped limpet.

DESCRIPTION: Shell exterior is white or pink with encrusting coralline algae. It is **cone-shaped with a very high profile**. Shell interior bears horseshoe-shaped muscle scar and a nearly central apex.

SIZE: Shell length to 2″ (5 cm).

HABITAT: On rocky beaches; low intertidal to shallow subtidal zones.

RANGE: Kiska Island, Aleutian Islands, Alaska, to Isla San Martin, Baja California, México.

NOTES: This limpet is often found covered in pink encrusting coralline algae, which also happens to be its prime food. The limpet's foot is strong enough to keep it from being washed away in the strongest of waves along the exposed coast.

Ringed Blind Limpet

Cryptobranchia concentrica

(Middendorff, 1847)

OTHER NAMES: Tiny white limpet; formerly classified as *Lepeta concentrica, Cryptobranchia caecoides*.

DESCRIPTION: The body is totally white without any pigmentation. The **exterior and interior of the shell is white**. The base is oval in shape with a moderate profile. The apex is positioned within the anterior third of the shell. Fine radial riblets are present.

SIZE: Shell length to 0.9″ (23 mm).

HABITAT: On rocks where mud accumulates; low intertidal zone to depths of 200′ (60 m).

RANGE: Arctic Ocean to central California; Japan.

NOTES: The ringed blind limpet is an uncommon species that is found at the lowest of tides. Just as its common name suggests the ringed blind limpet does not have eyes. It feeds upon microalgae. It also lacks gills, so it relies on the diffusion of oxygen over the body surface to breath.

SIMILAR SPECIES: Pustulate blind limpet *Lepeta caeca* is a similar species; however, it has pustules on the shell surface.

Giant Owl Limpet

Lottia gigantea Gray in G. B. Sowerby I, 1834

OTHER NAMES: Owl limpet, solitary giant owl limpet.

DESCRIPTION: The **sides of the foot and head are black to gray in color** with an orange to yellow sole. Shell exterior is marked in brown with white mottling. The **large shell** has a low profile and the **apex is positioned one-eighth from the anterior** portion of the shell. Shell interior is marked with a large, black **owl-shaped muscle scar** that is positioned centrally.

SIZE: Length to 4.25″ (10.8 cm).

HABITAT: On vertical surfaces of rocks at exposed, wave-swept shores; high to mid-intertidal zone.

RANGE: Neah Bay, Washington, to Bahía Tortugas, Baja California, México; uncommon north of San Francisco, California.

NOTES: The giant owl limpet feeds on a variety of tiny algae growing on rock. It is a loner, known to bulldoze limpets, mussels and sea anemones off the rock within its home territory—about 1 square foot (1,000 cm²). This large species is often harvested for human consumption which has reduced its numbers.

Shield limpets live in a wide variety of habitats including on the sea palm.

Shield Limpet

Lottia pelta (Rathke, 1833)

OTHER NAMES: Californian shield limpet; formerly classified as *Acmaea pelta*, *Collisella pelta*.

NOTE: The shield limpet is a species that has developed several forms that vary greatly in their appearance and size due to habitat. To identify this species in each of its forms, they have been separated by habitat.

ALL FORMS

All forms have several characteristics that are in common with each other.

DESCRIPTION: The body is totally white and lacks all pigmentation. No oral lappets (flaps of tissue next to mouth) present. The shell interior color is **bluish-white with an irregular brown central spot** (occasionally not present) **and a narrow brown margin**. The **apex is positioned slightly forward in the anterior third portion of the shell**. The **shell profile is high**. The apex often erodes to brown.

SIZE: Shell length to 1.75″ (4.5 cm) on rocks; to 1″ (2.5 cm) on mussels; 0.4″ (10 mm) on turbans; 0.6″ (15 mm) on kelp and feather boa.

RANGE: Aleutian Islands, Alaska, to Punta Rompiente, Baja California, México; Japan.

NOTES: The shield limpet is a common species that is found in many habitats. With each habitat, its shell characteristics (shell coloration, size and shape) are modified to better suit that environment. It has been suggested by some researchers that each form could be considered a separate species. To make things even more interesting, its coloration and patterning change when an individual moves from one habitat to another! The largest specimens of the rock form are present at northern localities. The shield limpet is most active during high tide when it moves about actively and feeds on cyanobacteria, diatoms and other microalgae and algae. The predators of the shield limpet include the purple star, mottled star, frilled dogwinkle, file dogwinkle, dire whelk, the hairy hermit, tidepool sculpin and northern clingfish.

ROCK FORM

DESCRIPTION: The color of the shell's exterior is quite variable and includes green, brown or grayish-black with a white checked pattern, white dots or rays radiating around the shell. The anterior, posterior and lateral slopes are all convex. The heavy shell's sculpture may be smooth or with broad radial ribs, equally developed on all surfaces, which are often eroded. Bumpy nodules may be present.

HABITAT: On rocks with no or very little macro-algae growth; mid- to low intertidal zone. This form is also found on the goose barnacle.

The rock form is the most commonly encountered form of the shield limpet.

MUSSEL FORM (*MYTILUS* FORM)

DESCRIPTION: **The exterior of the shell varies from brown or gray to blue-black with little patterning.** The apex may be eroded to white. The anterior slope is straight (the posterior and lateral slopes are convex). The shell sculpture is rough and may include very fine radial riblets. Shell features a moderately high profile.

HABITAT: On aggregations of Pacific blue mussels and California mussels; mid- to low intertidal zone.

Mussel form.

TURBAN SNAIL FORM (*TEGULA* FORM)

DESCRIPTION: The exterior of the shell varies from brown or gray to blue-black and the **shell interior is white.** The shell features a moderate profile. The posterior and lateral slopes are convex and the apex is just ahead of center. This form is very similar to the mussel form in its shape and color. It can be very common at some locations and may be present with the black limpet.

HABITAT: On the shells of the black turban; high- to mid-intertidal zone.

Feather boa kelp form.

FEATHER BOA KELP FORM (*EGREGIA* FORM) AND KELP FORM (*LAMINARIA* FORM)

DESCRIPTION: The exterior of the shell is brown overall with several white triangular-shaped markings. The apex tends to remain brown without significant wearing. The profile is lower than the rock form. Small individuals are characteristically black. Shell features a moderate to low profile for the *Egregia* form. The *Laminaria* form often grows with a higher profile and a saddle-shape to fit the algae it grows on. The anterior slope is concave while the posterior and lateral slopes are convex. The shell's sculpture includes **both fine radial riblets & concentric growth lines**. The shell's **lateral edges are almost parallel**; narrowing slightly toward the anterior.

HABITAT: On the stipe of the feather boa kelp, and several kelp species including *Laminaria* spp.; low intertidal zone. This species feeds on the stipe of these algae, creating a furrow as it feeds.

EELGRASS FORM (*ZOSTERA* FORM)

OTHER NAMES: Pacific eelgrass limpet, *Lottia parallela* is now believed to be an ecotype (form) of the plate limpet *Lottia pelta*. Research is ongoing.

DESCRIPTION: The body is totally white and lacks pigmentation. The exterior of the shell is light brown to dark brown marked with a **radial or checkerboard pattern in white**. The **profile is low**; apex positioned at the anterior third of the shell; shell base is oval in outline. The shell interior is bluish-white with a brown central stain; external marks visible through the thin shell.

SIZE: Length to 0.5″ (13 mm).

HABITAT: Only found on eelgrass in protected waters; low intertidal zone to shallow subtidal depths.

Ribbed Limpet

Lottia digitalis (Rathke, 1833)

Cluster of ribbed limpets on rock.

OTHER NAMES: Finger limpet; fingered limpet; formerly classified as *Acmaea digitalis*, *Collisella digitalis*.

ALL FORMS

DESCRIPTION: The body is totally white and lacks pigmentation. The **shell interior is white with a dark-brown apex area.** The **shell has conspicuous radial ribs primarily at the posterior end.**
SIZE: Shell length to 1.3″ (3.5 cm) on rocks; to 0.4″ (10 mm) on mussels and goose barnacles.
HABITAT: In the high to mid-intertidal zone.
SIMILAR SPECIES: Dwarf ribbed limpet.

ROCK FORM

DESCRIPTION: The exterior color of the shell ranges from brown to grayish-green or dark olive with white blotches or checkering. The interior color of the shell is white or bluish-white with an irregular central brown stain and a dark margin with or without white markings. Shell features a high to medium profile with the **apex is positioned in the anterior quarter of the shell.** The anterior slope of the shell is concave and the apex may overhang. The posterior and lateral slopes are convex. The **shell's sculpture is noticeably ribbed,** often creating a crenulated edge.
HABITAT: On vertical or overhanging rocks; splash zone to high intertidal zone, often in the shade.

MUSSEL FORM (*MYTILUS* FORM)

DESCRIPTION: Shell is dark overall and in larger specimens **white radial markings are present on the margins.** The shell surface is rough, lacking sculpture.
HABITAT: On the exposed and protected outer coast; on rocks, goose barnacles and mussel shells; splash zone to high intertidal zone.

GOOSE BARNACLE FORM (*POLLICIPES* FORM)
DESCRIPTION: External shell color ranges from **white to buff with irregular dark brown chevrons on the lower portion of the shell.** (These markings closely resemble the plate sutures of the barnacles.) The shell profile is typically higher in this habitat.
HABITAT: On the plates of gooseneck barnacles; in the mid-intertidal zone.
RANGE: Aleutian Islands, Alaska, to Cabo San Lucas, Baja California, México.
NOTES: The ribbed limpet is very common and found on three different habitats: on rock, goose barnacles and mussels. Those individuals living on goose barnacles (the goose barnacle form) are distinctive, with their coloration closely matching the plate sutures of these barnacles. They are so well camouflaged that they are often very difficult to find. In a study conducted in Oregon this species was shown to home (return to its "normal" resting spot) approximately 5″ (13 cm) for each feeding foray. The shape of the shell's outer edge matches precisely the rock area that is its home. This close fit is very helpful in preventing a predator from removing the limpet from its substrate. This limpet, as well as the dwarf ribbed limpet, are often infected with a common fungus, *Pharcidia balani*, which causes pitting and erosion of the shell. Other species such as the shield limpet are rarely infected with it.

....

Dwarf Ribbed Limpet

Lottia paradigitalis (Fritchman, 1960)

OTHER NAMES: Formerly classified as *Acmaea paradigitalis*, *Collisella paradigitalis*, *Lottia strigatella* of various authors (not of Carpenter, 1864); formerly and incorrectly considered to be a synonym of *Collisella borealis*, *Lottia borealis*.
DESCRIPTION: The body is totally white and lacks pigmentation. Shell exterior is highly variable in color from gray to green or brownish-gray, often with patterned markings and rays. Some specimens display white marks along the outer edge of the shell. The top portion of the **shell is normally pitted and eroded** from a fungus, revealing a white shell color. **Shell interior lacks a central dark stain** and is white or bluish-white, often with a narrow, dark band at the edge, which may be solid or broken. If exterior markings are present, they show through the shell to the interior. Shell features a medium profile with the **apex situated in the anterior quarter**. The anterior slope of the shell is straight or convex, lateral slopes straight and the posterior slope is convex. Normally, **radial ribbing is absent** but may be present on larger individuals.

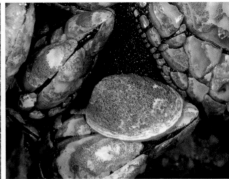

Dwarf ribbed limpet on rock.

Dwarf ribbed limpet on goose barnacles.

SIZE: Shell length to 0.8″ (20 mm) on rocks; to 0.4″ (10 mm) on mussels and turbans.

HABITAT: On vertical surfaces of rocks on exposed to protected shores as well as on goose barnacles, mussel shells and turban shells; high to mid-intertidal zones.

RANGE: Aleutian Islands, Alaska, to Point Conception, California.

NOTES: The dwarf ribbed limpet was once believed to be a hybrid between 2 species—the ribbed limpet and the shield limpet. It was eventually determined to be a unique species. It is a common and abundant species that is easily overlooked. It somewhat resembles a "dwarf" version of a ribbed limpet that lacks ribbing. It is often found living on rocks in the high intertidal region side by side with ribbed limpets or on the shells of the California mussel. It has also been confused with a small shield limpet. This species varies considerably throughout its range.

SIMILAR SPECIES: Ribbed limpet.

....

Rough Limpet

Lottia scabra (Gould, 1846)

OTHER NAMES: Formerly classified as *Acmaea scabra, Collisella scabra, Patella scabra.*

DESCRIPTION: The body is white overall with black speckles present on the head and sides of the foot. The exterior of the shell is gray to greenish-white, mottled with brown and pale-colored ribs. The shell's interior is white, normally with a brownish spot at the apex, and brown spots are positioned at the shell margin between ribs.

Several **strong, raised ribs radiate from the apex creating a saw-toothed edge.** The heavy shell has a low profile with an oval opening. The apex is positioned at the anterior third portion of the shell.

SIZE: Length to 1.2″ (3 cm).

HABITAT: On horizontal rock surfaces or gentle sloped rocks of exposed shores; splash zone to mid-intertidal zone.

RANGE: Port Orford Head, Oregon, to Baja California, México; rare north of California.

NOTES: The rough limpet is primarily a southern species that feeds on the algal film found on horizontal and angled rocks in the upper intertidal zone. The similar-looking ribbed limpet feeds on the algal film that clings to vertical rocks in the same intertidal zone. The rough limpet is known to return to its home scar daily at each low tide. A home scar is clearly visible when its owner is not resting on it. The rough limpet is believed to live as long as 11 years.

SIMILAR SPECIES: Ribbed limpet.

File Limpet

Lottia limatula (Carpenter, 1864)

OTHER NAMES: California file limpet; *Acmaea limatula, Collisella limatula*; occasionally misspelled *Acmae limatula*.

DESCRIPTION: The body is white except for the **black pigmentation on the dorsal surface of the head and the sides of its foot.** Shell exterior is tan to cream-brown. Shell interior margin is solid or with streaks and the central area white. The shell is **sculptured with fine riblets that radiate from the off-center apex.** The shell features a low profile and the anterior slope is straight.

SIZE: Shell length to 2″ (5 cm).

HABITAT: On rocks of the exposed and protected outer coast; mid- to lower intertidal zones.

RANGE: Southern British Columbia to Baja California, México.

NOTES: This is an uncommon species in the northern portion of its range. In the past, the file limpet has been observed from Newport, Oregon, to Baja California. The author has found individuals as far north as southern BC. Most limpets are vegetarians and as such have no proboscis, which flesh-eating molluscs do. Individuals are found as separate sexes and their young start out life as free-swimming organisms. Occasionally albino specimens of this limpet are found.

Black Limpet

Lottia asmi (Middendorff, 1847)

OTHER NAMES: Formerly classified as *Acmaea asmi, Collisella asmi.*

DESCRIPTION: The body is totally white and lacks pigmentation. The shell **exterior varies from dark brown to black**. The **interior of the shell is brown or black throughout**. Shell features a **high profile** with the apex placed in the anterior third of the shell. The shell's sculpture includes **fine riblets**. The slopes are all convex.

SIZE: Shell length to 0.4″ (10 mm); height to 0.3″ (8 mm).

HABITAT: On the shells of the black turban, California mussels and on rocks and crevices; low to mid-intertidal zone.

RANGE: Sitka, Alaska, to Punta Pequefia, Baja California, México.

NOTES: The black limpet is a small species that normally lives on the black turban, feeding on its film of microscopic algae. This limpet freely transfers from one black turban host to another. It, however, is not the only limpet that may be found here. Young shield limpets, ribbed limpets, and dwarf ribbed limpets may also be found. As these species gain size they move off their black turban hosts.

SIMILAR SPECIES: Shield limpet; dark juveniles are also often found on black turbans. Although they are very similar looking, their profile is much lower than that of the black limpet. The inside of the shield limpet's shell is light colored with a dark margin and center spot.

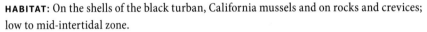

Fenestrate Limpet

Lottia fenestrata (Reeve, 1855)

OTHER NAMES: Formerly *Acmaea fenestrata, Notoacmea fenestrata, Patella fenestrata, Tectura fenestrata.*

DESCRIPTION: The body is totally white and lacks pigmentation. The exterior color of the shell is dark gray to brown, often with white markings at the margins; **apex erodes to brown; interior of shell is brown**. The **shell base is broadly oval to nearly round**; medium profile. The slopes are all straight to slightly convex.

SIZE: To 1.5″ (3.8 cm) long.

HABITAT: On smooth rocks and boulders that are embedded in sand or mud or in aggregations on outcroppings of rock; high to low intertidal zone.
RANGE: Alaska to northern Baja California, México.
NOTES: The fenestrate limpet is common but easily missed as it is normally found on rocks that are partially embedded in sand or mud. When the tide recedes, however, the animals often crawl back down into the sand, burying themselves, and as a result their presence often goes unnoticed.

Mask Limpet

Lottia persona (Rathke, 1833)

OTHER NAMES: Speckled limpet, masked limpet, large variegated limpet, inflated limpet; formerly *Acmaea persona, Notoacmea persona, Tectura persona.*
DESCRIPTION: The body is totally white and lacks pigmentation. Color of shell exterior varies from **blue-gray** to brownish, with light gray rays originating from the apex or a pattern of light gray spots. Several tiny white spots are found on top of shell. The shell has a dark stain at the interior apex that sometimes resembles a mask. **Apex is markedly off-center with a slight hook-like shape near the tip.**
SIZE: To 1.5″ (4 cm) long.
HABITAT: Prefers the dark of rock crevices or similar areas in the high to mid-intertidal zones but comes out at night to feed.
RANGE: Alaska to central California.
NOTES: Once the sun has set and darkness prevails, this limpet is busy feeding on algae. It has been calculated that a limpet of 1 square inch (6.5 cm^2) requires a browsing area of encrusting seaweed covering 75 square inches (484 cm^2) per year to survive.
SIMILAR SPECIES: Shield limpet.

Pacific Plate Limpet

Lottia scutum (Rathke, 1833)

OTHER NAMES: Plate limpet; formerly classified as *Acmaea scutum*, *Notoacmaea scutum*, *Tectura scutum*.

DESCRIPTION: Color of **top of head and tentacles are brown** (the only species with colored tentacles in the Pacific Northwest). The color of the shell's exterior is variable—tan, brown to gray-green; with checkered white spots, bars or rays. Shell interior is white with a brown border that is checkered with white. An irregular brown spot is found in the center. Shell features a **very low profile** with the apex position changing as this species gets larger. Smaller individuals have their apex toward the anterior third of the shell. As this limpet ages its shell apex moves toward the center. The shell's sculpture includes fine radial riblets on young individuals. The slopes of the shell are all convex and **the edge is knife-thin and very fragile**.

SIZE: Shell length normally to 2″ (5 cm), occasionally to 2.4″ (6 cm).

HABITAT: On rocks and in tidepools on the exposed and protected outer coast; mid- to low intertidal zone.

RANGE: Aleutian Islands, Alaska, to San Pedro, California; Japan.

NOTES: The Pacific plate limpet is a common species that remains inactive when exposed to the air at low tide. This species is active primarily after nightfall when it is submerged. Researchers have noted this species shows a rapid running response to several sea star predators including the purple star and sunflower star. Limpets use scent receptors located along the margin of the mantle to detect approaching sea stars. It is believed that this response has influenced the predators' preferences in choosing their prey; they simply go for slower prey like the shield limpet.

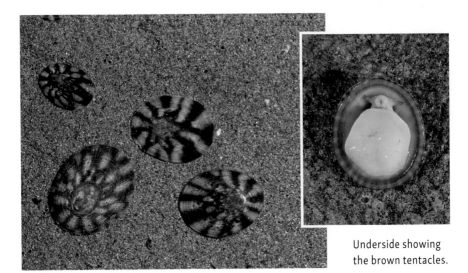

Underside showing the brown tentacles.

Seaweed Limpet

Discurria insessa (Hinds, 1842)

OTHER NAMES: Kelp limpet, feather-boa limpet; formerly *Acmaea insessa, Collisella insessa, Notoacmaea insessa, Patella insessa.*
DESCRIPTION: The body is totally white and lacks pigmentation. Shell exterior is light brown and glossy; **interior is light brown with a white ring at its edge. Apex is high near the front of the shell.** The shell sculpture includes many fine concentric lines. The anterior slope is straight and all others are convex. The shell is elongated lengthwise with **parallel edges.**
SIZE: Shell to 0.9″ (22 mm) long.
HABITAT: On algae in the low intertidal zone.
RANGE: Cape Arago, Oregon, to Bahía Magdalena, Baja California Sur, México.
NOTES: This limpet is commonly found on feather boa kelp, where it moves freely from one frond to another and eats a depression in the central stipe. Larger, older individuals orient themselves in the same direction as the stipe.

Surfgrass Limpet

Lottia paleacea (Gould, 1853)

OTHER NAMES: Chaffy limpet; formerly classified as *Notoacmaea paleacea, Tectura paleacea.*
DESCRIPTION: The body is totally white and lacks pigmentation. Exterior of the shell is light brown to reddish-brown; interior is bluish-white with a brown margin and **no central stain.** Shell features a **high profile;** the apex placed in the anterior quarter of the shell. The shell's sculpture includes fine, rounded, radial riblets. The slopes are all straight to convex. The aperture is an elongated oval since the **sides of the shell are parallel.** A small notch is present on the right anterior edge and occasionally on the left side of the shell.

SIZE: Shell length to 0.4″ (10 mm), width to 0.1″ (3 mm).

HABITAT: On the blades of surfgrass of exposed rocky shores; low intertidal zone.

RANGE: Cape Arago, Oregon, to Camalu, Baja California, México.

NOTES: This tiny limpet is very selective about its habitat, living only on the blades of surfgrass. Research on this limpet has shown that it synthesizes chemicals called flavonoids, which are stored in its shell (not its body). These chemicals are also found in surfgrass, so it avoids the predatory six-rayed stars by using chemicals to disguise itself. The sea stars do not detect this limpet because it smells like surfgrass! It is so effective at its disguise that the limpet simply hunkers down on the leaf, remaining motionless while the sea star crawls over it, unaware of its presence. Surfgrass limpets feed only on the plant's outer tissue, which leaves grazing scars on the plant. To find this small limpet, watch for signs of this grazer's presence!

....

Unstable Limpet

Lottia instabilis (Gould, 1846)

OTHER NAMES: Unstable seaweed limpet, yellow limpet; formerly classified as *Acmaea ochracea*, *Collisella instabilis*, *Collisella ochracea*.

DESCRIPTION: Body is totally white, lacking pigmentation. Shell exterior is brown and adorned with fine, regularly spaced **riblets that radiate from the apex**. The **base is elongate in shape with parallel sides**. The shell of the kelp form is unique with a **raised front and back that gives it a**

Kelp form crawling on rock.

saddle shape. There are also two additional forms found on rock: a solid form (pale yellow to red) and a tessellate form (patterned with regular white markings that become finer toward the apex).

SIZE: Shell length to 1.5″ (3.5 cm).

HABITAT: On stipes of brown algae and rock; low intertidal zone to depths of 240′ (73 m).

RANGE: Aleutian Islands, Alaska, to Cedros Island, central Baja California, México.

NOTES: The unstable limpet is a highly variable limpet that is known to have five forms. The most common ecotype is the kelp form, with that shell displaying parallel sides and a raised front and back. This unique shape is due to the limpet living on the round stipes of various species of kelp and growing to fit the round shape of their stipe. As a result, the empty shell will rock on a flat surface making it a unique shell to identify. Other forms, however, are not as easy to identify but the riblets will be present.

Flat Hoofsnail

Antisabia panamensis (C. B. Adams, 1852)

OTHER NAMES: Ancient hoof shell, hoof shell, horse's hoofsnail, hoof snail, Washington hoof shell, white hoofsnail; formerly classified as *Antisabia cranioides, Hipponix antiquatus, Hipponix cranioides, Hipponix serratus,* occasionally misspelled *Hipponix cranoides.*

DESCRIPTION: Shell is white with a brownish periostracum. Shell is **cap-shaped with a pedestal-like base** that is flat and circular and lacks any internal calcareous structures. **Muscle scar inside shell is horseshoe-shaped.** Apex is blunt and located at one end.

SIZE: Shell to 1″ (2.5 cm) in diameter.

HABITAT: On the under-surfaces of rocks and shells in areas of heavy surf; low intertidal zone to shallow subtidal depths.

RANGE: Vancouver Island, British Columbia, to México and possibly farther south; Florida to the West Indies.

NOTES: The flat hoofsnail is often found living in colonies. This species secretes and sits on a calcareous slab or shell base that it is not attached to but perfectly conforms to its upper shell. The animal feeds on detritus and coralline algae fragments by extending its long proboscis. Its skin-like periostracum is usually rubbed off on individuals that are washed up on the beach.

Pacific Half-slippersnail

Crepipatella lingulata (Gould, 1846)

OTHER NAMES: Pacific half-slipper shell, half-slipper snail, half-slipper shell, Pacific half-slipper, wrinkled slipper shell, wrinkled slippersnail; not the same as *Crepipatella dorsata* (a tropical species).

DESCRIPTION: The shell exterior is **radially striped or speckled with brown and white.** The shell interior is shiny white. A yellowish periostracum is also present. The shell is round overall, flat and brittle with **a small shelf on the inside of the shell that is only attached on one side.**

SIZE: Shell to 0.8″ (20 mm) high.
HABITAT: On shells and rocks; low intertidal zone to depths of 330′ (100 m).
RANGE: Alaska to Peru.
NOTES: This species is a filter feeder, consuming plankton and organic detritus suspended in the water. Empty shells are sometimes found washed ashore after a storm. Very little is known about its natural history.

....

Onyx Slippersnail

Crepidula onyx Sowerby, 1824

OTHER NAMES: English onyx slippersnail, onyx slipper snail, onyx slippershell; formerly classified as *C. cerithicola*, *C. lirata*.
DESCRIPTION: Shell exterior is brownish covered with a light brown periostracum. Shell interior is chocolate brown to pale brown with a glossy finish and a white shelf, with a sinuous (curved) edge also present. The shell is oval overall with a pointed apex.

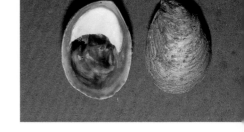

SIZE: Shell to 2.75″ (7 cm) high.
HABITAT: On rocks, shells and similar hard objects; low intertidal zone to depths of 295′ (90 m).
RANGE: Puget Sound, Washington (introduced), to Chile; Japan; Southern China; Korea.
NOTES: The onyx slippersnail is a native species from California to Costa Rica. Its range has expanded recently to numerous localities worldwide due to shipping vessels originating from San Diego. This species is often found with smaller males stacked on top of larger females.

....

Hooked Slippersnail

Garnotia adunca Sowerby, 1825

OTHER NAMES: Hooked slipper snail, hooked slipper shell, hooked slipper-shell, hooked slipper limpet, hooked slipper, turban slipper shell; formerly classified as *Crepidula adunca*.

A small male rides the shell of a large female.

DESCRIPTION: Shell exterior is dark brown; interior is white with a yellowish periostracum. A beak-like hook at the apex overhangs the posterior edge of shell.
SIZE: Shell to 1″ (2.5 cm) high.
HABITAT: On rocks or on shells of other snails; mid-intertidal zone to depths of 62′ (19 m).
RANGE: Haida Gwaii (Queen Charlotte Islands), British Columbia, to Punta Santo Tomás, Baja California, México.
NOTES: The hooked slippersnail is epibiotic—living on various snails, including the black turban, which also may be used by hermit crabs. Slippersnails have both male and female organs but become only one sex at a time. Large slippersnails are females waiting for smaller male suitors. They prepare several small egg capsules, placing approximately 250 eggs in each. The capsules are attached to the surface on which the female resides and guarded for about one month until the eggs hatch. Smaller slippersnails are males, which will become females and lay eggs as they grow older.

Atlantic Convex Slippersnail ⓘ

Crepidula convexa
Say, 1822

OTHER NAMES: Convex slipper shell, faded slipper shell; formerly classified as *Crepidula glauca*.
DESCRIPTION: Shell exterior is yellowish to dark brown and the interior is dark brown. Apex is strongly arched forward over the edge; shelf edge is slightly concave or nearly straight. The opening or base is oval.
SIZE: Shell to 1″ (2.5 cm) high.
HABITAT: On shells, rocks and similar hard objects; in quiet bays and lagoons; low intertidal zone to shallow subtidal waters.

RANGE: Southern British Columbia to southern California; Massachusetts to Caribbean.
NOTES: The Atlantic convex slippersnail is a protandrous hermaphrodite—an individual that changes from male to female after it grows to reach a minimum size. Hormones dictate which sex it will become when mating with another individual. This species was introduced from the Atlantic and is now found at several sites in the Pacific Northwest.

Northern White Slippersnail

Crepidula nummaria Gould, 1846

OTHER NAMES: Northern white slipper shell, western white slippersnail, western white slipper shell, western white slipper-shell, white slipper, white slipper shell, white slipper limpet, white slipper snail.
DESCRIPTION: Color of **shell's exterior is white**, covered with a **shaggy yellowish-brown periostracum. Shell interior is shiny white.** The shell is quite variable in **shape** but generally it **is flat and broad.** A shelf is also present with a concave edge.
SIZE: Shell to 1.5″ (4 cm) high.
HABITAT: On protected rocks and empty shells; low intertidal zone to shallow subtidal depths.
RANGE: Alaska to Panama.
NOTES: The northern white slippersnail can be found living inside and outside large snail shells, but individuals living in these situations grow to only 0.6″ (16 mm) long. Females release more than 5,000 eggs with each spawning. When the larvae settle by a functional female, they become males. However, a male will develop into a female if there are no functional females nearby.
SIMILAR SPECIES: Western white slippersnail.

Western White Slippersnail

Crepidula perforans (Valenciennes, 1846)

OTHER NAMES: Western white slipper-shell, western white slipper snail.
DESCRIPTION: The exterior of the shell is white and the interior is glossy white, often

with some reddish-brown at one end. The periostracum is light colored. The **shell is quite variable in shape but tends to be thin and elongated**. The shelf is slightly convex.

SIZE: Shell to 2.2″ (5.5 cm) high, but normally much smaller.

HABITAT: Beneath rocks, on clam shells, in abandoned snail shells, and in the holes of boring clams on the outer coast; low intertidal zone to shallow subtidal depths.

RANGE: Kodiak, Alaska, to Baja California, México.

NOTES: The western white slippersnail is normally a small species that finds itself in a wide variety of habitats and as a result its shape varies considerably. It is sometimes found sharing a shell with hermit crabs.

SIMILAR SPECIES: Northern shite slippersnail.

Cup-and-saucer Snail

Calyptraea fastigiata Gould, 1846

OTHER NAMES: Pacific Chinese-hat snail, Pacific Chinese hat, Pacific Chinese-hat.

DESCRIPTION: Exterior color is white overall, often with a darker apex. Shell is conical with a circular base and a smooth outer surface. A spiral septum or shelf with a twisted edge is found on the interior of the shell. The shell is thin and quite fragile.

SIZE: Diameter to 1″ (2.5 cm).

HABITAT: On rocks, shells and crabs; low intertidal zone to depths of 450′ (137 m).

RANGE: Central Alaska to southern California.

NOTES: The cup-and-saucer snail feeds on various seaweeds that they encounter. They lay their eggs in capsules that they protect with their foot until they are able to hatch and leave by swimming away.

Reticulate Button Snail

Trimusculus reticulatus (Sowerby, 1835)

OTHER NAMES: Button shell, reticulate gadinia; formerly classified as *Gadinia reticulata*.
DESCRIPTION: Shell is white occasionally tinted with orange, pink or green. The shell is **circular with radiating ribs from a low apex** and concentric striations may be present. Underside of the **empty shell bears a horseshoe-shaped scar**. The eyes are located at the base of the tentacles.
SIZE: Shell to 0.75″ (20 mm) in diameter.
HABITAT: On rocks in the mid-intertidal zone.
RANGE: Olympic Peninsula, Washington, to Acapulco, México; Chile.
NOTES: The reticulate button snail is often overlooked because of its secretive habits. It is a locally common species that lives in colonies and hides in crevices, caves and in the abandoned burrows of rock-boring bivalves. This air-breathing snail lives above the water more than below and often remains in one place for extended periods of time—sometimes a number of months. They feed entirely on particles (primarily diatoms) that are suspended in the water.

....

Northern Abalone

Haliotis kamtschatkana Jonas, 1845

Shell.

OTHER NAMES: Pinto abalone, Japanese abalone.
DESCRIPTION: Shell has reddish or mottled exterior and beautiful mother-of-pearl interior. **Shell is ear-shaped** normally with **3–6 respiration holes and no obvious muscle scar** on the shell.
SIZE: Shell to 6.7″ (17 cm) long.
HABITAT: Low intertidal zone to water 50′ (15 m) deep.
RANGE: Aleutian Islands, Alaska, to San Pedro, California.
NOTES: This abalone is thought to live to 50 years. A wide variety of marine life can often be found growing on the shell of this species. Its predators include the sea otter, red rock crab, cabezon, octopus and humans. In the past, coastal Indigenous people ate abalone

and used the shells to make ornaments and fish hooks. In the last century or so, people have harvested this and other abalone species to the extent that populations are extremely reduced. Northern abalone is now totally protected from harvesting in the hope that its numbers will increase.

SIMILAR SPECIES: Red abalone.

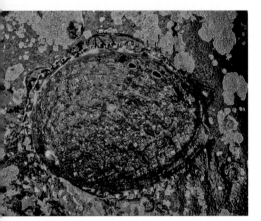

Red Abalone

Haliotis rufescens Swainson, 1822

DESCRIPTION: Outer shell is brick red but often covered with a wide variety of algae. Inner shell surface iridescent green, pink and copper with a **prominent central muscle scar. Shell is ear-shaped**, normally with **3–4 oval holes with raised edges** on the upper surface. Tentacles are dark black, and epipodium (fringe of skin circling the foot) is black, sometimes with alternating gray stripes.

SIZE: Shell to 12″ (30 cm) long, 9.25″ (23 cm) wide and 3″ (7.6 cm) high.

HABITAT: In rock crevices with heavy surf, from the low intertidal zone to water 600′ (180 m) deep.

RANGE: Coos Bay, Oregon, to Bahía Tortugas, Baja California, México.

NOTES: The red abalone is the largest species of abalone in the world. It is also a commodity prized by humans and by the sea otter. Other predators include a variety of sea stars, crabs and octopuses. This abalone feeds on loose algae fragments, including giant perennial kelp and bull kelp. The yellow boring sponge sometimes makes its home on the shell's exterior, which can drastically reduce its strength. The red abalone is known to live longer than 20 years.

SIMILAR SPECIES: Northern abalone.

Purple-ring Topsnail

Calliostoma annulatum (Lightfoot, 1786)

OTHER NAMES: Ringed top shell, purple-ringed topsnail.

DESCRIPTION: The foot is bright orange touched with black. Shell exterior is orange-yellow with bands of bright purple or mauve. Shell interior is white. The **shell is conical** with **8 or 9 whorls that are strongly beaded. The body whorl is very sharply angled**. No umbilicus is present.

SIZE: Shell to 1.25″ (3 cm) high.

HABITAT: On rocks of exposed shorelines; low intertidal zone to depths of 140′ (42 m).

RANGE: Southern Alaska to northern Baja California, México.

NOTES: This snail is usually associated with kelp, on which it feeds. It also eats hydroids, encrusting bryozoans and detritus. In the northern portion of its range, this species is occasionally found intertidally, but this is not the case farther south. It is often observed by divers in subtidal waters.

SIMILAR SPECIES: Blue topsnail.

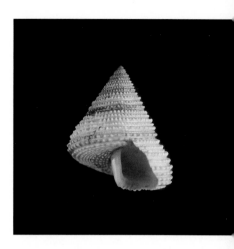

Blue Topsnail

Calliostoma ligatum (Gould, 1849)

OTHER NAMES: Costate top shell, western ribbed topshell, western ridged top shell; formerly classified as *Calliostoma costatum*.

DESCRIPTION: The snail body varies from brown to black and the bottom of the foot is orange. Shell exterior is brown to pinkish-brown overall with very light spiral ridges. The **conical shell is rounded** with approximately **6 convex whorls that are covered with smooth, rounded spiral cords**. No umbilicus is present.

SIZE: Shell to 1″ (2.5 cm) high.

HABITAT: Among algae and under rocks; low intertidal zone to depths of 100′ (30 m).

RANGE: Prince William Sound, Alaska, to San Diego, California.

NOTES: This species gets its name because of the pearly bluish color that is only revealed when its outer shell layer is worn away. This snail feeds on diatoms, kelp, detritus, hydroids and bryozoans. Its enemies include the multi-track six-rayed star and the purple star, and it has been found in the stomachs of lingcod. If the presence of a predatory sea star is detected, the speed of the blue topsnail doubles to 0.1″ (3 mm) per second.

Channelled Topsnail

Calliostoma canaliculatum (Lightfoot, 1786)

OTHER NAMES: Channelled top snail, channelled top shell, channelled top-shell, channelled top; formerly classified as *Calliostoma doliarum*.

DESCRIPTION: The exterior of the shell varies from rich brown to light tan with white spiral cords covering the whorls. A small bluish area is present near the columella. Shell interior is pearly. The **conical shell is sharp-edged** and graced with **7 whorls, each bearing several strong spiral cords.** The upper whorls are often beaded. No umbilicus is present.

SIZE: Shell to 1.5″ (3.8 cm) high and in diameter.

HABITAT: On rocks or on the blades of kelp; low intertidal zone to depths of 82′ (25 m).

RANGE: Sitka, Alaska, to Camalu, Baja California, México.

NOTES: The channelled topsnail is a univalve that is sometimes encountered by tidepoolers in the northern portion of its range, as it tends to live in deeper waters in the south where it is occasionally found washed ashore after a storm.

SIMILAR SPECIES: Blue topsnail.

Red Turban

Pomaulax gibberosa (Dillwyn, 1817)

OTHER NAMES: Red turban snail, red western turban, red top snail; formerly classified as *Astraea gibberosa*, *Astraea inaequalis*, *Lithopoma gibberosa*.

DESCRIPTION: The animal's foot is yellowish. Exterior of the **shell is reddish-brown** with a brown paper-like periostracum; shell interior is white. The **shell is a short and wide cone with flat-edged body whorls. Axial ribs are strong and transverse, producing a scalloped ridge** and prominent knobs that run around the shell. The calcareous operculum is thick, oval, smooth, pointed at one end and white with some brown toward one end.

SIZE: Shell to 2.25″ (5.7 cm) high; 3″ (7.5 cm) in diameter.

HABITAT: On rocks of the outer coast; low intertidal zone to depths of 270′ (80 m).

RANGE: Southern southeast Alaska to Bahía Magdalena, Baja California Sur, México.

NOTES: This large, distinctive snail is often covered with coralline algae. It is often found on small giant kelp, which provides both food and a home. Indigenous peoples of British Columbia and Alaska used both the shell and operculum as personal ornaments.

....

Dusky Turban

Promartynia pulligo (Gmelin, 1791)

OTHER NAMES: Dusky tegula, northern brown turban; formerly classified as *Tegula pulligo*.

DESCRIPTION: The animal's cephalic tentacles and dorsal side of head are black; the foot is also black but with a border of purplish or reddish-brown blotches. **Exterior of shell is brown overall**, often with purple mottling and orange streaks present. Shell interior is pearly. The conical shell is made up of 7 smooth and somewhat flattened whorls. The **body whorl is strongly angled. The umbilicus is open and deep.**

SIZE: Shell to 1.6″ (4 cm) high; slightly wider in diameter.

HABITAT: On rocks of open coasts; low intertidal zone to depths of 10′ (3 m).

RANGE: Sitka, Alaska, to Baja California, México.

NOTES: The dusky turban often has algae growing on its shell, giving it a somewhat thick and rusty appearance. This species prefers to live on various large brown algae; however, it is occasionally found on red seaweeds.

Brown Turban

Chlorostoma brunnea (Philippi, 1848)

OTHER NAMES: Brown tegula, brown turban snail, dusky tegula, dusky turban, dusky turban snail, northern brown turban; formerly known as *Tegula brunnea*.

DESCRIPTION: Foot has dark **brown to black sides and is light beneath**. Exterior of the shell is brown to orange-brown and shell interior is white. The conical shell has 6 **smooth and rounded whorls** with diagonal folds. The columella has one tooth present. **No umbilicus, or "navel," is present**; instead a slight depression is present.

SIZE: Shell to 1.2″ (3, cm) high.

HABITAT: On kelp from the low intertidal zone to shallow subtidal waters.

RANGE: Cape Arago, Oregon, to Santa Barbara Islands, California.

NOTES: The brown turban is a common species in California but it is uncommon in Oregon. It lives at lower levels than the dusky turban. Brown algae are believed to be its main food. Primary predators include the purple star and giant pinkstar.

SIMILAR SPECIES: Dusky turban.

Black Turban

Chlorostoma funebralis (A. Adams, 1855)

OTHER NAMES: Black tegula, black turban snail; formerly classified as *Tegula funebralis*.

DESCRIPTION: The animal is nearly totally black, but the bottom of the foot is white. **Shell exterior is purplish-black above, often with an eroded apex.** Shell interior and the columella base are pearl white. The shell is **stout and top-shaped with 4**

or 5 slightly convex and nearly smooth whorls of which the body whorl dominates. The umbilicus is closed.

SIZE: Shell to 1.75″ (4.4 cm) high.

HABITAT: On rocky shores, high to mid-intertidal zones.

RANGE: Vancouver Island, British Columbia, to central Baja California, México.

NOTES: This snail is one of the more common species found on the shores of the Pacific Northwest. It often congregates in great numbers on rocky shores. The black turban feeds only upon soft seaweed, using a specialized tongue (radula). Black turbans are believed to live as long as 30 years. This is likely one reason why the tops of their shells are almost always worn to the underlying white shell layer. This species is often found with adult black limpets and several species of juvenile limpets.

Dark Dwarf-turban

Homalopoma luridum (Dall, 1885)

OTHER NAMES: Dall's dwarf turban, dwarf turban, dark dwarf-turban, northern dwarf turban; formerly classified as *Homalopoma carpenteri*, *Homalopoma juanensis*.

DESCRIPTION: Shell exterior is pinkish-red to reddish-brown with a red lip margin. Shell interior is pearly. Shell shape is **globose** with approximately **4 rounded whorls, each of which is covered with several distinct spiral cords.** The body whorl is large, taking up most of the shell. The apex is low but sharp. The calcareous operculum is white and pearly, and almost round. **No umbilicus, or navel, is present.**

SIZE: Shell to 0.4″ (10 mm) high and wide in diameter.

HABITAT: Under rocks in protected waters; mid-intertidal zone to subtidal depths.

RANGE: Sitka, Alaska, to Isla San Geronimo, Baja California, México; Panama.

NOTES: As the common name of this species indicates, this species is easily missed due to its small size. It is often found inhabited with very small hermit crabs.

Spiral Margarite

Margarites helicinus (Phipps, 1774)

OTHER NAMES: Smooth top shell, smooth helical top shell, smooth margarite, helicina margarite; formerly classified as *Helix margarita, Margarita arctica, Margarita campanulata, Margarites diaphana, Trochus helicinus, Trochus helicinus* var. *fasciata, Turbo helicinus.*

DESCRIPTION: The gray-brown to yellowish-brown translucent shell has an iridescent blue or pinkish-brown finish. The shell is smooth with about **5 convex whorls that are smooth and glossy.** The spire is low and somewhat flat. The body whorl is very large and expands rapidly. Interior of the shell is pearly. The **umbilicus, or navel, is narrow and deep.**

SIZE: Shell to 0.33″ (8 mm) high.

HABITAT: On sandy shores; low intertidal zone to depths of 600′ (183 m).

RANGE: Arctic Ocean to southern California and Massachusetts; northern Europe.

NOTES: This species is found intertidally in the northern portion of its range but deeper in the southern portion. These very small, exquisite snails are gems to view. Its scientific name *helicinus* refers to the spiral nature of its shell. Spiral margarite feeds on algal growth.

....

Puppet Margarite

Margarites pupillus (Gould, 1849)

OTHER NAMES: Little margarite, margarite snail, pink topsnail; formerly classified as *Margarites pupilla, Margarites salmoneus.*

DESCRIPTION: Exterior of the shell varies from chalky gray to yellowish and wearing to pink. The aperture edge is slightly iridescent and the shell interior is often pinkish. The shell is conical and comprised of **4 or 5 convex whorls, each decorated with several fine spiral cords.** Sharp sutures separate the whorls. **There is a small, narrow umbilicus** at the base of the shell, which may be closed in larger northern specimens.

SIZE: Shell to 0.3″ (8 mm) high; 0.4″ (10 mm) in diameter.

HABITAT: On sand, mud, stones or rubble at sheltered sites; low intertidal zone to depths of 1,312′ (400 m).

RANGE: Circumboreal; Nunivak Island, Alaska, to San Diego, California; Arctic to Massachusetts; Japan.

NOTES: The puppet margarite has been found to crawl at a maximum rate of almost 0.08″ (2 mm) per second. This is accomplished by using its foot to contract in wave-like motions that pass from the rear of the foot to the front (direct waves). This species attains its largest size in the northern portion of its range.

....

Checkered Periwinkle

Littorina scutulata (Gould, 1849)

The tentacles are the most reliable feature for identification.

OTHER NAME: Checkered littorine.

DESCRIPTION: The **tentacles are normally patterned with dark, broken, transverse bands that frequently alternate**. Spots may also be present with these bands. Shell exterior is variable, often with a checkerboard pattern of white on a dark brown, purple or black background that may include spots. Shells may also be banded with a lighter color or a solid color including brown or black. It is best to view wet shells to see colors and patterning. Shell color banding may also be present. Shell interior is almost always purple. **No cream-colored basal band is present on the body whorl**. The shell is **conical in shape**, with 4 whorls, and has no strong spiral sculpture. Shells are frequently eroded or encrusted with algae. All characteristics may not be present in all individuals, so we must view more than one.

SIZE: Shell height normally to 0.4″ (10 mm), occasionally to 0.7″ (18 mm).

HABITAT: On rocks and pilings; high intertidal zone.

RANGE: Sitka, Alaska, to Cabo San Lucas, Baja California, México.

NOTES: The largest checkered periwinkles are often found much higher up on shore than smaller individuals. Their enemies include several carnivorous gastropods and the multi-track six-rayed star. This family of snails has a unique foot, which is divided into 2 separate parts that move alternately. Some scientists believe land snails may have evolved from periwinkles.

SIMILAR SPECIES: Little checkered periwinkle is a smaller species with tentacles that have a dark, wide central stripe.

A single dark unbroken stripe is present on the tentacles.

Little Checkered Periwinkle

Littorina plena Gould, 1849

OTHER NAMES: Black periwinkle, starry periwinkle; formerly included with *Littorina scutulata*.

DESCRIPTION: The **tentacles are normally patterned with a single dark, unbroken, longitudinal stripe.** Transverse bands may also be present. Some individuals have tentacles that are completely dark. **Shell exterior** is variable but normally **black to dark brown, often adorned in white in a small checkerboard pattern.** A distinct, **cream-colored band is often present at the base of the body whorl** along with a basal ridge. Shell color banding is also often present. It is best to view wet shells to see colors and patterning. Shell interior is almost always purple. The **shell is conical in shape**, with four whorls. No strong spiral sculpture is present and it is frequently eroded or encrusted with algae. All characteristics may not be present in all individuals so view more than one.

SIZE: Shell height normally to 0.35″ (9 mm), occasionally to 0.4″ (11 mm).

HABITAT: On rocks and pilings of both exposed and protected shorelines as well as in salt marshes; high intertidal zone.

RANGE: Sitka, Alaska, to Cabo San Lucas, Baja California, México.

NOTES: The little checkered periwinkle is a common species that often lives alongside its close relative, the checkered periwinkle. These 2 species are not easily differentiated since they are so similar in appearance. The pattern on the tentacles is one of the best and most reliable identification points. A 10× magnification loupe is very helpful. Additional differences have also been noted, including egg capsules, but they have not been included here. The difference in the size of the checkers is also helpful.

SIMILAR SPECIES: Checkered periwinkle is a larger species with a checkerboard pattern whose checkers are four times larger.

Sitka Periwinkle

Littorina sitkana Philippi, 1845

OTHER NAMES: Sitka littorine; formerly classified as *Littorina sitchana*.

DESCRIPTION: The tentacles and fleshy body are black. Shell exterior color varies widely from gray or black to reddish-brown, frequently with white, yellow or orange spiral bands. Shell interior is brown or orange. The **globose shell has a body whorl that is as tall as its spire**. Two forms may be found with the **shell smooth or with strong spiral ribbing**.

SIZE: Shell to 0.9″ (22 mm) high.

HABITAT: On rocks, pilings, eelgrass and kelp of protected and slightly exposed shorelines; splash zone to mid-intertidal zone.

RANGE: Bering Sea to Cape Arago, Oregon; Siberia, Japan and Sea of Okhotsk.

NOTES: The Sitka periwinkle is a rather squat species that can survive out of water about 50 percent of the time; in fact, it will actually suffocate if submerged under water for too long. This species does not move around much, with most individuals moving less than 1 m (39″) per month. Large numbers of Sitka periwinkles often congregate in moist shady crevices in bedrock to avoid desiccation. The Sitka periwinkle lives about 2 years.

SIMILAR SPECIES: Checkered periwinkle always has a shell with a conical (more elongated) shape.

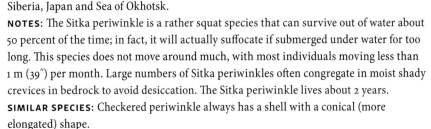

Flat-bottomed Periwinkle

Littorina keenae Rosewater, 1978

OTHER NAMES: Eroded periwinkle, gray periwinkle, gray littorine; formerly classified as *Littorina planaxis*.

DESCRIPTION: Shell exterior is grayish-brown with scattered whitish spots and flecks, but often eroded. Shell interior is chocolate-brown. The shell is **broadly conical with convex whorls** that are normally badly eroded, and it features **an eroded, flattened, white inner lip and columella** on the body whorl.

SIZE: Shell to 0.9″ (23 mm) high.

HABITAT: On rocks of the exposed coast from the splash zone to high intertidal zone.

RANGE: Charleston, Oregon, to Bahía Magdalena, Baja California Sur, México.

NOTES: This large, southern periwinkle is found only as far north as Oregon. If you ever wonder if sea anemones feed upon snails, this species shows some insight. A flat-bottomed periwinkle was fed to a short plumose anemone in an aquarium. After several hours the anemone disgorged the periwinkle that was tightly closed shut but was fine and able to resume its normal life. Its shell, however, was very clean and polished! But this outcome may not be the case for all snails.

Salt Marsh Periwinkle

Littorina subrotundata (Carpenter, 1864)

OTHER NAMES: Newcomb's periwinkle; formerly classified as *Algamorda subrotundata*; occasionally misspelled *Algamorda subrotunda*, *Littorina subrotunda*.

DESCRIPTION: Color of tentacles is black. Shell color is a **light brown with 2 bands of dark brown**. The thin periostracum is also brown. The thin shell is globose with well-rounded whorls, and normally features 9 or 10 **coarse spiral ribs on the largest whorl** and a thin outer lip. A flange-like lip partially covers the umbilicus.

SIZE: Shell to 0.8″ (21 mm) high.

HABITAT: In salt marshes or among mussels, barnacles or rocks; high intertidal zone.

RANGE: Aleutian Islands, Alaska, to Cape Arago, Oregon.

NOTES: The salt marsh periwinkle can be found in 2 different habitats. This periwinkle is found more easily in salt marshes at the highest of tides, but it can also be found on rocky shores amid barnacles and mussels. Males of this species have been found to seek out the largest females for reproduction, thus ensuring a better chance for more of their young to survive.

Variable Lacuna

Lacuna variegata Carpenter, 1864

OTHER NAMES: Carpenter variegated chink-shell, variegate lacuna, variegated lacuna, variegated chink-shell.

DESCRIPTION: The exterior of the shell is **brownish with lighter and darker bands, smooth and fragile with a glossy finish.** Aperture is rounded, with the height of the aperture slightly more than half the shell height. The whorls are well rounded. **The ubilicus is a wide chink that runs along the columella.**

SIZE: Shell to 0.7″ (18 mm) high.

HABITAT: On seaweeds and eelgrass on rocky shorelines; low intertidal zone to shallow subtidal depths.

RANGE: Drier Bay, Prince William Sound, Alaska, to southern California; more common from Puget Sound and north.

NOTES: Lacunas are aquatic snails that remain underwater much of the time and as a result you will find them at lower levels on the beach. The variable lacuna often deposits its distinctive yellow rings of eggs on eelgrass and kelp that are about 0.25″ (6 mm) across.

SIMILAR SPECIES: Wide lacuna.

Wide Lacuna

Lacuna vincta (Montagu, 1803)

OTHER NAMES: Carinate lacuna, carinate chink shell, chink shell, common northern chink-shell, common northern chink shell, common northern lacuna, northern lacuna, northern chink shell, wide chink shell, wide chink snail, wide chinkshell, wide-chink snail; formerly classified as Epheria vincta, *Lacuna carinata, Lacuna divaricata, Lacuna solidula.*

DESCRIPTION: The shell is normally **tan to brown colored with a white spiral band and a thin, glossy tan periostracum.** The conical shell holds 5 **whorls that are well rounded and separated by somewhat deep** sutures. The aperture's height is slightly more than half the shell height.

SIZE: Shell to 0.6″ (16 mm) high.

HABITAT: On various seaweeds of rocky shores; low intertidal zone to shallow subtidal depths.

RANGE: Alaska to California, uncommon south of Puget Sound; Labrador to New Jersey; northern Europe.

NOTES: This species is occasionally found in abundance. Females lay their eggs in jelly-like masses on the blades of seaweeds. The impressive list of common names for this species is a good reason why there are scientific names for organisms.

SIMILAR SPECIES: Variegated lacuna.

Mudflat Snail ⓘ

Batillaria attramentaria (G. B. Sowerby I,1855)

OTHER NAMES: False-cerith snail, screw shell; formerly classified as *Batillaria cumingi*, *Batillaria zonalis*.

DESCRIPTION: Exterior of the shell is extremely variable from gray to brown often with white stripes and or black bands. Interior is dark brown to black. The shell is turriform in shape with a spire of 8–9 **slightly convex whorls** that taper to a sharp apex. The **whorls are patterned with several flattened spiral cords**. Axial ribs are often also present, creating a beaded effect along the ridges. A short canal is present and twisted to the left.

SIZE: Shell normally to 1.4″ (3.5 cm) high, occasionally to 2″ (5 cm).

HABITAT: On mudflats and sand-mud protected shorelines; high to mid-intertidal zone.

RANGE: Central British Columbia to central California.

NOTES: This prolific species was accidentally introduced with oysters from Japan. Its common name is an excellent choice since it is frequently found on mudflats. This snail has been found to reach incredible densities—7,000 individuals per square meter in ideal habitats. The mudflat snail's life span is estimated to be as long as 10 years.

....

Threaded Bittium

Neostylidium eschrichtii
(Middendorff, 1849)

OTHER NAMES: Giant Pacific bittium, giant Pacific coast bittium, threaded horn shell, screw snail; formerly classified as *Bittium eschrichtii*, *Stylidium eschrichtii*.

DESCRIPTION: Shell exteriors are grayish or reddish-brown. Shell is turriform in shape with a spire of about

9 slightly **swollen whorls** that taper to a sharp apex. The base is large, due to the size of the body whorl, which is patterned with 8 flattened spiral cords. The smaller whorls have approximately 4 flattened spiral cords. No axial grooves are present. The **sutures are indistinct**. The aperture is small and oval with a thin outer lip.

SIZE: Shell to 0.75″ (20 mm) high.

HABITAT: On coarse sand or on and under rocks; low intertidal zone to depths of 180′ (55 m).

RANGE: Sitka, Alaska, to Baja California, México.

NOTES: The threaded bittium is a very common species on rocky beaches at low tide. This species lays gelatinous egg masses from February to May in Washington state.

SIMILAR SPECIES: Slender bittium *Lirobittium attenuatum* (Carpenter, 1864) features an elongated shell with beaded cords at the apex and distinct sutures.

....

Common Purple Sea-snail

Janthina janthina (Linnaeus, 1758)

OTHER NAMES: Common janthina, common violet sea snail, janthina, purple snail, round violet snail, violet snail; formerly classified as *Janthina prolongata*.

DESCRIPTION: Body is **overall violet to blue in color.** The foot is large and conspicuous. **Shell ranges from violet to blue** in color. The smooth shell is well rounded with a typical gastropod coil and a low spire.

SIZE: Shell to 1.5″ (3.8 cm) high.

HABITAT: Floats on tropical and semitropical oceanic waters.

RANGE: Southern British Columbia (occasionally) to Brazil: Cape Cod to Florida and Texas; worldwide in all tropical and subtropical waters.

NOTES: The common purple sea-snail, like all members of the genus *Janthina*, releases a violet pigment when disturbed. The Greeks used this pigment as a dye for their clothing. Like most snails, the common purple sea-snail is heavier than water, but unlike most species, it is able to produce a bubble raft that is entrapped in mucus to keep it afloat. Suspended upside down from a frothy bubble raft on the ocean surface, these floating snails are predators to other pelagic organisms, including the by-the-wind sailor, and Portuguese man-of-war.

Boreal Wentletrap

Opalia wroblewskyi (Mörch, 1875)

OTHER NAMES: Wroblewski's wentletrap; formerly classified as *Opalia chacei, Opalia borealis*.
DESCRIPTION: Exterior of the shell is **chalky white**. The body is white with pearly swellings. Shell is turriform and adorned with approximately 7 strong, **blunt axial ribs** per whorl, and one spiral ridge next to the base of the lowest whorl.
SIZE: Height to 1.3″ (3.2 cm).
HABITAT: In sand, or similar material near aggregating anemones; low intertidal zone to depths of 590′ (180 m).
RANGE: Forrester Island, Alaska, to Baja California, México.
NOTES: The boreal wentletrap is one species that is more often found on the beach as an empty shell than a live animal. It is active at high tide, feeding on the tentacles of sea anemones. At low tide it retreats into the sand near its food source, thus is not often observed live. The boreal wentletrap is reported to have a purple dye gland that is used for its defense.

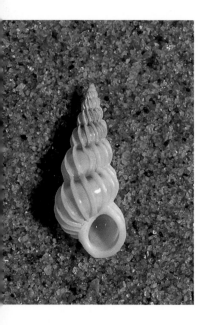

Tinted Wentletrap

Epitonium tinctum (Carpenter, 1864)

OTHER NAMES: Painted wentletrap, white wentletrap; formerly classified as *Nitidiscala tincta*.
DESCRIPTION: **The shell is white with a purple-brown band on whorls below the suture in fresh specimens.** The shell is high-spired, conical, stout and graced with 8–12 raised vertical ribs.
SIZE: Height to 1.3″ (32 mm).
HABITAT: Among rocks or in tidepools; the low intertidal zone to water 150′ (46 m) deep.
RANGE: Forrester Island, Alaska, to Bahía Magdalena, Baja California Sur, México.
NOTES: The tinted wentletrap is a relatively small species that lives near its food source, aggregating

anemones and giant green anemones. It feeds on the tentacles of these and other anemones when the tide covers them. When the tide is out, it hides in the sand. It avoids the short plumose anemone, however, because it occasionally falls prey to it. If you handle a live tinted wentletrap, it may irritate your skin. A purple dye may also be secreted if the animal is disturbed. The beautiful, delicate shells of wentletraps are favorites with shell collectors.

SIMILAR SPECIES: Money wentletrap.

Money Wentletrap

Epitonium indianorum (Carpenter, 1865)

OTHER NAMES: Indian wentletrap; formerly classified as *Nitidiscala indianorum*.

DESCRIPTION: Shell **exterior and interior are white**. Shell is turriform and adorned with a total of approximately 8 to 10 convex whorls. It is **an elongated shell with very rounded whorls and a rounded aperture**. The whorls are graced with 10 to 17 costae that continue over the sutures and are bent slightly backwards.

SIZE: Shell to 1.5" (3.5 cm) high.

HABITAT: On sandy mud; low intertidal zone to depths of 600′ (180 m).

RANGE: Forrester Island, Alaska, to Todos Santos Bay, Baja California, México.

NOTES: The money wentletrap was used as money by some Indigenous people, hence its common name. This species feeds upon anemones including the warty painted anemone and white-spotted anemone. It locates its prey by following its "scent." Wentletrap shells are also known as staircase shells.

British Columbia Balcis

Vitreolina columbiana (Bartsch, 1917)

OTHER NAMES: British Columbian balcis, Columbian cucumber sucker; formerly classified as *Balcis columbiana*, *Melanella columbiana*, *Vitreolina columbiana*.

DESCRIPTION: Shell is **translucent** (alabaster-like) and glossy. Seven smooth whorls are present that do not bulge (difficult to see), **slightly curved with a sharp spire.**
SIZE: Shell to 0.3″ (8 mm) high.
HABITAT: In mud but more often attached to sea cucumbers; low intertidal zone to shallow subtidal depths.
RANGE: Baranoff Island, Alaska, to Departure Bay, British Columbia.
NOTES: The British Columbia balcis is a parasite that clings to and sucks the blood of various sea cucumbers including the false white sea cucumber, tiny black sea cucumber and giant black cucumber. The easiest method to finding the British Columbia balcis is to locate a sea cucumber and look for the balcis either attached or nearby in the mud. This species has only been found on the very lowest of intertidal levels.

Lewis's Moonsnail

Neverita lewisii (Gould, 1847)

OTHER NAMES: Lewis's moon shell; formerly classified as *Euspira lewisii*, *Lunatia lewisii*; *Polinices lewisii*.
DESCRIPTION: The body is creamy white to purplish-white and it is enormous. Shell exterior and interior varies from yellowish-white to light brown. A thin, brownish-gray periostracum may be present on fresh shells. The **heavy shell** is globular with 5–6 smooth whorls, of which the body whorl is massive, taking up most of the shell. The apex is made up of a very low spire, and the aperture is large. The **umbilicus is deep and narrow and partially covered by a parietal callus.**
SIZE: Shell to 5.5″ (14 cm) high.
HABITAT: In sand and mud; low intertidal zone to depths of 300′ (91 m).

The egg case has a distinctive shape.

The Lewis's moonsnail drills through clam shells to feed on the meal inside.

RANGE: Ketchikan, Alaska, to Baja California, México.

NOTES: This active carnivore plows through the sand, preying upon clams and other bivalves by drilling a hole in the shell of the prey. To protect itself, the foot contracts by ejecting water from perforations around the edge. This enables the animal to retreat inside, filling most of the shell. This species is also known for its distinctive large egg case, or "sand collar." Females crawl higher up on muddy sand beaches in the spring and summer to lay their eggs. It has been found to feed upon approximately one clam every four days. This is the largest living moonsnail in the world!

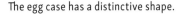

Aleutian Moonsnail

Cryptonatica aleutica (Dall, 1919)

OTHER NAMES: Aleutian moon snail, closed moonsnail; formerly classified as *Natica aleutica, Natica clausa*.

DESCRIPTION: The body is creamy-white to yellowish with small brown to purple blotches. Shell exterior is cream-coloured with a thin brown periostracum. The shell is globose with smooth, convex whorls, occasionally with very fine, wavy spiral grooves; body whorl is evenly rounded. The **umbilicus is closed with a glossy white callus**. A sharply demarcated white patch is adjacent to the umbilicus. The operculum is thick and calcareous.

SIZE: Shell to 2.4″ (6 cm) high.

HABITAT: In sand; low intertidal zone to depths of 1,650′ (500 m).

RANGE: Circumpolar; Arctic to southern California.

NOTES: The Aleutian moonsnail is primarily a northern resident of sandy intertidal sites, as its name suggests. This species is common in the low intertidal areas of southeast Alaska; however, these snails are usually completely buried under the sand.

SIMILAR SPECIES: Arctic moonsnail *Cryptonatica affinis* is a smaller animal (shell to 1″ (2.5 cm) high) with a body that is pure white. The umbilicus is completely covered with a white, calcareous callus.

Eggs.

Oregon Triton

Fusitriton oregonensis (Redfield, 1848)

OTHER NAMES: Hairy Oregon triton, hairy triton.

DESCRIPTION: Exterior of this sturdy shell is white (color not visible when animal is living) and covered with **dark brown bristles on a thick yellowish periostracum,** which separates from the shell and falls off after the animal dies. Shell interior is white. The spindle-shaped shell has a prominent spire and 6–7 whorls that are separated by prominent sutures. **Many axial ribs are crossed by several paired spiral cords.** The **elongated aperture** is about two-fifths of the height of the shell and the open siphonal canal is about a third the height of the aperture.

SIZE: Shell to 6″ (15 cm) high.

HABITAT: On rocky shorelines; extreme low intertidal zone to depths of 600′ (180 m).

RANGE: Bering Sea to San Diego, California; northern Japan.

NOTES: The Oregon triton is our largest intertidal snail. It is both a carnivore and predator, feeding primarily at night on a variety of prey items including sea squirts, gastropods and sea urchins. This snail has a proboscis gland that is capable of secreting an anesthetic to immobilize its prey. To feed upon its hard-shelled prey it uses its biting jaws as well as its radula. Sulfuric acid from its salivary glands is likely used as well to assist in the drilling of calcareous shells. This large snail is not harvested for human consumption because a pathogen in its salivary glands can be deadly.

SIMILAR SPECIES: Checkered hairysnail.

Checkered Hairysnail

Trichotropis cancellata Hinds, 1849

OTHER NAMES: Checkered hairy snail, cancellate hairysnail, hairy shell, cancellate hairy-snail, cancellated trichotropsis, dwarf hairy triton; occasionally misspelled *Trichotropis cancellata*.

DESCRIPTION: Body is white. Exterior of the shell is yellowish-white with a **brownish periostracum that is covered in bristles**; 5–7 whorls are accented with 4–5 strong spiral cords that are separated by deep sutures. **Weak axial ribs are often present resulting in a checkered appearance. Shell aperture is round and approximately a third the height of the shell.**

SIZE: To 1.6″ (4 cm) high.

HABITAT: On rocky shorelines with strong currents; low intertidal zone to depths of 660′ (200 m).

RANGE: Bering Sea to Oregon.

NOTES: The checkered hairysnail is a male for the first year of its life then it changes into a female, but it keeps its penis, which is located behind the right eye. This type of sex change is referred to as protandry. This unusual species is a filter feeder and, as a result, does not need to be very active.

SIMILAR SPECIES: Oregon triton with an elongated shell aperture.

....

Angular Unicorn

Acanthinucella spirata (Blainville, 1832)

OTHER NAMES: Angular thorn drupe, spotted thorn drupe, thorn snail; formerly classified as *Acanthina spirata*.

DESCRIPTION: Shell exterior is pale gray to yellowish-white with brown lines that cover much of the surface. The aperture is yellowish-white. Shell is elongate in shape with 5–6 whorls and **a prominent keel at the shoulder.** Light-colored spiral cords circle the shell with **interrupted dark reddish-brown grooves between. A sharp tooth** is also present on the lip of the aperture but small specimens may lack it.

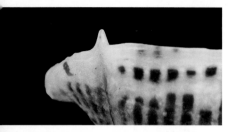

A tooth is found on the aperture lip.

SIZE: Shell to 1.6″ (4 cm) high.
HABITAT: On protected rocks and pilings; high to mid-intertidal zone.
RANGE: British Columbia to Camalu, Baja California, México; uncommon north of California.
NOTES: The angular unicorn is a predator of barnacles and molluscs. It has been shown to use its horn-like spine, located on the outer edge of its aperture, as a ram against the plates of its barnacle prey. It was discovered that in approximately 40 percent of cases of an attack, the result is spine breakage. Luckily their spines are regrown in about 4 weeks.

Eggs.

Leafy Hornmouth

Ceratostoma foliatum (Gmelin, 1791)

OTHER NAMES: Foliate thornmouth, foliated thorn purpura, leafy hornmouth, murex; formerly classified as *Purpura foliata*.
DESCRIPTION: Exterior of the shell varies from white or gray to yellowish-brown, often with brown banding. The shell is ovate with conical spire and **3 exaggerated flanges**, as well as several strong spiral cords. Mature specimens have a **distinctive tooth on the outer lip** of the aperture. The operculum is not calcified and the siphonal canal is a closed tube.
SIZE: Shell to 4″ (10 cm) high.
HABITAT: On and among rocks; low intertidal zone to depths of 200′ (60 m).
RANGE: Prince William Sound, Alaska, to San Diego, California.
NOTES: The leafy hornmouth is one of our more impressive gastropods. It is a generalist predator that prefers to feed upon barnacles and bivalves. It uses its labial spine as a wedge to open bivalves or mussels, enabling the insertion of the proboscis. They are known to live to 16 years.
SIMILAR SPECIES: Japanese oyster drill.

Frilled Dogwinkle

Nucella lamellosa (Gmelin, 1791)

OTHER NAMES: Frilled whelk, purple whelk, wrinkled dogwinkle, wrinkled purple, wrinkled whelk; formerly classified as *Thais lamellosa*.

DESCRIPTION: Color of shell exterior is variable, ranging from white or gray to brown, orange, purple or banded with a variety of colors. **Shell is** normally **high-spired** with an ovate shape and heavy and **may be smooth or highly ornamented with frills.** A total of 5–7 whorls are present and there may be spiral ribs on some shells. Shell can be smooth in exposed situations while several elaborate frills are often present in sheltered areas. The aperture is ovate in shape and reaches about half the shell length. **A broadly flared outer lip is present.** This species is likely our most variable shelled univalve in the Pacific Northwest!

SIZE: Height to 3.25″ (8 cm).

HABITAT: On rocks; low intertidal zone to depths of 33′ (10 m).

RANGE: Aleutian Islands, Alaska, to Central California.

NOTES: Large congregations of frilled dogwinkles are often found at the low tide mark in winter. At this time they breed, laying hundreds of yellow spindle-shaped eggs attached to the sides and undersides of rocks. These eggs are sometimes referred to as "sea oats." Each female is capable of laying up to 1,000 eggs per year, but maturity is reached at 4 years. The frilled dogwinkle is a predator, like the rest of its clan, feeding on a variety of prey including barnacles, mussels and other molluscs. Researchers have observed that it required 6.7 hours for an acorn barnacle to be drilled and eaten while a total of 17.4 hours were required to finish a thatched barnacle.

SIMILAR SPECIES: Leafy hornmouth.

Breeding masses in winter.

Frilled form.

Smooth form.

Northern Channelled Dogwinkle

Nucella canaliculata (Duclos, 1832)

OTHER NAMES: Channelled dogwhelk, channelled dogwinkle, channelled purple snail, channelled thais, channelled whelk; formerly classified as *Thais canaliculata, Purpura canaliculata*.

DESCRIPTION: Shell exterior ranges in color from whitish to orange. The shell is spindle-shaped with **a short spire** and 14–16 **nearly equal, spiral ribs with deep channels separating each rib**. The aperture is less than half the shell height.

SIZE: Height to 1.5″ (3.5 cm).

HABITAT: On rocks and barnacles near waters swept by tidal currents; mid-intertidal zone.

RANGE: Ketchikan, Alaska, to Fidalgo Island, Washington.

NOTES: The northern channelled dogwinkle is a species that is currently under study. Its previous range was thought to be from Alaska to California. Ongoing research is now revealing that another similar species, the lined dogwinkle, replaces the northern channelled dogwinkle in the southern portion of that range. The northern channelled dogwinkle is often found feeding on barnacles, its main prey item.

SIMILAR SPECIES: Lined dogwinkle.

Lined Dogwinkle

Nucella analoga (Forbes, 1852)

OTHER NAME: Previously included with *Nucella canaliculata*.

DESCRIPTION: Exterior of the shell ranges in color from whitish to orange and the interior is white. The shell is spindle-shaped with **several alternating thick and thin spiral cords that are separated with shallow channels** rather than deep furrows between the cords.

SIZE: Height to 1.5″ (3.5 cm).

HABITAT: On rocks in semi-protected and exposed rocky shores; mid-intertidal zone.

RANGE: Bering Sea to Point Conception, California: common in Oregon to northern California.

NOTES: This species lives on the exposed outer coast where it feeds on mussels. Marine researchers noted that former designations for this group of dogwinkles were not correct or complete. Additional research is being conducted to finalize the differences in this species complex. It seems that the more we find out about some species the more we realize how little we really know about them.

....

Northern Striped Dogwinkle

Nucella ostrina (Gould, 1852)

OTHER NAMES: Formerly included with *Nucella emarginata*, a species that is found as far north as southern Oregon; occasionally misspelled *Nucella osterina*.

DESCRIPTION: Shell exterior color varies greatly from white to black, brown or yellow. Color banding is frequently observed and the interior is often purple. Shell is spindle-shaped with a high, **slender spire** and **smooth whorls or with 5–6 spiral cords that are irregular in size, broad and frequently well separated**. Frills may also be present on the ribs. **The aperture is widely flared.** The egg capsules for this species are vase-shaped, with a long neck.

SIZE: Height to 1.25″ (3 cm).

HABITAT: On rocks of semi-protected and exposed shorelines; high to mid-intertidal zones.

RANGE: Northern Alaska to northern California.

NOTES: The variability of the northern striped dogwinkle makes it one of the more difficult species to identify. Its egg capsules are often used in identification.

SIMILAR SPECIES: Emarginate dogwinkle.

....

Emarginate Dogwinkle

Nucella emarginata (Deshayes, 1839)

OTHER NAMES: Emarginate dogwinkle; *Purpura emarginata*; formerly included with *Nucella ostrina*.

DESCRIPTION: Exterior of the shell varies from yellowish to gray or brown and occasionally banded. Shell interior is purple. The shell is globose with 4–5 whorls including the very large body whorl and **a very short spire**, and is decorated with **4–5 major spiral**

cords; some specimens may have minor cords between. Irregular nodes are often present on the spiral cords. The aperture is large with a wavy outer lip and 5 teeth on large specimens.

SIZE: Shell to 1.4″ (3.5 cm) high.

HABITAT: On rocky shorelines; mid-intertidal zone.

RANGE: Southern Oregon to Punta Eugenia, Baja California, México.

NOTES: The emarginate dogwinkle was formerly believed to be included with the northern striped dogwinkle. Recent studies have now separated the two distinct species, although it can be difficult to identify individuals living where both species exist.

SIMILAR SPECIES: Northern striped dogwinkle.

File Dogwinkle

Nucella lima (Gmelin, 1791)

OTHER NAMES: Purple thais, rough purple, rough purple whelk, uniform purple snail; formerly classified as *Thais lima*.

DESCRIPTION: Exterior shell color is variable, ranging from whitish to orange or brown, and is often banded. The shell is spindle-shaped with a **short spire**, 17–20 **alternating thick and thin spiral ribs with deep channels** that separate each rib from the next. The **aperture is tall** and ranges from a little greater than half to two-thirds of the shell height and is approximately half the shell's diameter.

SIZE: To 2″ (5 cm) high.

HABITAT: On rocky shorelines with a preference for exposed coastlines; mid-intertidal zone to shallow subtidal depths.

RANGE: Aleutian Islands, Alaska, to British Columbia; uncommon south of the northern end of Vancouver Island; Japan.

NOTES: The file dogwinkle drills the shells of barnacles and mussels to feed on the delicacies inside. Its predators include the purple star and the mottled star. Female file dogwinkles lay yellowish egg capsules that are somewhat ridged, called "sea oats." Each egg capsule contains approximately 500 to 900 eggs but 95 percent of these become nurse eggs that are consumed by developing embryos.

SIMILAR SPECIES: Channelled dogwinkle with spiral ribs that are nearly equal in size; lined dogwinkle with shallow channels between the spiral cords rather than deep furrows.

Sculptured Rocksnail

Ocinebrina interfossa Carpenter, 1864

OTHER NAMES: Carpenter's dwarf triton, sculptured rock shell, sculptured rock snail, sculptured whelk; formerly classified as *Ocenebra interfossa, Ocenebra atropupurea,Tritonalia interfossa.*

DESCRIPTION: Color of shell exterior is grayish-brown to yellow and the interior white or yellow. Each whorl, with a shoulder that is flattened below the suture, features **8–11 distinct axial ribs that are crossed by strong spiral cords.** Shells exhibit great variability.

SIZE: To 1″ (2.5 cm) high.

HABITAT: On and among rocks on rocky beaches; low intertidal zone to depths of 328′ (100 m).

RANGE: Semidi Islands, Alaska, to Baja California, México.

NOTES: The sculptured rocksnail lives in somewhat exposed seashores but keeps within sheltered microhabitats. This carnivorous snail feeds on molluscs and barnacles, first drilling through their shells. This species crawls with muscular contractions by using wave-like motions from front to rear of the foot. In addition, the waves on the opposite sides of the foot are out of phase. This technique is effective for its travels both above and below the water.

SIMILAR SPECIES: Lurid rocksnail.

Japanese Oyster Drill ⓘ

Ocenebra inornata (Récluz, 1851)

OTHER NAMES: Japan rock shell, Japanese dwarf triton, Japanese oyster drill, Japanese rocksnail; formerly classified as *Ceratostoma inornata, Cerotostoma inornatum,*

Ocenebra inornatum, Ocenebra japonica, Ocinebrina inornata, Ocinebrellus inornatus, Pteropurpura inornata.

DESCRIPTION: Shell exterior varies greatly from whitish to yellow or brown and occasionally orange to pink. It has a chalky texture. Shell interior, or aperture, is brown or yellow. The shell is solid and **spindle-shaped with 5–7 whorls, each with squared-off profile**, and is sculptured with **3–11 axial ribs** crossed by alternating strong and weak spiral cords. **Fairly sizable frills may be present on some individuals**. The canal is short and open when young but closed at maturity. No periostracum is present. The aperture is oval, with a very thick lip (up to half the width of the aperture) at or near maturity.

SIZE: Shell to 2.4″ (6 cm) high.

HABITAT: On gravel, mud and sand beaches; intertidal zone.

RANGE: British Columbia to California (introduced); Japan; North China.

NOTES: The Japanese oyster drill was introduced from Japan earlier than 1929. It is a predator of primarily oysters, both our native Olympia oyster and the Pacific oyster. It feeds on them by drilling a small hole into the shell and rasping out the soft body inside. This species does not spread through its own distribution because it does not have pelagic larva. Considerable care is taken not to bring this species to new areas where oysters are present.

SIMILAR SPECIES: Leafy hornmouth, a larger species with more ornamentation.

Atlantic Oyster Drill ⓘ

Urosalpinx cinerea (Say, 1822)

OTHER NAMES: Eastern drill, eastern oyster drill, oyster drill; formerly classified as *Urosalpinx cinera, Urosalpinx cinereus*.

DESCRIPTION: Shell varies from gray to yellowish-white, often with brownish spiral bands and the aperture is often purple. The spindle-shaped shell includes a **total of 5–6 whorls and numerous fine spiral cords that ornament the 9–12 axial ribs on each whorl**. There are often 2–7 small teeth inside the outer aperture, and the outer lip is sometimes thickened.

SIZE: Shell normally to 0.75″ (20 mm) high; occasionally to 1.75″ (4.4 cm) high.

HABITAT: On rocks, in oyster beds, and in similar areas in the sheltered waters of bays and similar areas; mid-intertidal zone to depths of 50′ (15 m).

RANGE: Vancouver Island, British Columbia, to Newport Bay, California; Gulf of St. Lawrence to northern Florida.

NOTES: Atlantic oyster drill was introduced from Europe over 100 years ago. As the common name suggests, this species is a major predator of young eastern oysters. Its presence is not widespread; it is found only at sites where it has been introduced.

Carinate Dovesnail

Alia carinata (Hinds, 1844)

OTHER NAMES: Carinate dove shell, keeled dove; formerly classified as *Mitrella gausapata, Mitrella carinata*.

DESCRIPTION: Exterior of the shell is brown to yellowish-brown and often mottled with white or dark brown, or covered with black seaside lichen, appearing all black. Shell interior is white; the **outer lip is chestnut-brown.** A thin brown periostracum is also present. The shell is stout and

ovate with a conical spire. Slightly inflated, the **body whorl is angled at the shoulder (best at aperture)** and often very smooth, but it can be strongly keeled.

SIZE: Shell to 0.4″ (10 mm) high.

HABITAT: On eelgrass and algae; mid-intertidal zone to depths of 49′ (15 m).

RANGE: Southern Alaska south to Baja California, México.

NOTES: Very little is known of the biology of the carinate dovesnail. It is believed to feed on the detritus that adheres to kelp blades where it is often found. It is also believed to be a micro-carnivore. In some locations the shells of this common species are a favorite home to tiny hermit crabs.

Violet-band Mangelia

Mangelia crebricostata Carpenter, 1864

OTHER NAMES: Formerly classified as *Kurtziella crebricostata, Kurtziella plumbea.*
DESCRIPTION: Exterior color ranges from white to cream-colored with a band of tan, brown or violet. The shell is **spindle-shaped with an elongated spire**. There are about 6 convex whorls that are sculptured with **several strong axial ribs**. The aperture is elongated and continuous with the open siphonal canal. The **siphonal canal bears faint or no spiral grooves**.
SIZE: Shell to 0.8″ (20 mm) high.
HABITAT: In sand and sandy mud; low intertidal zone to depths of 280′ (85 m).
RANGE: Cook Inlet, Alaska, to northern Washington.
NOTES: The violet-band mangelia is a small species that is not easily found in sandy mud. There it feeds upon a variety of tube worms.

Variegated Amphissa

Amphissa versicolor Dall, 1871

OTHER NAMES: Joseph's coat amphissa, variegate amphissa; formerly classified as *Amphissa incisa, Amphissa lineata.*
DESCRIPTION: Exterior color of the shell varies widely from white or gray to yellow and brown; mottling or dark spiral lines are often present. The shell is slender, high-spired and elongate; covered with 4–5 whorls and several weak axial ridges. Many fine **longitudinal ribs run at a distinct angle to the axis** from apex to mid-body whorl with spiral threads. A distinct notch is present rather than a siphonal canal.
SIZE: Shell to 0.5″ (13 mm) high.

HABITAT: On rocks and similar areas less protected from the surge; low intertidal zone to depths of 150′ (46 m).

RANGE: Central British Columbia to Isla San Martin, Baja California, México; rare north of California.

NOTES: The variegated amphissa is more commonly found in the southern than the northern portion of its range. As its scientific name *versicolor* indicates, it occurs in many different colors, including white, gray, yellow, red and brown. Empty shells are often found washed up on the shore after a storm. Like its close relative the wrinkled amphissa, this species is a scavenger and sometimes observed with its long siphon extended as it moves about.

SIMILAR SPECIES: Wrinkled amphissa.

....

Wrinkled Amphissa

Amphissa columbiana Dall, 1916

OTHER NAMES: Columbian amphissa, wrinkled dove snail, wrinkled snail.

DESCRIPTION: The animal is white with dark spots. Exterior of the shell varies greatly from orange to pink or yellowish-green, mauve or light brown, often with brownish spots. The shell is slender, high-spired and elongate; covered with 6–7 whorls and several weak axial ridges. **Many fine longitudinal ribs run parallel to the axis** from apex to mid-body whorl, with uniform even-spaced spiral threads. A distinct notch is present rather than a siphonal canal.

SIZE: Shell to 0.7″ (18 mm) high.

HABITAT: On and under rocks and in mud; low intertidal zone to depths of 100′ (30 m).

RANGE: Kodiak Island, Alaska, to southern California.

NOTES: The wrinkled amphissa gets its name from the ribs on the exterior of its shell. Its siphon or feeding tube is often seen extended while it searches for its next meal of carrion. This scavenger has also been found to be attracted to the food remains left by giant Pacific octopus (*Enteroctopus dofleini*) at its den.

SIMILAR SPECIES: Variegated amphissa.

Baer's Buccinum

Buccinum baeri (Middendorff, 1848)

OTHER NAMES: *Buccinum baerii*; formerly classified as *Volutharpa morchiana*.

DESCRIPTION: Exterior of the shell ranges from yellowish-brown to rich brown and the aperture is orange. The periostracum, if present, is very thin, translucent and light brown. Shell is **high spired, thin-shelled and smooth with a large, broad body whorl**. The operculum is oval and very small (one-fifth the size of the aperture).

SIZE: To 2.2″ (5.4 cm) high.

HABITAT: On sand or under rocks; low intertidal zone to water 50′ (15 m) deep.

RANGE: Bering Sea to Southeast Alaska.

NOTES: Baer's buccinum is a common species in Alaska. Details of this carnivore's habits, food and enemies seem to be a mystery as they have not been investigated. Its empty shells are often found washed up on the beach. Perhaps your observations will add an insight into this species' natural history!

SIMILAR SPECIES: Big-mouth whelk.

Big-mouth Whelk

Volutharpa ampullacea
(Middendorff, 1848)

OTHER NAMES: Alaskan volute, Baer's cousin, paper whelk; formerly classified as *Bullia ampullacea*.

DESCRIPTION: The body is speckled. Exterior and interior of the shell vary from grayish-brown to purplish-brown and are rich and shiny. There is also a brown, velvety periostracum. **Shell is globular, thin and fragile** with about 4 whorls in which the body whorl is massive. The height of the **aperture takes up approximately four-fifths of the shell**. The spire is very short.

SIZE: Shell to 1.5″ (3.5 cm) high.

HABITAT: On rocks; low intertidal zone to shallow subtidal depths.

RANGE: Bearing Sea to Vancouver Island, British Columbia; Japan and Korea.

NOTES: The big-mouth whelk is a common species in southeast Alaska. Researchers have found that only 15 percent of the population have an operculum or trap door. The remainder have either no operculum or region responsible for producing an operculum. **SIMILAR SPECIES:** Baer's buccinum.

....

Dire Whelk

Lirabuccinum dirum (Reeve, 1846)

OTHER NAMES: Elongate dire whelk, spindle shell, spindle snail, spindle whelk; formerly classified as *Searlesia dira*, *Kelletia dira*; sometimes misspelled as *Searlisia dira*.
DESCRIPTION: The body of this species is white. Shell exterior is bluish-gray to yellowish-brown. The spindle-shaped shell is elongate with a high spire. The first (smallest) whorls have strong rounded axial ribs crossed by strong spiral cords, which often become obscure as the animal ages. **Body whorl is adorned with equally spaced, flat, spiral cords without axial ribs**. The siphonal canal is well developed and open but short; aperture is nearly half the total height of the shell.
SIZE: Shell to 2″ (5 cm) high.
HABITAT: On rocky shores; mid-intertidal zone to depths of 115′ (35 m).
RANGE: Aleutian Islands, Alaska, to Monterey, California.
NOTES: The dire whelk is both a carnivore and scavenger. As a carnivore it prefers limpets and snails but it has also been observed feeding on the black Katy chiton, thatched barnacle and common acorn barnacle. This univalve also scavenges the carcasses of fish and crabs. This species does not drill its prey as most other predatory snails. Instead it uses its extensible proboscis that allows it to probe under and between shells. Dire whelks are believed to live to more than 15 years.

Western Lean Nassa

Hima mendica (Gould, 1849)

OTHER NAMES: Lean dog whelk, lean nassa, lean basketsnail, western lean dogwhelk; formerly classified as *Nassarius mendicus, N. cooperi.*
DESCRIPTION: The body is white overall. Shell exterior is yellowish-brown with a brown periostracum; aperture is bluish-white and **about one-third the shell's height**. The shell is narrowly ovate and slender with a high spire and about 7 convex whorls. **The axial ribs are crossed with numerous spiral cords, creating a beaded effect.**
SIZE: Shell to 0.9″ (22 mm) high.
HABITAT: On sand, mud and rocks; low intertidal zone to depths of 250′ (75 m).
RANGE: Kodiak Island, Gulf of Alaska, to Isla Asunción, Baja California Sur, México.
NOTES: The western lean nassa prefers to move about above the surface of the mud and sand searching for its next meal. Its close relatives the giant western nassa and western fat dog nassa, on the other hand, prefer to move about just beneath the surface of the substrate.
SIMILAR SPECIES: Japanese nassa.

Japanese Nassa

Hima fratercula (Dunker, 1862)

OTHER NAME: Formerly classified as *Nassarius fraterculus.*
DESCRIPTION: The foot is bluish-gray with white spots and its tentacles are translucent green with white spots. Exterior of the shell is brown with light yellowish-brown **banding**. The **aperture is usually yellowish with a dark band, and half the height of the shell**. The shell is narrowly ovate and slender with a high spire and 6 convex whorls. Axial ribs are prominent at a slight angle and faint spiral grooves are present.

SIZE: Shell to 0.6″ (15 mm) high.

HABITAT: In protected bays; on sand, often found under dead crabs; mid- to low intertidal zone.

RANGE: Southern British Columbia to northern Washington; Japan.

NOTES: The Japanese nassa was introduced into Bayview State Park, Washington prior to 1960. Since that time this alien has slowly expanded its range and will likely move farther into suitable habitats.

SIMILAR SPECIES: Western lean nassa.

Giant Western Nassa

Nassarius fossatus (Gould, 1850)

OTHER NAMES: Channelled basketwhelk, channelled dogwhelk, channelled dog whelk, channelled dog whelk, channelled basket snail, channelled basket shell, channelled basketshell, basket shell, nassa, channelled nassa, channelled nassa, giant western dogwelk; formerly classified as *Nassa fossata*.

DESCRIPTION: Exterior of the shell ranges in color from gray to yellowish-brown or orange-brown. **The callus is yellow to bright orange.** The ovate **shell is large and plump with an acute spire.** A total of about 7 whorls are complemented with numerous low, rounded axial ribs that are crossed with 5 spiral cords, creating a delicate beaded effect. The prominent siphonal canal is notched and turns upward.

SIZE: Shell to 2″ (5 cm) high.

HABITAT: On sand and mud shorelines with soft bottoms in protected sites; low intertidal zone to depths of 60′ (18 m).

RANGE: Southern Alaska to Laguna San Ignacio, Baja California, México.

NOTES: The giant western nassa is both carnivore and scavenger. The escape response of this snail has been observed when pursued by the giant pink star. It responds with rapid rocking and twisting of its shell as well as somersaulting with its foot. It clearly produces one of the more active predatory responses that has been observed in the Pacific Northwest. The pattern of spiral cords that are crossed with numerous fine axial ribs give the shell a basket-like appearance and as a result it is sometimes called a basket snail.

SIMILAR SPECIES: Western fat nassa.

Western Fat Nassa

Caesia perpinguis (Hinds, 1844)

OTHER NAMES: Western fat nassa; formerly classified as *Nassarius perpinguis*.

DESCRIPTION: Exterior of the shell is yellowish-white, often with spiral bands of orange-brown including one at the border of the suture. The **callus is white**. The shell is elongately ovate and **stout with a high spire**. There are about 5 whorls that are adorned with numerous axial ribs and equally prominent spiral cords that intersect to form a **beaded axial ridge** over all whorls. Inner lip includes fine ridges.

SIZE: Shell **to 1″ (2.5 cm) high**.

HABITAT: On sand; low intertidal zone to depths of 250′ (76 m).

RANGE: Puget Sound, Washington, to Isla Cedros, Baja California, México.

NOTES: The western fat nassa displays much finer sculpture than the giant western nassa. It is also wider in proportion to overall height and is much smaller, with drabber colors. This species is more common in the southern portion of its range.

SIMILAR SPECIES: Giant western nassa.

....

Eastern Mud Snail

Tritia obsoleta (Say, 1822)

OTHER NAMES: Common mud snail, eastern mud nassa, mud dog whelk, mud basket shell; formerly classified as *Ilyanassa obsoletus, Nassarius obsoletus, Ilyanassa obsoleta*.

DESCRIPTION: Exterior of the shell is **light brown, reddish-brown or dark brown and covered with a thick black periostracum**. The inside of the aperture is purplish-brown. Shell is ovate and stout with a high, rounded spire. A total of 6 whorls are marked with numerous, unequal, **faint revolving cords crossed by faint axial ribs**. The outer lip is thin, sharp and strongly arched with a fold at front. Siphonal canal is simply a notch.

SIZE: Shell to 1.25″ (3.2 cm) high.

HABITAT: On mudflats in quiet bays; high low
intertidal zone to shallow subtidal depths.
RANGE: British Columbia to central California;
Gulf of St. Lawrence to Florida.
NOTES: This species was accidentally
introduced to California from the Atlantic coast
before 1911. It feeds on both organic material
and carrion, and buries itself in the mud when
the tide goes out. Under the right conditions
it can be found in accumulations numbering
into the thousands. It is thought to have a life
span of 5 years. Its thick black periostracum is
probably the main reason it is sometimes rated
as the most unattractive snail found along the Pacific coast.

Eggs of eastern mud snail.

Purple Olive

Callianax biplicata (Sowerby I, 1825)

OTHER NAMES: Purple olivella, purple olive snail,
purple olive shell, purple dwarf olive; formerly
classified as *Olivella biplicata*.
DESCRIPTION: The foot and mantle are white to
cream-colored. Exterior of the shells vary in color
from white or lavender-grey to dark purple with a
glossy finish. The shell is ovate (**diameter is a third of
height**) and quite sturdy with an elongated aperture.
**A fine, dark line is present below the suture and an
orange line is found at upper edge of the purplish
siphonal band**. The whorls are nearly straight-sided
with very narrowly channeled sutures.
SIZE: Shell to 1.5″ (3.8 cm) high.
HABITAT: In sand on the open coast; low intertidal
zone to depths of 150′ (46 m).
RANGE: Southern Alaska to Bahía Magdalena, Baja California Sur, México.
NOTES: The purple olive is often first encountered as a moving "bump" under the sand at
low tide. This species is a common inhabitant of open sandy beaches where it normally
plows through the sand, just under the surface, searching for its next meal. Individuals live
in colonies and have an average life span of between 8 and 15 years.
SIMILAR SPECIES: Baetic olive.

Baetic Olive

Callianax baetica (Carpenter, 1864)

OTHER NAMES: Carpenter little olive, little olive; sometimes erroneously called the Beatie dwarf olive; formerly classified as *Olivella baetica*.

DESCRIPTION: The exterior of the shell varies from gray-brown to tan with purple-brown spots, streaks or bands below the suture. The shell is overall glossy, **elongate ovate (diameter is two-fifths of height)** and quite sturdy with an elongated aperture. The siphonal band is marked in white and often edged with brown.

SIZE: Shell to 1.1″ (2.7 cm) high.

HABITAT: In sand, mud or rubble; low intertidal zone to depths of 200′ (60 m).

RANGE: Kodiak Island, Alaska, to Cabo San Lucas, Baja California, México.

NOTES: A similar species, the purple olive, is a wider and larger snail often found on the same beaches. Like all *Callianax* species, the baetic olive has no eyes: it burrows in the sand most of its life so it does not need to see.

SIMILAR SPECIES: Purple olive.

Zigzag Olive

Callianax pycna Berry, 1935

OTHER NAMES: San Pedro dwarf olive; formerly classified as *Olivella pycna, Olivella pedroana*.

DESCRIPTION: Exterior of the shell is overall glossy buff, gray, or olive-gray with **distinct zigzag lines running lengthwise.** The shell is elongate ovate and very sturdy with an elongated aperture and a white callus.

SIZE: Shell to 0.6″ (15 mm) high.

HABITAT: In sand; low intertidal zone to depths of 90′ (27 m).

RANGE: Northern British Columbia to Baja California, México; uncommon north of Oregon.

NOTES: North of Oregon the shell of the zigzag olive is more likely found on a sandy beach than as a live snail. Beached shells are often paler in color than live shells. Shells of this species are occasionally found washed up on the beach with empty shells of the purple olive. The shells from various olive snails were once popular with coastal Indigenous people for making necklaces.

SIMILAR SPECIES: Baetic olive.

Gray Snakeskin-snail

Ophiodermella inermis

(Reeve, 1843)

OTHER NAMES: Formerly classified as *Ophiodermella ophiodermella*, *Ophiodermella halcyonis*, *Ophiodermella incisa*, *Ophiodermella montereyensis*, *Ophiodermella ophioderma*.

DESCRIPTION: Exterior of the shell is **gray to light brown overall, marked with several fine, brown- to black-incised lines**. The slender, high-spired shell displays an anal notch at the widest part of the aperture.

SIZE: Shell to 1.5″ (3.7 cm) high.

HABITAT: On sandy sites; low intertidal zone to depths of 230′ (70 m).

RANGE: Skidegate, Haida Gwaii (Queen Charlotte Islands), British Columbia, to Rancho Inocentes, Baja California Sur, México.

NOTES: This snail feeds on polychaete worms. Because it cannot detect its prey chemically from any distance, it moves against the current until it reaches its quarry. The red rock crab is a major predator. Gray snakeskin-snails reproduce from October to July. The egg capsules are usually laid in February, and each one holds several hundred eggs. The beautiful shell of this snail is sometimes found washed up on the beach after a storm.

Pacific Falselimpet

Siphonaria thersites Carpenter, 1864

OTHER NAMES: Carpenter's falselimpet, Carpenter's false limpet, siphon shell; formerly classified as *Liriola thersites*.
DESCRIPTION: The large foot is dark brown in color and is visible while the animal is active. **The foot is larger than the thin and fragile shell**. Shell exterior is black to reddish-brown covered by a reddish-brown periostracum. The interior is smooth, dark and reddish-brown with a lighter edge. The **shell is asymmetrical in shape** with an apex that is pushed to the left. There are two ribs that radiate from the apex to the right side of the shell, creating a wavy edge.
SIZE: Shell height to 0.5″ (13 mm); body to 0.6″ (15 mm) long.
HABITAT: On rocks or algae (including *Ulva* spp. *Fucus* spp. and others) of moderately exposed shores; high to mid-intertidal zones.
RANGE: Aleutian Islands, Alaska, to Puget Sound, Washington.
NOTES: The Pacific falselimpet is not a limpet but appears limpet-like. This species can become very abundant in some places, with population densities reaching 225 per ft² (2,500 per m²). This species has both gills and a lung enabling it to obtain oxygen whether in or out of the water—a handy attribute for an intertidal species! Researchers have discovered that it produces mucus that contains polypropionates, substances that are toxic to predators. The Pacific falselimpet feeds on Pacific rockweed, sea sacs and sea lettuce. This species is active only during the lowest of the two low tides of each day. Individuals are simultaneously hermaphroditic (both male and female at the same time), but to reproduce they exchange spermatophores (packaged sperm).
SIMILAR SPECIES: Leather limpet.

Leather Limpet

Onchidella borealis Dall, 1872

OTHER NAME: Northwest onchidella.
DESCRIPTION: The body varies and may include yellowish-green, olive, reddish-brown or

brownish-black. It is also patterned with mottling and occasionally white spots. **No shell is present; small, blunt tubercles are found along the body margin.**

SIZE: Body to 0.5″ (13 mm) long.

HABITAT: On and among the holdfasts of various algae on exposed coasts as well as on rocks of more protected shorelines; high to mid-intertidal zone.

RANGE: Alaska to San Luis Obispo County, California.

NOTES: The common name for this species is well chosen for its texture is leathery. It has a lung that is similar to land snails and slugs that it uses for respiration. It is

related closer to the sea slugs than land snails and slugs. This species feeds on diatoms that are epiphytic on algae.

SIMILAR SPECIES: Pacific falselimpet.

Spiral Velvet Snail

Velutina velutina (O.F. Müller, 1776)

OTHER NAMES: Smooth velvet shell, velvet shell, smooth velutina, smooth lamellaria; formerly classified as *Velutina laevigata*.

DESCRIPTION: The animal has a white foot without additional coloration on the foot. Shell exterior is a translucent amber and with a brown periostracum. The **shell is ear-shaped with 3 whorls and relatively flat.** Spiral ridges are present on the surface.

SIZE: Shell to 0.9″ (22 mm) high.

HABITAT: On rock; low intertidal zone to depths of 738′ (225 m).

RANGE: Circumpolar; Northern Alaska to central California; Arctic Canada to Cape Cod, Massachusetts; the Mediterranean.

NOTES: The spiral velvet snail is a species that is occasionally found intertidally on rocks where its prey, tunicates, are near. This distinctive mollusc is a simultaneous hermaphrodite.

Stearn's Ear Shell

Marsenina stearnsii (Dall, 1871)

OTHER NAMES: Formerly classified as *Lamellaria steamsii, Marsenina orbiculata.*
DESCRIPTION: The color of the mantle ranges from **white to pinkish-white with a smooth finish and pores that match the pink leathery tunicate's surface.** The shell is white and ear-shaped with a widely flaring aperture.
SIZE: Shell to 0.6″ (15 mm) high.
HABITAT: On tunicates; very low intertidal zone to depths of 62′ (19 m).
RANGE: Central Alaska to Islas Marías, México.
NOTES: The Stearn's ear shell is well known for its habit of living on or very near its main food, the pink leathery tunicate, *Trididemnum opacum.* Other species of tunicate may also be eaten but it has never been observed. Its appearance closely matches the tunicate that it lives with. This uncommon species feeds at night using its proboscis to eat.

Nudibranchs & Allies

SUBCLASS OPISTHOBRANCHIA

This subclass of gastropods is extremely diverse. Most individuals do not possess a shell, or if they do, it is normally quite small. Nudibranchs means "naked gills" which refer to their external respiratory organs which form a tuft-like branchial plume at the back end of the animal or a group of club-like projections along its dorsal side. Other nudibranch-like organisms are also present from several different orders, each of which differs from "true" nudibranchs.

Nudibranch Allies

Several nudibranch-like organisms are present on the Pacific Northwest Coast. This is a group of diverse molluscs that includes bubble snails and barrel-bubbles (order Cephalaspidea), sea hares (order Anaspidea), berthellas (order Notaspidea) and planctonic opistobranchs (order Thecosomata).

White Bubble Snail

Haminoea vesicula (Gould, 1855)

OTHER NAMES: Blister glassy-bubble, blister paper bubble, Gould's paper bubble, Gould's paper-bubble, white bubble shell, white bubble.
DESCRIPTION: The **body is tan to light brown and shaped similar to a slug**. Shell color is light brown, glassy and translucent, and it covers only a portion of the body. A thin, rusty-brown or yellowish-orange, speckled periostracum covers the shell. The thin, fragile shell is bubble-shaped with a sunken spire and an **aperture that is less than half the diameter of the shell**.
SIZE: Shell height to 0.8″ (19 mm); body to 1.7″ (4.2 cm) long.
HABITAT: On algae, eelgrass or mud in the muddy and brackish waters of protected shores; low intertidal zone; seasonally abundant.
RANGE: Ketchikan, Alaska, to Bahía Magdalena, Baja California Sur, México.
NOTES: The internal shell of this species is almost completely covered by its body. Its deep yellow egg ribbons can sometimes be seen in July on sandy-bottom shores. If you are lucky enough to find a particularly light specimen of this species, it is possible to observe the pulsing of its heart through the shell.
SIMILAR SPECIES: Japan's bubble snail; green bubble snail.

Japanese Bubble Snail ⓘ

Haminoea japonica (Pilsbry, 1895)

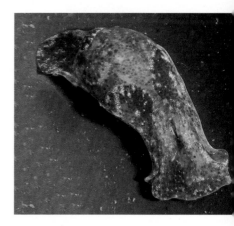

OTHER NAMES: Oval bubble shell, Japan's bubble snail; *Haminoea callidegenita* is likely a junior (= invalid) synonym.
DESCRIPTION: The **body is gray to light brown with several dark brown spots and edged with white spots. The cephalic shield is divided into two from above**. Shell color ranges from white

to reddish-white. The shell closely resembles the white bubble snail, however, the shell of Japan's bubble snail is narrower and more ovate.

SIZE: Shell height to 0.5″ (13 mm); body to 1.1″ (2.8 cm) long.

HABITAT: On various algae, surfgrass or silty substrates; high intertidal zone to shallow subtidal depths.

RANGE: Boundary Bay, British Columbia, to San Francisco Bay, California; Atlantic coast of Spain; Venice Lagoon; Japan and Korea (endemic).

NOTES: Japan's bubble snail was accidentally introduced from Japan and Korea. Its presence is causing some concern in the Pacific Northwest. In Boundary Bay, British Columbia, the white bubble snail was a very common species with densities reaching 200 individuals per m^2. After the arrival of the Japanese bubble snail, the white bubble snail has disappeared. It is not known with certainty if the two occurrences are coincidence or cause-and-effect. In San Francisco Bay, California, the presence of the Japanese bubble snail has been linked, as an intermediate host for a parasite, to outbreaks of cercarial dermatitis (swimmer's itch) in humans.

SIMILAR SPECIES: White bubble snail.

Green Bubble Snail

Haminoea virescens (Sowerby, 1833)

OTHER NAMES: Green bubble, green paper bubble, Sowerby's paper bubble; formerly classified as *Haminoea cymbiformis*.

DESCRIPTION: **The body is green overall** and shaped somewhat like a slug, and the parapodia display yellow and white mottling. The shell is yellowish-brown and thin. The **shell aperture width is more than half the diameter of the shell**.

SIZE: To 0.7″ (18 mm) long.

HABITAT: **On rocks of exposed coast** and occasionally in bays; intertidal zone.

RANGE: Southern Alaska to Bahía de Panama, Panama.

NOTES: The green bubble snail is occasionally seen in abundance on open rocky shores. The shells of the bubble snails are the most reliable method to determine species.

SIMILAR SPECIES: White bubble snail.

Pleatless Barrel-bubble

Acteocina eximia (Baird, 1863)

OTHER NAMES: Barrel bubble, excellent lathe-shell, intermediate barrel-bubble, pillow barrel-bubble; formerly classified as *Bullina eximia, Acteocina culcitella intermedia, Acteocina intermedia, Utriculastra (Tornastra) eximia*; occasionally misspelled *Torantina culcitella*.

DESCRIPTION: The exposed top surface of this species is opaque white with white spots. Its rounded head has a central cleft. The shell is white and covered with an orange to straw-colored periostracum. The surface is covered with wavy, revolving striae, a feature that is often difficult to view. **Shell is cylindrical with a spire that is depressed**; aperture is long and wider at the anterior end. The outer lip is very thin and fragile.

SIZE: Shell height to 0.5″ (13 mm); body to 0.8″ (19 mm) long.

HABITAT: On sand and mud of protected shorelines including shallow bays; low intertidal zone to depths of 150′ (46 m).

RANGE: Kodiak Island, Alaska, to Monterey, California.

NOTES: The pleatless barrel-bubble is an uncommon species that feeds on other gastropods. This species uses its fleshy head shield to plow through the mud or sand just beneath the surface of the substrate. Its shells are found more often than the animal.

SIMILAR SPECIES: Western barrel-bubble *Acteocina culcitella* (Gould, 1853) has a larger shell, to 1″ (2.5 cm) with a somewhat tall spire. It can be found in bays with sand or mud bottoms in the low intertidal zone to subtidal waters. Its columellar fold or pleat is prominent.

....

Spotted Aglajid

Aglaja ocelligera (Bergh, 1893)

OTHER NAMES: Eyespot aglaja, yellow spotted aglaja, yellowspotted aglaja, yellow-spotted aglaja; formerly classified as *Aglaja phocae, Chelidonura ocelligera, Chelidonura phocae, Doridium ocelligera, Doridium ocelligerum, Doridium adellae*.

DESCRIPTION: The body is **brownish-black with numerous small, light yellowish to white spots**. This species has a small, vestigial internal shell.

SIZE: Body to 1.6″ (4 cm); normally to 0.9″ (24 mm) long.

HABITAT: On muddy sand at sheltered locations; low intertidal zone to depths of 65′ (20 m).
RANGE: Sitka, Alaska, to Mission Bay, San Diego, California.
NOTES: The spotted aglaja is a seasonally common species during the summer months. Adults dine on bubble snails without damaging their fragile shell, which is disgorged. In Washington state their pear-shaped egg masses are produced during June through August. This species lacks a radula or rasping tongue, and so it sucks in its prey whole. It is unclear, however, what its prey is, as little is known about its biology. Some believe that it feeds on bubble snails while others speculate that it feeds on polychaete worms or flatworms. More research is needed.

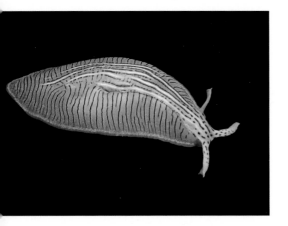

Taylor's Sea Hare

Phyllaplysia taylori Dall, 1900

OTHER NAMES: Taylor's seahare, green sea slug, zebra leafslug.
DESCRIPTION: Body is a **bright green with black and white stripes**. The body is flattened dorso-ventrally to closely mimic eelgrass.
SIZE: Length normally to 1.7″ (4.5 cm); occasionally to 3.2″ (8 cm).
HABITAT: On eelgrass in bays and estuaries; low intertidal zone to shallow subtidal depths. Often found wedged between the lower portions of eelgrass blades.
RANGE: Esperanza Inlet, Vancouver Island, British Columbia, to San Diego, California.
NOTES: Taylor's sea hare is the only species of sea hare found north of California. Sea hares and all opisthobranchs (nudibranchs and allies) are hermaphroditic, capable of producing both eggs and sperm at the same time. Copulation may be reciprocal with two individuals laying their eggs simultaneously, each through a single reproductive duct that is used for incoming and exiting sperm as well as for outgoing previously fertilized eggs.

California Berthella

Berthella californica (Dall, 1900)

OTHER NAMES: California sidegill, California sidegill slug, white berthella; formerly classified as *Pleurobranchus californica, Pleurobranchus californicus*.
DESCRIPTION: The background color of the **dorid-shaped body is white overall with bright white spots**. A white border is present on the dorsal shield. The rhinophores are shaped like a roll.
SIZE: Length to 2″ (5 cm).
HABITAT: On rocks; low intertidal zone to depths of 110′ (33 m).
RANGE: Point Craven, Alaska, to Panama; Islas Galapagos, Ecuador; Russia.
NOTES: The California berthella is deceptively shaped like a nudibranch, however, it is actually a member of another order Notaspidea—the sidegills. It lacks a flower-shaped gill or branchial plume at the rear. Instead it has a prominent branchial plume that projects from its right side. Members of this genus are known for their fiery nature—attacking fish, other members of the opisthobranch clan and even other individuals of the same species.

Spectacular Corolla

Corolla spectabilis Dall, 1871

OTHER NAME: Sea butterfly.
DESCRIPTION: The pelagic animal is butterfly-like, gelatinous in nature and transparent with a yellowish coloration and small spots. The pseudoconch ("false shell") is **gelatinous and slipper-shaped with a series of lumps** on the exterior.
SIZE: Pseudoconch length to 1″ (2.5 cm); "wing span" of animal to 3.1″ (8 cm) across.
HABITAT: Pelagic.

Pseudoconch.

RANGE: British Columbia to Monterey, California; Japan; North Atlantic Ocean.
NOTES: The distinctive pseudoconch of this species is occasionally found washed up on the shore. This is the only member of this genus that is present in eastern Pacific waters. This pelagic species feeds on plankton.

Nudibranchs (Order Nudibranchia)

The nudibranchs, or "sea slugs," are favorites of divers, beachcombers and snorkelers because many of them display such spectacular colors and patterns. Others have coloring that allows them to match their environments very closely. The nudibranch has a shell early in its life, but the shell is soon lost. Predators are few and far between. Many nudibranchs have chemical defenses or discharge stinging cells called nematocysts. All nudibranchs have a pair of intricate projections near the head, called rhinophores, which help them detect chemicals in the water. Some of these chemicals can help lead the nudibranch to food sources.

Nudibranchs can be divided into a few groups, or suborders. Dorids, suborder Doridacea, are primarily those species with their gills forming a circlet around the anus. There are a few species that do not conform to this, however. The next suborder is Dendronotacea, which have a row of cerata-like gills along the margins of the dorsal surface. The suborder Arminacea includes those nudibranchs that feature true cerata on their dorsal surface. Aeolids, suborder Aeolidacea, are those species that feature clusters, groups or rows of elongated, finger-like, smooth dorsal cerata.

DORIDS (SUBORDER DORIDACEA)

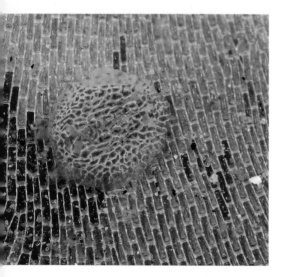

Cryptic Nudibranch

Corambe steinbergae (Lance, 1962)

OTHER NAMES: Joan Steinberg's corambe, Steinberg's dorid; formerly classified as *Doridella steinbergae*, *Paracorambe steinbergae*, *Suhinia steinbergae*.

DESCRIPTION: The background color of the flattened body is nearly transparent marked with reticulated lines that match the pattern of the substrate on which it lives. Reddish-brown speckles are also found on the dorsal surface. **No prominent notch is present at the posterior end**. It also has long, smooth rhinophores, which are difficult to see.

SIZE: Length to 0.7″ (18 mm).

HABITAT: On kelp encrusting bryozoan; low intertidal zone.

RANGE: Katmai National Park, Alaska, to Estero del Coyote, Baja California, México.

NOTES: This nudibranch is easy to miss unless you are looking for it. Its only food source, the kelp encrusting bryozoan, lives on bull kelp and a few other seaweeds. Check the bryozoan closely, as the tiny cryptic nudibranch spends most of its life there.

SIMILAR SPECIES: Frost-spot nudibranch.

Eggs.

Frost-spot Nudibranch

Corambe pacifica

MacFarland & O'Donoghue, 1929

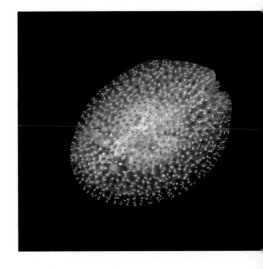

OTHER NAMES: Frost-spot corambe, frost spot, Pacific corambe, translucent gray nudibranch; formerly classified as *Gulbinia pacifica*.

DESCRIPTION: The background color of the flattened body is nearly transparent marked with reticulated lines that match the pattern of the substrate on which it lives. **A prominent notch is found at its posterior end**.

SIZE: Length to 0.6″ (15 mm).

HABITAT: On kelp encrusting bryozoan; low intertidal zone.

RANGE: Southern Alaska to Bahía de Banderas, México.

NOTES: The frost-spot nudibranch is a tiny species of nudibranch that lives on kelp encrusting bryozoan. There it feeds by sucking out the soft parts, and there too it lays its eggs. A 10× magnifying lens will certainly help to view and identify this tiny species.

SIMILAR SPECIES: Cryptic nudibranch.

Hudson's Horned Dorid

Acanthodoris hudsoni (MacFarland, 1905)

OTHER NAMES: Hudson's dorid, Hudson's spiny doris, Hudson's yellow margin nudibranch, yellow margin dorid.

DESCRIPTION: The background color of this dorid's body is translucent white overall with normally yellow-tipped rhinophores and papillae. The **rhinophores are elongated and the papillae are noticeably pointed**. The outer edge is also highlighted with a yellow band around the dorsal edge.

SIZE: Length to 1.5" (4 cm).

HABITAT: On rocks or similar objects; low intertidal zone to depths of 83' (25 m).

RANGE: Southern Alaska to southern California.

NOTES: Hudson's horned dorid is an uncommon species at intertidal sites. This dorid features noticeably large rhinophores and pointed papillae. The similar-looking yellow-edged nudibranch has rounded tubercles on its dorsal side and shorter rhinophores. The Hudson's horned dorid is believed by some to have a mild cedar odor.

SIMILAR SPECIES: Yellow-edged nudibranch.

....

Rufus Tipped Nudibranch

Acanthodoris nanaimoensis O'Donoghue, 1921

OTHER NAMES: Nanaimo nudibranch, Nanaimo dorid, red gilled dorid, red-gilled dorid, wine-plume dorid, wine-plumed doris, wine-plumed spiny doris; formerly classified as *Acanthodoris columbina*.

DESCRIPTION: The background color of this dorid-shaped body is white or gray, covered with yellow-tipped projections. **Red tips grace the antennae-like rhinophores** and edges of the gills.

SIZE: Length to 1" (2.5 cm).

HABITAT: On rocks and similar objects; low intertidal zone to depths of 83' (25 m).

RANGE: Baranof Island, Alaska, to Santa Barbara, California.

NOTES: There are two distinct color phases for this species. In the light phase the body is typically white overall, while the darker form is mottled with dark gray. In both phases, distinctive yellow-tipped projections cover the entire body and red is present on the gills and the tips of the rhinophores. This nudibranch feeds on bryozoans and colonial ascidians.

....

Hopkin's Rose

Okenia rosacea (MacFarland, 1905)

OTHER NAMES: Rose nudibranch, rosy-pink nudibranch; formerly classified as *Hopkinsia rosacea*.
DESCRIPTION: The background color of **this dorid is entirely rose pink**. Its **elongated papillae cover the body** and tend to hide the shorter brachial plume.
SIZE: Length to 1.25″ (3 cm).
HABITAT: On rocky shorelines; low intertidal zone to depths of 20′ (6 m).
RANGE: Coos Bay, Oregon, to Puerto Santo Tomas, Baja California, México.
NOTES: The impressive Hopkin's rose feeds on the derby hat bryozoan by scraping a hole in its outer crust and sucking out the soft inner tissues. This species obtains its striking color from the carotenoid pigment, hopkinsiaxanthin, from its prey. Its eggs are laid in a spiraling, pink to rose-colored ribbon and deposited in a counter-clockwise pattern. This seasonally common nudibranch secretes substances that apparently repel predators.

....

Barnacle-eating Dorid

Onchidoris bilamellata (Linnaeus, 1767)

OTHER NAMES: Barnacle-eating onchidoris, many-gilled onchidoris, rough-mantled sea slug, rough mantled sea slug, rough mantled doris, rough-mantled doris; formerly classified as *Onchidoris fusca*.
DESCRIPTION: The background color of this dorid is creamy-white **with chocolate to rusty-brown markings. Numerous colorless, club-shaped tubercles cover the dorsal surface** and two half rings of 16–32 simple feathery gills grace the rear.

SIZE: Length to 1.2″ (3 cm).
HABITAT: Undersides of rocks and similar hard objects near mud bottoms; rocky shorelines; mid-intertidal zone to depths of 100′ (30 m).
RANGE: Hagemeister Island, Alaska, to Baja California, México; both sides of North Atlantic.
NOTES: Adult barnacle-eating dorids feed on barnacles, including the common acorn barnacle and little brown barnacles by using a specialized pumping mechanism to suck the soft tissues from their hard outer coverings. Juveniles, however, feed on encrusting bryozoans.

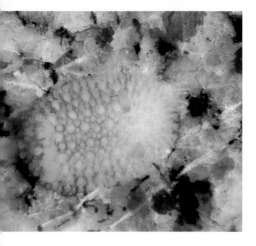

Fuzzy Onchidoris

Onchidoris muricata (O. F. Müller, 1776)

OTHER NAMES: White onchidoris; formerly classified as *Onchidoris hystricina*.
DESCRIPTION: Background color is **light yellow to orange overall**. Rhinophores are yellow-orange with yellow tips and the tubercles are orange at the tip. **Numerous club-shaped tubercles cover the body.**
SIZE: Length to 0.6″ (15 mm).
HABITAT: On kelp primarily; low intertidal zone to depths of 59′ (18 m).
RANGE: Kiska Island, Aleutian Islands, Alaska, to Baja California, México; France to Russia; Greenland to Connecticut.
NOTES: The fuzzy onchidoris feeds upon encrusting bryozoans such as the kelp encrusting bryozoan. Researchers in Washington state discovered that from January to April this dorid reproduces, depositing eggs in a long ribbon in the shape of a whorl. The eggs vary from white to pale orange.

Salt-and-pepper Nudibranch

Aegires albopunctatus MacFarland, 1905

OTHER NAMES: Salt-and-pepper doris, small white nudibranch, white knight, white knight nudibranch, white-spotted doris.
DESCRIPTION: Background color of the torpodeo-shaped body varies overall from **white to**

yellowish, along with several black
to brown spots. Several cylindrical
tubercles cover the dorsal surface
arranged in irregular rows.

SIZE: Length to 0.9″ (23 mm).

HABITAT: Undersides of rocks, in
tidepools and on pilings at sheltered
sites; low intertidal zone to depths of
100′ (30 m).

RANGE: Mountain Point, Ketchikan,
Alaska, to Bahía de los Angeles, Baja
California, México.

NOTES: The salt-and-pepper
nudibranch is aptly named with
its salt and pepper coloration. This
species is known to feed on sponges. Its white eggs are deposited in somewhat spiraled
bands. It produces a non-acid secretion, which is known to repel predators.

Cockerell's Dorid

Limacia cockerelli

(MacFarland, 1905)

OTHER NAMES: Cockerell's
nudibranch, lalia doris, orange
spotted nudibranch; formerly
classified as *Laila cockerelli*.

DESCRIPTION: Background color of
the sausage-shaped body is white.
Background color of the bulbous-
tipped tubercles and rhinopores
varies from yellow to orange. These
projecting tubercles often form a row
around the dorsal side of the animal.

SIZE: Length to 1″ (2.5 cm).

HABITAT: On rocky shores and in tidepools; low intertidal zone to depths of 115′ (35 m).

RANGE: Southern Alaska to Cabo San Lucas, Baja California, México.

NOTES: The colorful Cockerell's dorid dines on bryozoans. It lays pale pink eggs in
long spirals that contain about 6,500 eggs. Spawning occurs from May to June in lower
British Columbia.

Sea-clown Nudibranch

Triopha catalinae (Cooper, 1863)

OTHER NAMES: Catalina triopha, clown dorid, orange-spotted nudibranch; formerly classified as *Triopha carpenteri*.

DESCRIPTION: Background color is translucent white to gray. Numerous bright orange blotches decorate the sausage-shaped body, along with orange papillae and orange or red rhinophores. The rear displays a circle of white gills that are tipped with orange as well. A series of orange tentacles are also present around the front.

SIZE: Length to 6″ (15 cm); intertidal specimens are normally to 2.75″ (7 cm).

HABITAT: On rocky shorelines and in tidepools; mid-intertidal zone to depths of 262′ (80 m).

RANGE: Amchitka Island, Alaska, to Baja California, México; Japan.

NOTES: The sea-clown nudibranch is a large, spectacular species that is not easily forgotten in a tidepool! It deposits its white to cream-colored eggs in a ribbon that is shaped into a loose coil. This colorful species feeds on bryozoans.

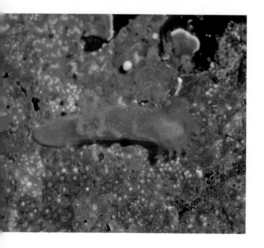

Spotted Triopha

Triopha maculata MacFarland, 1905

OTHER NAMES: Blue-spotted nudibranch, maculated triopha, maculated doris, spotted dorid, speckled triopha; formerly classified as *Triopha grandis*.

DESCRIPTION: Background color of this variable species includes yellow to orange and brown. The tube-shaped body is decorated with a series of white to light blue spots. **A series of red to orange appendages are present along the dorsal edges of the body and frontal area.** The rhinophores and gills are variable as well but are often red to orange-red.

SIZE: Length to 7″ (18 cm); intertidal specimens to 2″ (5 cm).

HABITAT: In rocky shores, mudflats, estuaries and eelgrass beds; low intertidal zone to depths of 110′ (33 m).

RANGE: Bamfield, Vancouver Island, British Columbia, to Punta Rosarito, Baja California, México; Siberia.

NOTES: The spotted triopha feeds on encrusting bryozoans and commonly deposits its eggs, in coiled ribbons, on various species of kelp. Smaller-sized juveniles of this nudibranch are normally found intertidally.

....

Cooper's Dorid

Aldisa cooperi Robilliard & Baba, 1972

OTHER NAMES: Cooper's aldisa; formerly classified as *Aldisa sanguinea cooperi*.

DESCRIPTION: Background color of this dorid varies from **yellow to orange**. A **row of fine black speckles** are positioned along the dorsal midline. The rhinophores and gills are yellow to orange, as found in the body color.

SIZE: Length to 1″ (2.5 cm).

HABITAT: On rocky shorelines; low intertidal zone to depths of 75′ (23 m).

RANGE: Hogan Island, Alaska, to Trinidad, California; Japan.

NOTES: The Cooper's dorid closely resembles the red sponge nudibranch, with the addition of a row of black speckles. This nudibranch feeds on and deposits its egg ribbons on an encrusting sponge.

SIMILAR SPECIES: Red sponge nudibranch.

....

Spotted Leopard Dorid

Diaulula odonoghuei (Steinberg, 1963)

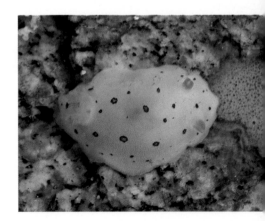

OTHER NAMES: Brown-spotted nudibranch, leopard nudibranch, ringed nudibranch, ring-spotted nudibranch, San Diego dorid, spotted nudibranch, ringed doris; formerly included with *Diaulula sandiegensis*

DESCRIPTION: Background color varies from white to yellow or light brown.

Chocolate-brown spots or ring shapes are present on the dorsal side that extend to the mantle margin.

SIZE: Length to 3″ (8 cm); intertidal specimens to 2″ (5 cm).

HABITAT: On and under rocks; mid-intertidal zone to depths of 115′ (35 m).

RANGE: Alaska to Bodega Bay, California.

NOTES: Recent DNA studies have documented this new intertidal species. It was once included with the ringed dorid. The spotted leopard dorid is normally spotted, while the ringed dorid is, as expected, normally ringed. The rings of the ringed dorid do not extend into the mantle margin as they do in the spotted leopard dorid.

SIMILAR SPECIES: Ringed dorid.

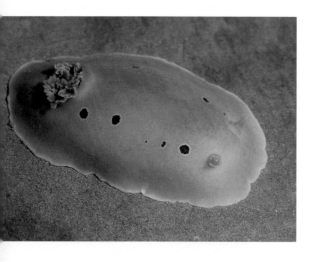

Ringed Dorid

Diaulula sandiegensis
(Cooper, 1863)

OTHER NAME: Formerly included with *Diaulula odonoghuei*.

DESCRIPTION: Background color ranges from white to light brown, highlighted with a few chocolate-brown to nearly black rings that do not reach as far as the mantle's margin.

SIZE: Length normally to 1″ (2.5 cm); occasionally to 6″ (15 cm) primarily in subtidal waters.

HABITAT: On rocks and in tidepools; very low intertidal zone to shallow subtidal depths.

RANGE: Southern British Columbia to Baja California, México.

NOTES: The ringed dorid is more common subtidally than its more common intertidal relative, the spotted leopard dorid. This nudibranch feeds on a variety of sponges including yellow-green encrusting sponge and purple encrusting sponge.

SIMILAR SPECIES: Spotted leopard dorid.

Monterey Sea Lemon

Doris montereyensis (Cooper, 1862)

OTHER NAMES: Dusty yellow nudibranch,
false lemon peel nudibranch, false sea lemon,
Monterey doris, Monterey sea lemon, Monterey
sea-lemon, sea lemon; formerly classified as
Archidoris montereyensis.

DESCRIPTION: Background color is lemon
yellow. Small **black speckles are present on the
tubercles** of the nudibranch's dorsal surface.

SIZE: Length to 6″ (15 cm); intertidal specimens
are much smaller.

HABITAT: On rocky shores; low intertidal zone to depths of 845′ (256 m).

RANGE: Kachemak Bay, Alaska, to San Diego, California.

NOTES: The Monterey sea lemon feeds on sponges as many nudibranchs do. It's truly a
mystery how this species, and others, can feed unharmed on organisms made up of a
network of sharp spicules. It has been speculated that nudibranchs may cover the spicules
in mucus to prevent damage to their intestines. Research is needed to answer this and so
many other questions.

SIMILAR SPECIES: Sea lemon.

Sea Lemon

Peltodoris nobilis (MacFarland, 1905)

OTHER NAMES: Lemon nudibranch, noble
Pacific doris, noble sea lemon, Pacific
sea lemon, Pacific sealemon, sea lemon
nudibranch, speckled sea lemon; formerly
classified as *Anisodoris nobilis.*

DESCRIPTION: Background color is lemon
yellow. Small **black speckles are present
between the tubercles** of the nudibranch's
dorsal surface.

SIZE: Length to 8″ (20 cm).

HABITAT: On rocky shorelines; low
intertidal zone to depths of 750′ (228 m).

RANGE: Kodiak Island, Alaska, to Baja California, México.

NOTES: The sea lemon is known to have a distinctive, persistent and fruity odor, which is thought to deter predators. This species, as many other nudibranchs do, dines on a wide variety of sponges including the bread crumb sponge and purple encrusting sponge.
SIMILAR SPECIES: Monterey sea lemon.

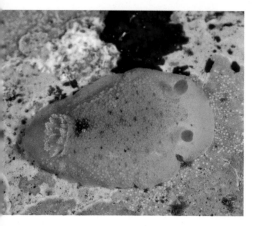

Heath's Dorid

Geitodoris heathi (MacFarland, 1905)

OTHER NAMES: Heath's doris, gritty dorid, gritty doris; formerly classified as *Discodoris heathi*, *Discodoris fulva*.
DESCRIPTION: Background color varies from white to yellowish-brown. **A concentration of dark speckles, appearing as a blotch, is found in front of the 8–10 gills.** Additional speckles may or may not be present on the dorsal side of the body.
SIZE: Length to 1.7″ (4.3 cm).
HABITAT: On rocky shores; mid-intertidal zone to depths of 65′ (20 m).
RANGE: Prince William Sound, Alaska, to Bahía San Quintin, Baja California, México.
NOTES: Heath's dorid closely resembles the Monterey Sea Lemon. This species is not often encountered on intertidal shores in the northern portion of its range.
SIMILAR SPECIES: Monterey sea lemon.

Red Sponge Nudibranch

Rostanga pulchra MacFarland, 1905

OTHER NAMES: Bright red nudibranch, bloody red dorid, crimson dorid, crimson doris, MacFarlane's pretty doris, red sponge doris, red nudibranch.
DESCRIPTION: The color of this **dorid is vivid orange-red.** No additional colors or markings are present.
SIZE: Length to 1.4″ (3.3 cm); intertidal specimens to 0.7″ (18 mm).

HABITAT: On rocky shorelines; low intertidal zone to depths of 335′ (102 m).
RANGE: Point Craven, Alaska, to Gulf of California, México; Chile; Argentina.
NOTES: This common nudibranch is an excellent example of camouflage. It incorporates into its own body the pigment of the red sponges on which it feeds, which helps it to blend in to the red sponge substrate. Its ring-like egg masses are also red and laid on sponges in spring or early summer so that they too blend in with the substrate. The species' whole life evolves around the red sponges on which it feeds. Studies have shown that some individuals move about a great deal, while others are much more sedentary. One individual was observed to have stayed on a sponge for 37 days.

This red nudibranch has laid its circular egg case on red encrusting sponge, its food source.

Yellow-edged Nudibranch

Cadlina luteomarginata MacFarland, 1966

OTHER NAMES: Common yellow-margin nudibranch, pale yellow nudibranch, yellow nudibranch, yellow margin dorid, yellow-edged cadlina, yellow-edged nudibranch, yellow-rim cadlina, yellow-rimmed doris, yellow-rimmed nudibranch; formerly classified as *Cadlina marginata*.
DESCRIPTION: This **dorid is translucent white. Bright yellow also graces this species as a narrow margin** around the body, as well as the tips of **short rounded tubercles** on its dorsal surface. The 6 gills form a typical rose shape to the rear that is white and tipped with yellow.
SIZE: Length to 3″ (7.5 cm); intertidal specimens to 1″ (2.5 cm).
HABITAT: On rocks and under rocky ledges, in tidepools; low intertidal zone to depths of 150′ (45 m).
RANGE: Lynn Canal, Alaska, to Punta Eugenia, Baja California, México.
NOTES: The yellow-edged nudibranch lays its eggs in very tightly coiled ribbons from autumn to spring. This delicate sea slug feeds on a variety of sponge species as most dorids do.
SIMILAR SPECIES: Hudson's horned dorid.

Yellow-spotted Cadlina

Cadlina flavomaculata MacFarland, 1905

OTHER NAME: Yellow spot cadlina.
DESCRIPTION: The **white body is edged with bright lemon-yellow trim**. A series of 6–11 yellow spots form a row along each side of the body. The **rhinophores vary in color from dark brown to black** and the gills are white to yellow.
SIZE: Length to 0.8″ (20 mm).
HABITAT: On and under rocks, in tidepools; low intertidal zone to depths of 66′ (20 m).
RANGE: Vancouver Island, British Columbia, to Punta Eugenia, Baja California, México; Costa Rica.
NOTES: The strikingly colored rhinophores are the most obvious feature that makes this uncommon species easily identifiable. Little is known about the yellow-spotted cadlina's natural history. It is sometimes found in groups and has been noted by some to be "sluggish."
SIMILAR SPECIES: Modest cadlina.

Modest Cadlina

Cadlina modesta MacFarland, 1966

DESCRIPTION: The body of this **dorid is translucent white**. A series of **yellowish spots are found randomly along the sides** of the dorsal side of the animal. The rhinophores vary from yellowish to light brown and the gills pale yellow to whitish.
SIZE: Length to 1.8″ (4.5 cm).
HABITAT: On rocky shorelines; low intertidal zone to depths of 165′ (50 m).
RANGE: Point Lena, Alaska, to Isla Guadalupe, Baja California, México.
NOTES: The modest cadlina is known to feed on sponges as many other nudibranchs do. It bears a somewhat close resemblance to the yellow-spotted cadlina.

White-spotted Sea Goddess

Doriopsilla albopunctata (Cooper, 1863)

OTHER NAMES: Salted yellow doris, salted doris, white spotted porostome, white speckled nudibranch, yellow porostome; formerly classified as *Dendrodoris albopunctata*, *Dendrodoris fulva*, *Doriopsis fulva*.

DESCRIPTION: Background color of this **dorid varies from yellow to yellow-orange or reddish-brown. It has white gills, and white spots are found only on the tips of the tubercles.**

SIZE: Length to 2.75″ (7 cm).

HABITAT: On rocky shores; low intertidal zone to depths of 150′ (46 m).

RANGE: Southern British Columbia to Punta Eugenia, Baja California, and Bahía de los Angeles, Gulf of California, México.

NOTES: The white-spotted sea goddess is a well-named treasure for beachcombers and divers alike. Its color is truly stunning! Darker-colored individuals are more common in the southern portion of its range. This striking species has only recently been found in British Columbia, which extends its range considerably.

SUBORDER DENDRONOTACEA

White Dendronotid

Dendronotus albus MacFarland, 1966

OTHER NAMES: White dendronotus, white frond-aeolis.

DESCRIPTION: Background color of this species is translucent white. The elongated body tapers to a fine point and is graced with **4–7 pairs of white cerata that are tipped with orange, red or brown;** a white line extends from the last cerata to the tail. In addition, **5 slender crown papillae adorn the anterior** region of the animal.

SIZE: Length to 1.5″ (3.5 cm).
HABITAT: On rocky shorelines with current-swept areas; low intertidal zone to depths of 100′ (30 m).
RANGE: Kenai Peninsula, Alaska, to Islas Coronado, México.
NOTES: The white dendronotid feeds on hydroids. In Washington state this species has been observed mating in March but the egg laying does not occur until October and November. This species has been noted for its swimming abilities.

Bushy-backed Nudibranch

Dendronotus frondosus (Ascanius, 1774)

OTHER NAMES: Bushy-backed sea slug, frond eolis, leafy dendronotid.
DESCRIPTION: Background color of this species varies from off-white to greenish or brownish. The elongated, tube-shaped body is **adorned with 2 rows of 5–8 bushy appendages**, which are positioned on its back in a comb-like arrangement.
SIZE: Length to 4.6″ (11.5 cm).
HABITAT: On rocks, floats or various seaweeds; low intertidal zone to depths of 1,320′ (400 m).
RANGE: Circumboreal; Northern Alaska to California and Chile; Arctic to New Jersey; Europe; Siberia; Japan.
NOTES: The bushy-backed nudibranch is often found in bays and on floats, especially during the summer months. It feeds primarily on hydroids. This common species is cosmopolitan throughout the northern hemisphere. *Dendronotus* means "tree-back," referring to the bushy appearance of its back.

Hooded Nudibranch

Melibe leonina (Gould, 1852)

OTHER NAMES: Lion nudibranch, melibe, translucent nudibranch.
DESCRIPTION: This species is translucent white with a network of greenish to brownish patterning that covers most of the dorsal surface. A very **large oral hood at the front bears 2 rows of short tentacles along its margin**. In addition there are 5–6 pairs of leaf-like, inflated projections found on the back.

SIZE: Length to 4″ (10 cm).

HABITAT: On rocks, eelgrass and kelp beds in sheltered bays; low intertidal zone to depths of 115′ (37 m).

RANGE: Kodiak Island, Alaska, to Bahía de los Angeles, Baja California, México.

NOTES: The hooded nudibranch is a remarkable predator of our waters. It lacks a radula for feeding; instead it uses its huge, flexible oral hood to trap its prey, which includes plankton, a variety of crustaceans, as well as molluscan prey items and even some small fish! To capture

these items it firmly attaches to a substrate and elevates its hood, which is expanded by its blood sinuses. There it remains motionless before it begins sweeping the water. Once it has captured its prey it sweeps the two sides of its hood together and the tentacles that line the hood interlock to close the trap and force the prey into the nudibranch's mouth.

....

White-and-orange-tipped Nudibranch

Janolus fuscus O'Donoghue, 1924

OTHER NAMES: Formerly classified as *Antiapella fusca*; formerly included with *Antiapella barbarensis* or *Janalus barbarensis*, *Janalus aureocinta*.

DESCRIPTION: Background color of the tube-shaped body is white. The body is covered with numerous unbranched **cerata that have a brown core, orange ends and white tips.** The dorsal surface also has a **reddish to orange line on the upper half of the center line.**

SIZE: Length to 2.4″ (6 cm); intertidal specimens to 1″ (2.5 cm).

HABITAT: On rocks, pilings, floats and kelp in sheltered sites such as bays and lagoons; low intertidal zone to depths of 100′ (30 m).

RANGE: Homer, Alaska, to San Luis Obispo, California; Japan.

NOTES: The white-and-orange-tipped nudibranch feeds on bryozoans. It is similar-looking to the opalescent nudibranch, but it does not have the electric blue or the bright white lines on its dorsal surface.

SIMILAR SPECIES: Opalescent nudibranch.

SUBORDER ARMINACEA

Frosted Nudibranch

Dirona albolineata MacFarland, 1905

OTHER NAMES: Alabaster nudibranch, chalk-lined dirona, white-streaked dirona, white-lined dirona.
DESCRIPTION: Background color of the elongated **body is a delicate translucent white, purple or orange**. It is adorned with numerous leaf-like projections that are **edged with a fine, brilliant white line**.
SIZE: Length to 7″ (18 cm); intertidal specimens to 1.5″ (4 cm).
HABITAT: On mudflats, bayside boat docks and in rocky tidepools; low intertidal zone to depths of 122′ (37 m).
RANGE: Kachemak Bay, Alaska, to San Diego, California; Barent's Sea, Russia; Japan.
NOTES: This strikingly beautiful nudibranch feeds on small snails by cracking their shells with its powerful jaws. Other foods include sea anemones, sea squirts and bryozoans. The frosted nudibranch is often found during very low tides. It occurs in 3 color phases: white, purple-tinged and orange-tinged.

Painted Nudibranch

Dirona picta MacFarland, 1905

OTHER NAMES: Colorful dirona, spotted dirona.
DESCRIPTION: Background color of the elongated body is pinkish-orange or light brown to yellowish-green with splotches of various colors. Numerous inflated cerata cover the body.
SIZE: Length to 4″ (10 cm); intertidal specimens to 1.2″ (3 cm).
HABITAT: On rocky shorelines; low intertidal zone to depths of 30′ (9 m).
RANGE: Cape Meares, Tillamook County, Oregon, to Isla Angel de la Guarda, Baja California, México; Sea of Japan.

NOTES: The painted nudibranch is aptly named with its wide-ranging colors. It is sometimes found in large numbers. The species feeds on bryozoans and hydroids. It is one of several nudibranch species that have been observed moving upside down along the surface of a tidepool.

AEOLIDS (SUBORDER AEOLIDACEA)

Spanish Shawl

Flabellina iodinea (Cooper, 1862)

OTHER NAMES: Elegant eolid, iodine eolis, purple aeolis, purple fan nudibranch, purple nudibranch, violet fan nudibranch; formerly classified as *Coryphella sabulicola*, *Flabellinopsis iodinea*.

DESCRIPTION: The elongated **body is deep purple**. On the dorsal surface numerous **cerata have a purple base with vivid orange tips.** The rhinophores are deep maroon.

SIZE: Length to 3.8″ (9 cm).

HABITAT: On rocks, pilings and in kelp beds; low intertidal zone to depths of 130′ (40 m).

RANGE: Vancouver Island, British Columbia, to Bahía San Quintin, Baja California, and Gulf of California, México; Galapagos Islands, Ecuador.

NOTES: Spanish shawl is a strikingly colorful species whose bright colors warn predators of its bad taste. This nudibranch can swim by making a series of quick lateral, U-shaped bends to its body, first to one side, then to the other. This is one spectacular display by one spectacular nudibranch!

Three-lined Aeolid

Flabellina trilineata (O'Donoghue, 1921)

OTHER NAMES: Three lined aeolid, threeline aeolis, three-stripe aeolid; formerly classified as *Caryphella fisheri*, *Coryphella piunca*, *Caryphella trilineata*.

DESCRIPTION: The color of the body is translucent white with **3 bright white stripes that extend most of the length of the animal**. Numerous cerata with interiors that are orange to red are found on the body.
SIZE: Length to 1.5″ (3.5 cm).
HABITAT: On rocky shores, mudflats and bayside docks; low intertidal zone to depths of 165′ (50 m).
RANGE: Lisianski Inlet, Alaska, to Bahía Tortugas, Baja California, México.
NOTES: The three-lined aeolid dines on several types of hydroids. This nudibranch is one of several species that extract unexploded nematocysts from hydroids and store them in the cerata for their own protection. Research with other species suggests that these nematocysts last only for approximately 3–5 days before they need to be replaced.

California Shag-rug Nudibranch

Aeolidia loui Kienberger, et al, 2016

OTHER NAME: Formerly included with *Aeolidia papillosa*.
DESCRIPTION: Background color varies widely from white to orange or brown. Many translucent gray-brown cerata are present on the dorsal surface, with a bald spot down the center. The cerata are bristle-like with pointed tips and **the rhinophores are covered with tiny wart-like coverings**.
SIZE: Length to 2.5″ (6.4 cm).
HABITAT: Beneath rocks and in tidepools; mid- to low intertidal zone.
RANGE: Washington to Punta Baja, Baja California, and Punta Norte, Isla de Cedros, México.
NOTES: The California shag-rug nudibranch is a newly discovered species that was once part of a species complex formerly included with *Aeolidia papillosa*. This new species is easily identified by its distinctive rhinophores.
SIMILAR SPECIES: Northern shag-rug nudibranch *Aeolidia papillosa* (Linnaeus, 1761) features rhinophores that are smooth, and cerata that are thin and elongated. Its range includes Cook Inlet, Alaska to Washington.

Opalescent Nudibranch

Hermissenda crassicornis (Eschscholtz, 1831)

OTHER NAMES: Horned nudibranch, long-horned nudibranch, opalescent sea slug, opalescent aeolid; formerly classified as *Flabellina opalescens, Hermissenda opalescens, Phidiana crassicornis.*

DESCRIPTION: Background color of body varies from translucent cream to brownish. **An orange line originates from the head region and trails toward the middle with electric blue edges.** The elongated body tapers to a fine point and is covered with numerous cerata that vary in coloration from translucent white to orange, often with a white central core and an orange tip. **The oral tentacles display a blue line on their dorsal surface.**

SIZE: Length to 3.25″ (8.3 cm); intertidal specimens much smaller.

HABITAT: On rocks, mudflats, wharf pilings and in tidepools; low intertidal zone to depths of 122′ (37 m).

RANGE: Kodiak Island, Alaska, to Bahía de los Angeles, Baja California, México; Japan.

NOTES: The opalescent nudibranch is known for its aggressive nature. It is often viewed fighting other individuals where biting and lunging are "normal." Its diet is wide-ranging and includes mainly hydroids; however, it also feeds on small sea anemones, bryozoans, colonial ascidians, annelids, crustaceans, minute clams and it scavenges dead animals. As with other aeolids, this one extracts the stinging cells from hydroids and anemones while feeding, then stores the cells in the cerata and uses them to repel predators.

Bivalves
CLASS BIVALVIA

Bivalves are members of a large group of animals, each of which is covered by a pair of shells (valves). There are some 10,000 species of bivalves worldwide, including mussels, oysters, clams, scallops and shipworms. Some live in fresh water, but the majority are found in saltwater environments, buried in sand and mud (clams), rock (piddocks) and wood (shipworms). Others have evolved to become mobile and capable of swimming (scallops). Bivalves have come to occupy very diverse environments, but remain relatively unchanged through time.

The world's largest bivalve, from the Indo-Pacific, grows to 5′ (1.5 m) long and can weigh as much as 650 lb. (295 kg). Locally, the Pacific geoduck can weigh up to 20 lb. (9 kg), while other species are as small as 0.01″ (2 mm) wide. Clams draw in water to feed and breathe, and expel wastes through siphons, special tubes that extend from the surface. The siphons range from very short, as in the Nuttall's cockle, to 3′ (1 m) long, as in the Pacific geoduck. Many species of bivalves have been, and continue to be, utilized for food.

....

Western Bittersweet

Glycymeris septentrionalis
(Middendorff, 1849)

OTHER NAMES: Northern bittersweet, California bittersweet; formerly classified as *Glycymeris subobsoleta*, *Glycymeris profunda*, *Pectunculus septentrionalis*.

DESCRIPTION: Shell exteriors are chalky white to pale brown, often with radiating or zigzag patterns. The shallow, flattened ribs are often worn smooth. The periostracum is thick and made up of numerous fine hairs. Shell interiors often have yellow or purple-brown stains. The **trigonal shell** is sculptured with numerous radiating lines on unworn specimens. **Numerous (15–16) small, fine teeth are present on the shell margin** and on both sides of the hinge.

SIZE: Shells to 1.75″ (4.5 cm) long.

HABITAT: In sand or gravel; low intertidal zone to depths of 180′ (55 m).

RANGE: Aleutian Islands, Alaska, to Baja California, México.

NOTES: The shell patterning of the western bittersweet is quite variable. This species is primarily found in shallow warm waters.

California Mussel

Mytilus californianus Conrad, 1837

OTHER NAMES: California sea mussel, ribbed mussel, sea mussel, surf mussel.
DESCRIPTION: Shell exteriors are blue-black with a heavy **dark brown periostracum**. Shell interiors are grayish to blue-gray and the meat color is bright orange. The elongated shells are triangular with a rounded hind end. The shells are **sculptured with irregular radiating ribs**.
SIZE: Shells to 10″ (25.5 cm) long.
HABITAT: On rocks of exposed shorelines; high intertidal zone to depths of 330′ (100 m).
RANGE: Cook Inlet, Alaska, to Islas Revillagigedo, México.
NOTES: This species has a high reproductive capability: one female can produce 100,000 eggs annually. The California mussel can grow 3.5″ (9 cm) in one year's time. When feeding, average-sized mussels filter between 2–3 liters of water per hour. Indigenous people of the West Coast used this species extensively, its flesh for food and its shells for implements. This bivalve is believed to be one of the richest species in vitamins.
SIMILAR SPECIES: Pacific blue mussel is smaller and lacks the flattened ribs.

Pacific Blue Mussel

Mytilus trossulus Gould, 1850

OTHER NAMES: Bay mussel, blue mussel, common blue mussel, edible mussel, foolish mussel; formerly incorrectly classified as *Mytilus edulis*.
DESCRIPTION: Shell exteriors are covered with a black, blue or brown periostracum. Shell interiors are dull blue with a dark margin and the flesh is bright orange. The triangular **shells are smooth without raised radiating ribs**. Shells and periostracum are thin.
SIZE: Shells to 5″ (13 cm) long.
HABITAT: On rocks and similar surfaces of protected shorelines; mid-intertidal zone to depths of 600′ (180 m).
RANGE: Uncertain—northern Alaska to central California (and probably to southern California); northern Europe.

NOTES: The Pacific blue mussel (and others) can produce a sticky substance that hardens into threadlike fibers, the byssus, with which the mussel attaches to substrates such as rocks. If you try to remove a mussel from its bed, you will discover how strong these fibers can be. Mussels feed on plankton by pumping up to 3 quarts (3 L) of seawater per hour through their gills. This flow is generated by the rhythmic movement of cilia. When the tide goes out, mussels close their shells tight to stop from drying out.
SIMILAR SPECIES: Mediterranean mussel.

Mediterranean Mussel

Mytilus galloprovincialis Lamarck, 1819

OTHER NAMES: Gallo's mussel; formerly classified as *Mytilus edulis diegensis*.
DESCRIPTION: Shells are dark blue with a light-colored hinge. The triangular **shells are broad, expanded dorsally; the narrow (anterior) end is pointed** rather than curved. Anterior muscle scar is tiny and posterior scar is broad.
SIZE: Shells to 6.5″ (16.6 cm) long.
HABITAT: On rocks; low intertidal zone to depths of 79′ (24 m).
RANGE: Southern British Columbia to México; the Mediterranean, western France, Britain and Ireland.
NOTES: This mussel was introduced after 1900 from the Mediterranean as well as from Britian, France and Ireland. It is currently being cultured commercially in Puget Sound, Washington. This species replaces the Pacific blue mussel from southern California to Baja California, but the two mussels cannot be distinguished by their shells alone, and they hybridize readily.
SIMILAR SPECIES: The Pacific blue mussel cannot be reliably separated by shell characteristics alone. Much hybridizing with other species has been occurring and will continue to occur.

Blue Mussel

Mytilus edulis Linnaeus, 1758

OTHER NAME: Edible mussel.
DESCRIPTION: Shell exteriors vary from bluish-black to black and are covered with a thin,

shiny, bluish-black periostracum. The interiors are bluish-white. Each shell is triangular, with the umbones forming an apex at its front end. **The ventral margins are straight or slightly curved**. Shell exteriors lack radial ribs but have many very fine concentric lines, giving it a smooth appearance.

SIZE: Shells to 5.25″ (13.3 cm) long.

HABITAT: On rocks, pilings and in tidepools; high intertidal zone to depths of 164′ (50 m).

RANGE: British Columbia; Arctic to South Carolina; both coasts of South America; Europe.

NOTES: The blue mussel has been introduced to

British Columbia for aquaculture. Blue mussels require 7 to 12 years to reach a 2.5″ (60 mm) size. Most have about a 12-year lifespan; however, some individuals have been recorded to reach more than 24 years old. Intertidal specimens grow slower since they can only grow when they are feeding underwater.

SIMILAR SPECIES: Pacific blue mussel.

California Datemussel

Adula californiensis (Philippi, 1847)

OTHER NAMES: Pea-pod borer; formerly classified as *Botula californiensis*.

DESCRIPTION: Shell exteriors are white with a brownish-black to reddish-brown shiny, smooth periostracum. Shell interiors are bluish-gray. The shells are **elongate, thin, cylindrical and rounded at both ends**. A hairy mat on the posterior slope is used to bind to its substrate.

SIZE: Shells to 2.5″ (6 cm) long.

HABITAT: Bores into clay, shale and other soft rocks; low intertidal zone to depths of 65′ (20 m).

RANGE: Graham Island, Haida Gwaii (Queen Charlotte Islands), British Columbia, to Point Loma, San Diego County, California.

NOTES: The valves of this datemussel are very fragile. It is an uncommon species that can sometimes be found at the same sites as other rock-boring bivalves. Scientists know little of its biology.

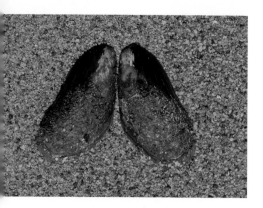

Northern Horsemussel

Modiolus modiolus (Linnaeus, 1758)

OTHER NAMES: Bearded mussel, common horse mussel, giant horse mussel, great horse mussel, horse mussel, northern horse mussel; formerly classified as *Volsella modiolus, Volsella modiola, Modiola modiola*.

DESCRIPTION: Shell exteriors are **violet, covered with a dark brown hairy periostracum.** The interiors are grayish-white. Shells are irregularly triangular with a curved outer margin and a narrowed front end.

SIZE: Shells to 9″ (23 cm) long.

HABITAT: Among gravel and rocks; to low intertidal zone to depths of 660′ (200 m).

RANGE: Circumboreal; St. Paul Island, Pribilof Islands, Alaska, to Monterey, California; Japan; Greenland to New Jersey; European coast to the Mediterranean.

NOTES: Unlike most mussels, northern horsemussels can burrow, and often cluster together in groups. Their byssus attaches to the surrounding rock and to their "buddies," anchoring them in place. This mussel has a circumpolar distribution. It is not considered a gourmet item. Pea crabs are often found inside the shells of this species.

SIMILAR SPECIES: Straight horsemussel.

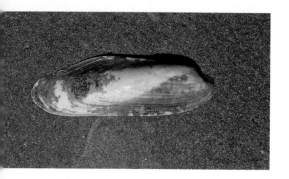

Straight Horsemussel

Modiolus rectus (Conrad, 1837)

OTHER NAMES: Fat horse mussel, fan mussel, fan-shaped horsemussel, fan-shaped horse mussel, fan horsemussel, straight horse mussel; formerly classified as *Volsella recta, Modiola recta*.

DESCRIPTION: Shell exteriors are white to bluish-white. The **periostracum is two toned with yellowish-brown on the rear two-thirds portion of the shell and a dark brown on the remaining section.** Shell interiors are white. The large shells are narrowly oblong with a lower edge that is straight or somewhat concave. Large umbones are present.

SIZE: Shells to 9″ (23 cm) long.

HABITAT: In mud and sand mixtures or gravel; low intertidal zone to depths of 150′ (46 m).

RANGE: Tow Hill, Haida Gwaii (Queen Charlotte Islands), British Columbia, to Peru.

NOTES: This horsemussel is found in quiet bays or lagoons, or in offshore areas. It is a solitary species that anchors itself in sand-mud substrates and lies buried with only its posterior tip left uncovered. Byssal threads keep this bivalve anchored in the sand or mud.

SIMILAR SPECIES: Northern horsemussel.

Olympia Oyster

Ostrea conchaphila (Carpenter, 1857)

OTHER NAMES: California oyster, lurid oyster, native Pacific oyster, native oyster; formerly classified as *Ostrea lurida*.

DESCRIPTION: Shell exteriors are gray to brownish-gray or purplish-brown. Shell **interiors are grayish-white, normally with a tint of green. Shells are circular to irregular** with the left (bottom) valve **normally cemented to a substrate over a broad area** and the top valve usually flattened. The outer sculpture may be wrinkled or scaly in a concentric pattern. Frills are normally not present.

SIZE: Shells to 3.5″ (9 cm) long.

HABITAT: On rock beds, mudflats or on gravel in estuaries or similar sheltered sites, often with freshwater seepage; low intertidal zone to depths of 165′ (50 m).

RANGE: Sitka, Alaska, to Panama.

NOTES: This native species is capable of changing its sex during spawning season. Like several other

species, this oyster is called a protandrous hermaphrodite. It is never totally male or female, but alternates between the two phases. The "female" then holds the young inside her mantle until their shells are developed. While the young develop, the male gonads begin the process of producing sperm. And so the phases alternate. Because of pollution, overharvesting and the species' slow growth (it requires 4 to 6 years to mature), its populations have declined sharply. A similar species, the introduced Pacific oyster, is a larger oyster with a fluted edge to its shells.

Pacific Oyster

Magallana gigas (Thunberg, 1793)

OTHER NAMES: Giant Pacific oyster, Japanese oyster; formerly classified as *Crassostrea gigas, Ostrea gigas.*
DESCRIPTION: Shell exteriors are grayish, often with touches of purplish-brown. Shell interiors are white. **An oval white or purplish muscle scar is present near the hind margin. The overall shape is narrow-elongate with a wavy margin and commarginal frills.**
SIZE: Shell normally to 12″ (30 cm) long; occasionally to 18″ (45 cm).
HABITAT: On rocky beaches or gravel; low intertidal zone to depths of 20′ (6 m).
RANGE: Prince William Sound, Alaska, to Newport Bay, California; Japan (native); Siberia to Pakistan; Europe; Australia.
NOTES: The Pacific oyster was introduced to BC and Washington in 1922. It can be harvested commercially after only 2 to 4 years but is known to live longer than 20 years. If harvesting this oyster, leave the shells on the beach. They provide attachment sites for new generations of oysters. Harvesters should possess a license and be aware of bag limits and closures, especially for red tide (PSP).
SIMILAR SPECIES: Olympia oyster.

Eastern Oyster

Crassostrea virginica (Gmelin, 1791)

OTHER NAMES: American oyster, Atlantic oyster, blue point oyster, commercial oyster, eastern American oyster, Virginia oyster; formerly classified as *Ostrea virginica.*
DESCRIPTION: Shell exteriors are tan to purple; **interior is white or yellow with an oval, black or purple muscle scar.**

The irregular shells widen from a **narrow beak to a broad, flat upper valve** and a cupped lower valve.

SIZE: Shells to 8″ (20 cm) long.

HABITAT: On both firm and soft substrates in sheltered sites such as estuaries; low intertidal zone to depths of 40′ (12 m).

RANGE: Southern British Columbia to California; Gulf of St. Lawrence to Brazil (native).

NOTES: The Eastern oyster, valued for its excellent flavour, was introduced from the east coast around 1870. Today few remnant populations may persist along the Pacific coast, including the Serpentine River, British Columbia, and a commercial operation at Tomales Bay, California. It is believed that the Atlantic oyster can live to 20 years, but individuals are large enough to be marketed at about age 3.

Smooth Pink Scallop

Chlamys rubida (Hinds, 1845)

OTHER NAMES: Reddish scallop, swimming scallop.

DESCRIPTION: The shells are nearly circular with the front ears approximately twice the length of the hind ears. **Left (upper) shell:** The exterior **varies in color from red to pink or orange.** It is sculptured with numerous (20–42) **smooth rounded radial ribs**, each of which has 1–2 barely discernible riblets between. **Right (lower) shell:** The exterior is normally white. The right shell is slightly flatter and sculptured with numerous (18–30) **flat radial ribs that split into two.**

SIZE: Shells to 2.8″ (7.1 cm) high.

HABITAT: On mud and gravel sites; in subtidal waters 3–660′ (1–200 m) deep.

RANGE: Kodiak Island, Alaska, to San Diego, California (uncommon south of Puget Sound); Bering Sea to northern Japan.

NOTES: The smooth pink scallop is more likely to be found as a shell cast on the shore after a storm than an intertidal specimen. The upper shell is normally the one that is found on the beach. Living specimens are often encrusted with sponges. This scallop and the spiny pink scallop are harvested by commercial and recreational fishers. The taste of fresh scallops is hard to beat!

SIMILAR SPECIES: Spiny pink scallop.

Spiny Pink Scallop

Chlamys hastata (G. B. Sowerby II, 1842)

OTHER NAMES: Pacific pink scallop, Pacific spear scallop, pink rough-margined scallop, spiny scallop, swimming scallop; formerly classified as *Chlamys hastatus, Pecten haustata.*

DESCRIPTION: The shells are nearly circular with the front ears greater than twice the length of the hind ears. Both valves vary in their exterior coloration from orange or yellowish to purple. **Left (upper) shell:** The **exterior is brightly colored** with purple, orange or yellow. The left shell is sculptured with numerous (8–20) **radial ribs armed with small scale-like spines.** There are also 1–10 riblets between each pair of ribs. **Right (lower) shell:** Often paler in coloration than the left. The right shell is sculptured with numerous (12–24) radial ribs with 3–4 riblets between each pair of ribs.

SIZE: Shells to 3.25″ (8.3 cm) high.

HABITAT: On rocks, sand or mud; very low intertidal zone to depths of 530′ (160 m).

RANGE: Afognak Island and the Kenai Peninsula, Alaska, to San Diego, California.

NOTES: This scallop is larger and more abundant than the smooth pink scallop. It is not found in the intertidal zone but its distinctive shells are sometimes found washed up on sandy, exposed beaches. This species is often covered in encrusting sponges. The spiny pink scallop reaches maturity at 2 years and lives to 6 years. The sexes are separate, with females possessing orange ovaries and males white testes. Specimens found on muddy substrates often have drab colors and short to nearly no spines.

SIMILAR SPECIES: Smooth pink scallop.

Giant Rock Scallop

Crassadoma gigantea (Gray, 1825)

OTHER NAMES: Giant scallop, purple-hinged rock scallop; formerly classified as *Hinnites giganteus.*

DESCRIPTION: **The shells of adults are thick and heavy.** When an adult is found attached to a rock its orange mantle can often be seen bearing numerous blue eyes. Juveniles are free-swimming and have much lighter shells. **Left (upper) shell:** The exterior of the shell varies from grayish to reddish-brown and is often covered with various organisms. The shell interior is white with **purple markings near the hinge. Right (lower) shell:** The irregularly shaped shell is normally difficult to view as it is attached to a rock or similar hard object. Interior is white with **purple markings near the hinge.**

JUVENILES

Shell exteriors of free-swimming juveniles are orange, cream or brownish. The thin, light shells have 8–16 radial ribs and reach as large as 1.75″ (4.5 cm) high.

ADULTS

Adult shell exteriors are grayish or reddish-brown with several crowded, scaly riblets. The heavy shells of adults are **irregularly shaped**, distorted and **cemented to the substrate** by the right valve. **Left (upper) shell:** The exterior of the shell varies from grayish to reddish-

Shells of juveniles.

brown and is often covered with various organisms. The shell interior is white with **purple markings near the hinge. Right (lower) shell:** The irregularly shaped shell is normally difficult to view as it is attached to a rock or similar hard object. Interior is white with **purple markings near the hinge.**

SIZE: Shells to 10″ (25 cm) high.

HABITAT: In crevices, on or under rocks in rocky shorelines; low intertidal zone to depths of 265′ (80 m).

RANGE: Prince William Sound, Alaska, to Isla Guadalupe, Baja California, México.

NOTES: This is a free-swimming species until it reaches approximately 1–1.75″ (25–45 mm) in diameter. At that time it usually attaches to a rock or shell where it remains for the rest of its life! An older individual may be found with encrusting algae or boring sponges growing on the shells. It can live as long as 50 years. This species is a gourmet item. If you harvest it, be aware of closures, bag limits and protected areas where harvesting is not allowed.

Weathervane Scallop

Patinopecten caurinus (Gould, 1850)

OTHER NAMES: Giant Pacific scallop; formerly classified as *Pecten caurinus.*
DESCRIPTION: The valves are circular in shape and the ears, or wings, are nearly equal in size. **Left (upper) shell:** The exterior of the left valve is reddish-brown; the interior

is white. Approximately 17 broad flattened ribs are present. **Right (lower) shell:** The exterior of the right valve is white near the hinge, reaching yellowish-brown on the outer margin; the interior is white. Approximately 24 broad flattened ribs are present.

SIZE: Shells to 11″ (28 cm) high.

HABITAT: On sand or gravel seafloors; in subtidal waters 60–300′ (18–91 m) deep.

RANGE: Aleutian Islands, Alaska, to Point Sur, California.

NOTES: This species is the largest living scallop in the world. It is not normally found in the intertidal zone, but during winter storms it can be unwillingly deposited, in large numbers, on surf-swept beaches. These stranded animals sometimes accumulate, lying stranded until the next tide takes them back into the ocean. Barnacles are often attached to the top shell of this impressive scallop.

....

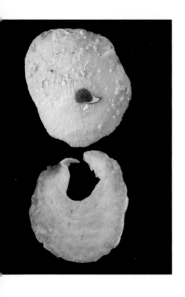

Green False-jingle

Pododesmus macrochisma (Deshayes, 1839)

OTHER NAMES: Blister shell, jingle shells, pearly monia, rock oyster; formerly classified as *Pododesmus cepio*.

DESCRIPTION: The circular shells have a polished interior with a green tinge. The mantle is bright orange. **Left (upper) shell:** The exterior of the left valve is grayish, often tinged in green and sculptured with light radiating lines. **Right (lower) shell:** The right valve is smaller in size and may be misshaped due to the substrate it is attached to. A **large pear-shaped opening is present in the center of the lower shell** to allow for the shell's attachment.

SIZE: Shells to 5.25″ (13 cm) long.

HABITAT: On rocks and pilings; low intertidal zone to depths of 300′ (90 m).

RANGE: Arctic Ocean to Guaymas, Sonora, México.

NOTES: This species is edible, though it is not an abundant intertidal species. The bright orange mantle is sometimes visible when the shells are open. Its distinctive shells are often washed up on beaches. Its name likely originates from the sound the shells make jingling in a beachcomber's pocket. The green shell color is believed to be a result of algae inside the shell matrix.

Western Ringed Lucine

Lucinoma annulatum (Reeve, 1850)

OTHER NAMES: Ringed lucina; formerly classified as *Lucina annulata*, *Lucinoma annulata*, *Lucinoma densilineata*, *Phacoides annulata*, *Phacoides annulatus*.
DESCRIPTION: Shell exteriors are dull gray, covered in a light to dark tan periostracum; **shells are nearly circular with numerous, regular, widely spaced, concentric ridges**, somewhat inflated.
SIZE: Shells to 3.3″ (8.2 cm) long.
HABITAT: In sand and mud bottoms; low intertidal zone to depths of 2,500′ (750 m).
RANGE: Prince William Sound, Alaska, to the Gulf of California.
NOTES: Finding shells like the one pictured here makes one wonder how it came to be on the beach and why the apex or umbo is broken off. Gulls often find stranded bivalves on the beach, pick them up with their bill and drop them onto rocks to break them open and feed on the animal inside. Perhaps that is the story behind this shell.

Kellyclam

Kellia suborbicularis (Montagu, 1803)

OTHER NAMES: North Atlantic kellia, suborbicular kellyclam, smooth kelly clam.
DESCRIPTION: Shells are white with a thin, yellowish periostracum. The **shells are globular in shape with prominent and incurved umbones**.
SIZE: Shells to 1″ (2.5 cm) long.
HABITAT: In crevices from the low intertidal zone to water 65′ (20 m) deep.
RANGE: Circumboreal; Prince William Sound, Alaska, to Peru; Mediterranean; New York, Japan.
NOTES: The kellyclam broods its young internally before releasing these tiny veligers into the ocean. The free-swimming young eventually settle down and attach themselves to rocks with their byssus threads. This clam is often found inside empty pholad (boring clam) holes as well as discarded bottles. It is circumboreal in its distribution.
SIMILAR SPECIES: Round diplodon lacks prominent umbones.

Mud Shrimp Clam

Neaeromya rugifera (Carpenter, 1864)

OTHER NAMES: Wrinkled lepton, wrinkled montacutid; formerly classified as *Pseudopythina rugifera, Orobitella rugifera*.

DESCRIPTION: Shell exteriors are white to yellowish and covered in a thick periostracum that ranges from yellow to dark brown. The shape is **quadrangular with a slight indentation on the lower margin**.

SIZE: Shells to 2″ (5 cm) long.

HABITAT: Attached to the abdomen of the blue mud shrimp; low intertidal zone to depths of 184′ (56 m).

RANGE: Kodiak Island, Alaska, to Punta Rompiente, Baja California, México.

NOTES: The mud shrimp clam is a remarkable species that attaches itself to the underside of the blue mud shrimp as well as the copper-haired sea mouse and related species. The females that are attached often house dwarf males inside their mantle cavity. This is not a common occurrence in bivalves but it does occur in a few species. This bivalve is classified as a protandrous hermaphrodite, meaning that individuals have both male and female organs and are capable of changing sex. How this all plays out in this species is not fully understood at the moment.

Little Heart Clam

Glans carpenteri (Lamy, 1922)

OTHER NAMES: Carpenter's cardita, little heart shell; formerly classified as *Lazaria subquadrata, Cardita subquadrata*.

DESCRIPTION: Shell exteriors are grayish-white with brown mottling and a thin brown periostracum. The interiors are cream colored with purplish markings. The **subquadrate (nearly square) shells are thick and sculptured with 14–15 prominent radial rays**.

SIZE: Shells to 0.6″ (15 mm) long.

HABITAT: Under rocks or among rocky debris; low intertidal zone to depths of 330′ (100 m).

RANGE: Frederick Island, British Columbia, to Punta Rompiente, Baja California Sur, México.

NOTES: The little heart clam produces eggs that are released into the mantle cavity. Here they are fertilized and brooded until they grow large enough to go out on their own. After emergence, a young clam has its shells and sometimes starts out attaching to its parent's shell. It is able to crawl about with its large foot, and to reattach elsewhere with byssal threads.

....

Boreal Astarte

Astarte borealis (Schumacher, 1817)

OTHER NAME: Boreal tridonta.

DESCRIPTION: Shell exteriors are white, covered in a fibrous olive-brown to black periostracum. Shell interiors are white. The oval to orbicular shells **feature several concentric ribs** that are most pronounced mid-shell. The shells bear a hinge with **thick teeth** and the **umbones are small, central and bent forward**.

SIZE: Shells to 2.2″ (5.5 cm) long.

HABITAT: In sand, mud or gravel; low intertidal zone to depths of 600′ (183 m).

RANGE: Circumboreal; Arctic to north-central British Columbia; the Bering Sea; Arctic to Massachusetts; Norway and Denmark.

NOTES: Shells of the boreal astarte are a relatively common find in southeast Alaska on muddy shorelines. The valves of this species vary considerably in their appearance and proportions.

....

Nuttall's Cockle

Clinocardium nuttallii (Conrad, 1837)

OTHER NAMES: Basket cockle, heart cockle, Nuttall cockle; formerly classified as *Cardium corbis*.

DESCRIPTION: Shell exteriors are yellowish-brown with patterns and mottling of

reddish-brown. The markings are often more prevalent in younger individuals. A thin and tough periostracum is present. Shell interiors range from whitish to yellowish-brown with a dark-brown central area. The shells are circular, thick and adorned with **34–38 strong radial ribs that cross concentric growth rings**. Elongated beads are positioned on the rays where the growth rings lie.

SIZE: Shells to 5.5″ (14 cm) long.

HABITAT: In sand or sand-gravel of sheltered sites; low intertidal zone to depths of 656′ (200 m).

RANGE: Bering Sea to San Diego, California; Kamchatka to Japan.

NOTES: Nuttall's cockle is a shallow burrower that is usually found on or near the surface of tidal flats because it has very short siphons. This species is preyed upon by the sunflower star. This clam, however, possesses a large, muscular foot, which it uses to flip itself onto the beach in a rather impressive escape response. Nuttall's cockle is a simultaneous hermaphrodite that becomes sexually mature in the summer of its second year. This cockle has been known to live 19 years.

SIMILAR SPECIES: Hundred-line cockle *Keenaea centifilosa* (Carpenter, 1864) has shells that are nearly round and thin with numerous (40+) fine, flat radial riblets.

....

Low-rib Cockle

Keenocardium blandum (Gould, 1850)

OTHER NAMES: Smooth cockle; formerly classified as *Clinocardium blandum*, *Clinocardium fucanum*.

DESCRIPTION: Shell exteriors vary from yellowish to dark brown. The shells are **thin and delicate** with a shape that is rounded and inflated to oval with approximately **45–50 delicate radiating ribs and narrow spaces between**. Large teeth are present at the hinge.

SIZE: Shells to 2″ (5 cm) long.

HABITAT: On mudflats or sand-mud sites; low intertidal zone to depths of 262′ (80 m).

RANGE: Pribilof Islands, Alaska, to Salt Point, Sonoma County, California.

NOTES: The low-rib cockle burrows just below the surface of the sediment. This species is more likely to be observed in the northern part of its range.

Fat Gaper

Tresus capax (Gould, 1850)

OTHER NAMES: Blue clam, fat horse clam, gaper clam, horseclam, horseneck clam, Alaskan gaper, northern gaper clam, otter clam, rubberneck clam, summer clam, Washington clam; formerly classified as *Schizothaerus capax*.
DESCRIPTION: Shell exteriors are chalky white with a dark brown periostracum. (Shells are often stained black from sulfides in the mud.) The interiors are white. The **ovate shells gape at the rear** to accommodate the huge, fused siphons. **Shell length is approximately one and a third times the height**. Both shells have a **chondrophore**. Siphon rim and tentacles are green to black with pads at tip and are smaller than Pacific gaper.
SIZE: Shells to 11″ (28 cm) long.
HABITAT: On beaches of sand-mud on protected shorelines; low intertidal zone to depths of 100′ (33 m).
RANGE: Kachemak Bay, Cook Inlet, Alaska, to Oceano, California.
NOTES: Several clam species, including the fat gaper, announce their presence at the beach by spouting a geyser as they retract their siphons in the sand. This is the sign to collectors that they have discovered a clam bed, but fat gapers are known for being tough to dig out. The Indigenous people of the West Coast also found this clam difficult to collect because of its ability to bury itself as far down as 20″ (50 cm). Some specimens in the Pacific Northwest have been estimated to reach 16 years old.
SIMILAR SPECIES: Pacific gaper.

Pacific Gaper

Tresus nuttallii (Conrad, 1837)

OTHER NAMES: Big-neck clam, great Washington clam, Pacific horse clam, horse clam, horse neck clam, ottershell clam, otter-shell clam, rubberneck clam, southern gaper clam, summer clam, otter clam, Washington clam; formerly classified as *Schizothaerus nuttallii, Tresus maximus, Tresus nuttalli*.
DESCRIPTION: Shell exteriors are white to yellowish with a dark brown periostracum. The

Siphons.

interiors are white. The **elongated ovate shells gape at the rear** to accommodate the huge, fused siphons. **Shell length is approximately one and two-thirds times the height**. Both shells have a chondrophore. Siphon rim and tentacles are tan to light orange with heavy pads at the tips.

SIZE: Shells to 9″ (22.5 cm) long.

HABITAT: In mud of protected bays and similar sites; mid-intertidal zone to depths of 262′ (80 m).

RANGE: Kodiak Island, Alaska, to Bahía Magdalena, Baja California Sur, México.

NOTES: This clam is noted for sporadically spurting jets of water approximately 3′ (1 m) into the air. It is believed to be a summer spawner. Usually it is found deeper, 36″ (90 cm), in the sand and lower on the beach than the similar fat gaper, and the fat gaper has broader, rounder shells. Indigenous people of the Northwest Coast dried the siphons of both of these species for winter food.

SIMILAR SPECIES: Fat gaper.

Hooked Surfclam

Simomactra falcata (Gould, 1850)

OTHER NAMES: Hooked surf clam; formerly classified as *Spisula falcata*, *Symmorphomactra falcata*.

DESCRIPTION: Shell exteriors are chalky white. A thin, highly polished, light-brown to reddish-brown periostracum covers the shells. The interiors are a shiny white. The shells are triangular in shape, and the anterior dorsal surface is slightly concave. **The condrophore does not project past hinge line of the shell's interior**.

SIZE: Shells to 3.5″ (9 cm) long.

HABITAT: In sand, normally on sheltered beaches; low intertidal zone to depths of 165′ (50 m).

RANGE: Rose Spit, Haida Gwaii (Queen Charlotte Islands), British Columbia, to Isla San Martin, Baja California, México.

NOTES: This clam builds a shallow burrow in the sand. It can close its shells tightly when required. Its thin, shiny shells are always a welcome sight to beachwalkers, as it is not commonly found.

SIMILAR SPECIES: Arctic surfclam.

Arctic Surfclam

Mactromeris polynyma (Stimpson, 1860)

OTHER NAMES: Hooked surf clam; surf clam, pinkneck clam, Stimpson's surf clam; formerly classified as *Spisula polynyma*.

DESCRIPTION: Shell exteriors are white with a varnish-like yellowish-brown or reddish-brown periostracum. The interiors are white. The shells are thick, flattened and triangular with a smooth surface. **The condrophore projects past the hinge line of the shell's interior.**

SIZE: To 5.5″ (14 cm) long.

HABITAT: In sand or muddy sand; low intertidal zone to depths of 365′ (110 m).

RANGE: Point Barrow, Alaska, to Neah Bay, Washington; Japan; north Atlantic to Rhode Island.

NOTES: The Arctic surfclam is found on both the Atlantic and Pacific coasts. Research on this species indicates that it is known to live to an amazing 73 years on the Atlantic coast. In Alaska, however, the oldest individuals are believed to reach 25 years.

SIMILAR SPECIES: Hooked surfclam.

Pacific Razor-clam

Siliqua patula (Dixon, 1789)

OTHER NAMES: Northern razor clam, Pacific razor, Pacific razor clam.

DESCRIPTION: Shell exteriors are white, covered with a periostracum that is thick, olive to dark brown, with a highly polished finish. A purplish coloration is also present near the beaks. The interiors vary from white to light pinkish. The **elongate-oblong shells are thin, rounded at the front end with a somewhat squared-off rear end.** An internal rib on the shell is positioned so that it projects anteriorly.

SIZE: Shells to 7.5″ (19 cm) long.

Dimple indicates presence of Pacific razor-clam below.

HABITAT: On surf-swept sandy beaches; low intertidal zone to depths of 180′ (55 m).
RANGE: Cook Inlet, Alaska, to Morro Bay, California.
NOTES: This clam is a very active digger with no permanent burrow. It has been observed to bury itself completely in sand in less than 7 seconds. To do so, the clam pushes its foot deeper into the sand while its fluids are displaced. The tip of the foot then expands, forming an anchor. Then, as the foot contracts, the animal draws deeper into the sand. Individuals have been known to live to 19 years of age. In the north, breeding probably occurs in July and August. Pacific razor-clams were traditionally gathered by Indigenous people in May and June, at low spring tides. Today, both recreational and commercial fishermen collect them. If you collect this species, be sure that the area is safe from red tide or PSP.
SIMILAR SPECIES: Alaska razor-clam *Siliqua alta* (Broderip & Sowerby, 1829) is found from the Bering Strait to Cook Inlet, Alaska. The posterior end of the shell is rounded and the interiors bears a rib that is vertical.

Sickle Jackknife-clam

Solen sicarius Gould, 1850

OTHER NAMES: Blunt jackknife clam, blunt razor-clam, fast jackknife clam, jackknife clam, sickle razor clam.
DESCRIPTION: Shell exteriors are white, often revealed when the periostracum is worn away. The periostracum is greenish-yellow to dark-brown and shiny. The interiors are white. The **valves are near rectangular and elongated with a rounded anterior end. The umbones are situated at the posterior.**
SIZE: Shells to 5″ (12.5 cm) long.
HABITAT: In sand-mud and eelgrass at sheltered sites; low intertidal zone to depths of 130′ (40 m).
RANGE: Haida Gwaii (Queen Charlotte Islands), British Columbia, to Bahía San Quintin, Baja California, México.
NOTES: The sickle jackknife-clam is often found near eelgrass beds, where it builds a permanent burrow to 14″ (35 cm) deep. In this burrow it can travel very rapidly. This species has also been known to bury itself completely in 30 seconds and to leap "several centimeters" from the sand while out of the water. It swims by jetting water from its siphons or the area around its foot. The latter method is likely useful in its rapid digging technique.

Rough Diplodon

Diplodonta impolita

S. S. Berry, 1953

OTHER NAME: Round diplodon.
DESCRIPTION: Shell exteriors vary
from chalky-white to gray. The
periostracum is dark brown overall
and thick with irregular growth lines.
The **shell is circular and inflated
without any surface sculpture**.
SIZE: Shells to 1.5″ (3.5 cm) long.
HABITAT: In sand, gravel or beneath
rocks; low intertidal zone to depths of 330′ (100 m).
RANGE: Kodiak Island, Alaska, to central Oregon.
NOTES: The rough diplodon is known to secrete a mucus channel, which reaches to the
surface. This species is more often found intertidally in the northern part of its range.

Northern Baltic Clam

Limecola balthica (Linnaeus, 1758)

OTHER NAMES: Tiny Baltic macoma, pink clam;
formerly classified as *Macoma balthica*, *Macoma
inconspicua*.
DESCRIPTION: Shell exteriors are often pink
but may also be blue, orange or yellow. The
interiors are white or pink. The shells are **small
and oval in shape**. Fine concentric lines are
present on the exterior.
SIZE: Shells to 1.5″ (3.5 cm) long.
HABITAT: In areas with mixed mud and sand,
mudflats and eelgrass beds; low intertidal zone
to depths of 130′ (39 m).
RANGE: Beaufort Sea to Oregon; throughout
northwest Europe and Britain.
NOTES: This common small species is often
found to be plentiful in muddy areas.

Oval Macoma

Macoma golikovi Scarlato & Kafanov, 1988

OTHER NAME: Originally mistaken for the Asian species, *Macoma incongrua*.

DESCRIPTION: Shell exteriors are calcareous white, often stained with brown to reddish-brown. The periostracum varies from yellowish-brown to brown. The **ovate shell is slightly inflated with its anterior end longer, and the posterior end abrupt.** The pallial sinus is deep in the left shell and moderate in the right shell and slightly detached for both.

SIZE: Shells to 2″ (5 cm) long.

HABITAT: In gravel or sand; low intertidal zone to depths of 656′ (200 m).

RANGE: Point Barrow, Alaska, to Puget Sound, Washington; Sakhalin Island, Russia, to the Sea of Japan.

NOTES: The oval macoma is more often found intertidally in the northern portion of its range. In Russia this bivalve has been associated with hydrothermal activity of a volcano. Members of the genus *Macoma* have two separate siphons—incurrent (to bring in water) and excurrent (to release water). The siphons extend to the surface for these species to feed, breathe and expel waste.

Bent-nose Macoma

Macoma nasuta (Conrad, 1837)

OTHER NAMES: Bent-nose clam, bent-nosed clam.

DESCRIPTION: Shell exteriors are grayish-white to yellowish-white and the periostracum is grayish-brown and fibrous. The interiors are white. The **shells are broadly ovate, thin and bend sharply to the right near the rear.** The siphons are orange. The pallial sinus is very deep in the left shell where it merges with the front muscle scar and in the right shell it is deep and connected.

SIZE: Shells to 4.3″ (11 cm) long.

HABITAT: In sand or silt; low intertidal zone to depths of 165′ (50 m).

RANGE: Cook Inlet, Alaska, to Cabo San Lucas, Baja California, México.

NOTES: This clam typically lies flat with its "nose" pointed upward, which allows its separate siphons to reach the surface and suck up sand, mud and nutrients "like a vacuum cleaner." This clam species is also known to be the most tolerant of stale water and soft mud. Lewis's moonsnail is known to be an important predator of this clam.

SIMILAR SPECIES: Pointed macoma is also a species with a bent nose, but to a much lesser extent.

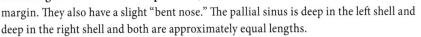

Pointed Macoma

Macoma inquinata (Deshayes, 1855)

OTHER NAMES: Fouled macoma, polluted macoma, stained macoma; formerly classified as *M. irus*, *M. arnheimi*, *Heteromacoma inquinata*.

DESCRIPTION: Shell exteriors are quite often stained with a yellowish-orange on the ventral portion, and covered in a flaky, grayish-brown periostracum. The shells are oval with a **wedge-shaped rear and they bear a slight indentation in the posterior,** ventral margin. They also have a slight "bent nose." The pallial sinus is deep in the left shell and deep in the right shell and both are approximately equal lengths.

SIZE: To 2.5″ (6.6 cm) long.

HABITAT: In silt; low intertidal zone to depths of 165′ (50 m).

RANGE: Bering Sea to San Pedro, California.

NOTES: The pointed macoma is a suspension feeder eating mainly small diatoms and some flagellates. It is rather unique in that it lies on its right side in the sediment, unlike other macomas that lie on their left sides or vertically. From this position it extends its siphons almost vertically up to 1″ (2.5 cm) above the surface of the sediment. The reason for this difference is unknown.

Sleek Macoma

Macoma lipara Dall, 1916

DESCRIPTION: The exteriors of the shiny shells vary from white to yellowish with a gray to olive-green periostracum. The interiors are white. The **ovate shells are heavy and solid with evenly rounded ventral margins.** The pallial

sinus is deep in the left shell and moderate in the right shell and very detached in both.

SIZE: Shells to 3″ (7.5 cm) long.

HABITAT: In silt and fine sand; in subtidal waters 65–850′ (20–260 m) deep.

RANGE: Northern Bering Sea south to Redondo Submarine Canyon, California.

NOTES: The sleek macoma is a large subtidal species that occasionally finds itself stranded on beaches after a storm.

Expanded Macoma

Rexithaerus expansa (Carpenter, 1864)

OTHER NAMES: Formerly classified as *Macoma expansa*, *Macoma liotricha*.

DESCRIPTION: Shell exteriors are white, as are their interiors. The periostracum is shiny, yellowish-brown and thin. The elongated **ovate shells are rounded at the anterior and slightly inflated**. The pallial sinuses of both shells meet the pallial line at approximately 90° and they are equal in size.

SIZE: Shells to 2″ (5 cm) long.

HABITAT: In sand in a variety of exposures; low intertidal zone to depths of 100′ (30 m).

RANGE: Bering Sea, Alaska, to Oceano, California.

NOTES: Although the expanded macoma is found on both exposed and sheltered beaches, it is more prevalent on exposed beaches.

White-sand Clam

Rexithaerus secta (Conrad, 1837)

OTHER NAMES: Cleft clam, sand clam, white sand macoma; formerly classified as *Macoma secta*, *Tellina secta*.

DESCRIPTION: Shell exteriors are glossy white to yellowish-white. The periostracum is thin and pale yellowish. The interiors are glossy white. Shell exteriors are patterned with fine, concentric growth lines. The broadly ovate shells are thin with a **distinctive ridge running**

at the rear of both shells. The left valve is flatter than the right and there is an abrupt notch behind the ligament. The pallial sinuses of both shells meet the pallial line at approximately 90° and are equal in size.

SIZE: Shells to 4.7″ (12 cm) long.

HABITAT: In sand and sand-mud at sheltered sites; low intertidal zone to depths of 152′ (46 m).

RANGE: Haida Gwaii (Queen Charlotte Islands), British Columbia, to Bahía San Carlos, Baja California, México.

NOTES: The white-sand clam favors sites with fine sand or sandy mud. It buries itself so deeply into the sand that few predators can reach it. There it lies on its flatter left side, extending 2 separate white siphons to the surface up to 2″ (5 cm) apart. The inhalant siphon acts like a vacuum cleaner, bringing organic detritus into the gut along with great quantities of sand. The second (exhalant) siphon returns all wastes to the sand's surface. Pea crabs are often found inside this clam.

....

Bodega Tellin

Megangulus bodegensis (Hinds, 1845)

OTHER NAMES: Bodega tellen, Bodegas tellin; formerly classified as *Moerella bodegensis*, *Tellina bodegensis*, *Tellina santarosae*.

DESCRIPTION: Shell exteriors are white; the interiors are normally white but often have a yellow to pinkish blush. The valves are **elongate with a rounded anterior end**. The exterior is smooth with a **polished surface and sculpted with fine concentric lines that are evenly spaced**.

SIZE: Shells to 2.5″ (6 cm) long.

HABITAT: Normally in sand on exposed beaches; low intertidal zone to depths of 328′ (100 m).

RANGE: Sitka, Alaska, to Bahía Magdalena, Baja California Sur, México.

NOTES: This is an uncommon species but its distinctive shells are sometimes found washed up on the beach. The bodega tellin has 2 separate siphons that extend to the surface. It is reportedly an excellent tasting clam but is too scarce to be harvested regularly.

Plain Tellin

Tellina modesta (Carpenter, 1864)

OTHER NAMES: Button tellin, modest tellin; formerly classified as *Angulus modestus*.
DESCRIPTION: Shell exteriors are white to yellow; interiors are white. The ovate-elongate shells are flat, shiny and slightly inflated with fine, concentric grooves covering the exterior. A **radial riblet is present on both shell interiors**, immediately behind the adductor muscle scar.
SIZE: Shells to 1″ (2.5 cm) long.
HABITAT: In sand; low intertidal zone to depths of 328′ (100 m).
RANGE: Cook Inlet, Alaska, to Bahía San Bartolome, Baja California, México.
NOTES: The plain tellin is a common bivalve that is frequently found on the beach. Its small shells are distinctive.

Purple Mahogany-clam

Nuttallia obscurata (Reeve, 1857)

OTHER NAMES: Dark mahogany-clam, dark mahogany clam, savoury clam, varnish clam; formerly classified as *Soletellina obseurata*.
DESCRIPTION: Shell exteriors are light purple covered with a thick, shiny brown periostracum. The interiors are a rich, dark purple. The ovate shells are very flat and the hinge ligament is external and prominent.
SIZE: Shells to 2.8″ (7 cm) long.
HABITAT: In sand or sand-gravel; high to mid-intertidal zone.
RANGE: Southern British Columbia, to Alsea Bay, Oregon; Korea; Japan.
NOTES: This clam was introduced into British Columbia from Japan in 1991 in ballast water. Since that time, it has spread rapidly south into Oregon. The purple mahogany-clam uses its long separate siphons to gather food and release wastes.

California Sunset Clam

Gari californica (Conrad, 1849)

OTHER NAMES: California sunsetclam, sunset clam; formerly classified as *Psammobia californica.*
DESCRIPTION: Shell exteriors are **white with radiating pink rays**, which may not always be present. The periostracum is yellowish-brown, thin and tends to remain attached at the edge of the shell. Shell interiors are glossy white. The shells are **elongate** with rounded ends with a relatively smooth surface. The **hinge ligament is external and prominent**, and the pallial sinus is nearly square.
SIZE: Shells to 6″ (15 cm) long.
HABITAT: In sand or gravel; low intertidal zone to depths of 918′ (280 m).
RANGE: Kachemak Bay, Alaska, to Bahía Magdalena, Baja California Sur, México; Japan.
NOTES: This clam is found both on the open coast and in entrances to bays. Its colorful shells are found frequently on sandy beaches. The clam burrows to 8″ (20 cm) deep where it extends 2 separate siphons to the surface of the substrate. There have been no observations of this species along the coasts of Washington or Oregon.
SIMILAR SPECIES: Rose-painted clam.

Rose-painted Clam

Semele rubropicta Dall, 1871

OTHER NAMES: Red-painted semele, rock semele, rose-painted semele, rose-petal semele, rose petal semele.
DESCRIPTION: Shell exteriors are **white with radiating pink rays**, which may not always be present. The periostracum is yellowish-brown, thin and tends to remain attached at the edge of the shell. Shell interiors are glossy white. The shells are **round** to **ovate** with a relatively smooth surface. The **hinge ligament is primarily internal**, and the pallial sinuses are deep and broad.
SIZE: Shells to 2″ (5 cm) long.
HABITAT: In sand, gravel and rubble; low intertidal zone to depths of 330′ (100 m).
RANGE: Kenai Peninsula, Alaska, to Bahía Willard, Baja California, México.

NOTES: This species is found more frequently in the intertidal region in the northern portion of its range. Many species in the family Semelidae are renowned for the bright coloration of their shells.

SIMILAR SPECIES: California sunset clam.

Rock Venus

Irusella lamellifera (Conrad, 1837)

OTHER NAMES: Lamellar venus; formerly classified as *Irus lamellifer.*

DESCRIPTION: Shell exteriors and interiors are white. Shells are nearly quadrate in shape and often distorted from nestling. Shell sculpture with **sharp, widely spaced concentric shelf-like ribs.**

SIZE: Shells to 2″ (5 cm) long.

HABITAT: Nesting in rock crevices and empty pholad burrows; low intertidal zone to depths of 328′ (100 m).

RANGE: Coos Bay, Oregon, to Isla San Martin, Baja California, México.

NOTES: The rock venus is a nestling clam that resides in the empty burrows of various rock-boring clams. The prominent ridges on the shell help the clam to brace itself in its environment.

Pacific Littleneck

Leukoma staminea (Conrad, 1837)

OTHER NAMES: Common Pacific littleneck, native little-neck clam, rock cockle, rock venus; formerly classified as *Venerupis staminea.*

DESCRIPTION: Shell exteriors vary from white to yellow or brown, often with chocolate brown angular patterns and zigzag markings. The interiors are white. The **oval to nearly round shells** are inflated and adorned with radiating ribs crossed with numerous concentric ridges creating a latticed sculpture. The umbo is prominent at the anterior ends of the shells. **The inside outer margins have many small teeth** that are easily felt.

SIZE: Shell normally to 1.6″ (4 cm) long; occasionally to 3.1″ (8 cm) long.

HABITAT: In sand-mud or gravel of protected bays; mid-intertidal zone to depths of 130′ (40 m).

RANGE: Aleutian Islands, Alaska, to Bahía Santa Maria and possibly Cabo San Lucas, Baja California, México; Japan.

NOTES: The Pacific littleneck is generally slow-growing, reaching legal harvestable size in 3 to 4 years, but living as long as 16 years. Breeding occurs during the summer months, after a maturation period of 3 to 5 years. A similar species, the Japanese littleneck, has more elongated shells. The Pacific littleneck is excellent eating when steamed. But you must have a sport fishing license to harvest them legally. Be sure to check with local officials to ensure the clams are safe to eat in the area you wish to harvest from.

SIMILAR SPECIES: Japanese littleneck.

....

Japanese Littleneck

Ruditapes philippinarum

(A. Adams and Reeve, 1850)

OTHER NAMES: Filipino venus, Japanese littleneck, Manilla clam, steamer clam; formerly classified as *Tapes japonica*, *Venerupis philippinarum*.

DESCRIPTION: Shell exteriors are often gray-brown, usually with brown, black or gray patterns and zigzag markings. **Shell interiors are** white to yellowish with **deep purple at the posterior end**. The **oblong shells** are inflated and adorned with radiating ribs crossed with numerous concentric ridges creating a latticed sculpture. The umbo is prominent at the anterior ends of the shells. The **inside outer margins are smooth**, lacking small teeth (that are present in the Pacific littleneck).

SIZE: Shells to 3″ (7.5 cm) long.

HABITAT: In muddy gravel of sheltered sites including bays and estuaries; high intertidal zone.

The patterns of juveniles are highly variable.

RANGE: Haida Gwaii (Queen Charlotte Islands), British Columbia, to Elkhorn Slough, California; Hawaii; Mediterranean; Siberia to China (native).

NOTES: This species was accidentally introduced to North America with oyster spat from Japan. It appears to be unable to withstand extreme temperature changes, as mass winter mortalities have been noted. This species requires only 2 years to reach legal harvestable size of 2″ (5 cm) and can live to 14 years. If you plan to harvest Japanese littlenecks, check with officials to ensure that the area is free from pollution and red tide.

SIMILAR SPECIES: Pacific littleneck.

Thin-shelled Littleneck

Callithaca tenerrima (Carpenter, 1857)

OTHER NAMES: Finest carpet shell, superlative rock venus, thin-shell littleneck, thin-shelled little-neck, thin-shelled littleneck clam.

DESCRIPTION: Shell exteriors are grayish-white to light brown. The interiors are white. The **solid shells are ovate with a delicate sculpture of sharp, widely spaced concentric ridges.** The pallial sinus is very deep.

SIZE: Shells to 6.3″ (16 cm) long.

HABITAT: In sand and gravel on sheltered beaches; low intertidal zone to depths of 165′ (50 m).

RANGE: Baranof Island, Sitka Sound, Alaska, to Bahía Thurloe, Baja California, México.

NOTES: The thin-shelled littleneck is a large and rather uncommon littleneck compared with its cousin the native littleneck. Its shells are often found with a very neat hole bored into them by the predatory Lewis's moonsnail. Another predator that has been known to dig up this bivalve is the sea otter.

Washington Butter Clam

Saxidomus gigantea (Deshayes, 1839)

OTHER NAMES: Butter clam, smooth Washington clam.

DESCRIPTION: Shell exteriors are white to gray; interiors are white. A thin periostracum may be present. The **solid and heavy shells are ovate with a prominent external hinge ligament**, fine concentric growth lines and a gape at the anterior end. Shell interiors have well-marked muscle scars.

SIZE: Shells to 5.4″ (13.6 cm) long.

HABITAT: In sand and gravel shores; mid-intertidal zone to depths of 130′ (40 m).

RANGE: Southeast Bering Sea, Alaska, to southern California.

NOTES: The Washington butter clam has been known to live for more than 20 years. It also has a long history of commercial use. To collect it, first ensure that the area is safe from red tide (PSP) and pollution. PSP toxins accumulate particularly in the dark tips of the siphons of the butter clam, so remove them before eating your catch, just to be extra safe. This species is also a host species for the gaper pea crab, a species that lives inside the clam's mantle cavity. There is no problem in eating an edible clam that hosts any of the many pea crabs.

Softshell-clam

Mya arenaria Linnaeus, 1758

OTHER NAMES: Eastern soft-shell clam, eastern soft shell, long clam, long-necked clam, mud clam, nanny nose, sand gaper, softshell, soft clam, soft-shelled clam, steamer clam.

DESCRIPTION: Shell exteriors are chalky white to gray with a yellow-brown periostracum that normally persists, at least at the edges. Shell interiors are white. The ovate shells have a somewhat pointed posterior end and are sculpted with **irregular concentric growth lines**. Valves are **thin, quite soft, brittle** and easily broken. A **large spoon-shaped erect chondrophore is positioned at the hinge of left valve.** The shells gape slightly at both ends. This species has dark siphons.

SIZE: Shells to 6" (15 cm) long.

The chondrophore on the left valve.

HABITAT: In the mud of sheltered bays and similar sites; mid-intertidal zone to to depths of 240′ (73 m).

RANGE: Circumboreal; Icy Cape, Alaska, to San Diego, California; Korea; Japan; Iceland to Spain and the Black Sea; Newfoundland to Virginia.

NOTES: The softshell-clam burrows in mud and sand in a unique way. It ejects water below its body, pushing sand out of the way as it digs deeper—a slow method of burrowing that is more effective in sand than in mud. This clam also has a special sac off the stomach that holds a food reserve. This species was accidentally introduced to California in 1874 with Eastern oysters.

SIMILAR SPECIES: California softshell-clam is similar in appearance but much smaller.

....

Truncated Softshell-clam

Mya truncata Linnaeus, 1758

OTHER NAMES: Blunt soft-shell clam; blunt gaper, truncate soft shell clam, truncated mya, mud gaper.

DESCRIPTION: Shell exteriors are dull white and covered by a yellowish-brown periostracum. The shells are nearly quadrate (squarish) with a wide flaring gap, a round anterior end, and **a truncated posterior end. A large chondrophore is found inside the hinge of the left valve.** The siphons are fused and small.

SIZE: Shells to 3.5″ (8.6 cm) long.

HABITAT: In mud and sand of protected shorelines; low intertidal zone to depths of 330′ (100 m).

RANGE: Circumboreal; Panarctic; Beaufort Sea to Puget Sound, Washington; New England; Japan; Western Europe.

NOTES: Empty shells of the truncated softshell-clam are often found washed up on the beach. The enormous siphons of the truncated softshell-clam are too large to be completely retracted into the shells of the live animal.

SIMILAR SPECIES: Pacific geoduck juveniles look somewhat similar.

California Softshell-clam

Cryptomya californica (Conrad, 1837)

OTHER NAMES: California glass mya, California softshell, false mya, glass mya.
DESCRIPTION: Shell exteriors are chalky white to gray and covered with a thin, yellowish-brown periostracum. Shell interiors are white. The valves are ovate, slightly inflated and sculptured with irregular growth lines. **The posterior ends are of the shells are slightly truncated.** A large spoon-shaped **erect chondrophore is found on the left valve.** The shells gape slightly at the siphonal end.
SIZE: Shells to 1.5" (3.7 cm) long.
HABITAT: In sand-mud or fine mud of estuaries or bays; low intertidal zone to depths of 265′ (80 m).
RANGE: Montague Island, Alaska, to Bayovar, Peru; Japan.
NOTES: The siphons of this small, mobile clam are only 0.05″ (1 mm) long, unusually short for a clam. This species lives deeper in the sand than its siphons would normally allow by living adjacent to the permanent burrows of the blue mud shrimp and bay ghost shrimp and using its short siphon to feed from the water circulating there.
SIMILAR SPECIES: Softshell-clam.

Boring Softshell-clam

Platyodon cancellatus (Conrad, 1837)

OTHER NAMES: Checked borer, checked softshell-clam, checked soft-shell clam, clay boring clam.
DESCRIPTION: Shell exteriors are gray, covered with a thin, yellowish-brown periostracum, which is often only present near the margin. The interiors are white. Shells are **subquadrate and sculptured with fine, sharp, evenly spaced concentric lines.** The siphons are dark, long and fused with two pointed pads visible near the tips.
SIZE: Shells to 3″ (7.6 cm) long.
HABITAT: Bores into hard-packed clay, soft sandstone

and mudstone at protected sites and bay entrances along the outer coast; mid-intertidal zone to depths of 65′ (20 m).

RANGE: Tlell, Haida Gwaii (Queen Charlotte Islands), British Columbia, to Isla Cedros, Baja California, México.

NOTES: This clam can bore directly into soft rock by shell rocking rather than a rotating motion. It does so by alternate contractions of muscles in the shells, which causes the shells to rock. As a result, it can bore holes that closely match the shape of its shells, rather than the round holes of other boring species. It is also reported to have been found boring into low-grade concrete. Historically, the Haida people on the Queen Charlotte Islands of BC harvested this clam.

Arctic Hiatella

Hiatella arctica (Linnaeus, 1767)

OTHER NAMES: Gallic saxicave, arctic nestler, arctic saxicave, arctic rock borer, little gaper, nestling clam, nestling saxicave, red nose.

DESCRIPTION: Shell exteriors are **chalky white.** The thin periostracum is yellowish. Shell **shape is oblong-ovate but highly variable** as it normally conforms to its rock environment. The **valves gape slightly** and the sculpture includes irregular concentric lines. The siphon tips are red-orange.

SIZE: Shells to 3.1″ (8 cm) long.

HABITAT: Bores into clay or limestone; low intertidal zone to depths of 3,930′ (1,190 m). Range: Worldwide; Point Barrow, Alaska, to Chile.

NOTES: The Arctic hiatella bores into soft rock using a rocking motion. It is an opportunist, often moving into the burrows of other boring clams. Adults can attach directly to rock surfaces with weak byssus threads. There is some evidence that there are actually 2 species involved; however, more research is required to determine if this is the case.

Siphons in tidepool.

Ample Roughmya

Panomya ampla Dall, 1898

OTHER NAMES: Ample rough mya, false geoduck.

DESCRIPTION: Shell exteriors are white to cream colored; interiors are white, often with yellowish tinges. A thick, light brown to black periostracum is also present. The thick shells are extremely variable in shape but generally **quadrate or squarish, chalky, with a pointed anterior end and a truncated posterior end.** The sculpture is simple with growth lines present and gaping at both ends. The **interiors of the shells bear 3–6 depressions.** The long, thick and fused siphons are rust-brown in color with pink-tinged ends and small white papillae.

SIZE: Shells to 2.75″ (7 cm) long.

HABITAT: In muddy-sand or gravel; low intertidal zone to depths of 492′ (150 m).

RANGE: Point Barrow, Alaska, to Puget Sound, Washington.

NOTES: As one of this clam's common names indicate, this species is often mistaken for the Pacific geoduck. This is especially true for the juveniles and their siphons.

SIMILAR SPECIES: Pacific geoduck.

Pacific Geoduck

Panopea generosa (Gould, 1850)

OTHER NAMES: Gooeyduck, king clam; occasionally misspelled *Panope generosa*.

DESCRIPTION: Shell exteriors are white and porcelaneous in juveniles; chalky white to grayish in adults. A thin, light-brown periostracum covers the shell but is easily worn off. Shell interiors are white. The **ovate shells are truncated at the posterior end and gape on all sides.** Shell sculpture consists of irregular growth lines. The siphons are fused and huge.

SIZE: Shells to 8″ (20 cm) long.

HABITAT: In sand and mud; very low intertidal zone to depths of 330′ (100 m).

RANGE: Kodiak Island, Alaska, to Newport Bay, California; Sakhalin Island, Russia, to Japan.

NOTES: This remarkable clam can extend its siphon nearly 3′ (1 m) to the surface, and as a result it is not easily collected. Because the siphon is too large to be retracted completely into the shell, the geoduck relies on its deep burrow for protection. The giant pink star feeds on the siphons of this clam by grasping them with its sticky tube feet. The Pacific geoduck is the largest burrowing clam in the world, weighing up to 20 lb. (9 kg). It is also extensively harvested commercially. The total number of eggs produced by a single female during one year has been calculated to exceed 50 million; few of these survive, but individuals of this species have been known to live up to 146 years.

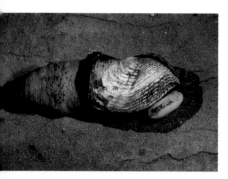

Rough Piddock

Zirfaea pilsbryi Lowe, 1931

OTHER NAMES: Pilsbry piddock, Pilsbry's piddock; formerly classified as *Zirfaea pilsbryii, Zirfaea gabbi*; occasionally misspelled *Zirphaea pilsbryi*.

DESCRIPTION: Shell exteriors are white and the periostracum is dark brown. The interiors are chalky white, often with some brown mottling. The valves are irregularly shaped with the posterior end truncated and the anterior end angled. A **diagonal division divides the shell exteriors into 2 separate sections**. The anterior end features teeth on the edges of the concentric growth rings and the posterior end displays wide concentric growth rings alone. The shells also gape at both ends. A myopore is present on the inside of both shells. The siphon tip is dark maroon with a pattern of white bumps.

SIZE: Shells to 5.75″ (14.5 cm) long.

Siphons underwater.

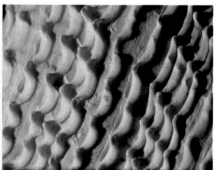

Detail of the rough piddock's cutting surface.

HABITAT: Burrows in limestone, shale, mud or clay; low intertidal zone to depths of 410′ (125 m).

RANGE: Point Lay, Arctic coast of Alaska, to Bahía Magdalena, Baja California Sur, México.

NOTES: The rough piddock rasps away at clay or soft rock to build its burrow with sharp, toothlike projections at the rear of the shells. As it digs it rotates, carving a circular burrow. This clam is a true "prisoner in its castle": it is embedded in its home until it dies. The rough piddock has been known to live 8 years.

SIMILAR SPECIES: Flat-tip piddock valves are divided into 3 sections.

Flat-tip Piddock

Penitella penita (Conrad, 1837)

Siphons underwater.

OTHER NAMES: Common piddock, flat-tipped piddock, flap-tip piddock, left paddock; formerly classified as *Pholadidea penita*.

DESCRIPTION: Shell exteriors and interiors are white. The periostracum is brown, thick and leathery. The shells are thin and elongated-ovate with the anterior bulbous and the **posterior truncated and extended with a leathery addition. The exteriors of the valves are divided into 3 separate surface sculptures with a near-triangular central section that separates the other two.** The mesoplax covers the hinge. The siphon is white overall with an orange tip.

SIZE: Shells to 3.75″ (9.5 cm) long.

HABITAT: Burrows in clay or soft rock; mid-intertidal zone to depths of 300′ (90 m).

RANGE: Prince William Sound, Alaska, to Punta Pequena, Baja California, México.

NOTES: This piddock lives in burrows with only its siphons exposed to obtain food and remove wastes. The opening in the rock is typically small, since the clam begins to burrow when it is quite small. Burrowing is accomplished by simple mechanical abrasion of the rock by the file-like shells. Since the animal is always growing, it must continually enlarge its burrow. Once it has reached its full size, its foot is no longer required; the foot degenerates and the shells overgrow it.

SIMILAR SPECIES: Rough piddock, with shells that are separated into just 2 sections.

Beaked Piddock

Netastoma rostratum (Valenciennes, 1846)

OTHER NAMES: Rostrate piddock; formerly classified as *Netastoma rostrata*, *Nettastomella rostrata*, *Pholadidea rostrata*.

DESCRIPTION: The exteriors and interiors of the shells are white. The outer surfaces are sculptured with a series of raised, concentric ridges. The valves are triangular and **a long tapering, calcareous extension** is distinctive for this species.

SIZE: Shells to 0.75″ (20 mm) long.

HABITAT: Burrows in soft rock, especially shale and occasionally dead shells; low intertidal zone to depths of 330′ (100 m).

RANGE: Barkley Sound, Vancouver Island, British Columbia, to Bahía San Cristobal, Baja California, México.

NOTES: The beaked piddock burrows into soft shale where it can become especially abundant. The shape of the shell is often somewhat irregular because of this boring activity. This small species is often found in the company of other rock-burrowing clams.

Feathery Shipworm

Bankia setacea (Tryon, 1860)

OTHER NAMES: Northwest shipworm, Pacific shipworm, shipworm, teredo.

DESCRIPTION: Superficially a **worm-like creature** with a pair of small white shells at the front end and **2 feather-like pallets or appendages at the rear.**

SIZE: Shells to 0.8″ (20 mm) long; animal to 39″ (1 m) long.

HABITAT: In wood; mid-intertidal zone to depths of 300′ (90 m).

RANGE: Bering Sea, Alaska, to San Diego, California; Kurile Islands to Sea of Japan.

NOTES: The young (veligers) of the feathery shipworm look like miniature clams in the first stages of development. Changes occur once they

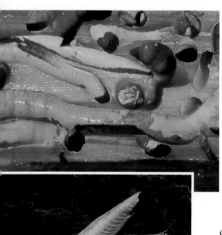

A pair of feathery pallets.

settle on a wood source to begin their "boring" life. They use the "teeth" on their shells to rasp away at the wood while they burrow. The 2 feather-like appendages that grace the rear can be used to stopper the burrow. Feathery shipworms produce a calcareous lining to their burrows, which is visible in the photo.

....

Punctate Pandora

Heteroclidus punctatus (Conrad, 1837)

OTHER NAMES: Dotted pandora; formerly classified as *Pandora punctata*, *Pandora punctatus*.

DESCRIPTION: Shell exteriors are white; interiors are white with a pearly finish. Both valves are crescent-shaped with a concave upper edge. The valves are not equal; the right is inflated while the left is not.

SIZE: Shells to 3″ (7.6 cm) long.

HABITAT: In mud; low intertidal zone to depths of 165′ (50 m) deep.

RANGE: Esperanza Inlet, Vancouver Island, British Columbia, to Punta Pequeiia, Baja California, México.

NOTES: Although this species is not often an intertidal one, their fragile, empty shells occasionally turn up on the shoreline. The curious shape of these shells makes them easy to identify.

....

Rock Entodesma

Entodesma navicula

(Adams & Reeve, 1850)

OTHER NAMES: Northwest ugly clam, ugly clam, rock-dwelling entodesma, rock-dwelling clam.

DESCRIPTION: Shell exteriors are white and covered with an orange-brown, thick periostracum. The interiors are yellow to brownish with a mother-of-pearl finish.

Juvenile.

Shell of adult.

The shells will grow to a pear shape unless their rock environment modifies their shape—which is very often the case. The thick periostracum often fractures the valves in shell collections as it dries. The red siphons cannot be completely retracted as the shell gapes.

SIZE: Shells to 6″ (15 cm) long.

HABITAT: Nestling in rock crevices or under rocks; mid-intertidal zone to depths of 200′ (60 m).

RANGE: Bering Sea to Point Lorna, California; Bering Sea to Japan.

NOTES: The young of this species look much different than adults. A light brown periostracum completely covers the shell of the young, giving it a unique appearance. Grains of sand often adhere to the shell by mucous produced by glands in the mantle. As this species is sometimes called the northwest ugly clam, you know it is not one of the prettier shells to collect.

....

California Lyonsia

Lyonsia californica Conrad, 1837

OTHER NAME: Puget Sound Iyonsia.

DESCRIPTION: Shell exteriors are pearly and very thin. The periostracum is yellowish-brown and very thin. The valves are elongate with a **flat-tipped beak** extension at the anterior end. The exterior is graced with numerous irregular concentric ridges. Several radial ribs may be visible.

SIZE: Shells to 1.7″ (4.2 cm) long.

HABITAT: In sandy mud; low intertidal zone to depths of 240′ (73 m).

RANGE: Kodiak Island, Alaska, to Acapulco, Guerrero, México.

NOTES: This distinctive bivalve buries itself close to the surface in mud or sandy mud, so that it can reach the surface with its 2 short siphons. It is a simultaneous hermaphrodite, releasing eggs and sperm alternately through the exhalant siphon. Sand particles tend to adhere to the periostracum of small individuals.

Octopods & Squids

CLASS CEPHALOPODA

The creatures in this group of molluscs have several remarkable characteristics. A total of 8 or more arms are positioned around the mouth, and 2 gills, 2 kidneys and 3 hearts are also present. A dark fluid is produced in some species, which can be released to aid in defense against predators.

....

Giant Pacific Octopus

Enteroctopus dofleini (Wülker, 1910)

OTHER NAMES: Giant octopus, north Pacific giant octopus; formerly classified as *Octopus dofleini*.
DESCRIPTION: Color ranges widely from **reddish-brown to red**, often including reticulating black lines. Color changes according to mood and background color. A total of eight equal-sized arms are present as well as a large body and head. Prominent **paddle-shaped skin projections cover the body. No "eyelash" projections are found beneath the eyes.**
SIZE: Arms of subtidal individuals spread to 10′ (3 m) across. At least one individual

measured 32′ (9.6 m) across; the beachcomber can expect to see intertidal specimens reaching to 5′ (1.5 m) across.

HABITAT: In rocky areas and tidepools; low intertidal zone to depths of 4,950′ (1,500 m).

RANGE: Northern Alaska to northern México; Japan; Siberia.

NOTES: This octopus is the largest in the world, with one individual recorded at a weight of nearly 600 lb. (272 kg). The giant Pacific octopus is often shy by nature or inquisitive. It is well known for its rapid color changes, caused by the presence of large pigmentation cells that can match the color of the animal's background. This octopus is known to live to 5 years. If you find it on the beach, do not pick it up. It can deliver a nasty bite.

SIMILAR SPECIES: Pacific red octopus *Octopus rubescens* Berry, 1953 is a muddy brown-colored octopus that features 3 eyelash-like flaps beneath each eye. This is an uncommon intertidal species.

....

Opalescent Squid

Doryteuthis opalescens (Berry, 1911)

OTHER NAMES: Calamari, calamary, common squid, market squid, opal squid, opalescent squid, sea arrow; *Loligo opalescens*.

DESCRIPTION: The animal can change its colors from translucent white to mottled reddish-brown. As with all squid there are 8 arms and 2 specialized tentacles, which are shorter. The translucent white egg capsules increase in size as they age. Each egg cluster is elongated and normally attached to seaweed or other objects with several other clusters.

SIZE: Squid length to 11″ (28 cm); egg capsule length varies from 2.75″ (7 cm) on day 1 and 5.75″ (14.7 cm) on day 19.

HABITAT: Pelagic.

RANGE: Southern Alaska to northern México.

NOTES: It is unlikely that you will observe opalescent squid on shore. It is more likely that you may find its egg capsules washed up on shore, or perhaps observe them from a dock at night. Large numbers of this species mate and lay their eggs together. Once the egg laying is finished the adults perish. Each egg capsule contains between 50 to 300 eggs; it can take the young up to 5 weeks to emerge.

Common lampshell,
Terebratalia transversa

Lampshells
PHYLUM BRACHIOPODA

Lampshells look somewhat like clams and were once classified as molluscs, but are now known to be a separate phylum. All lampshells are marine filter-feeders that collect diatoms and detritus from the water with cilia. The animal is protected by 2 shells and attached to a substrate with a stalk. Fossil records indicate that there were once more than 30,000 species, but today only 325 species survive.

Common Lampshell

Terebratalia transversa (Sowerby, 1846)

OTHER NAMES: Common Pacific brachiopod, lamp shell, lampshell, scalloped lamp shell, transverse lamp shell; formerly classified as *Terebratalia caurina*.

DESCRIPTION: Color varies greatly from gray to yellow or red. The shells are hinged together and may display ribs. The valves are attached to rock by a fleshy stalk or pedicel.

SIZE: Shells to 2.25″ (5.6 cm) wide.

HABITAT: On rocks in clean, quiet water; low intertidal zone to depths of 6,000′ (1,820 m).

RANGE: Alaska to Baja California, México.

NOTES: This brachiopod is thought to resemble an Aladdin's lamp, hence its name. Its chief enemies are crabs, which chip away at the shell to reach a tender meal inside. Fortunately for the common lampshell, it is usually attached to a rock in a covered or hidden location. A full 10 years is required for this brachiopod to reach its maximum size.

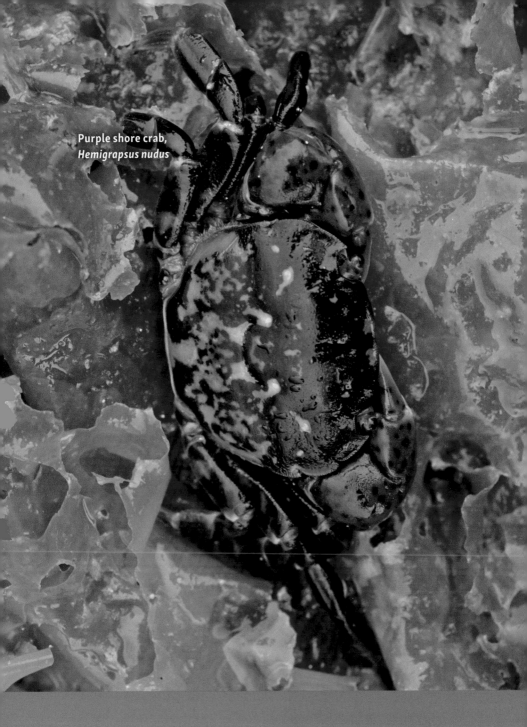

Purple shore crab,
Hemigrapsus nudus

Arthropods

PHYLUM ARTHROPODA

Arthropods are acclaimed to be the most widespread group of creatures in the animal kingdom. Marine arthropods include barnacles, isopods, amphipods, shrimps and crabs. All members of this large group, phylum Arthropoda, have "jointed limbs" and an exoskeleton, or a skeleton that covers their body like armor.

Arachnids
CLASS ARACHNIDA

This class contains spiders, mites, ticks and closely related species. Most adult members have eight legs. Additional appendages are used for feeding, reproduction and other activities. Their bodies are divided into two sections, and all species have an exoskeleton.

Red Velvet Mite
Neomolgus littoralis (Linnaeus, 1758)

OTHER NAMES: Red mite, intertidal mite.
DESCRIPTION: Color is red overall. The abdomen has several ridges on its dorsal side, and the legs have numerous hairs. The snout is noticeably elongated.
SIZE: Length to 0.1″ (2 mm).
HABITAT: On various shorelines; high intertidal to splash zone.
RANGE: Circumpolar; Alaska to Gulf of California; Arctic to Maine; Japan; Europe.

NOTES: Although the red velvet mite is small, it is an interesting arthropod to observe. With a hand lens, you will discover it is covered with tiny white hairs. It is one of the most widely distributed of all intertidal mites. This species does not avoid bright light. In fact, it is actively wandering about both day and night. It feeds on kelp flies, midges and occasionally dead insects. When the tide goes out, males deposit their stalked spermatophores on rock surfaces, which females later pick up.

Barnacles

CLASS CIRRIPEDIA

Barnacles have modified legs (cirri) that sweep through the water like a net to collect tiny planktonic food. Most species reach sexual maturity at approximately 80 days and their reproduction is unusual. Males may become females and vice versa at any time. To reproduce, the male must locate a female close enough for his penis to reach, as barnacles are unable to move from their substrate. The penis, however, can reach up to 20 times the length of the barnacle's body. All barnacles in the genus *Balanus* possess a calcareous base that leaves a white scar when knocked off the rock where it is living, an important fact to aid in identifying barnacles.

Little Brown Barnacle

Chthamalus dalli Pilsbry, 1916

OTHER NAMES: Little acorn barnacle, small acorn barnacle, brown buckshot barnacle, buckshot barnacle, small northern barnacle, Dall's barnacle, brown barnacle.
DESCRIPTION: The overall color is a uniform grayish-brown. A membranous (non-calcified) base is present. There is a relatively large central opening with a cross pattern where cover plates meet. The lateral edges of the rostrum are positioned above the adjacent plates, rather than beneath them as found in all species of *Balanus*.
SIZE: To 0.25" (6 mm) in diameter; 0.2" (4 mm) high.
HABITAT: On rocks of protected shores including bays; high intertidal zone.
RANGE: Unalaska Island, Alaska, to San Diego, California.
NOTES: The little brown barnacle is distinctive in that it does not crowd into spaces in such a way that produces elongated individuals. But under ideal conditions, it can reach populations of 60,300/yd² (72,000/m²). This species is known to grow higher on intertidal rocks than any other barnacle, so it must tolerate very long periods of exposure in the hot sun. Some individuals can lose up to 40 percent of the water in their bodies in less than 9 hours.

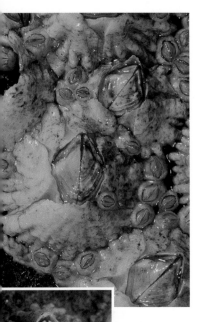

Northern Rock Barnacle

Semibalanus balanoides (Linnaeus, 1767)

OTHER NAMES: Rock barnacle; formerly classified as *Balanus balanoides*.

DESCRIPTION: The plates are grayish-white and smooth, with much folding. The shells are tubiferous (hollow chambers are present in a cross-section.) **The lateral plates overlap only one of the adjoining plates. No calcareous base is present.**

SIZE: To 0.6″ (15 mm) in diameter; 1″ (25 mm) high.

HABITAT: On rocks; mid-intertidal zone.

RANGE: Ketchikan, Alaska, to Washington (uncommon in Washington and British Columbia); Arctic Ocean to Cape Hatteras, North Carolina.

NOTES: The northern rock barnacle is a common species in the northern portion of its range. However, it is easily outcompeted for new space by the common acorn barnacle. This barnacle often makes its home where a stream or other freshwater source is located. It is interesting to note that its profile changes depending upon its site of attachment—at the top of a boulder it is flat and elsewhere it is conical, unless it is in a crowded situation in which it becomes nearly tubular. This likely occurs with most barnacle species.

SIMILAR SPECIES: Common acorn barnacle.

Thatched Barnacle

Semibalanus cariosus (Pallas, 1788)

OTHER NAMES: Thatched acorn barnacle, rock barnacle, horse barnacle; formerly classified as *Balanus cariosus*.

DESCRIPTION: Color white to gray overall. A membranous (non-calcified) base is present and **numerous downward-pointing spines cover the steep walls** of uncrowded individuals. The walls of the shells are very thick and porous.

SIZE: Uncrowded individuals to 2″ (5 cm) in diameter; 1.2″ (3 cm) high; in crowded situations to 1.4″ (3.5 cm) in diameter; 4″ (10 cm) high.
HABITAT: On rocks of exposed shorelines; mid-intertidal zone to shallow subtidal depths.
RANGE: Bering Sea and Aleutian Islands, Alaska, to California; Japan.
NOTES: The spines covering the walls of this barnacle give it a "thatched" look. This species often forms column-like shapes under crowded conditions, which makes it more difficult to identify. The purple star is the main predator and often limits

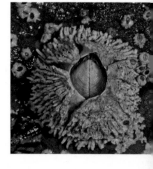

the depth to which this barnacle is found. Females are known to brood their young over the winter months and release them when spring arrives. Individuals can live for 10 to 15 years.

....

Common Acorn Barnacle

Balanus glandula Darwin, 1854

OTHER NAMES: Sharp acorn barnacle, acorn barnacle, white buckshot barnacle, common barnacle; formerly classified as *Balanus glandulus*.
DESCRIPTION: The white or gray shell is conical under normal conditions. **Each scutum displays a smudged black triangular pit** in small (young) specimens. The **shell has a calcified base**, as do all members of the genus *Balanus*.
SIZE: To 0.9″ (22 mm) in diameter; height to 0.5″ (13 mm).

Crowded conditions.

Smudged black triangles are visible on the scuta of this specimen.

HABITAT: On rocks, pilings, floats, ship bottoms and various hard-shelled animals in both exposed and protected sites; high and mid-intertidal zones.

RANGE: Aleutian Islands to Baja California, México.

NOTES: The common acorn barnacle is likely the most common species of intertidal barnacle found on the Pacific coast of North America. It often grows into elongated columns under crowded conditions, somewhat like the larger thatched barnacle. This barnacle produces between 2 and 6 broods per year during the cooler months, and each brood can contain as many as 30,000 young. Individuals reach adult size within 2 years and live to about 10 years, occasionally to 15 years.

SIMILAR SPECIES: Northern rock barnacle.

Crenate Barnacle

Balanus crenatus Brugiere, 1789

DESCRIPTION: The white to yellowish barnacle has a conical shape with a **squat profile** under normal conditions. This species features a **rhomboidal orifice** and the terga are rather short and blunt. The shell has a calcified base, like all members of the genus *Balanus*. Mature specimens have a crenate-like basal edge.

SIZE: To 0.8″ (20 mm) in diameter.

HABITAT: On shells of molluscs and crabs, ship bottoms and similar objects in protected shorelines; low intertidal zone to depths of 597′ (182 m).

RANGE: Alaska to Santa Barbara, California; Japan; North Atlantic.

NOTES: The crenate barnacle is a subtidal species that often attaches its shell on various shells of molluscs and arthropods that venture into the low intertidal zone. This too is the reason it often fouls the bottoms of boats. Its predators include the mottled star.

Rostrate Acorn Barnacle

Balanus rostratus Hoek, 1883

DESCRIPTION: Color is white. The shell is **conical with steep walls and rugged.** It lacks any ribbing and the **entire shell leans toward the carina** where the shell is nearly vertical.

SIZE: Normally to 1.2″ (3 cm) in diameter; occasionally to 2″ (5 cm).

HABITAT: On rocks and shells of molluscs; low intertidal zone to depths of 1,115′ (338 m).

RANGE: Aleutian Islands, Alaska, to Puget Sound, Washington; Japan.

NOTES: The rostrate acorn barnacle is known as a variable species. It is much more common at subtidal levels than in the intertidal zone.

Giant Acorn Barnacle

Balanus nubilus Darwin, 1854

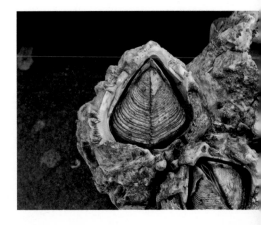

OTHER NAMES: Giant barnacle, horse barnacle; occasionally misspelled *Balanus nubilis.*

DESCRIPTION: Exterior is a dirty white color with **bright purple, yellow or red tissue near the beak-like central plates.** A calcified base is present that displays a large, flaring central opening (aperture). The casings are often eroded.

SIZE: To 3.1″ (8 cm) in diameter, 4.9″ (12 cm) high.

HABITAT: On rocks, docks or pilings; mid-intertidal zone to water 300′ (91 m) deep.

RANGE: Alaska to Baja California, México.

NOTES: The giant acorn barnacle is sometimes observable while attached to pilings and

With feeding cirri visible.

rocks in the low intertidal zone. The feeding appendages reach out a full 2″ (5 cm) or more with sweeping movements in an effort to feed. This action can sometimes be observed even while the barnacle is out of water. Barnacle casings are sometimes found on beaches after being tossed there during winter storms. Coastal Indigenous people traditionally roasted giant acorn barnacles in embers as a food source. This is one of the largest barnacles in the world!

Hydrocoral Barnacle

Solidobalanus engbergi (Pilsbry, 1921)

OTHER NAME: Formerly classified as *Balanus engbergi*.
DESCRIPTION: The white shell is **steep-walled and displays deep furrows**. It is very often **covered with the hydrocoral it is growing on**. Its small orifice is oval.
SIZE: To 0.75″ (20 mm) in diameter.
HABITAT: Almost always associated with hydrocorals; low intertidal zone and subtidal depths.

RANGE: Alaska to Seal Rocks, Oregon.
NOTES: The hydrocoral barnacle is primarily a subtidal species that is found on or encased in hydrocoral, just as its common name suggests. At times it is very nearly completely encased with this species. This barnacle is normally found in association with the purple encrusting hydrocoral at intertidal sites.

Goose Barnacle

Pollicipes polymerus Sowerby, 1833

OTHER NAMES: Goose-neck barnacle, goose neck barnacle, leaf barnacle, Pacific goose barnacle, stalked barnacle; formerly classified as *Mitella polymerus*.
DESCRIPTION: Barnacles in this group are composed of two parts: the capitulum (head) and the peduncle (stalk). The plates on the **capitulum are chalky white and the peduncle is dark brown and covered with small calcareous scales**.
SIZE: Total length to 6″ (15 cm).
HABITAT: On rocks or similar hard objects; high intertidal zone to depths of 100′ (30 m).
RANGE: Southeast Alaska to Punta Abreojos, Baja California, México.
NOTES: The presence of this species indicates you are in an area subject to harsh ocean waves. Each year mature goose barnacles can produce 3–7 broods, each with approximately 100,000 to 240,000 larvae per brood. The goose barnacle is edible and has been exported from North America to Europe as a delicacy. Birds, including surfbirds (*Aphriza virgata*), Western gulls (*Larus occidentalis*) and Glaucous-winged gulls (*Larus glaucescens*), find this a tasty species and can consume it in large numbers.

....

Smooth Pelagic Goose Barnacle

Lepas anatifera Linnaeus, 1758

OTHER NAMES: Blue goose barnacle, common goose barnacle, goose neck barnacle, pelagic barnacle, pelagic goose-neck barnacle, pelagic stalked barnacle.
DESCRIPTION: Barnacles in this group are composed of two parts: the capitulum (head) and the peduncle (stalk). The plates on the **capitulum vary from white to pale blue, edged with a wide, bright orange band, and the stalk is dark purplish-brown**. No spines are present on the capitulum. The plates are smooth without ridges. The peduncle is long, dark, flexible and rubber-like, and able to attach to hard surfaces.
SIZE: Total length to 8″ (20 cm).
HABITAT: Normally on driftwood, floating in the

open ocean. Small individuals are sometimes found attached to seaweed, stranded on the beach.

RANGE: Cosmopolitan: Alaska to South America.

NOTES: This gregarious barnacle is a creature of the high seas. The young are attracted to floating objects, which become home to hundreds or thousands of these barnacles. Once the "colonies" have been afloat for some time, they mature and produce their young. To locate this species, walk on the beach after a storm and look for a stranded float, bottle or log on which these barnacles have settled.

Isopods
ORDER ISOPODA

Scavenging Isopod

Cirolana harfordi (Lockington, 1877)

OTHER NAMES: Dark-backed isopod, dark-backed rock louse, Harford's greedy isopod, marine pillbug, swimming isopod.

DESCRIPTION: The color is variable from gray or black to tan with a two-toned pattern. The body is **oval shaped with a triangular terminal segment as well as a pair of two-part, paddle-like appendages that create a fan at the tail**.

SIZE: Length to 0.75″ (19 mm).

HABITAT: Under rocks, between barnacles and in mussel beds; mid-intertidal zone to subtidal depths.

RANGE: British Columbia to Baja California, México.

NOTES: The scavenging isopod is an opportunist that eats various segmented worms, amphipods or any other dead organisms, locating its food by chemoreception. It is well known for its ability to consume great quantities of food in a short period of time and often occurs in great numbers.

Oregon Pill Bug

Gnorimosphaeroma oregonensis (Dana, 1853)

OTHER NAMES: Pill-bug, stubby isopod.
DESCRIPTION: The coloration is normally gray
to black overall, often with white mottling.
The body is **oval in shape with an anterior
pair of antennae separated at the base.** The
terminal segment is rounded and not separated
into lobes.
SIZE: Length to 0.4″ (10 mm).
HABITAT: Under rocks, algae and driftwood;
mid- to low intertidal zone.
RANGE: Alaska to Monterey Bay, California.
NOTES: The Oregon pill bug is often one of the most common, and at times abundant,
intertidal species that can be encountered on our seashores. This species is capable of
protogynous (female to male) sex change. Females are capable of having a brood then
moult a number of times before changing into sexually mature males.

Smooth-tailed Isopod

Dynamenella glabra (Richardson, 1899)

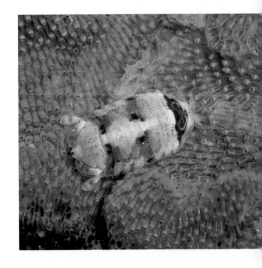

OTHER NAME: Formerly classified as
Dynamene glabra.
DESCRIPTION: Color is variable,
frequently cream to gray. This species has
a short body that is ovate with a smooth
surface and small head. The **terminal
segment is smooth with no tubercles or
ridges present**.
SIZE: Length to approximately 0.3″ (8 mm).
HABITAT: On various surfaces; low
intertidal zone to depths of 230′ (70 m).
RANGE: British Columbia to San Diego,
California.
NOTES: This is one of several small species of isopods that may be encountered. There are
no obvious differences between the sexes other than that the males are larger.

Pencil Isopod

Idotea fewkesi Richardson, 1905

OTHER NAME: Fewke's isopod.
DESCRIPTION: Coloration of this species varies greatly. The **elongated body is made up of several segments that are all equal in width. The terminal segment has an elongated central portion of the tip.**
SIZE: Length to 1.7″ (4 cm).
HABITAT: On algae on outer rocky shorelines; low intertidal zone to depths of 35′ (11 m).
RANGE: Alaska to central California.
NOTES: The pencil isopod has been found to reproduce during the summer and autumn months in California. This is one of the more distinctive isopods that may be encountered at the seashore.

Shouldered Isopod

Idotea urotoma Stimpson, 1864

OTHER NAMES: Formerly classified as *Idotea rectiline*; ocassionally misspelled *Idotea rectilineata*.
DESCRIPTION: Coloration is extremely variable, often with more than one color. The body is **slender and elongated with a spade-shaped terminal segment displaying a blunt tooth in the center.**
SIZE: Length to 0.6″ (15 mm).
HABITAT: Beneath rocks, often with encrusted bryozoans on exposed rocky shores; mid-intertidal zone to depths of 46′ (14 m).
RANGE: Puget Sound, Washington, to Baja California, México.
NOTES: The many colors that this species exhibits are truly amazing, and there does not seem to be any reason for this variability. Researchers have found that the northern clingfish is one of its predators. It is likely, however, that other species of fish prey upon this isopod at subtidal levels.

Monterey Isopod

Pentidotea montereyensis Maloney, 1933

DESCRIPTION: Color ranges widely from green to red, or brown, often including patterns of black and white. The **body is elongated to 4 times the width**. The **end of the terminal segment forms a slightly rounded and tapering central point**.

SIZE: Length to 0.6″ (15 mm).

HABITAT: On various red algae and surfgrass of exposed rocky shorelines; mid-intertidal zone to depths of 365′ (110 m).

RANGE: Central Alaska to Point Conception, Santa Barbara County, California.

NOTES: Research has found that this species is a master of color change. It is capable of matching its environment with the use of various pigments present in its cuticle. Different pigments match red substrates or green ones. If it changes its substrate it will mold its cuticle to change its color.

SIMILAR SPECIES: Vosnesensky's isopod.

Eelgrass Isopod

Pentidotea resecata Stimpson, 1857

OTHER NAMES: Concave isopod, cut-tailed isopod, kelp isopod, seaweed isopod, transparent isopod; formerly classified as *Idothea resecata, Pentidotea resecata*.

DESCRIPTION: Two color variations are commonly encountered—green and yellow-brown. The body is elongated with a slight widening in the center. **The outer edges of the terminal segment are elongated to points**.

SIZE: Length to 1.6″ (4 cm).

HABITAT: On eelgrass and brown algae; low intertidal zone to depths of 60′ (19 m).

RANGE: Prince William Sound, Alaska, to Mazatlan, México.

NOTES: Despite its name, the eelgrass isopod is found on a variety of algae as well as common eelgrass. The reverse is also true, with several species of isopods living on eelgrass. The color variability of this species is due to its habitat selection and its environment.

Small-eyed Isopod

Pentidotea stenops (Benedict, 1898)

OTHER NAMES: Featherboa isopod; formerly classified as *Idotea stenops*.

DESCRIPTION: Color varies from olive-green to reddish-brown. Body is oblong-ovate. A rectangular terminal segment has an acute point that is centrally located. **Its distinctive eyes are very elongated** (width is 5 times the height) **and small in relation to the body size.**

SIZE: Length to 2.4″ (6 cm).

HABITAT: Under rocks and boulders or on various algae, especially feather boa kelp; mid-intertidal zone to shallow subtidal depths.

RANGE: Alaska to Punta Eugenia, Baja California, México.

NOTES: The small-eyed isopod is our largest isopod. This species has been found in the stomach of at least one species of fish. Even though it is large, this isopod is not found very often. Its colors seem to work very well in keeping it camouflaged, especially on feather boa kelp, one of its favorite habitats.

SIMILAR SPECIES: Vosnesensky's isopod.

Vosnesensky's Isopod

Pentidotea wosnesenskii (Brandt, 1851)

OTHER NAMES: Green isopod, kelp isopod, olive green isopod, rockweed isopod, round-tailed isopod; formerly classified as *Idotea wosnesenskii*.

DESCRIPTION: Color ranges widely from green to red, as well as brown and black. **The body is robust and elongated, about 3 times the width.** The terminal segment is rounded with a tiny tooth at the tip.

SIZE: Length to 1.6″ (4 cm).

HABITAT: On various seaweeds, under rocks and in mussel beds; high intertidal zone to depths of 52′ (16 m).

RANGE: Prince William Sound, Alaska, to San Luis Obispo County, California; Sea of Okhotsk, Russia.

NOTES: Vosnesensky's isopod is very well adapted for living among seaweed and rocks. It is a master of disguise, usually cryptically colored and difficult to find. Algae are the mainstay of its diet. This isopod was named in recognition of the work that the Russian zoologist Ilya Gavrilovich Vosnesensky conducted in Siberia, Alaska and California.

Sea Slater

Ligia pallasii Brandt, 1833

OTHER NAMES: Northern sea roach, rock louse, sea roach.
DESCRIPTION: Color varies from gray-brown to slate gray with various mottling. The body is ovate and flat with 7 thoracic segments. The length of the **forked tail appendages (uropods) are short, reaching approximately half the width of the animal.** Each uropod has a basal segment that is almost as long as it is wide. The males are larger and broader than the females.
SIZE: Length to 1.5″ (3.7 cm).
HABITAT: On and under rocks, on cave walls and cliffs of both exposed and protected shores; splash and spray intertidal zones.
RANGE: Aleutian Islands, Alaska, to Santa Cruz County, California.
NOTES: The sea slater is a nocturnal isopod that favors cool and moist habitats. Often individuals are found that have undergone only half of their molting—the rear half of the body is noticeably narrower than the front. After a few days this condition will be restored to normal as the moult is completed. The sea slater feeds on algae and dead plant matter. Its predators include gulls and the striped shore crab.
SIMILAR SPECIES: Western sea roach.

Western Sea Roach

Ligia occidentalis (Dana, 1853)

OTHER NAME: Rock louse.
DESCRIPTION: The color varies from gray to yellow-brown. It is also paler at night, becoming darker during daylight hours. The body is ovate and flat with 7 thoracic segments. The **uropods are long, reaching about the same length as the width of the animal.**

Juvenile.

Each uropod has a basal segment that is much longer than it is wide.

SIZE: Length to 1″ (2.5 cm).

HABITAT: Under rocks and in crevices; spray to high intertidal zone.

RANGE: Southern British Columbia to Central America.

NOTES: The western sea roach is the cockroach of the seashore. This essentially terrestrial species was thought to be found only as far north as southern Oregon. The adult pictured here is one of numerous individuals that were found by the author in southern British Columbia. This is either a large-range extension for the species or perhaps an isolated population that has found a haven at this location.

SIMILAR SPECIES: Sea slater.

Mud Shrimp Parasitic Isopod ⓘ

Orthione griffenis Markham, 2004

OTHER NAMES: Griffen's isopod, mudshrimp parasitic isopod; occasionally misspelled Griffon's isopod.

DESCRIPTION: The male is cream-colored and the female is two-toned cream with yellow-brown to pink. Males are elongated and grub-like with a terminal segment that has a slightly pointed end. Females are ovoid to round in shape and many times larger than males.

SIZE: Length of females to 0.8″ (20 mm); males to 0.4″ (10 mm).

HABITAT: **Parasitic on the blue mud shrimp living on sand and mud beaches**; mid- to low intertidal zone.

RANGE: British Columbia to Baja California, México; China; Japan.

NOTES: The mud shrimp parasitic isopod was first discovered on the Pacific coast of North America in 1988. Since that time it has spread across much of the Pacific coast. It is a parasite of the blue mud shrimp. This parasite is an invader from China that appears to castrate males and prevent the reproduction of its host. Numbers of blue mud shrimp have dropped dramatically since this parasite's arrival in Oregon.

Amphipods
ORDER AMPHIPODA

....

California Beach Hopper

Megalorchestia californiana Brand, 1851

OTHER NAMES: California beach flea,
long-horned beach hopper; formerly
classified as *Orchestoidea californiana*.
DESCRIPTION: Coloration is ivory-white.
Immature individuals display a dark
butterfly-like pattern and dark mid-dorsal
line on their dorsal side. The body is ovate
and generally heavy. The **antennae are red
in adults, orange in juveniles, and longer
than the body**.
SIZE: Length to 1.6″ (4 cm).
HABITAT: On fine sandy beaches of exposed shores; high intertidal zone and higher.
RANGE: Vancouver Island, British Columbia, to Laguna Beach, Orange County, California.
NOTES: The California beach hopper is one of many beach hoppers that can be found on
our sandy beaches. This large species is distinctive, however, with its colorful, immense
antennae. They dig burrows that sometimes reach 2′ (60 cm) and are elliptical in cross
section. A plug closes the burrow's entrance.

....

Blue-horned Beach Hopper

Megalorchestia columbiana (Bousfield, 1958)

OTHER NAMES: Pale beach hopper; formerly classified as *Orchestoidea columbiana*.
DESCRIPTION: Color of the body varies from cream to light blue. **Large antennae are
bluish**. The body is not armed with spines on the segment margins.
SIZE: Length to 0.75″ (18 mm).
HABITAT: On sandy beaches on the outer coast; high intertidal zone.
RANGE: Aleutian Islands, Alaska, to central California.

NOTES: The blue-horned beach hopper is a common species that is easy to observe on sandy beaches. It energetically digs its burrows first in one direction, throwing sand onto the beach, then turns 180 degrees to do the same in the opposite direction. No mounds are present at the burrow entrance.

Pink Beach Hopper

Maera danae (Stimpson, 1853)

OTHER NAMES: Beach hopper; formerly classified as *Leptothoe danae*.
DESCRIPTION: Color is pink overall, with small black eyes. The first antennae are noticeably longer than the second antennae and nearly half the body length. The telson is deeply bilobed—each lobe bears many setae (bristles).
SIZE: Length to 0.75″ (18 mm).
HABITAT: Among rocks and gravel, often when mud has accumulated; low intertidal zone to water 328′ (100 m) deep.
RANGE: Point Barrow, Alaska, to Monterey Bay, California; Gulf of St. Lawrence to Cape Cod; Siberia.
NOTES: This colorful amphipod is one of the more common species found in the low intertidal zone. Female pink beach hoppers carry their eggs from March to May along the Atlantic Coast of the United States. Their lifespan is likely one or two years.

Skeleton Shrimp

Caprella spp. Lamarck, 1801

OTHER NAME: Phantom shrimp.
DESCRIPTION: Color is variable from green to brown. The **elongated body bears 4 pairs of leg-like appendages and grasping claws.**
SIZE: Length to 2″ (5 cm).

HABITAT: On hydroids, eelgrass and seaweed near the low-tide level and below in shallow water.
RANGE: Aleutian Islands, Alaska, to central California.
NOTES: The skeleton shrimp is not a shrimp at all, but an amphipod. These active creatures feed upon tiny plants and animals. Females with obvious brood pouches can sometimes be found. The pouches are located on the third and fourth thoracic segments, as are the gills.

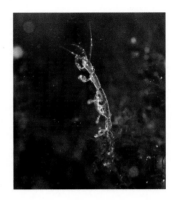

Shrimps & Crabs
ORDER DECAPODA

Smooth Bay Shrimp

Lissocrangon stylirostris (Holmes, 1900)

OTHER NAMES: Smooth crangon; formerly classified as *Crangon stylirostris*.
DESCRIPTION: The color is light brown to gray with mottling to exactly match its environment. The body is very "stocky" overall with a **carapace that has no central dorsal spine**.
SIZE: Length to 2.4″ (6 cm).
HABITAT: On wave-swept beaches with high energy; surf zone to depths of 156′ (47 m).
RANGE: Unalaska Island, Alaska, to Bahía Todos Santos, Baja California, México.
NOTES: This species can be separated from several members of the genus *Crangon* by its lack of a dorsal spine on the carapace. This shrimp is capable of lightning-fast movements, aiding it in avoiding predators. Watch carefully and you will notice that this species prefers to bury itself in the sand whenever possible. It can hide itself almost completely by pushing sand over its body with its long antennae, leaving only a tiny portion of its head uncovered. Very small clams and crustaceans form the bulk of this species' diet.

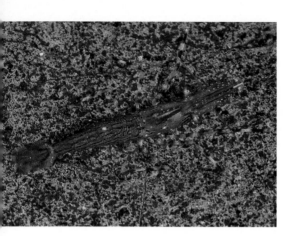

Dock Shrimp

Pandalus danae Stimpson, 1857

OTHER NAMES: Coonstripe.
DESCRIPTION: Color varies from tan to dark brown and red, frequently with brilliant blue spots. The **abdomen features broken diagonal stripes**.
SIZE: Length to 5.5″ (14 cm).
HABITAT: On rocks and algae; low intertidal zone to depths of 863′ (263 m).
RANGE: Alaskan Peninsula to Point Loma, California.
NOTES: The dock shrimp is often seen on dock pilings, which influences its common name. This species hides by day among algae or in rock crevices. At night it ventures out to feed upon a variety of marine annelid worms. The pattern on its abdomen is distinctive.

....

Stout Shrimp

Heptacarpus brevirostris (Dana, 1852)

OTHER NAMES: Shortspine shrimp, shortspined shrimp, stout coastal shrimp.
DESCRIPTION: Body colors vary widely from various browns or greens to orange and red, with stripes, patterns or mottling of white. The **rostrum is short, with the tip projecting just barely past the eye**. Several tiny spines are present at the basal portion of the first antenna.
SIZE: Length to 2.4″ (6 cm).
HABITAT: In tidepools; low intertidal zone to depths of 420′ (128 m).
RANGE: Attu, Aleutian Islands, Alaska, to Tanner Bank, California.
NOTES: This is one of the common species of *Heptacarpus* shrimp that beachcombers encounter. It is often difficult to identify the species found. The stout shrimp is one of the larger intertidal species and the most likely to be observed in tidepools if you watch carefully and wait patiently—these shrimp hide by day and may not move for extended periods of time. Stout shrimp are active by night when they come out to feed in tidepools.
SIMILAR SPECIES: Shorthorn shrimp.

Shorthorn Shrimp

Heptacarpus taylori (Stimpson, 1857)

OTHER NAMES: Shortnose shrimp, Taylor coastal shrimp.
DESCRIPTION: Body colors vary widely from reddish-brown or green with a mottling of color or a carapace that is white. **The rostrum is very short, not projecting past the eye.** A single spine is present at the basal portion of the first antenna.
SIZE: Length to 1.1″ (2.8 cm).
HABITAT: Under rocks, among algae, in tidepools and on pilings on exposed shorelines; low intertidal zone to depths of 42′ (13 m).
RANGE: Olympic Peninsula, Washington, to Bahía Magdalena, Baja California Sur, México.
NOTES: The shorthorn shrimp is a common shrimp that is more often found in the southern portion of its range.
SIMILAR SPECIES: Stout shrimp.

Barred Shrimp

Heptacarpus pugettensis Jensen, 1983

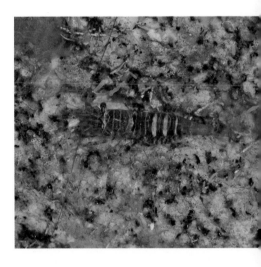

DESCRIPTION: Body coloration is translucent overall with **3 wide greenish-yellow bars located on the ventral abdomen. The dorsal surface is adorned with stripes of red and yellow.** The rostrum is short, projecting to the end of the eye.
SIZE: Length to 0.8″ (20 mm).
HABITAT: Under rocks; very low intertidal zone to depths of 60′ (18 m).
RANGE: Sitka, Alaska, to Morro Bay, California.
NOTES: The barred shrimp is a small species that is distinctively colored with its barring. It is shy and prefers to hide in daylight. It also responds to being uncovered from beneath a rock by simply clinging to the rock rather than jumping off to escape like most shrimp do.

Sitka Shrimp

Heptacarpus sitchensis (Brandt, 1851)

OTHER NAMES: Common coastal shrimp, red-banded transparent shrimp, Sitka coastal shrimp; formerly classified as *Heptacarpus picta*.
DESCRIPTION: The abdomen color varies from bright green to dark brown. The carapace is all white or marked with diagonal red lines. The entire body can be transparent when algae numbers are low. The **rostrum is shorter than the remainder of its carapace.**
SIZE: Length to 1.3″ (3.3 cm),
HABITAT: In gravel and sand beaches as well as eelgrass areas and under rocks; mid-intertidal zone to depths of 40′ (12 m).
RANGE: Resurrection Bay, Alaska, to Cabo Thurloe, Baja California, México.
NOTES: Female Sitka shrimp have been seen carrying their eggs during May, June and September. Transparent individuals can be found when algae are rather scarce. The males are much smaller in size than females and were once classified as a separate species, Heptacarpus littoralis.

Smalleyed Shrimp

Heptacarpus carinatus Holmes, 1900

OTHER NAMES: Small-eyed coastal shrimp, smalleye coastal shrimp, smalleye shrimp.
DESCRIPTION: Body color ranges from bright green to red, often with a white dorsal stripe. Specimens living among dark, small perennial kelp or giant perennial kelp are also dark brown and covered with tiny turquoise spots. The **rostrum is very long** with its dorsal half lacking teeth. **The eyes are noticeably small.**
SIZE: Length to 2.3″ (6 cm).
HABITAT: In tidepools and shallow waters near surfgrass or algae on exposed shorelines; low intertidal zone to depths of 90′ (27 m).
RANGE: Dixon Harbor, Alaska, to Point Loma, California.

NOTES: The smalleyed shrimp is a distinctive species that is often found among surfgrass and algae and in tidepools along the exposed coast. Its body colors closely match that of the surrounding vegetation. It is often found in the company of several other shrimps. As with many shrimp species, the female is larger than the male.

Blue Mud Shrimp

Upogebia pugettensis (Dana, 1852)

OTHER NAMES: Marine crayfish, mud shrimp, Puget Sound ghost shrimp.

DESCRIPTION: Body **coloration varies from gray to blue-gray.** There is a prominent rostrum with a rounded front. **Two equal-sized claws are present**. The walking legs and claws are covered in fine hairs.

SIZE: Length normally to 3.9″ (10 cm); occasionally to 6″ (15 cm).

HABITAT: On mud and sandy mud beaches at sheltered sites; low intertidal zone to depths of 67′ (20 m).

RANGE: Sawmill Bay (near Valdez), Alaska, to Morro Bay, California.

NOTES: Although this species has the common name of blue mud shrimp, it is rarely found in the blue color phase. A pair of blue mud shrimp live in a permanent Y-shaped burrow. They continually fan water through their burrow to obtain microscopic food. Hairs on the first two pairs of legs are used to strain this food from the water. In the fall these shrimp lay yellow eggs, which develop slowly and hatch in the spring. Entrances to their burrows lack the distinctive volcano shape of the bay ghost shrimp's burrow. Numerous species live with this species in its burrow, including the mud shrimp clam and the newly introduced mud shrimp parasitic isopod.

SIMILAR SPECIES: Bay ghost shrimp.

The blue mud shrimp's burrow partially excavated.

Bay Ghost Shrimp

Neotrypaea californiensis (Dana, 1854)

OTHER NAMES: California ghost shrimp, ghost shrimp, pink sand shrimp, pink mud shrimp, red ghost shrimp, sand shrimp; formerly classified as *Callianassa californiensis*.
DESCRIPTION: Body **color varies from orange or pink**, often with a yellow tint. **One claw is much larger than the other, especially in the male**, and it is white. There is a big gap in the larger claw.
SIZE: Length to 4.8″ (12 cm).
HABITAT: In sand and mud on sheltered beaches; high to low intertidal zone and possibly to depths of 85′ (26 m).
RANGE: Mutiny Bay, Alaska, to Bahía de San Quintin, Baja California, México.
NOTES: The bay ghost shrimp may live to 10 years in its Y-shaped burrow. A characteristic volcano-shaped mound indicates each burrow entrance. These non-permanent burrows may be as deep as 30″ (75 cm). At least 9 different tenant species are known to live in the burrows while the owner is present. This shrimp lays its eggs in the spring and the female carries them until they hatch from June through August.
SIMILAR SPECIES: Blue mud shrimp.

 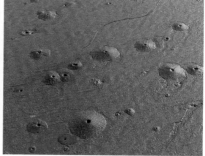

A pair, including male with large pincer above.   The distinctive burrows of this species.

Pacific Red Hermit

Elassochirus gilli (Benedict, 1892)

OTHER NAMES: Red hermit crab, orange hermit; formerly classified as *Eupagurus gilli*.
DESCRIPTION: Color of **body overall is a uniform red or orange**. Its carapace has a smooth surface and its right claw is enlarged.

SIZE: Carapace length to 1.5″ (3.8 cm).
HABITAT: In rocky areas with good currents; low intertidal zone to depths of 656′ (200 m).
RANGE: Pribilof Islands, Alaska, to Puget Sound, Washington; Bering Island to the Sea of Japan.
NOTES: Viewing the vivid color of this striking hermit will make any trip to the seashore a special treat! In Alaska it often uses the shells of the Aleutian moonsnail as its home. Little is known about its diet or other natural history details.

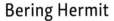

Gold Ring Hermit

Pagurus hemphilli (Benedict, 1892)

OTHER NAMES: Maroon hermit; formerly classified as *Eupagurus hemphilli.*
DESCRIPTION: Color of the body is a uniform dark red or red overall with granules of red or blue. The **eyes are distinctive with gold rings highlighting the cornea**.
SIZE: Carapace length to 1″ (2.5 cm).
HABITAT: On rocky shorelines of the open coast; low intertidal zone to depths of 165′ (50 m).
RANGE: Klokachef Island, Alaska, to Diablo Cove, California.
NOTES: This hermit is striking in appearance with its dark reddish coloration and its unique eyes! No other species can be confused with it. It often makes its home from the shells of top snails and turban snails like the one pictured here, the dusky turban.

Bering Hermit

Pagurus beringanus (Benedict, 1892)

OTHER NAMES: Bering hermit crab; formerly classified as *Eupagurus newcombei, Pagurus newcombei.*
DESCRIPTION: The **walking legs of adults are pale blue or green to white and highlighted**

with red spots and banding. Juveniles are yellowish overall with legs that are adorned with a dark band. The right claw is much larger than the left.

SIZE: Carapace length to 1″ (2.5 cm).

HABITAT: Near rock formations of protected or semi-protected shores; low intertidal zone to depths of 1,193′ (364 m).

RANGE: Amchitka Island, Alaska, to Monterey, California.

NOTES: The Bering hermit adds a splash of color to the low intertidal zone. It tends to use large, heavy shells, such as frilled dogwinkle and dire whelk, in which it can hide completely inside. During low tides this species is often attracted to shady rock crevices.

SIMILAR SPECIES: Grainyhand hermit.

Blueband Hermit

Pagurus samuelis (Stimpson, 1857)

OTHER NAMES: Blue-clawed hermit crab, blueband hermit crab, blue-handed hermit crab.

DESCRIPTION: Walking legs are a dull green with **bright blue bands near the tips**. Young have white bands on walking legs. **Antennae are bright red and unbanded**.

SIZE: Carapace length to 0.75″ (19 mm).

HABITAT: In outer coast situations near rocks, often in tidepools; high intertidal zone.

RANGE: Nootka Sound, British Columbia, to Baja California, México.

NOTES: The blueband hermit eats both plant and animal material. Most feeding activity occurs during the darkness of night. This hermit crab usually uses the abandoned shells of the black turban and striped dogwinkle. Shells constantly change ownership in the world of hermit crabs. As a crab grows, it is ever watchful for a new shell, even if that shell is currently being used by a neighboring hermit.

SIMILAR SPECIES: Hairy hermit.

Grainyhand Hermit

Pagurus granosimanus (Stimpson, 1859)

OTHER NAMES: Grainy hermit crab, grainyhand hermit crab, granular hermit crab, hermit crab; formerly classified as *Eupagurus granosimanus*.

DESCRIPTION: Body overall is dull green in color, with **blue or whitish spots or granules. Antennae are orange or red and unbanded.** Juveniles are yellow (or pale) with the merus of the claw dark.

SIZE: Carapace length to 0.75″ (19 mm).

HABITAT: In rocky, gravel and sandy areas and tidepools of protected shores; mid-intertidal zone to depths of 118′ (36 m).

RANGE: Unalaska Island, Alaska, to Ensenada, Baja California, México.

NOTES: This common species recycles larger empty shells such as the black turban and frilled dogwinkle. The antics of this hermit crab, the clown of

the seashore, can often be observed in tidepools. It reacts to the slightest movement by withdrawing into its shell, then falls and rolls to the bottom of its home, at which time it comes back out to do it all over again. This species is found lower intertidally than the hairy hermit crab.

....

Greenmark Hermit

Pagurus caurinus Hart, 1971

OTHER NAME: Greenmark hermit crab.

DESCRIPTION: **The walking legs have conspicuous white bands** without any blue markings. **The antennae are orange and unbanded** and the claws have orange tips.

SIZE: Carapace length to 0.4″ (10 mm).

HABITAT: In sandy and rocky sites of both exposed and sheltered locations; low intertidal zone to depths of 413′ (126 m).

RANGE: Port Gravina, Alaska, to San Pedro, California.

NOTES: This common hermit crab is often overlooked due to its small size, or thought to be the hairy hermit. The red antennae and absence of blue on the walking legs of the greenmark hermit crab help to confirm its identity.

SIMILAR SPECIES: Hairy hermit.

Hairy Hermit

Pagurus hirsutiusculus (Dana, 1851)

OTHER NAMES: Hairy hermit crab, hairy-legged hermit crab, little hairy hermit crab.
DESCRIPTION: Walking legs have a **conspicuous white band on lower portion of each leg** and a blue spot on upper portion of the same segment. Juveniles bear more white bands on the claws and legs. The **brownish antennae have several white bands**. Much of the crab is **often covered with hair**.
SIZE: Carapace length to 1.25″ (3.2 cm).
HABITAT: In tidepools with rock bottoms, in protected rocky areas; high to mid-intertidal zone.
RANGE: Pribilof Islands, Alaska, to Monterey, California; Japan.
NOTES: The hairy hermit chooses a variety of empty shells, including striped dogwinkle, purple olive and occasionally those of various turbans *Tegula* spp. This hermit often abandons its shell altogether after it has been picked up. This provides an excellent opportunity to see the entire body, normally hidden inside the shell, particularly the soft, coiled abdomen.

Pacific Mole Crab

Emerita analoga (Stimpson, 1857)

OTHER NAMES: Sand crab, common sand crab, mole crab, Pacific sand crab; formerly classified as *Hippa analoga*.
DESCRIPTION: External color varies from gray to light brown. The **body is a distinctive egg shape**. Its shell is smooth, and the legs are flattened and without claws.
SIZE: Carapace length to 1.33″ (3.3 cm).
HABITAT: On open sandy beaches; high to low intertidal zones.
RANGE: Kodiak, Alaska, to Bahía Magdalena, Baja California Sur, México.
NOTES: This crab burrows into the sand backwards so that only its head and antennae are exposed at the surface. It uses its long, feathery antennae to catch plankton and detritus, its primary food. If disturbed, these crabs disappear into the sand in mere seconds—truly

amazing to watch. Temporary populations have been found north of Oregon. These only begin when larvae reach new sites via ocean currents, then individuals successfully grow to maturity but cannot reproduce, and the colony eventually disappears.

Thick-clawed Porcelain Crab

Pachycheles rudis Stimpson, 1859

This individual is missing one claw.

OTHER NAMES: Big-claw porcelain crab, lumpy porcelain crab, thick clawed porcelain crab, rough mottled porcelain crab, thick clawed crab.
DESCRIPTION: Overall color varies from dull brown or gray to white (juveniles). The **carapace** is roughly square in shape **with a rough, granular surface.** The **claws are unequal, also with a granular surface** and scattered hairs.
SIZE: Carapace to 0.75″ (19 mm) wide.
HABITAT: Under rocks, in rock crevices and holes, in kelp holdfasts and empty shells of the giant acorn barnacle; low intertidal zone to depths of 96′ (29 m).
RANGE: Kodiak, Alaska, to Bahía Magdalena, Baja California Sur, México.
NOTES: This crab uses its specialized mouthparts to filter out plankton and other microscopic food from the water. Unlike many types of crabs, males and females of this species grow to the same size, and live in pairs in a variety of situations around rock.

Flat Porcelain Crab

Petrolisthes cinctipes (Randall, 1840)

OTHER NAMES: Porcelain crab, smooth porcelain crab.
DESCRIPTION: Carapace color ranges from light brown to reddish-brown and blue. Carapace is flat and nearly circular, with long whip-like antennae. **The mouthparts are red** and there is a **red spot at the base of the movable part of each claw.** The **carpus of the claw appears broad** as its length is about 1.5 times its width.
SIZE: Carapace to 0.9″ (24 mm) wide.

HABITAT: Beneath rocks and in California mussel beds on the outer shores; high to low intertidal zones.

RANGE: Porcher Island, British Columbia, to Santa Barbara, California.

NOTES: This crab is sometimes found in high numbers in beds of the California mussel. In some ideal locations, they have been calculated to reach 3,304 individuals per square yard (3,933 per m²). This crab, like all porcelain crabs, sheds its brittle claws or legs easily when it feels threatened. The missing appendages grow back after several molts.

SIMILAR SPECIES: Flattop crab.

Flattop Crab

Petrolisthes eriomerus Stimpson, 1871

OTHER NAMES: Blue-mouth crab, flat-topped crab, porcelain crab, porcellanid crab.

DESCRIPTION: Overall color ranges from brown to blue. Carapace is flat and nearly circular, with long whip-like antennae. **Mouthparts are blue** and there is **a blue spot at the base of the movable part of each claw.** The **carpus of claw appears narrow** as its length is about 2 times its width. **Outer edges of the carpus run parallel** to each other.

SIZE: Carapace to 0.75″ (19 mm) wide.

HABITAT: Beneath rocks; low intertidal zone to depths of 282′ (86 m).

RANGE: Chichagof Island, Alaska, to La Jolla, California.

NOTES: Flattop crabs are known to live together in groups of males, females and young. One dominant male does all or most of the breeding. Females often have 2 broods of young per year, each consisting of 10 to 1,580 eggs. In addition to filter feeding with its mouthparts, this species has claws with tufts of fine hairs, used to gather food from rock surfaces at night. Like all porcelain crabs, this crab has only 3 visible pairs of walking legs.

SIMILAR SPECIES: Flat porcelain crab.

Granular Claw Crab

Oedignathus inermis (Stimpson, 1860)

OTHER NAMES: Blue lithode crab, hole-loving crab, papillose crab, paxillose crab, soft-bellied crab; formerly classified as *Hapalogaster inermis*.

DESCRIPTION: The carapace is pear-shaped with a flattened top and ranges in color from grayish-brown to brown with darker brown to reddish-brown granules. The **circular granule-covered surface of the large right claw** has a bluish to purple coloration. Patterned granules cover the dorsal surface of the carapace.

SIZE: Carapace to 1″ (2.5 cm) wide.

HABITAT: Inside rock crevices and similar situations at sheltered sites along the outer coast; mid-intertidal zone to depths of 164′ (50 m).

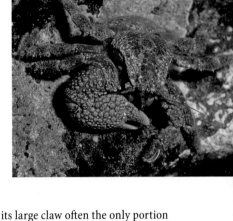

RANGE: Dutch Harbor, Alaska, to Pacific Grove, California; Japan.

NOTES: This crab is well protected within crevices, its large claw often the only portion visible. A pair of these crabs often takes up residence in the same cavity. The crab uses its large, clumsy but powerful claw to crush small mussels. The smaller left claw is used effectively for grabbing, scraping and other feeding motions. The black oystercatcher *Haematopus bachmani* is known to prey upon this crab found in mussel beds.

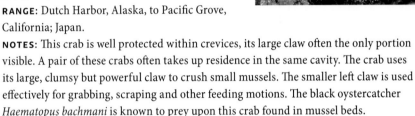

Scaled Crab

Placetron wosnessenskii Schalfeew, 1892

OTHER NAMES: Scaly lithodid; formerly classified as *Leiopus forcipatus, Leiopus forcipulatus.*

DESCRIPTION: The carapace varies widely in its coloration from gray to orange, and is **bottle shaped and covered with plates that are scale-like. The claws are long, with spoon-shaped fingers** that are close to equal in size.

SIZE: Carapace to 3.1″ (7.8 cm) wide.

HABITAT: On and around boulders; very low intertidal zone to depths of 600′ (185 m).

RANGE: Pribilof Islands, Alaska, to Octopus Hole, Hood Canal, Washington.

NOTES: The scaled crab is an arthropod that is not often found at intertidal levels. They feed on a wide array of foods including shrimp, amphipods, crabs and small fish. It would be interesting to discover how these crabs use their unique claws with their spoon-like fingers.

Hairy Crab

Hapalogaster mertensii Brandt, 1849

OTHER NAMES: Fuzzy crab, hairy lithode, hairy Iithodid, red-brown bristly crab, tuft-haired crab.
DESCRIPTION: Overall color varies from brown to reddish-brown. Its carapace is ovate and its **body is covered in tufts of long hair**. The fingers on the claws are frequently orange.
SIZE: Carapace to 1.4″ (3.5 cm) wide.
HABITAT: Underside of algae and beneath piled-up rocks; low intertidal zone to depths of 180′ (55 m).
RANGE: Atka, Alaska, to Port Orford, Oregon.
NOTES: The hairy crab appears to have only 3 pairs of legs, and 3 pairs are apparently sufficient for all its normal activities. This crab is an omnivore, feeding on algae and small invertebrates. It is also capable of filter feeding. A parasite called the hairy crab parasitic barnacle *Briarosaccus tenellus* has been found on the underside of this crab. This is truly a specialized barnacle that lives on this crab.

Umbrella Crab

Cryptolithodes sitchensis Brandt, 1853

OTHER NAMES: Flaring turtle crab, Sitka crab, turtle crab, umbrella-backed crab.
DESCRIPTION: Carapace color is variable including bright red, orange, gray or white, often with blotches. The flattened and flared **carapace conceals the crab's legs when viewed from above**. Shell also includes a distinctive **rostrum that is square and widest at the front**.
SIZE: Carapace to 3.6″ (9 cm) wide.
HABITAT: On bedrock or gravel bottoms of semi-protected shores; low intertidal zone to depths of 121′ (37 m).
RANGE: Sitka, Alaska, to Point Loma, California.
NOTES: This slow-moving crab is a great treat to find at the lowest of tides. It remains motionless, and its many color phases help it blend in well with its surroundings, so it often goes unnoticed. The umbrella crab feeds on a wide variety of organisms, including calcareous red algae. Little else is known about the biology of this species.

SIMILAR SPECIES: Butterfly crab *Cryptolithodes typicus* Brandt 1848 is similar-looking with a **rostrum that is square and narrowest at the front**.

....

Red King Crab

Paralithodes camtschaticus (Tilesius, 1815)

OTHER NAMES: Alaska king crab, king crab, Kamchatka crab, Russian crab; formerly classified as *Lithodes japonicas, Paralithodes camtschatica, Paralithodes rostrofalcatus.*

DESCRIPTION: The color varies from brownish-red to purple. The **carapace, legs and claws are covered with distinctive conical spines**.

SIZE: Carapace to 11″ (28 cm) wide.

HABITAT: In areas with rocks and algae (juveniles) and open sand or mud bottoms (adults); low intertidal zone (juveniles) to depths of 1,200′ (366 m).

RANGE: Bering Sea to Haida Gwaii (Queen Charlotte Islands), British Columbia.

NOTES: Those visiting the seashore at the lowest of tides may be rewarded with the sight of a juvenile of this well-known crab. The red king crab is world renowned for its quality and abundance. This species reaches sexual maturity at 5 to 6 years. Males are polygamous and may mate with 7 or more females annually. Prior to mating, the male embraces the female for 1–16 days, releasing her after she molts and after he has spread his spermatophores. She then extrudes her eggs, which become attached to her abdomen. The red king crab may live 15 to 20 years and weigh as much as 26 Ib. (11.8 kg).

....

Purple Shore Crab

Hemigrapsus nudus (Dana, 1851)

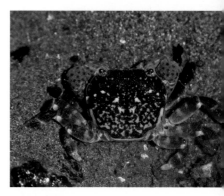

OTHER NAMES: Purple beach crab, purple rock crab, purple shore-crab; formerly classified as *Pseudograpsus nudus.*

DESCRIPTION: Typical specimens are purple overall with **purple spots on the claws**. Other color varieties include olive green, reddish-brown overall. Juvenile specimens vary greatly in color and patterning. The **carapace is**

Purple phase.

Green phase.

square-shaped and flat and the walking legs are hairless. Three teeth are present on the carapace behind the eye.

SIZE: Carapace to 2.3″ (5.8 cm) wide.

HABITAT: Underneath and between rocks of exposed shorelines; high to mid-intertidal zone.

RANGE: Yakobi Island, Alaska, to Bahía de Tortuga, México.

NOTES: The purple shore crab feeds mainly at night, consuming green algae such as sea lettuce. When this crab is discovered under a rock, it often walks sideways in an effort to escape and find a new hiding spot. Predators of adult crabs include the glaucous-winged gull *Larus glaucescens* and white-winged scoter *Melanitta fusca*.

SIMILAR SPECIES: Hairy shore crab.

Hairy Shore Crab

Hemigrapsus oregonensis (Dana, 1851)

OTHER NAMES: Green shore crab, hairy shore-crab, mud flat crab, mud-flat crab, mud crab, Oregon shore crab, yellow shore crab, yellow shore-crab; formerly classified as *Pseudograpsus oregonensis*.

DESCRIPTION: The carapace is normally gray-green but may also be yellow, or a variety of colors in juveniles. Mottling may be present on the carapace. The walking legs with dark spots are noticeably hairy. The carapace has a small notch between the eyes; 3 teeth are present on the carapace behind each eye.

SIZE: Carapace to 1.9″ (5 cm) wide.

HABITAT: Beneath or between rocks on mud or sand substrates of protected shores; high intertidal zone to depths of 79′ (24 m).

RANGE: Resurrection Bay, Alaska, to Bahía San Juanico, Baja California, México.

NOTES: This crab is primarily a herbivore, feeding on green algae such as sea lettuce. It is also a predator of numerous invertebrates, a scavenger of small organisms as well as a

filter-feeder, separating food particles from the water with special parts of its mouth. A variety of predators are known to feed upon the hairy shore crab, including birds and fish.
SIMILAR SPECIES: Purple shore crab.

Striped Shore Crab

Pachygrapsus crassipes Randall, 1840

OTHER NAMES: Green-lined shore crab, lined shore crab, lined rock crab.
DESCRIPTION: The overall color is normally green but may also be red or purple with **prominent black stripes**. Two teeth are present on the carapace behind the eye.
SIZE: Carapace to 1.9″ (5 cm) wide.
HABITAT: In rock crevices and tidepools on rocky shores; high to mid-intertidal zone.
RANGE: Barkley Sound, British Columbia, to the Gulf of California; Japan; Korea.
NOTES: This crab is often found in tidepools. Well adapted to life outside the water, it comes out in large numbers to feed, especially among eelgrass. Its primary food is algae, which it picks up and brings to its mouth with alternating claws, seemingly shoveling it in with salad forks! There is also a report of this lively species capturing flies at low tide. Its main predators are gulls and raccoons. Striped shore crabs engage in interesting courtship behavior. The female releases a chemical (pheromone) to attract males. Then a sort of dance begins, in which a male turns over onto his back and the female walks over him. The female produces approximately 50,000 eggs once or twice a year.

Black-clawed Crab

Lophopanopeus bellus (Stimpson, 1860)

OTHER NAMES: Black clawed crab, black clawed mud crab, black-clawed pebble crab, black-clawed shore crab, blackclaw crestleg crab, black-fingered crab, northern black-clawed crab.
DESCRIPTION: Overall color is variable, including purple or orange to white and brown. Specimens may be mottled or not and normally

the **fingers of claws are very dark to black**. The carapace is ovate and widest at the front with 3 teeth on the carapace margin behind each eye.

SIZE: Carapace to 1.6″ (4 cm) wide.

HABITAT: Beneath rocks or buried beneath sand or gravel; low intertidal zone to depths of 260′ (80 m).

RANGE: Resurrection Bay, Alaska, to Bahía Tortugas, Baja California, México.

NOTES: The black-clawed crab eats a variety of food, including algae, mussels and barnacles. The female is known to have 2 broods of young a year, each consisting of 6,000–36,000 eggs. Males are nearly twice the size of females.

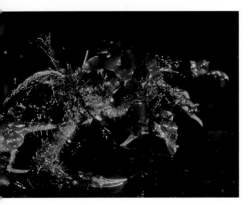

Graceful Decorator Crab

Oregonia gracilis (Dana, 1851)

OTHER NAMES: Decorator crab, slender decorator crab, spider crab; formerly classified as *Oregonia hirta*, *Oregonia longimana*.

DESCRIPTION: The carapace varies from tan or light brown to gray or white with patches of brown. There may also be red spots or markings present. The **rostrum (nose) has long, thin parallel horns**. The carapace is triangular with only one spine behind each eye. Walking legs are long and thin.

SIZE: Carapace to 1.5″ (3.9 cm) wide.

HABITAT: Among dense algae at intertidal sites; low intertidal zone to depths of 1,430′ (436 m).

RANGE: Nunivak Island, Alaska, to Monterey, California; Japan.

NOTES: This species is known for its very elaborate camouflage, which is made of seaweeds, hydroids, sponges, bryozoans and virtually anything available. These it carefully fastens on its upper shell or carapace and legs with small, curved setae. This is likely the most elaborately decorated crab intertidal explorers will encounter.

Northern Kelp Crab

Pugettia producta (Randall, 1840)

OTHER NAMES: Kelp crab, shield back crab, spider crab, shield-backed kelp crab; formerly classified as *Epialtus producta*, *Epialtus productus*.

DESCRIPTION: The overall color ranges from brown to red on the dorsal side. The **carapace is shield-shaped with a smooth surface.**
SIZE: Carapace to 4.3″ (11 cm) wide.
HABITAT: In kelp beds and dock pilings; low intertidal zone to depths of 240′ (73 m).
RANGE: Bertha Bay, Chichagof Island, Alaska, to Punta Asunción, Baja California, México.
NOTES: This crab feeds primarily on kelp or large brown seaweed, but will eat a variety of organisms if kelp is not available. The smooth carapace closely matches the algae it is often found upon. In the winter the kelp dies back,

and this species switches their foods to barnacles and mussels. Occasionally barnacles grow on the backs of adults, but this species does not camouflage itself as other related species do. Be sure to check pilings while at the dock, where large adults can often be found.

· ·

Graceful Kelp Crab

Pugettia gracilis Dana, 1851

OTHER NAMES: Graceful spider crab, graceful rock crab, kelp crab, slender crab, slender kelp crab, spider crab; formerly classified as *Pugettia lordii, Pugettia quadridens gracilis.*
DESCRIPTION: Carapace color is quite variable, including greenish to brown or white, pink, red or blue. The carapace is **covered with tubercles.** The rostrum is equipped with a pair of large, divergent horns. Claw **fingers are gray to blue, tipped with orange.** Walking legs are stout.
SIZE: Carapace to 1.5″ (4.5 cm) wide.
HABITAT: On rocky shores and among algae and eelgrass; low intertidal zone to depths of 1,204′ (367 m).
RANGE: Attu, Aleutian Islands, to Monterey, California.
NOTES: This crab adds a few decorations to its rostrum. As with all crabs, the eggs are kept on the female until the young are ready to hatch. They are attached in such a way that oxygen can reach each egg while water circulates.
SIMILAR SPECIES: Cryptic kelp crab.

Cryptic Kelp Crab

Pugettia richii Dana, 1851

OTHER NAMES: Kelp crab, spider crab; incorrectly *Pugettia richi*.
DESCRIPTION: Carapace color varies from from dark brown to red. The claws' **fingers are violet or reddish, tipped with white**. The carapace is **lumpy with several spines**, and the rostrum is equipped with a pair of large, divergent horns. Walking legs are slender.
SIZE: Carapace to 1.6″ (4 cm) wide.
HABITAT: Rocky shorelines along the outer coast; low intertidal zone to depths of 318′ (97 m).
RANGE: Prince of Wales Island, Alaska, to Isla San Geronimo, Baja California, México.
NOTES: Like other kelp crabs, this species adorns itself with bits of seaweed, bryozoans and hydroids. The cryptic kelp crab, however, tends to decorate only its rostrum. It also commonly hides in kelp holdfasts, especially perennial kelp.
SIMILAR SPECIES: Graceful kelp crab.

Foliate Kelp Crab

Pugettia foliata (Stimpson, 1860)

OTHER NAMES: Foliate spider crab, mimicking crab, sponge crab, sponge-covered kelp crab; formerly classified as *Mimulus foliatus*.
DESCRIPTION: The colors of this species are as variable as it can get, including brown, white, gray, yellow, orange or red. The rostrum is equipped with a pair of short horns. The **carapace is hexagonal, wider than long, with a smooth surface**.
SIZE: Carapace to 1.6″ (4.2 cm) wide.
HABITAT: Among kelp holdfasts and rocks along the outer coast; low intertidal zone to depths of 420′ (128 m).
RANGE: Attu, Aleutian Islands, Alaska, to San Diego, California.
NOTES: The foliate kelp crab is a species that sometimes decorates its rostrum with various bryozoans or sponges. Its diet consists primarily of drifting pieces of kelp. Researchers in California have found females brooding their eggs year-round.

Sharp-nosed Crab

Scyra acutifrons Dana, 1851

OTHER NAMES: Intertidal masking crab, masking crab, sharpnose spider crab, sharp-nosed masking crab.
DESCRIPTION: The color of the carapace varies from white or gray to tan, red, brown or purple, and it is triangular to pear-shaped with a surface that is somewhat rough. The chelipeds are normally brown or white with some red or orange (and enlarged in adult males). Fingers of the claws show small amounts of orange or red. **Rostrum is equipped with a pair of short, flat horns that are rounded and widest near the center.**
SIZE: Carapace to 1.7″ (4.5 cm) wide.
HABITAT: On rocky sites, pilings, at the base of large anemones in protected shores and the outer coast; low intertidal zone to depths of 720′ (220 m).
RANGE: Kodiak, Alaska, to Punta San Carlos, México; Japan.
NOTES: The sharp-nosed crab feeds upon detritus and various sessile invertebrates. Its enemies include a variety of fish. In Puget Sound, females of this species were found brooding eggs every month of the year except April and May.

....

Helmet Crab

Telmessus cheiragonus (Tilesius, 1812)

OTHER NAMES: Bristle crab, bristly crab, horse crab; formerly classified as *Cancer cheiragonus*, *Telmessus serratus*.
DESCRIPTION: Overall color is yellowish-green with dark fingers on the claws. The carapace is near pentagonal or **helmet shaped. Stiff, bristly hairs cover the entire body.** There are a total of 6 large teeth on each side of the carapace with the 4th being the largest.
SIZE: Carapace to 4″ (10.2 cm) wide.
HABITAT: In eelgrass beds or near rocks with thick algae; low intertidal zone to depths of 590′ (180 m).
RANGE: Chukchi Sea, Alaska, to Monterey, California; uncommon south of Puget Sound; Japan.
NOTES: During the early spring, this crab is often observed intertidally, typically in areas with an abundance of seaweed where it can hide. It is known to feed on eelgrass, algae, snails, bivalves and worms. In turn it is preyed upon by a wide range of other invertebrates, mammals and fish.

Dungeness Crab

Cancer magister Dana, 1852

OTHER NAMES: Commercial crab, common edible crab, edible cancer crab, edible crab, market crab, Pacific crab, Pacific edible crab; occasionally misspelled Dungeoness crab; *Metacarcinus magister*.

DESCRIPTION: Carapace color varies from reddish-brown to purplish. **Carapace is large**, ovate in shape and **widest at its 10th tooth (a prominent and final tooth) behind the eye**.

SIZE: Carapace to 10″ (25.4 cm) wide.

HABITAT: On sand or muddy-sand; mid-intertidal zone to depths of 750′ (230 m).

RANGE: Pribilof Islands, Alaska, to Santa Barbara, California.

Juvenile.

NOTES: The Dungeness crab is harvested both commercially and recreationally. Females lay 1–2 million eggs per brood on average. This species is known to live at least 6 years. It is an active carnivore that feeds on at least 40 different species including shrimp, small clams, oysters, worms and fish. The Dungeness crab spends a great deal of time buried in the sand. In the spring, this species can often be found in the low intertidal zone buried in sand in tidepools. Females can retain the sperm from a male for at least 2.5 years to fertilize future eggs.

SIMILAR SPECIES: Graceful crab *Cancer gracilis* Dana, 1852 is a smaller species that is widest at its 9th tooth.

Male underside.   Female underside.

Red Rock Crab

Cancer productus Randall, 1840

OTHER NAMES: Brick red cancer crab, red cancer crab, red crab; formerly classified as *Cancer perlatus*.

DESCRIPTION: The carapace of an **adult ranges from brick red to dark red**. Juveniles may display a wide range of colors including solid white to yellow or blue-gray, red with white zebra stripes and many other combinations. Carapace is **widest at its 8th tooth (the final tooth) behind the eye**.

SIZE: Carapace to 7.8″ (20 cm) wide.

HABITAT: On rocky shores, especially with gravel or boulders on protected shorelines; low intertidal zone to depths of 260′ (79 m).

RANGE: Kodiak, Alaska, to Isla San Martin, Baja California, México.

Juvenile.

NOTES: The red rock crab, like all of the *Cancer* clan, is a carnivore. Its heavy claws are strong enough to crack open the shells of barnacles and snails. It is an opportunist, also feeding on small living crabs and dead fish. The young of this native species are often found in the intertidal zone. Their coloration ranges from stripes of various colors to near white, and the shape of their carapace changes dramatically, narrowing as they age. The red rock crab is popular in the sport fishery.

SIMILAR SPECIES: Dungeness crab.

....

Pygmy Rock Crab

Cancer oregonensis (Dana, 1852)

OTHER NAMES: Hairy cancer crab, Oregon crab, Oregon cancer crab, Oregon rock crab, pygmy cancer crab; formerly classified as *Glebocarcinus oregonensis*.

DESCRIPTION: Color of the carapace is normally purplish-red to orange, occasionally with colored mottling or stripes. The carapace is nearly round in shape with numerous symmetrical bumps and groves, **and is widest at its 7th or 8th tooth behind the eye**.

SIZE: Carapace to 1.9″ (5 cm) wide.

HABITAT: Beneath rocks, in empty giant barnacles and piddock holes; low intertidal zone to depths of 1,428′ (435 m).

RANGE: Pribilof Islands, Alaska, to Palos Verdes, California.

NOTES: Chivalry is not dead in the world of crabs. The male pygmy rock crab grasps a female and carries her for several days before she molts. Mating follows after she has molted. The diet of the pygmy rock crab is wide ranging and includes barnacles, snails, worms and bivalves, as well some green algae.

Spot-bellied Rock Crab

Romaleon antennarium (Stimpson, 1856)

OTHER NAMES: Brown rock crab, common rock crab, edible rock crab, California rock crab, Pacific rock crab, red rock crab, red-spotted cancer crab, rock crab; formerly classified as *Cancer antennarius*.

DESCRIPTION: The dorsal side of the carapace is reddish-brown and **the underside is light colored with reddish spots.** The **large claws have black tips.** The points along the anterior edge of the carapace are curved. Hair is present on the carapace of juveniles and as a fringe on the underside of adults.

SIZE: Carapace to 7″ (17.8 cm) wide, intertidal specimens much smaller.

HABITAT: Among and beneath rocks primarily on the outer coast; low intertidal zone to depths of 294′ (90 m).

RANGE: Virago Sound, Haida Gwaii (Queen Charlotte Islands), British Columbia, to Cabo San Lucas, México.

NOTES: The spot-bellied rock crab feeds on a wide variety of animals, including snails and carrion. This species is remarkable in its ability to collect foods and store them on its body. It collects hermit crabs by sitting on them and uses its body to create a "cage," where it stores them for when it's time to eat! It uses its large claws to chip away at hermit crab shells and remove the contents for dinner.

European Green Crab ⓘ

Carcinus maenas (Linnaeus, 1758)

OTHER NAMES: European shore crab, green crab.

DESCRIPTION: Carapace color is greenish, mottled with black above and yellowish below. Behind both eyes there are **5 large teeth on outer edge of carapace and 3 teeth between eyes.** Last pair of legs are relatively flattened.

SIZE: Carapace to 3.9″ (10 cm) wide.

HABITAT: On rocks, mudflats of sheltered bays and estuaries, and tidepools; from the intertidal zone to depths of 20′ (6 m); to depths of 656′ (200 m) in Europe.

RANGE: Nootka Sound, British Columbia, to Morro Bay, California; Nova Scotia to New Jersey; Europe (native); Australia, South Africa; Panama; Brazil.

NOTES: The European green crab was accidentally introduced to San Francisco Bay in 1989 and since then its range has rapidly expanded. It is an adaptable invader, and has been introduced to many areas around the globe including Australia, South Africa and both coasts of the USA. Often described as a voracious omnivore, this crab feeds on a wide variety of plants and animals, including clams, mussels, other crabs, small fish and almost anything else.

....

Gaper Pea Crab

Pinnixa littoralis Holmes, 1895

OTHER NAME: Pea crab.

DESCRIPTION: Carapace color ranges from white to gray with bands of dark brown. The carapace is ovate and smooth with a soft body in the female and hard in the male. The dactyls (last segment) of walking legs are noticeably bent backwards and very pointed. The **female's claws have a gap (opening) when the claw is closed.** Females are larger than males. The male's third walking leg is proportionately much larger than that of the mantle pea crab (see similar species below).

SIZE: Carapace to 1″ (2.5 cm) wide.

HABITAT: Inside the mantle of the fat gaper and other bivalves; low intertidal zone to depths of 300′ (91 m).

RANGE: Hawkins Island, Prince William Sound, Alaska, to Bahía Santa Maria, Baja California, México.
NOTES: Gaper pea crabs live in pairs, inside the cavities of clams. The young are sometimes found in the cavities of many species of clams as well as in larger limpets. Adults may be found in various larger clams, including Nuttall's cockle.

A pair of gaper pea crabs inside a fat gaper clam.

SIMILAR SPECIES: Mantle pea crab *Pinnixa faba* is normally orange with black markings. Its claws do not gape when they are closed. It lives in the mantle of the fat gaper as well as several other clam species.

··

Tube-dwelling Pea Crab

Pinnixa tubicola Holmes, 1895

OTHER NAMES: Burrow crab, pea crab, polychaete worm pea crab.
DESCRIPTION: Color of shell exterior varies from white to brown with darker markings. The **third walking leg is noticeably the largest**. Carapace is oblong-ovate and smooth. As is the case with most pea crabs, females are larger and proportionately wider than long.

SIZE: Carapace to 0.7″ (18 mm) wide.
HABITAT: Inside the tubes created by several large tubeworms; mid-intertidal zone to depths of 574′ (175 m).
RANGE: Sitka, Alaska, to Bahía Blanca, Baja California, México.
NOTES: Tube-dwelling pea crabs are found in pairs inside the tubes of various tubeworms. Occasionally males are found outside of their "normal" habitat as was the individual illustrated here. It is interesting that females have not been observed outside.

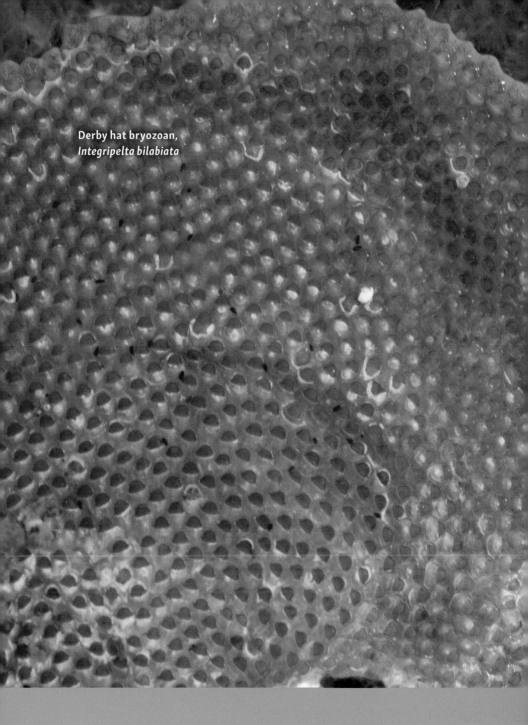
Derby hat bryozoan,
Integripelta bilabiata

Moss Animals

PHYLUM BRYOZOA

Moss animals or bryozoans comprise a group of nearly 2,000 different species. They live hanging from marine algae, encrusting on rocks and shells, or growing upright from a rock crevice. A bryozoan colony contains thousands of individuals. The colony reproduces and grows by budding. Some species are rigid, others are flexible and sway in the water, and still others are gelatinous. The bryozoan has a primitive nerve system but lacks a heart and vascular system. They feed by bringing in water to filter the detritus that attaches to micro-algae and bacteria.

Pacific Staghorn Bryozoan

Heteropora pacifica Borg, 1933

OTHER NAMES: False coral, northern staghorn bryozoan, staghorn bryozoan; possibly includes *Heteropora magna*.
DESCRIPTION: Color varies from **yellowish-green** to gray and occasionally with pink-tinged tips. This is an **erect, calcified bryozoan colony**. The branches may reach 0.2″ (5 mm) in diameter.
SIZE: Colony height to 4″ (10 cm).
HABITAT: Undersides of rocks on exposed shores; low intertidal zone to depths of 90′ (27 m).
RANGE: Alaska to central California.
NOTES: The Pacific staghorn bryozoan is an uncommon intertidal resident that is very distinctive. The Pacific Northwest hosts a few staghorn bryozoans but more research is required to determine their species status.

Branched-spine Bryozoan

Flustrellidra corniculata (Smitt, 1872)

OTHER NAMES: Branch-spine bryozoan, spiny leather bryozoan.
DESCRIPTION: Color ranges from dark brown to tan. The colonies are fleshy and flattened

or cylindrical in shape. **Tall, dark brown, branched spines originate from special zooids** within the colony to give it an overall "fuzzy" appearance.

SIZE: Colony to 2.4″ (6 cm) long.

HABITAT: On the stipes of various algae including *Laminaria* spp. and erect coralline algae; low intertidal zone to depths of 246′ (75 m).

RANGE: Point Barrow, Alaska, to San Luis Obispo County, California; northern Europe.

NOTES: The branched-spine

bryozoan is thought to appear leather-like to some and fuzzy to others; either way this is a distinctive species to identify. Each spine of this northern species includes 1–6 branches.

Kelp Encrusting Bryozoan

Membranipora membranacea

(Linnaeus, 1767)

OTHER NAMES: Encrusting bryozoan, jackfrost bryozoan, kelp-encrusting bryozoan, kelp lace, kelp lace bryozoan, kelp lacy bryozoan, lacy crust, lacy-crust bryozoan, tree bryozoan, white-encrusting bryozoan; formerly classified as *Flustra membranacea*.

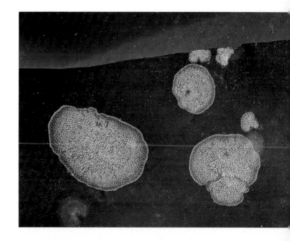

DESCRIPTION: This species is white in color. Each colony forms a crust that is often circular in shape, **a single layer thick with a regular, reticulating honeycomb pattern**.

SIZE: Colony to 8″ (20 cm) across.

HABITAT: On the blades of various algae including bull kelp and various other objects; low intertidal zone to depths of 600′ (180 m).

RANGE: Alaska to California; Atlantic North America; Caribbean; Europe.

NOTES: The kelp encrusting byrozoan is found most often from spring to fall. This beautifully patterned species starts growing from the center, reproduces by budding and radiates outward from the oldest portion. The cryptic nudibranch sometimes lives on this bryozoan, but careful inspection is required to see it.

....

Sea-lichen Bryozoan

Dendrobeania lichenoides

(Robertson, 1900)

OTHER NAMES: Leaf bryozoan, leaf crust bryozoan, lichen bryozoan, sea lichen bryozoan, sea lichen, sea mat bryozoan.

DESCRIPTION: Color of colony varies from tan to brown. The colony is a **flexible, leaf-shaped structure that is thin** and bears a single layer of patterned zooids on its surface. Spines are often present.

SIZE: Frond to 1″ (2.5 cm) across.

HABITAT: On rocks and other hard objects; low intertidal zone to depths of 330′ (100 m).

RANGE: British Columbia to southern California.

NOTES: This species attaches to a wide variety of substrates including shells, rocks and worm tubes. Bryozoans are made up of many individual animals called zooids that are tightly packed together. Countless numbers of microscopic tentacles cover bryozoans. These tentacles are used to filter feed on phytoplankton, bacteria and detritus, the food being moved to the central mouth of each individual by tiny hairs on the tentacles.

....

Fluted Bryozoan

Primavelans insculpta

(Hincks, 1883)

OTHER NAMES: Fluted coral bryozoan, sculptured bryozoan; formerly classified as *Hippodiplosia insculpta*.

DESCRIPTION: Color ranges from

light yellow to light tan or orange. The colony consists of **hard fronds that are double-layered and leaf-like** in appearance.

SIZE: Colony to 2″ (5 cm) high; width to 6″ (15 cm).

HABITAT: On rocks and occasionally algae; low intertidal zone to depths of 770′ (235 m).

RANGE: Alaska to Gulf of California; Isla del Coco, Costa Rica.

NOTES: This bryozoan is hard to the touch. In cooler waters to the north, colonies are comprised of larger individuals (zooids).

....

Orange Encrusting Bryozoan ⓘ

Schizoporella japonica
Ortmann, 1890

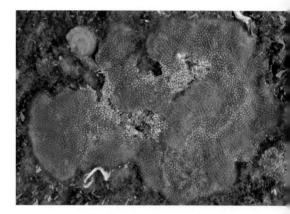

OTHER NAMES: Orange crust bryozoan; formerly classified as *Schizoporella unicornis*, *Schizoporella unicornis* var. *japonica*.

DESCRIPTION: Color in the Pacific Northwest is **bright orange** but elsewhere it ranges from whitish-pink to deep red. This **encrusting species** is normally one layer thick with a distinctive pattern of zooids radiating from a central point.

SIZE: Colonies to 2″ (5 cm) across.

HABITAT: On shells, rocks and algae; low intertidal zone to depths of 197′ (60 m).

RANGE: Alaska to Point Conception, California; China; Japan.

NOTES: The orange encrusting bryozoan is an introduced species that is now considered to be the dominant encrusting bryozoan found in intertidal waters of the Pacific Northwest. It is believed to have arrived from Japan with introduced Pacific oysters.

....

Derby Hat Bryozoan

Integripelta bilabiata (Hincks, 1884)

OTHER NAMES: Rosy bryozoan; formerly classified as *Eurystomella bilabiata*.

DESCRIPTION: Color of colony is a **rosy red**. This encrusting species is one layer thick with **individual zooids that resemble derby hats**.

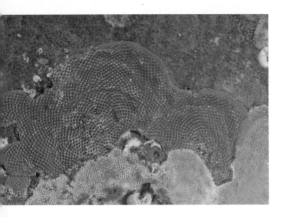

SIZE: Colony to 2″ (5 cm) or more across.
HABITAT: On rocks and shells; low intertidal zone to depths of 782′ (237 m).
RANGE: Alaska to Bahía de Tenacatita, México; Japan.
NOTES: The wonderful common name, derby hat bryozoan, originates from the shape of this species' operculum or trap door, which closes to protect the zooid after it has retreated into its home. Many individuals live side by side on a solid substrate to form a colony. The colony expands when individuals bud off, producing new zooids.

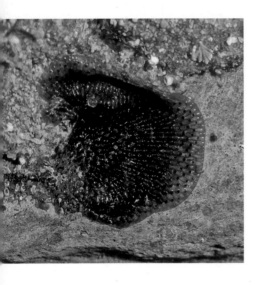

Black and Red Encrusting Bryozoan

Watersipora cucullata (Busk, 1854)

OTHER NAME: Formerly classified as *Watersipora subovoidea*.
DESCRIPTION: Color overall is **brownish-orange to orange-red with a dark brown to black operculum**. This calcified, **encrusting** bryozoan varies in appearance with its environment. It is an encrusting species in quiet waters but grows leaf-shaped in other areas.
SIZE: Colonies to 8.5″ (22 cm) across; 2.5″ (6 cm) high.
HABITAT: On rocks, shells, docks, kelp, pilings and similar objects; low intertidal zone.
RANGE: Cosmopolitan; northern Washington to Baja California, México; Hawaii; Florida to Brazil; Australia; New Zealand; Europe; South Africa.
NOTES: There is much confusion regarding the black and red encrusting bryozoan at the present time. It is part of a species complex that requires more scientific study. It is noted to be an early successional species that colonizes new surfaces quickly.

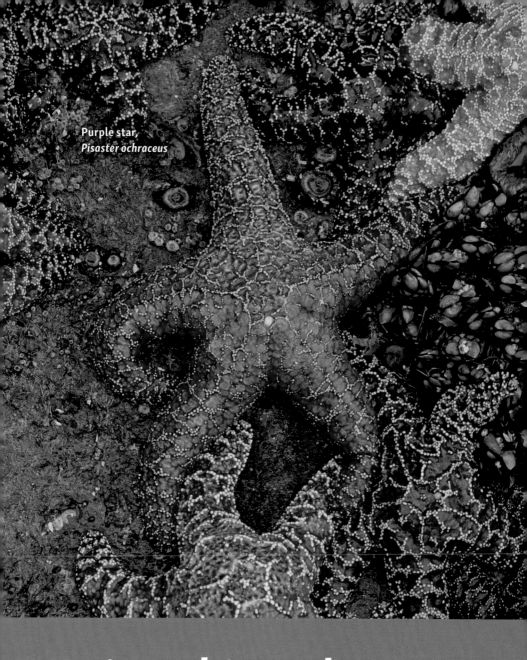

Purple star,
Pisaster ochraceus

Spiny-skinned
Animals

PHYLUM ECHINODERMATA

The echinoderms (spiny-skinned animals) comprise a large group in which all members have calcareous plates covered with a soft layer of skin. The size of the plates varies from large and conspicuous, as in most species (e.g. sea urchins), to inconspicuous (e.g. sea cucumbers). Locally the echinoderms consist of sea stars, brittle stars, sea urchins, sand dollars and sea cucumbers.

Sea Stars
CLASS ASTEROIDEA

Sea stars were once referred to as starfish, but sea star is a much better name as no individuals in this group can swim, have scales or are edible. Sea stars feed on a wide variety of foods. Some of the more active species can actually capture live snails or other stars, while some slower species feed on various seaweeds. Movement is made possible by many small tube feet on the underside of each ray. Animals in this class have truly remarkable powers of regeneration. Entire limbs can be regenerated, and in some species whole sea stars can be regenerated from a single ray with a portion of the central disc or body.

Vermilion Star

Mediaster aequalis Stimpson, 1857

OTHER NAMES: Equal arm star, equal arm starfish, equal-arm star, red sea star, vermilion starfish; occasionally misspelled vermillion star.
DESCRIPTION: The aboral (dorsal) surface is red-orange. The **5 arms** are tapered and medium length. **Numerous plates cover the dorsal surface in a regular pattern** and a **single row of larger plates form around the perimeter**.
SIZE: To 8″ (20 cm) in diameter.
HABITAT: On rocky shores; low intertidal zone to depths of 1,650′ (503 m).

RANGE: Chignik Bay, Alaska Peninsula to southern California.

NOTES: The vermillion star is an uncommon species to intertidal explorers. It dines on a wide range of invertebrates including encrusting sponges, bryozoans and sea squirts, as well as carrion. Its main predator is likely the morning sun star.

....

Bat Star

Patiria miniata (Brandt, 1835)

OTHER NAMES: Bat starfish, broad disc sea star, broad-disc sea star, broaddisk starfish, sea bat, webbed star, webbed sea star, webbed starfish; formerly classified as *Asterina miniata*.

DESCRIPTION: The aboral surface includes nearly every color of the rainbow and some individuals are mottled. **Normally 5 short, broad, webbed arms**, but occasionally 4–9 arms. There are no spines or pincers present.

SIZE: To 10″ (25 cm) in diameter.

HABITAT: On rock, sand, mud or algae in sheltered areas along the outer coast; low intertidal zone to depths of 1,000′ (302 m).

RANGE: Sitka, Alaska, to Islas de Revillagigedo, México.

NOTES: The bat star eats surfgrasses, as it is able to digest the cellulose. This omnivore also feeds on various algae, sponges, sea urchins, squid eggs and colonial tunicates. This distinctive species is thought to live up to 30 years. The bat star worm *Ophiodromus pugettensis*, a segmented worm, is often found living commensally on the underside of this sea star.

....

Leather Star

Dermasterias imbricata (Grube, 1857)

OTHER NAMES: Garlic sea star, garlic star, leather sea star, leather starfish.

DESCRIPTION: The aboral surface is **blueish-gray overall and mottled with reddish-orange.** A large lemon yellow madreporite is also present. The 5 rays

Underwater view.

are medium in length. The surface is always **slippery to the touch**.

SIZE: To 12″ (30 cm) in diameter.

HABITAT: On rocky shores; low intertidal zone to depths of 299′ (91 m).

RANGE: Prince William Sound, Alaska, to Point Loma, San Diego County, California.

NOTES: This common species is easily recognized. The leather star feels like wet leather and often smells like garlic or sulphur. The diet of this carnivore includes the giant green anemone, proliferating anemone, stubby rose anemone, purple sea urchin and several other invertebrates that it swallows whole and digests internally. The leather star is also one of the hosts of the red-banded commensal scaleworm.

Rose Star

Crossaster papposus (Linnaeus, 1767)

OTHER NAMES: Common sun star, rose sea star, rose starfish, snowflake star, snowflake sea star, spiny sun star, spiny sunstar; formerly classified as *Asterias papposus*, *Solaster papposus*.

DESCRIPTION: The spiny aboral surface is scarlet, with concentric banding of yellow, white, pink or red. A **net-like pattern with raised ridges** is also present over the short rays and large central disk. There are **normally 11 short arms** but this can range from 8 to 14 rays.

SIZE: To 14″ (34 cm) in diameter.

HABITAT: On various shores; very low intertidal zone to depths of 3,937′ (12,000 m).

RANGE: Circumpolar; Bering Sea to Puget Sound, Washington; Arctic to Gulf of Maine; Britain.

NOTES: The striking colors of the rose star make this uncommon intertidal species truly beautiful. This species is a top predator feeding on bivalves, nudibranchs, bryozoans, sea squirts and sea stars. This species lives for at least 20 years.

Morning Sunstar

Solaster dawsoni Verrill, 1880

OTHER NAMES: Dawson's sea star, Dawson's sun star, morning sunstar, morning sun sea star, morning sun starfish.

DESCRIPTION: The aboral surface varies from gray to yellow, brown or red. There are **normally 11–13 slender, elongated arms** but this can range from 8 to 15 rays.

SIZE: To 16″ (40 cm) in diameter.

HABITAT: On rocks, sand, mud or gravel; low intertidal zone to depths of 1,386′ (420 m).

RANGE: Aleutian Islands, Alaska, to Monterey Bay, California.

NOTES: This sea star, one of more than 2,000 species of stars found throughout the world, specializes in feeding on other sea stars. Included in its menu are the striped sun star, mottled star, leather star, Pacific blood star, and occasionally even its own species. It has also been known to feed on the stiff-footed sea cucumber.

SIMILAR SPECIES: Northern sunstar.

Northern Sunstar

Solaster endeca (Linnaeus, 1771)

OTHER NAMES: Northern sun star, northern sun sea star, purple sun star, smooth sunstar; formerly classified as *Asterias endeca*.

DESCRIPTION: The aboral surface varies from red to orange or pink. Sometimes a purple stripe is found down each ray. There are **normally 9–11 chunky, elongated arms** but this can range from 7 to 13 rays.

SIZE: To 16″ (40 cm) in diameter.

HABITAT: On rocky shorelines; low intertidal zone to depths of 1,558′ (475 m).

RANGE: Circumboreal; Bering Sea to Puget Sound, Washington; Arctic Ocean to Cape Cod, and to Great Britain.

NOTES: Just like its close cousin, the morning sunstar, this species is a specialist feeder that eats primarily sea stars. Included in this carnivore's diet are the blood star, leather star, mottled star, rose star, striped sunstar, sunflower star and vermilion star, as well as cannibalizing its own species. To add variety to its diet, it also includes a number of sea cucumbers.

SIMILAR SPECIES: Morning sunstar.

Striped Sunstar

Solaster stimpsoni Verrill, 1880

OTHER NAMES: Orange sun star, Stimpson's sun star, Stimpson's sunstar, Stimpson's star, Stimpson's sea star, striped sun starfish, sun star, sun sea star, sun starfish.
DESCRIPTION: The aboral surface varies from red to orange, blue green or yellow with **a blue-gray stripe stripe radiating down the center of each ray.** There are **normally 10 tapering, elongated arms** but this can range from 9–11 rays.
SIZE: To 20″ (50 cm) in diameter.
HABITAT: On rocks and sand; low intertidal zone to depths of 2,001′ (610 m).
RANGE: Commander Islands, Bering Sea, to Trinidad Head, Humboldt County, California; Japan.
NOTES: The striped sun star has a feeding preference for sea cucumbers but will also feed on a variety of invertebrates, including lampshells and tunicates. This distinctive species is occasionally found in the intertidal zone. Its chief enemy is the morning sun star.

Pacific Blood Star

Henricia leviuscula (Stimpson, 1857)

OTHER NAMES: Blood red star, blood sea star, blood star, blood starfish, Pacific henricia, red sea star.
DESCRIPTION: The **aboral surface is bright red to reddish-orange.** There are **5, or occasionally 4–6, thin, elongated rays that taper gradually** and are smooth to the touch.

SIZE: To 13″ (32 cm) in diameter; intertidal specimens are much smaller.
HABITAT: On rocky shorelines; low intertidal zone to depths of 1,320′ (400 m).
RANGE: Aleutian Islands, Alaska, to Bahía de Tortuga, Baja California, México.
NOTES: The Pacific blood star is a free-spawning species (releases eggs directly to the ocean). This common star feeds primarily on sponges, including the bread crumb sponge. The smooth surface of this species is due to the lack of long spines and pedicellariae, which are not present in the genus *Henricia*. The vivid color of this sea star is often the reason beachcombers take it home, but its color fades when it dries. Rather than removing it from its habitat, try taking a photograph or making a sketch.

Dwarf Mottled Henricia

Henricia pumila

Eernisse, Strathmann & Strathrnann, 2010

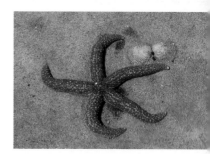

OTHER NAME: Mottled henricia; formerly included with *Henricia leviuscula*.
DESCRIPTION: The aboral surface varies from **yellow to orange, mottled with brown or orange**. This **small species normally has 5 short, tapering arms** but individuals with 6 rays have been observed.
SIZE: To 2″ (5 cm) in diameter.
HABITAT: On the underside of rocks of exposed shorelines; low intertidal zone.
RANGE: Sitka, Alaska, to Punta Banda, Baja California, México.
NOTES: The dwarf mottled blood star is a small, newly described species that is easily distinguished from its well-known cousin, the Pacific blood star. This sea star has been observed brooding its eggs from January to April in the San Juan Islands and central California. Little is known about this species at the present time.

Mottled Star

Evasterias troschelii (Stimpson, 1862)

OTHER NAMES: False ochre sea star, false ochre star, mottled starfish, slender-rayed star, slender-rayed sea star, Troschel's star, Troschel's sea star, true star; formerly classified as *Evasterias troscheli*.
DESCRIPTION: The aboral surface varies from

brown to orange, green or blue-gray with numerous tiny spines that form **a net-like pattern**. There are **normally 5 tapering, elongated arms**. The **central disk is smaller and the rays are slimmer** than those of the purple star.

SIZE: To 24″ (60 cm) in diameter.

HABITAT: On rocks or sand on protected shores; low intertidal zone to depths of 250′ (75 m).

RANGE: Pribilof Islands, Alaska, to Monterey Bay, California; uncommon south of Puget Sound, Washington.

NOTES: The colors of the mottled star are often drab in comparison to many of the other stars found in this region. This species is found in sheltered areas—a useful identifying feature when distinguishing this star from the similar purple star, which often makes its home in areas with heavy surf. The mottled star feeds on a wide variety of invertebrates, including bivalves, limpets, barnacles, snails, tunicates and brachiopods.

SIMILAR SPECIES: Purple star.

Single-track Six-rayed Star

Leptasterias hexactis species complex
(Stimpson, 1862)

OTHER NAMES: Drab six-armed star, rough six-armed sea star, six ray star, spiny drab six ray star; species complex includes *Leptasterias hexactis* (in part) and *Leptasterias epichlora*.

DESCRIPTION: The aboral surface varies greatly from grey to green, pink, purple and orange, and patterns are often present. The arms are rather short and appear "stubby" looking. **A single row of larger spines is present in the center of the aboral surface of each ray**. Typically there are **6 rays** present but individuals may have from 5 to 7.

SIZE: To 4″ (10 cm) in diameter.

HABITAT: Beneath rocks; low intertidal zone to depths of 150′ (45 m).

RANGE: Aleutian Islands, Alaska, to southern Vancouver Island, British Columbia.

NOTES: The single-track six-rayed star species complex is a group of similar sea stars that were once lumped together with other six-rayed sea stars. This large group of six-rayed sea stars have been broken down into 3 smaller species complexes. Future research will likely determine species within each of these complexes. The multi-track six-rayed star and Alaskan six-rayed star are two other species complexes (see next 2 species).

SIMILAR SPECIES: Multi-track six-rayed star.

....

Multi-track Six-rayed Star

Leptasterias aequalis species complex

(Stimpson, 1862)

OTHER NAMES: Broad six-rayed star, brooding star, colorful six-rayed star, delicate six-armed star, six-armed star, six-rayed star; species complex includes *Leptasterias aequalis aequalis*, *Leptasterias aequalis nana*.

DESCRIPTION: The aboral surface varies greatly from grey to green, pink, purple and orange, and patterns are often present. Each ray is short with a broad base. **Several rows of larger spines are present on the aboral surface of each ray** creating an overall rough appearance. Normally there are **6 rays** present.

SIZE: To 4″ (10 cm) in diameter.

HABITAT: Beneath rocks; low intertidal zone to depths of 150′ (45 m).

RANGE: Vancouver Island, British Columbia, to Santa Catalina Island, California.

NOTES: This sea star is quite variable in its appearance, just as its close relative, the single-track six-rayed star.

SIMILAR SPECIES: Single-track six-rayed star is a similar-looking species that features a single line of spines down each ray.

....

Alaskan Six-rayed Star

Leptasterias alaskensis species complex (Verrill, 1909)

OTHER NAMES: Species complex includes *Leptasterias hexactis* (in part) and *Leptasterias hexactis aspera*.

DESCRIPTION: The aboral surface varies greatly from pinkish to brown, or bluish, and patterns are often present. **No rows of spines are present on the aboral surface of any rays** creating an overall smooth appearance. Normally there are **6 rays** present.

SIZE: To 4.3″ (11 cm) in diameter.
HABITAT: Beneath rocks of protected shorelines; low intertidal zone to shallow subtidal depths.
RANGE: Southern Alaska to British Columbia.
NOTES: Like other six-rayed stars, this species gathers in numbers to breed. A female produces hundreds of large eggs, which are brooded under her arched back. These eggs can often be viewed in early spring. After 3 months the miniature sea stars leave the safety of their parent to venture on their own.

Painted Star

Orthasterias koehleri (deLoriol, 1897)

OTHER NAMES: Long rayed star, rainbow sea star; formerly classified as *Asterias koehleri, Orthasterias columbiana.*
DESCRIPTION: The aboral surface varies from **pink or red, banded** with yellow or blue. This species normally has **5 long, slender, tapering arms** with a small central disk. Several rows of sharp spines are also present on the aboral surface.
SIZE: To 24″ (60 cm) in diameter.
HABITAT: On rock, sand, mud or algae; low intertidal zone to depths of 2,190′ (668 m).
RANGE: Aleutian Islands, Alaska, to Santa Rosa Island, California.
NOTES: This beautiful sea star is a carnivore, feeding on small snails, limpets, clams, scallops, barnacles, tunicates and other similar invertebrates. Like several other stars, this species pushes its stomach between the shells of a clam to begin digesting its meal.

Giant Pink Star

Pisaster brevispinus (Stimpson, 1857)

OTHER NAMES: Pink sea star, pink star, short-spined sea star, spiny pink star.
DESCRIPTION: The **aboral surface is always pink** with numerous **tiny spines** and plates

that form **a rough pattern and a central row on each ray**. This species normally has **5 long, tapering arms**.

SIZE: To 25″ (65 cm) in diameter.

HABITAT: On various soft substrates of quiet waters; low intertidal zone to depths of 600′ (182 m).

RANGE: Sitka, Alaska, to San Diego County, southern California.

NOTES: The giant pink star is one of the larger sea stars found in the Pacific Northwest. This species feeds on the Pacific geoduck, giant acorn barnacle and eccentric sand dollar, among other species. The size of the individual sea star determines the size of its prey.

SIMILAR SPECIES: Purple star.

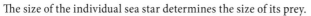

Purple Star

Pisaster ochraceus

(Brandt, 1835)

OTHER NAMES: Common sea star, common purple star, ochre star, ochre sea star, ochre sea star, ochre starfish, Pacific sea star, purple sea star, purple starfish, common sea star, warty sea star; formerly classified as *Asterias ochracea*; occasionally misspelled *Pisaster ochraceous*.

The purple star feeds on the California mussel.

DESCRIPTION: The **aboral surface varies from purple to orange, yellow or brown with numerous white spines that form a reticulated pattern**. There are **5 tapering arms** and a central disk with a high profile.

SIZE: To 20″ (50 cm) in diameter.

HABITAT: On rocks of exposed shorelines; mid-intertidal zone to depths of 289′ (88 m).

RANGE: Prince William Sound, Alaska, to Baja California, México.

NOTES: This is the most common sea star found in our intertidal zones. It feeds on mussels, abalone, chitons, barnacles and snails. Many prey species can detect this star when it's nearby and they are able to escape. But its favorite prey species, including the California mussel and the goose barnacle, are attached and are unable to flee. The purple star is one of at least 20 species of sea stars that have been affected by the sea star wasting disease, which has existed for at least 72 years or more. Past outbreaks have been observed but never to the extent of the outbreak that started in 2013. The cause is believed to be the sea star-associated densovirus (ssaDV). Young sea stars have been found in abundance since the initial outbreak, but the disease still occurs at the time of this writing (2018). What caused the outbreak is a question that goes unanswered. Hopefully with time the numbers of sea stars will return to normal. It has been said that this viral outbreak is among one of the worst ever wildlife die-offs from Alaska to Mexico.

SIMILAR SPECIES: Mottled star.

Sunflower Star

Pycnopodia helianthoides
(Brandt, 1835)

OTHER NAMES: Many rayed star, sunflower sea star, sunflower starfish, twentyarm star, twenty-rayed star, twenty-rayed sea star; formerly classified as *Asterias helianthoides*.

DESCRIPTION: The aboral surface varies from purple to orange, yellow or reddish-brown. The **surface is soft to the touch** or "flabby." Adults have up to **24 long arms** but juveniles may have as few as 5. The central disk is relatively large.

SIZE: To 39″ (1 m) in diameter.

HABITAT: On rock, sand, mud or gravel and in tidepools; low intertidal zone to depths of 1,427′ (435 m).

RANGE: Unalaska Island, Alaska, to Baja California, México.

NOTES: A good-sized sunflower star has an estimated 15,000 tube feet on its body. It is the largest and fastest sea star found in the world. Researchers in Alaska noted that marked sunflower stars were located 2 miles (3 km) from their original location. It is a voracious feeder, preying on many large clams and crustaceans. It has also been observed to feed on dead squid, ingesting the indigestible squid pen as well. The pen is too large to pass normally from the star—instead it is extruded through the soft upper part of the star's body.

Brittle Stars

CLASS OPHIUROIDEA

Most species of brittle stars have five long rays joined to a flattened central disc; however, some species have more arms. They are called brittle stars because their rays often break when being handled.

....

Daisy Brittle Star

Ophiopholis aculeata

(Linnaeus, 1767)

OTHER NAMES: Painted brittle star, painted brittlestar, painted serpent star, rusty-red brittle star, serpent star, ubiquitous brittle star.

DESCRIPTION: The colors and patterns of the aboral (dorsal) side are highly variable and the arms are frequently banded. Rays are long and wider than most brittle stars. **Central disc is scallop shaped with bulges between the arms.**

SIZE: Disc to 0.9″ (22 mm) in diameter; arms to 3.5″ (9 cm) long. **Length of arms 3.5–4 times diameter of disc.**

HABITAT: Under stones, in algal holdfasts and along rocky shores, low intertidal zone to depths of 3,300′ (1,000 m).

RANGE: Bering Sea to south of Santa Barbara, California; Arctic to Cape Cod; Europe; Russia.

NOTES: This common species, whose name comes from the flower-like shape of its disc, is more abundant in the northern part of its range. Like other brittle stars, it feeds by scraping minute organisms from rock with its specialized tube feet. The food then enters the stomach, which fills up most of the body cavity. Unlike a sea star, the brittle star cannot extrude its stomach to feed. Strangely enough, there is no intestine or anus; food is absorbed along the alimentary canal and wastes go back out the mouth.

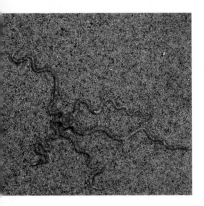

Western Long-armed Brittle Star

Amphiodia occidentalis (Lyman, 1860)

OTHER NAMES: Burrowing brittle star, long-armed brittle star, snaky-armed brittle star.

DESCRIPTION: The color of the aboral side is gray to tan, yellow or bluish, mottled with various colors. **Rays are extremely long and slender. The disk is nearly circular and smooth. A pair of dark spots is found on the disk at the base of each arm.** The spines on the arms are thick, flattened and blunt.

SIZE: Disc to 0.5″ (13 mm) in diameter; arms to 6.3″ (16 cm) long. **Length of arms 9–15 times diameter of disc.**

HABITAT: In sand, a sand and shell debris mix or buried under rocks and seagrass, or tidepools; low intertidal zone to depths of 1,210′ (369 m).

RANGE: Kodiak Island, Alaska, to central California.

NOTES: The western long-armed brittle star is a delicate and well-named creature. Its long arms are extremely fragile and easily fragmented. This species often burrows just beneath the surface of the sand or mud. With its tube feet moving up and down, it literally descends, disappearing from view. The tips of the arms, however, are often still exposed; they are used to feed at night.

SIMILAR SPECIES: Common long-armed brittle star.

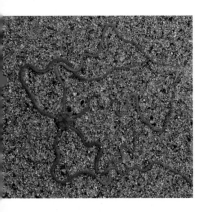

Common Long-armed Brittle Star

Amphiodia periercta H.L. Clark, 1911

OTHER NAMES: Burrowing brittle star, long arm brittle star; formerly classified as *Amphiodia pelora*; not *Amphiodia untica*.

DESCRIPTION: The color of the aboral side of the disk is reddish-brown to yellowish-brown with white markings and traces of red. **Rays are extremely long and slender.** The disk is nearly circular and smooth. The spines on the arms are oval-shaped (in cross section), slightly flattened and sharp.

SIZE: Disc to 0.6″ (15 mm) in diameter; arms to 18″ (45 cm) long. **Length of arms 15–20 times diameter of disc.**

HABITAT: Buried in silty, sandy mud; low intertidal zone to depths of 302′ (92 m).

RANGE: Aleutian Islands, Alaska, to central California; Southern Kuril Islands to Sea of Japan.

NOTES: The common long-armed brittle star is one of several long-armed species that bury themselves in sandy mud and similar substrates. This species is the most common, and one of the largest, species found in that environment.

SIMILAR SPECIES: Western long-armed brittle star.

Black and White Brittle Star

Amphipholis pugetana (Lyman, 1860)

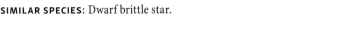

OTHER NAMES: Dwarf brittle star, Puget dwarf brittle star, Puget Sound dwarf brittle star.

DESCRIPTION: The color of the aboral side is variable and includes the disk of white to reddish-brown, and the arms are normally lighter with blotches of various colors. The **spines on the arms are very long and stout**.

SIZE: Disc to 0.5″ (13 mm) in diameter; arms to 1.5″ (3.8 cm) long. **Length of arms 7–8 times diameter of disc.**

HABITAT: Beneath rocks often in tidepools; high intertidal zone to depths of 3,949′ (1,204 m).

RANGE: Gulf of Alaska to southern California.

NOTES: The black and white brittle star is a small species that has been found to emit a yellow-green luminescence if stimulated by mechanical means. It also fluoresces after its luminescence has been initiated. This species and the dwarf brittle star are found higher on the beach than other brittle stars. The arms of this hardy species do not fall off as easily as those of other species. This brittle star does not brood its young.

SIMILAR SPECIES: Dwarf brittle star.

Dwarf Brittle Star

Amphipholis squamata (Delle Chiaje, 1828)

OTHER NAMES: Brooding brittle star, holdfast brittle star, small brittle star, small serpent star, serpent star; formerly classified as *Axiognathus squamata*.

DESCRIPTION: The color of the disk's aboral side is normally dark gray with a white spot

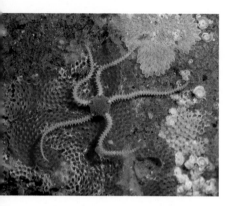

at the base of each arm. The arms are colored lighter and may be tan, gray, lavender or orange. The **disk is nearly circular** and flat, and its surface is covered with fine scales.

SIZE: Disc to 0.2″ (5 mm) in diameter; arms to 1″ (2.5 cm) long. **Length of arms 3–4.5 times diameter of disc.**

HABITAT: Under rocks, in rock crevices, algal holdfasts and gravel debris and in tidepools; high intertidal zone to depths of 4,362′ (1,330 m).

RANGE: Cosmopolitan.

NOTES: The dwarf brittle star is ovoviviparous, a species that broods its young in bursal pockets (slits on both sides of the base of each arm). The spines on the arms can produce a greenish luminescence that is visible in darkness. This species disperses by attaching to various types of debris and floating in the prevailing currents.

....

Flat-spined Brittle Star

Ophiopteris papillosa (Lyman, 1875)

OTHER NAME: Blunt-spined brittle star.

DESCRIPTION: The color of the disk's aboral side varies from chocolate-brown to yellowish-brown or red. The arm's aboral side is similarly colored with prominent banding. The side (or lower) **spines on arms are flat, blunt and very long** (3 times the width of arm joint).

SIZE: Disc to 0.5″ (13 mm) in diameter; arms to 2″ (5 cm) long. **Length of arms 3–4.5 times diameter of disc.**

HABITAT: Under rocks in holdfasts and tidepools; low intertidal zone to depths of 549′ (140 m).

RANGE: Barkley Sound, British Columbia, to Isla Cedros, Baja California, México; uncommon north of southern Oregon.

NOTES: This very active brittle star readily drops arms when disturbed or attacked. The flat-spined brittle star is able to feed in two very different ways. It can simply capture suspended particles with its tube feet, which form a comb-like net, and pass them to its mouth. It is also a carnivore that uses the spines on its arms to break small chunks of food it holds in its jaws.

Sea Urchins & Sand Dollars

CLASS ECHINOIDEA

Sea urchins and sand dollars are covered with movable spines, which come in a wide range of colors and can be blunt or sharp, long or short. Urchins make their way into our kitchens on occasion: their roe (see red sea urchin) are eaten raw in sushi, they are sautéed or added to omelettes or soups, and they are cooked in a variety of other ways.

Green Sea Urchin

Strongylocentrotus droebachiensis
(Müller, 1776)

OTHER NAME: Green urchin.
DESCRIPTION: The exterior is **greenish-brown overall**, often with dark bands created by vertically arranged rows of brown tube feet. The test is normally purple rather than green.
SIZE: Animal to 3.25″ (8.3 cm) in diameter; to 1.5″ (3.8 cm) high. **Spine length varies from one-fifth to one-third diameter of test.**
HABITAT: On rocky shorelines and among kelp; low intertidal zone to depths of 3,937′ (1,200 m) in the Atlantic.
RANGE: Arctic Ocean to Washington state; Hudson Bay to Chesapeake Bay; Japan; Greenland, Iceland, Europe.
NOTES: The green sea urchin, our smallest urchin, feeds primarily on algae, especially kelp including bull kelp. It will also feed on other species such as encrusting coralline algae and sea lettuce. At times it is opportunistic and feeds on slow-moving animals such as the black Katy chiton. It is also known to be a scavenger.

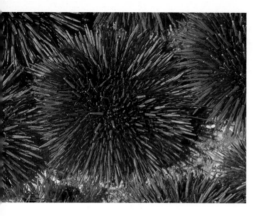

Purple Sea Urchin

Strongylocentrotus purpuratus
(Stimpson, 1857)

OTHER NAMES: Purple-spined sea urchin, purple urchin.
DESCRIPTION: Exterior is **a rich purple overall in adults and green in juveniles.** Their **spines are relatively short.** The test is normally greenish, often with bluish tones. (See Plate 15.)
SIZE: Animal to 4″ (10.2 cm) in diameter; to 1.75″ (4.4 cm) high. **Spine length varies from one-quarter to one-third diameter of test.**
HABITAT: On rocky sites of exposed shorelines; low intertidal zone to depths of 525′ (160 m).
RANGE: Cook Inlet, Alaska, to Baja California, México.
NOTES: The purple sea urchin is a herbivore that dines on both red and brown algae. This common species is well known for its ability to erode shallow burrows in soft rock using its spines and possibly its teeth. In many areas this ability has transformed rock into urchin condos. Broken spines are regenerated in time, and their teeth continually grow. This species is believed to live to 30 years, enough time to make its burrow reasonably deep, which gives the urchin an advantage against both predators and wave action.
SIMILAR SPECIES: Giant red sea urchin is a species that can also be purple overall.

Two color phases of the giant red sea urchin.

Giant Red Sea Urchin

Mesocentrotus franciscanus (Agassiz, 1863)

OTHER NAMES: Giant red urchin, red sea urchin, red urchin; formerly classified as *Strongylocentrotus franciscanus*.
DESCRIPTION: **The exterior is vivid purple or red overall. The spines are very long.** The test is normally purple.
SIZE: Animal to 5″ (12.7 cm) in diameter; to 2″ (5.1 cm) high. **Spine length to two-thirds diameter of test.**
HABITAT: On rocks in protected sites on the exposed coast; low intertidal zone to depths of 410′ (125 m).
RANGE: Kodiak Island, Alaska, to Isla Cedros, Baja California, México; Japan.

NOTES: The diet of the red sea urchin, like our other urchins, includes various species of red and brown algae, however, it also includes sea lettuce. The spines of this giant urchin reach an impressive length up to 3″ (7.6 cm) long. Research on this species suggests that it may live to more than 100 years. The reproductive organ (roe) of the red sea urchin is harvested for shipment to Japan. This delicacy is eaten raw as a garnish for sushi and numerous other dishes.

SIMILAR SPECIES: Purple sea urchin.

Eccentric Sand Dollar

Dendraster excentricus (Eschscholtz, 1831)

OTHER NAMES: Common sand dollar, Pacific sand dollar, sand cookie, sand dollar, sea biscuit, West Coast sand dollar.

DESCRIPTION: Color of living animal is dark purple and the test is normally off-white. The test is flat and nearly circular. Minute spines and tube feet cover the animal, giving it a velvety appearance. A 5-petaled leaf pattern is found on the dorsal side, toward the posterior margin.

SIZE: Test diameter to 3″ (7.6 cm); height to 0.25″ (6 mm).

HABITAT: In sand; low intertidal zone to depths of 295′ (90 m).

RANGE: Juneau, Alaska, to northern Baja California, México.

NOTES: These familiar residents of our sandy beaches will bury themselves when the tide exposes them. At high tide, however, they position their posterior half at an angle into the waves. This allows them to capture food suspended in the water, including dinoflagellates, tiny crustaceans, diatoms and pieces of algae. In subtidal areas, the density of sand dollars can be staggering—more than 523 per square yard (625/m²), a great deal more than are found intertidally. Long-lived eccentric sand dollars may reach 9 years.

Test.

Sea Cucumbers

CLASS HOLOTHUROIDEA

Sea cucumbers are echinoderms (spiny-skinned animals) that are related to sea urchins. Most species have separate sexes. Reproduction occurs in two ways: some species produce many small eggs, which eventually develop into pelagic larvae; other species produce a few rather large yolk-filled eggs, which hatch directly into small cucumbers.

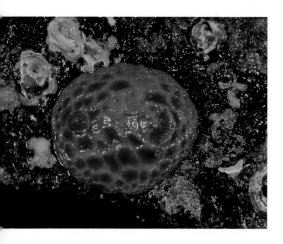

Creeping Pedal Sea Cucumber

Psolus chitonoides Clark, 1901

OTHER NAMES: Creeping pedal cucumber, armored sea cucumber, armored cucumber, creeping armored sea cucumber, creeping armored cucumber, slipper sea cucumber; formerly classified as *Psolus californicus*

DESCRIPTION: The color ranges from **bright red** to orange or yellow with red tentacles and white tips. **Flat body is covered with several calcareous plates.** A total of **10 equal-sized tentacles** are used for feeding.

SIZE: To 5″ (12.5 cm) in diameter.

HABITAT: On rocks free of sediment in exposed sites and sheltered inlets; low intertidal zone to subtidal water 815′ (247 m) deep.

RANGE: Pribilof Islands and Gulf of Alaska to Baja California, México.

NOTES: Out of the water, this cucumber resembles a chiton. In the water, however, its feeding tentacles are extended and become visible. Each tentacle holds a sticky pad that is used to catch tiny food particles from the water. The tentacles are then inserted in the mouth to be cleaned off. Various sea stars and the red rock crab feed on this sea cucumber and some fish nibble on its tentacles, even though it produces various toxic chemicals to deter predators.

Pale Creeping Pedal Sea Cucumber

Psolidium bidiscum Lambert, 1996

OTHER NAME: Incorrectly thought to also be *Psolidium bullatum*.

DESCRIPTION: Color ranges from **pink to white. Flat body is covered with several calcareous plates**. A total of **10 tentacles (8 large and 2 smaller)** are used for feeding.

SIZE: To 1.25″ (3 cm) in diameter.

HABITAT: On rocks, shells and similar objects especially when covered with sediment; low intertidal zone to depths of 725′ (220 m).

RANGE: Southeastern Alaska to central California.

NOTES: The pale creeping pedal sea cucumber prefers sites with sediment. This recently described species is distinctive in its shape and color. It is occasionally found at very low tides.

SIMILAR SPECIES: Creeping pedal sea cucumber.

California Sea Cucumber

Apostichopus californicus
(Stimpson, 1857)

OTHER NAMES: California cucumber, California stichopus, common sea cucumber, giant sea cucumber, giant red sea cucumber, giant red cucumber, large red cucumber; formerly classified as *Parastichopus californicus, Stichopus californicus.*

DESCRIPTION: Overall color is **orange-brown to reddish-brown**. During the first year the body is reddish. The body is cylindrical with tapering ends with numerous tube feet on the ventral side. The **feeding end includes 20 mop-like tentacles**.

SIZE: Length to 20″ (50 cm).

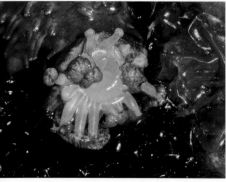
Mop-like feeding tentacles.

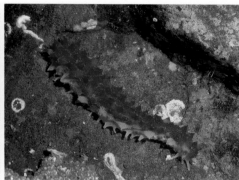
Juvenile in tidepool.

HABITAT: On rocky and sandy substrates at sheltered sites; low intertidal zone to depths of 817′ (249 m).

RANGE: Gulf of Alaska to Cedros Island, Baja California, México.

NOTES: The California sea cucumber is the largest sea cucumber in the Pacific Northwest. Both male and female specimens of this species mature at 4 years. The animal is harvested for the thin muscles running along the inside of the body wall. This sea cucumber reacts to its chief predator, the sunflower star, in an interesting manner when in extreme danger. The internal organs are ejected from the anus, producing a sticky pile of viscera that could distract a predator. These organs may be regenerated within 6–8 weeks.

....

Orange Sea Cucumber

Cucumaria miniata (Brandt, 1835)

OTHER NAMES: Red sea cucumber, red sea gherkin, vermilion sea cucumber.

DESCRIPTION: Overall color varies from **orange to orange-brown**. The body is cylindrical with tapering ends with numerous **tube feet placed in 5 evenly spaced bands along the body**. There are **10 equal-sized tentacles** present at the feeding end.

SIZE: Length to 10″ (25 cm).

HABITAT: Beneath rocks of protected shores; low intertidal zone to depths of 738′ (225 m).

RANGE: Amaknak Island, Aleutian Islands, Alaska, to Cambria, California.

NOTES: The orange sea cucumber is a common species in protected waters. Its body rests beneath rocks while its feeding tentacles are exposed for collecting tiny plankton or detritus from the water. Once the cucumber detects a food particle it slowly retracts the tentacle to wipe off the food particle and swallows it with its mouth. These tentacles may be brilliant orange or darker orange-brown. This sea cucumber possesses hemoglobin for the absorption and transport of oxygen to its cells.

Feeding tentacles underwater.

Giant Black Sea Cucumber

Cucumaria cf. *frondosa japonica* (Gunnerus, 1767)

OTHER NAME: Giant black cucumaria.
DESCRIPTION: Color of the entire **body is black**, the tentacles and areas around the mouth region can be white or red. There are 10 equal-sized tentacles present at the feeding end.
SIZE: To **12″ (30 cm) long or more.**
HABITAT: On rocky seashores; very low intertidal zone to depths of 425′ (130 m).
RANGE: Alaska to Fitzhugh Sound (near Bella Bella), British Columbia.
NOTES: No research has been done to date on the giant black sea cucumber. It is closely related to a similar sea cucumber on the east coast of North America as well as a subspecies found in Japan. If you look for this species in the low intertidal zone be sure to search carefully as it may be totally covered with algae. The British Columbia balcis is also often found feeding on or lying beside this species.

Alaska Tar Spot Sea Cucumber

Cucumaria vegae Théel, 1886

OTHER NAMES: Northern tar spot sea cucumber, tiny black sea cucumber.

DESCRIPTION: Color of the body is **black overall**. This **small species** includes **8 large, equal-sized tentacles and 2 smaller tentacles** present at the feeding end. Additional differences require a microscope. The **range of this species** helps greatly for identification.

SIZE: To 1.6″ (4 cm) long.

HABITAT: On rocks of exposed and protected shores and among California mussel beds; low intertidal zone.

RANGE: Aleutian Islands, Alaska, to Haida Gwaii (Queen Charlotte Islands), British Columbia; Japan.

NOTES: The Alaska tar spot sea cucumber is a northern species that is virtually identical in appearance to the tar spot sea cucumber. In the Juneau area of Alaska the tiny black sea cucumber forms dense mats on rocks in the lower intertidal zone. For those viewing intertidal marine life in southeast Alaska, the look-alike species, the tar spot sea cucumber, does not occur and so the identity of this species is not in question. For the sites where both species live, the identification can only be determined by examining their skin ossicles under a microscope.

SIMILAR SPECIES: Tar spot sea cucumber.

....

Tar Spot Sea Cucumber

Cucumaria pseudocurata Deichmann, 1938

DESCRIPTION: The body is **black overall**. The **tube feet are placed in rows on the dorsal side** of the body. There are **eight large and two small tentacles** at the mouth region. Additional differences require a microscope. The **range of this species** helps greatly for identification.

SIZE: To 1.5″ (3.5 cm) long.

HABITAT: Normally found living with the California mussel on exposed rocky shores; mid- to low intertidal zone.

RANGE: Central coast of British Columbia and northern Vancouver Island to Monterey Bay, California.

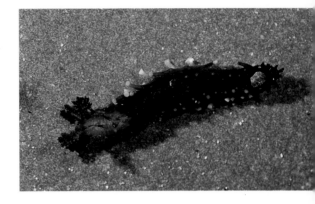

NOTES: The tar spot sea cucumber is found living among California mussel clusters. Their distribution is patchy as it can be abundant in one area of the mussel bed and totally absent in another. Under ideal conditions their densities can reach 4,000 individuals per/m². The tar spot sea cucumber and the black sea cucumber brood their eggs below the body for approximately one month.

SIMILAR SPECIES: Black brooding sea cucumber *Pseudocnus curatus* (Cowles, 1907) is a black species with scattered tube feet on its dorsal side and ten equal-sized tentacles.

··

False White Sea Cucumber

Eupentacta pseudoquinquesemita
Deichmann, 1938

OTHER NAME: White sea cucumber.
DESCRIPTION: The color is white overall with 5 rows of tube feet. **Its body feels soft** and bits of **debris including shell fragments often adhere to its tube feet**. At the feeding end of the body there are 8 large and 2 small tentacles. **The tube feet are very fine and numerous**. There are additional differences in the skin ossicles but a microscope is required for observing these.
SIZE: To 4 in (10 cm) long.
HABITAT: Under and between rocks; low intertidal zone to 660′ (200 m).
RANGE: Aleutian Islands, Alaska, to Puget Sound, Washington.
NOTES: Identification of this species can be difficult because a microscope is required to

confirm it. In southeast Alaska the false white sea cucumber is more common intertidally; in British Columbia the stiff-footed sea cucumber is more common.

SIMILAR SPECIES: Stiff-footed sea cucumber.

....

Stiff-footed Sea Cucumber

Eupentacta quinquesemita (Selenka, 1867)

OTHER NAMES: Stiff-footed cucumber, white sea cucumber, white cucumber, white sea gherkin, white gherkin; formerly classified as *Cucumaria quinquesemita, Cucumaria chronhjelmi.*

DESCRIPTION: Body is white to cream-colored, with traces of yellow or pink at base of tentacles. The body is cylindrical with elongated ends, it **does not feel soft** and **no debris normally adheres to its tube feet, which are coarse and numerous.** The body feels slightly firm to the touch. The feeding end includes 8 large and 2 smaller branched tentacles

SIZE: To 4″ (10 cm) long.

HABITAT: Under or between rocks on rocky shores; mid-intertidal zone to depths of 183′ (55 m).

RANGE: Sitka, Alaska, to Baja California, México.

NOTES: Stiff-footed sea cucumber and the false white sea cucumber are very similar species that are difficult to identify with certainty without the use of a microscope to look at the skin ossicles. As the name of this species indicates, the tube feet feel stiff due to the abundance of calcareous skin plates located within the skin and feet. The body wall of both this species and the false white sea cucumber can kill fish due to the presence of a poison.

SIMILAR SPECIES: False white sea cucumber.

Mushroom tunicate,
Distaplia occidentalis

Tunicates

PHYLUM CHORDATA,
SUBPHYLUM TUNICATA

At the seashore, there are three types of tunicates or ascidians that may be found there: solitary, colonial and compound. All are covered with an exterior coating called a tunic, hence the name tunicate. Solitary species are oval, elongated or irregular in shape, and an individual is usually attached directly to the substrate by a base. All tunicates have two siphons, one to draw in water for food and gas exchange, and the other to expel water and non-food particles. Colonial or social tunicates reproduce by budding or cloning to produce additional individuals from a single original member. Compound sea squirts are much different—many individuals (zooids) are packed together and form a fleshy common tunic. All individuals work together to ensure the survival of the compound organism.

It is truly remarkable that the simple-looking tunicates comprise one of the most advanced group of organisms found in the intertidal zone. Animals in the phylum Chordata have a primitive nerve cord (notochord), and they are distantly related to fish, whales and man. A unique feature of a tunicate is the heart, which reverses its beating every few minutes to change the direction in the flow of blood. Any advantage this system provides is currently unknown.

Solitary Sea Squirts

Solitary sea squirts are normally large individuals that have a tough leathery outer skin (tunic). Members of this group are often ovoid or irregular in shape.

Spiny-headed Sea Squirt

Boltenia villosa (Stimpson, 1864)

OTHER NAMES: Bristly tunicate, hairy sea squirt, hairy tunicate, shaggy tunicate, spiny-headed tunicate, stalked hairy sea squirt, strawberry sea squirt; formerly classified as *Cynthia castaneiformis, Cynthia villosa, Halocynthia castaneiformis, Halocynthia villosa*.
DESCRIPTION: Overall color varies from orange to reddish or tan. The tunic (body) is **globular shaped with short siphons and attached to a slender stalk** that varies greatly in

length and is occasionally absent. **Bristles are distributed in an irregular fashion over the tunic** and may have secondary bristles attached.

SIZE: Body length to 1.2″ (3 cm); stalk length to 1.6″ (4 cm).

HABITAT: On rocks or similar hard surfaces in areas with strong currents on the outer coast; low intertidal zone to depths of 328′ (100 m).

RANGE: Alaska to San Diego, California.

NOTES: This sea squirt and the long-stalked sea squirt have been found to extract vanadium (a metal element used in the manufacture of various alloys) from the environment and to concentrate it in their bodies. The leather star and painted sea star are known predators of this tunicate.

··

Long-stalked Sea Squirt

Styela montereyensis (Dall, 1872)

OTHER NAMES: Baseball club tunicate, California styela, Monterey tunicate, Monterey stalked tunicate, Monterey stalked sea squirt, stalked sea squirt, stalked simple tunicate, stalked tunicate, tidepool tunicate.

DESCRIPTION: Color ranges from yellowish to dark reddish-brown. The **tunic is elongated and cylindrical with longitudinal ridges and grooves**. The stalk is narrower, elongated and also cylindrical. The surface of the tunic is smooth.

SIZE: Total height to 12″ (30 cm).

HABITAT: On rock or similar object in both calm and rough locations; low intertidal zone to depths of 100′ (30 m).

RANGE: Hope Island, British Columbia, to Isla San Geronimo, Baja California, México.

NOTES: The long-stalked sea squirt is the largest solitary tunicate found on our shores. Its distinctive shape makes it one of the easier species to identify. Those individuals found in quiet bays grow to a larger size than those found in exposed locations. One individual has been known to reach 9″ (23 cm) in height in 3 years. The body of this tunicate may be pointed straight up or at right angles to the stalk. This species can absorb and store vanadium from its environment. See spiny-headed sea squirt.

Warty Sea Squirt

Pyura haustor (Stimpson, 1864)

OTHER NAMES: Decorator tunicate, solitary tunicate, solitary sea squirt, warty tunicate, wrinkled sea squirt, wrinkled seapump.
DESCRIPTION: The tunic is reddish-brown and the siphons are bright red. Much of the creased globular body is normally obscured with debris and encrusting organisms. The **2 exposed red siphons are normally extended** and often the only recognizable part of this species visible.
SIZE: Height to 3.2″ (8 cm).
HABITAT: On rocks, pilings, floats and similar objects, and in tidepools; low intertidal zone to depths of 660′ (200 m).
RANGE: Shumagin Islands, Aleutian Islands, Alaska, to San Diego, California.
NOTES: The warty sea squirt may be difficult to find or observe at low tide as it normally withdraws its siphons when the water recedes. Those in tidepools and similar situations are easier to view. This tunicate is one species that does not concentrate vanadium. The striped sun star is its well-known predator.

Brooding Transparent Sea Squirt

Corella inflata Huntsman, 1912

OTHER NAMES: Brooding transparent tunicate, transparent sea squirt, transparent tunicate; early records refer to this species as *Corella willmeriana*, which is now known to be a similar-looking, deep-water species.
DESCRIPTION: The **tunic is transparent**, allowing the viewer to observe the internal organs of the animal. White flecks are often present on the tunic. The cubic shaped body may be smooth to rough.
SIZE: Height to 1.1″ (2.8 cm).
HABITAT: On rocks and similar hard objects as well as floats in protected waters; low intertidal zone to depths of 59′ (18 m).

RANGE: Hope Island, British Columbia, to Puget Sound, Washington.

NOTES: Much of the information published on the brooding transparent sea squirt refers to a similar-looking species that lives in deeper waters. The transparent sea squirt, *Corella willmeriana*, is a similar-looking species with an elongated tunic. As the common name of this species suggests, it broods its eggs until they hatch.

Shiny Red Sea Squirt

Cnemidocarpa finmarkiensis
(Kiaer, 1893)

OTHER NAMES: Brilliant red hide tunicate, broad-base sea squirt, broad base sea squirt, broadbase tunicate, Finmark's tunicate, red sea squirt, shiny orange sea squirt, shiny red tunicate, solitary tunicate.

DESCRIPTION: Color of the tunic ranges from pink to **red or orange**. The **squat body is smooth without wrinkles**. The 2 **siphons are short** and retractable.

SIZE: Width to 2″ (5 cm); to 1″ (2.5 cm) high.

HABITAT: On rock, gravel or on shell debris and in tidepools; low intertidal zone to depths of 165′ (50 m).

RANGE: Circumboreal; Alaska to Point Conception, California; Japan.

NOTES: This solitary sea squirt has been reported to live as deep as 1,782′ (540 m) in Japan. It is also found in both the Canadian and European Arctic. It is sometimes seen on rocks covered with many other small organisms. Two crater-like siphons provide the means by which all sea squirts obtain water for both food and respiration. The painted sea star is a predator.

Disc-top Tunicate

Chelyosoma productum Stimpson, 1864

OTHER NAMES: Flattop sea squirt, horseshoe ascidian, horseshoe sea squirt; formerly classified as *Chelyosoma producta*.

DESCRIPTION: The color changes from transparent in young individuals to

yellowish-brown in older individuals. The surface also changes from smooth to rough and wrinkled as it ages. The tunic is **cylindrically shaped with a flat, disk-shaped top** and attached at one end to a hard surface.

SIZE: Height to 2.5″ (6 cm); to 2″ (5 cm) in diameter.

HABITAT: On rocks and similar objects including pilings and floats; low intertidal zone to depths of 164′ (50 m).

RANGE: Prince William Sound, Alaska, to southern California.

NOTES: Research has shown that this species feeds upon the larvae of barnacles, copepods, gastropods and ascidians. Breeding happens in the spring when both the eggs and sperm are shed into the ocean. This distinctive ascidian is known to live at least 3 years. Its predators include the painted star and the Oregon triton.

Social Ascidians

Members of this group are colonial tunicates that form clusters of individuals, which are separated or occasionally joined at a base.

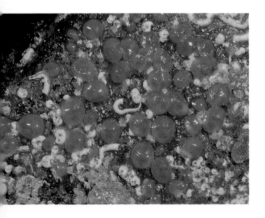

Taylor's Social Tunicate

Metandrocarpa taylori Huntsman, 1912

OTHER NAMES: Orange social ascidian, orange social sea squirt, orange social tunicate, red sea buttons, Taylor's colonial tunicate.

DESCRIPTION: The tunic varies in color from **bright red to orange** and sometimes yellow or green. The shape of **individual zooids may be round or oval**.

SIZE: Individual height to 0.3" (8 mm); width to 0.2" (5 mm); colony diameter; 8" (20 cm).
HABITAT: On rocks in well-circulated waters; low intertidal zone to depths of 100' (30 m).
RANGE: China Hat, British Columbia, to San Diego, California.
NOTES: Taylor's social tunicate is a colonial organism that appears to be a group of simple tunicates. These individuals are actually joined by a thin basal sheet that is not easily observed, creating a colony of social tunicates. In old established colonies the individual zooids may be packed together because budding individuals have filled the gaps left by earlier individuals. Taylor's social tunicate reproduces both asexually—by budding—and sexually all year long.

Lightbulb Tunicate

Clavelina huntsmani Van Name, 1931

OTHER NAMES: Light bulb ascidian, light bulb tunicate.
DESCRIPTION: The zooids are **transparent with 2 parallel orange or pink longitudinal bands present** inside the tunic that resemble the filaments of a lightbulb.
SIZE: Individual height to 2" (5 cm); colony to 20" (50 cm) wide.
HABITAT: On rocks in areas of exposed ocean; low intertidal zone to depths of 100' (30 m).
RANGE: Barkley Sound, British Columbia, to Monterey Bay, California.
NOTES: The individuals comprising this colonial ascidian are not dependent upon each other as adults. When the zooids are young, however, the colony is connected by a thin basal sheet. This is an annual species that is abundant in the spring and summer.

Compound Ascidians

This group of colonial ascidians comprises many individuals or zooids that are embedded within a common tunic or covering.

California Sea Pork

Aplidium californicum
(Ritter and Forsyth, 1917)

OTHER NAMES: Sea pork; formerly classified as *Amaroucium californicum*.
DESCRIPTION: Overall color ranges from **gray to opalescent white**, yellowish, or transparent. The colony forms a smooth, sand-free and somewhat **thick slab or sheet** that can cover a small area.
SIZE: Colonies to 1.25″ (3 cm) thick; to 12″ (30 cm) across.
HABITAT: On rocks, shells and similar hard surfaces in protected sites along the outer coast; mid-intertidal zone to depths of 276′ (84 m).
RANGE: Alaska to Gulf of California, México; Galapagos Islands, Ecuador.
NOTES: California sea pork, a very common, large colonial tunicate, is found on rocks in areas protected from the surf. Its name comes from its color and slab-like shape, which resemble pork fat. Enemies of this species include the leather star, bat star and other sea stars.
SIMILAR SPECIES: Red sea pork.

Red Sea Pork

Aplidium solidum
(Ritter and Forsyth, 1917)

OTHER NAMES: Red ascidian; formerly classified as *Amaroucium solidum*.
DESCRIPTION: Overall color ranges from bright red or orange-brown. The colony forms a smooth, sand-free and somewhat bulky, irregular slab or sheet that can cover a small area, often with pits present.
SIZE: Colonies to 2″ (5 cm) thick and 8″ (20 cm) across.
HABITAT: On rocks and pilings in sheltered and circulating water; low intertidal zone to depths of 130′ (40 m).
RANGE: Vancouver Island, British Columbia, to San Diego, California.

NOTES: Red sea pork is found in sheltered areas where a current is present. It is a common ascidian, most abundant in spring and summer but present year-round. The opalescent nudibranch is known to feed on this species in California and likely elsewhere.
SIMILAR SPECIES: California sea pork.

Yellow-lobbed Tunicate

Eudistoma ritteri Van Name, 1945

OTHER NAMES: Clubbed sea squirt; formerly classified as *Archidistoma ritteri*.
DESCRIPTION: The colony color ranges normally from **yellowish to gray or transparent** but on occasion can also include dusky orange. Colony shape is normally **mushroom-like pendant lobes with a distinct stalk**. In cave-like situations they may simply form sheets.
SIZE: Colonies normally to 1.6″ (4 cm) high and 0.6″ (15 mm) across; individual lobes to 2″ (5 cm) high.
HABITAT: On rock near surfgrass and on channel and cave walls; low intertidal zone to depths of 66′ (20 m).
RANGE: Vancouver Island, British Columbia, to San Diego, California.
NOTES: The yellow-lobbed tunicate prefers to live on the outer coast where there are strong currents, including surge channels and in sea caves. It reproduces both sexually and asexually. Research has found that this species concentrates several rare metals inside its tissues. "Astonishing concentrations" of vanadium, chromium and titanium are removed from the environment and stored in living specimens. The reason for this is unknown.

Mushroom Tunicate

Distaplia occidentalis Bancroft, 1899

OTHER NAMES: Mushroom ascidian, western distaplia; formerly classified as *Distaplia californica*.
DESCRIPTION: Color is variable and includes **purple, red, pink, yellow, gray or white**. Various color combinations are also possible. **Several mushroom-like bodies together form a colony**. Each small zooid bears a **mushroom-like shape** on a stalk when underwater.

Purple form with closed siphons.   Orange form with open siphons.

SIZE: Colonies to 1.5″ (4 cm) high and 4″ (10 cm) across; individual bodies to 0.5″ (13 mm) across.

HABITAT: On rock in areas with good circulation but without heavy surf; low intertidal zone to depths of 49′ (15 m).

RANGE: Chichagof Island, Alaska, to San Diego, California.

NOTES: The mushroom tunicate is a compound tunicate made up of several individuals. This conspicuous species is known for its bright and varied colors and it gets its name from the shape of its small colonies when under water. The zooids collectively produce an oral siphon to admit water into the colony. Smaller, separate siphons pass the water out of the body, once the food has been filtered out. It is believed that this tunicate's high acid content may help protect it from its enemies.

....

Multi-lobed Tunicate

Ritterella aequalisiphonis
(Ritter and Forsyth, 1917)

OTHER NAMES: Orange mushroom compound tunicate; formerly classified as *Amaroucium aequalisiphonis*, *Sigillinaria aequalisiphonis*.

DESCRIPTION: Overall color is **orange-brown**. Several club-shaped lobes are **clustered into colonies** (loose groups). Each lobe is normally **heavily sand-encrusted** and has a basal network that keeps the colony together.

SIZE: Colonies to 0.8″ (20 mm) high and 3″ (8 cm) across; individual (head) to 0.3″ (8 mm) across.

HABITAT: On rock of sheltered to moderate shores; low intertidal zone to depths of 49′ (15 m).

RANGE: Puget Sound, Washington, to San Diego California; possibly Japan.

NOTES: The multi-lobed tunicate forms several hemispherical shapes that together form a larger colony. Several species of marine life are often found in the sheltered environment between the lobes.

White Glove Leather

Didemnum albidum

(Verrill, 1871)

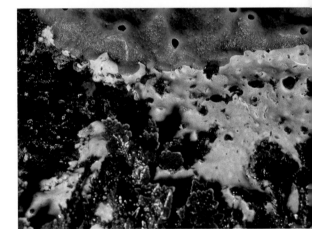

OTHER NAME: Formerly classified as *Leptoclinum albidum* (in part).

DESCRIPTION: This **white** encrusting species is **thin and leather-like, and it clings to the substrate**.

SIZE: Colonies to 0.1″ (3 mm) thick and 4″ (10 cm) across.

HABITAT: On rocks and similar hard surfaces; low intertidal zone to depths of 50′ (15 m) and lower.

RANGE: Circumpolar; Bering Sea to Washington; Arctic to Cape Cod; Europe.

NOTES: This ascidian is one of several similar-looking species that may be encountered along our coast. Most of these species, however, are subtidal. A microscope is required to correctly identify the species present.

Carpet Tunicates

Didemnum spp. Savigny, 1816

OTHER NAME: White crusts.

DESCRIPTION: The wide-ranging colors include white, yellow, reddish and brown. Colonies are tough crusts. No arrangement of zooids is apparent and the apertures may not be obvious.

SIZE: Colonies to 0.2″ (5 mm) thick and 8″ (20 cm) across.
HABITAT: On rocks, shells, pilings, algae and similar objects; low intertidal zone to depths of 1,350′ (411 m).
RANGE: British Columbia to northern California; the entire Atlantic Coast of North America.
NOTES: Carpet tunicates are invasive species that have invaded a significant portion of the Pacific Northwest as well as the entire Atlantic Coast and many other waters. Their crust-like colonies incorporate minute calcareous spicules too small to see. The identification of most species requires a microscope.

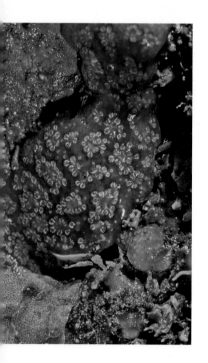

Harbour Star Ascidian

Botryllus schlosseri (Pallas, 1766)

OTHER NAMES: Eyed tunicate, golden star tunicate.
DESCRIPTION: Color ranges widely and includes yellow, orange, red and gray. The body is flat, **encrusting with star-shaped or round patterns** visible on the surface. **A large central opening is present** in the middle of each star or round shape.
SIZE: Colonies to 0.2″ (5 mm) high and 6″ (15 cm) across.
HABITAT: On rock, boat bottoms, floats, pilings and eelgrass; low intertidal zone to depths of 60′ (18 m).
RANGE: British Columbia to Baja California, México; Bay of Fundy, Nova Scotia, to Gulf of Mexico; Europe; Mediterranean.
NOTES: This introduced tunicate is originally from Europe and is noted for its rapid growth during the warmer summer months. Its unique patterning makes it one of the easier tunicate species to identify. Each zooid draws in water for food and respiration separately, and each colony collectively removes the wastes, indigestible particles and water through a common opening.

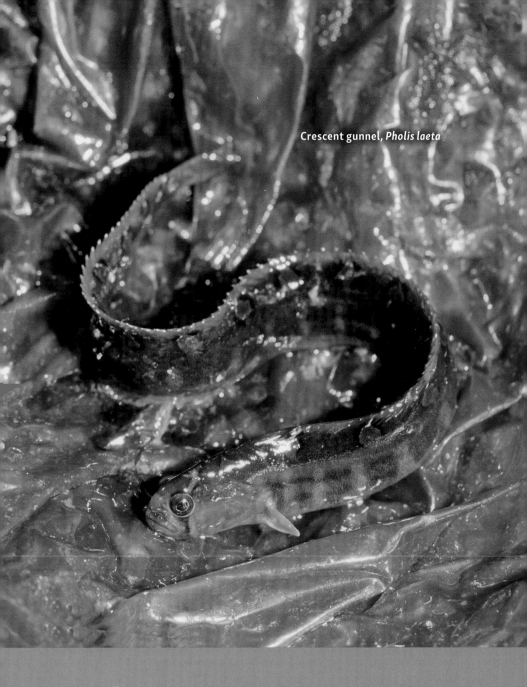

Crescent gunnel, *Pholis laeta*

Fishes

PHYLUM CHORDATA,
SUBPHYLUM VERTEBRATA

F ish can be found in all marine habitats from tidepools to deep subtidal waters. It is one of our more important foods and various species have been harvested for centuries. Although a number of species occur in the intertidal habitat, few species have been harvested.

Cartilaginous Fishes
CLASS CHONDRICHTHYES

Big Skate

Raja binoculata Girard, 1855

OTHER NAMES: Pacific great skate, Pacific barndoor skate.

ANIMAL

DESCRIPTION: Color of the dorsal surface ranges widely from gray to various shades of brown, or blackish, frequently with rosettes of white, occasionally with dark spots. The flattened body is diamond-shaped and slightly wider than it is long. Spines are found in a row from the tail extending to the body.

SIZE: Length 8′ (2.4 m).

EGG CASE

DESCRIPTION: The egg case turns black when dry. It is a compact shape lacking any attachment fibers and the surface is very smooth. The anterior apron is concave and the **dorsal surface features two prominent ridges** creating a concave area.

SIZE: Length (includes the aprons but not the horns) to 11″ (28 cm).

HABITAT: Egg cases are washed up on beach; high to low intertidal zone.

RANGE: Bering Sea and southeast Alaska to Baja California, México.

NOTES: The tidepooler probably won't come across any live skate on the shore; it is much more likely that an empty egg case ("mermaid's purse") will be found there. The light, empty cases are occasionally blown high up on the beach after a storm. The big skate is the only species of skate that contains multiple embryos in each egg case. The number of embryos per case ranges from 2–7. This species probably produces the largest egg case of any skate in the world.

Longnose Skate

Raja rhina Jordan & Gilbert, 1880

ANIMAL

DESCRIPTION: Color of the dorsal surface ranges widely from brown to bluish or gray with a dark ring at the base of each pectoral fin.

SIZE: Length to 4.8′ (1.5 m).

EGG CASE

DESCRIPTION: This egg case is a golden brown when fresh then turns to black when dry. The overall shape is rectangular and flat. The dorsal surface is often etched with a very thin, dense fibrous texture. **Both the anterior and posterior tendrils (horns) possess an inner keel. Attachment fibers (found on the lateral edges of the egg case) are present.** The posterior apron is almost straight, as well as broad. The tendrils are medium length.

SIZE: Egg case length (includes the aprons but not the horns) to 12″ (30 cm).

HABITAT: Egg cases are washed up on beach; high to low intertidal zone.

RANGE: Bering Sea and Unalaska Island, Alaska, to Cedros Island, Baja California, México.

NOTES: The egg case of the longnose skate is the most common egg case or "mermaid's purse" that washes up on the beach in the Pacific Northwest. There are a total of 11 species of skates that are found in the waters of this region.

Bony Fishes
CLASS OSTEICHTHYES

Egg clusters of Pacific herring.

Pacific Herring
Clupea pallasii Valenciennes, 1847

OTHER NAME: Formerly classified as *Clupea harengus pallasi*.
DESCRIPTION: Color of the fish is basically **silvery without spots**. It bears **no scales on the head and side of the tail**. Large scales are found on the body.
SIZE: Fish to 18″ (46 cm) long; eggs to 0.05″ (1.5 mm) across.
HABITAT: This fish spawns on various algae and seagrasses; low intertidal zone to shallow subtidal depths.
RANGE: Bering Sea to Baja California, México; Arctic Ocean to Korea and Japan.
NOTES: The Pacific herring is a remarkable fish that is of major importance to many species living in the oceans, including the humpback whale *Megaptera novaeangliae* and Pacific white-sided dolphin *Lagenorhynchus obliquidens*. Its numbers have had dramatic fluctuations due to overfishing and other causes. It is a spring spawner that times the laying of its eggs with the local conditions of the season. In the Pacific Northwest, that typically happens in February and March. This timing varies considerably up and down our coast, starting as early as October in California and as late as July in Alaska, depending upon the year's conditions.

Plainfin Midshipman
Porichthys notatus Girard, 1854

OTHER NAMES: Midshipman, northern midshipman.
DESCRIPTION: Color is grayish-brown with purple tones along with **rows of tiny silvery dots**. The **body is plump** and rectangular shaped, and the first dorsal fin is very small.

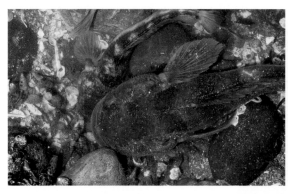

Large male with visiting female.

Eggs.

SIZE: Length to 15″ (37.5 cm).
HABITAT: Beneath large rocks and boulders; low intertidal zone to depths of 1,200′ (366 m).
RANGE: Central British Columbia to Baja California, México.
NOTES: The plainfin midshipman gets its common name from the rows of silvery dots found on its body. These are luminous organs that have some resemblance to the row of buttons found on former jackets of the naval marine midshipmen. This fish is well known for the male's ability to create a resonating hum in his bid to attract a mate. The hum is produced by quickly contracting the muscles around his swim bladder, the organ used to adjust the fish's buoyancy underwater. The male waits under a large rock for a female to visit and lay her yellow eggs on the underside of the rock, which he will watch over for weeks.

Northern Clingfish

Gobiesox maeandricus (Girard, 1858)

OTHER NAMES: Common cling fish, flathead clingfish.
DESCRIPTION: Color ranges from gray to brown or occasionally red often with bold patterning. The body is stocky with a flat head. A **large circular adhesive disc that extends across the total width is present** on the underside.

SIZE: Length to 6.5″ (16.5 cm).
HABITAT: On the underside of rocks; low intertidal zone to depths of 65′ (20 m).
RANGE: Southeastern Alaska to northern Baja California, México.

NOTES: This fish usually uses its adhesive disc to cling to the underside of a rock, where it waits for food to arrive. Its diet includes the white-lined chiton, lined chiton, shield limpet, plate limpet, ribbed limpet, masked limpet and tiny red rock crab, but it also feeds on other fish including sculpins and clingfish. If you find this species hiding under a rock, be sure to return the rock to its original position.

SIMILAR SPECIES: Tidepool snailfish has small adhesive suckers on the underside of its body, extending to about ⅓ the width of the fish.

Longfin Sculpin

Jordania zonope Starks, 1895

OTHER NAME: Band-eye sculpin.

DESCRIPTION: Bright color overall from olive green to brown or red, with bands around the head and **3 bars radiating downward from the eye.** The body is elongated and slender, and **the head bears noticeably long cirri.**

SIZE: Length to 6″ (15 cm).

HABITAT: In caves, caverns and crevices; very low intertidal zone to depths of 60′ (18 m).

RANGE: Baranoff Island, Southeast Alaska, to Point Lobos, California.

NOTES: The longfin sculpin is an uncommon but striking visitor to the intertidal zone. Its distinctive coloration is always a pleasant sight for the observant beachcomber.

Tidepool Sculpin

Oligocottus maculosus Girard, 1856

OTHER NAMES: Tide-pool sculpin, tidepool johnny.

DESCRIPTION: Color of the dorsal surface varies from **green to reddish-brown with 5 darker saddle-like blotches on its back.** The ventral side is lighter. A single, slim, forked spine is found on the gill cover.

SIZE: Length to 3.5″ (9 cm).

HABITAT: Under rocks and in tidepools; mid-intertidal zone to shallow subtidal depths.
RANGE: Bering Sea and the Aleutian Islands, Alaska, to southern California.
NOTES: The tidepool sculpin is probably our most common resident fish of the tidepools in this area. It has been well studied by biologists, who have found it to be very tolerant of extreme changes in temperature, from the heat of tiny tidepools in direct sun to the cool waters of high tide. This sculpin is able to use its sense of smell to "home" back to its original tidepool if displaced.

Tidepool Snailfish

Liparis florae (Jordan & Starks, 1895)

OTHER NAME: Shore liparid.
DESCRIPTION: Overall color is variable from yellow to green, purplish-brown or reddish-brown. Reddish spots may be present on the sides of the body and the fins may feature dark speckles. The tail is short and the head is compressed with small eyes. Both the dorsal fin and anal fin are elongated. **A small adhesive disc is found between the two pelvic fins.**
SIZE: Length to 7.3″ (18.3 cm).
HABITAT: Beneath rocks and among algae and surfgrasses on exposed shores; mid-intertidal zone to shallow subtidal depths.
RANGE: Bering Sea to southern California.
NOTES: The tidepool snailfish can change its color somewhat, turning lighter or darker to match its environment. Its eyes are noticeably small for its size. It feeds primarily on shrimp and similar animals living in its rocky habitat.

High Cockscomb

Anoplarchus purpurescens Gill, 1861

OTHER NAMES: Cockscomb, cockscomb prickleback, crested blenny.
DESCRIPTION: Color varies greatly from dark brown to purple or blackish, often with mottling. Males during breeding season are adorned with vivid orange pectoral and anal

fins. The body is elongated with a head that bears a **fleshy crest resembling a cockscomb**.

SIZE: Length to 7.8″ (20 cm).

HABITAT: Under rocks or among algae; low intertidal zone to depths of 100′ (30 m).

RANGE: Attu Island, Aleutian Islands, Alaska, to California.

NOTES: The beachcomber is most likely to find this fish under an intertidal rock, where several individuals are often grouped together. In the darkness of night, the high cockscomb comes out from hiding to feed. Green algae, worms, molluscs and crustaceans are important foods. Females grow to be larger than males. They are known to release up to 2,700 eggs, which they wrap their bodies around to guard and aerate. The common garter snake (*Thamnophis sirtalis*) is a predator of this species.

Mosshead Warbonnet

Chirolophis nugator (Jordan & Williams, 1895)

OTHER NAME: Mosshead prickleback.

DESCRIPTION: Overall color varies from orange-brown to reddish-brown or red. The body is elongated and the **top of its head is graced with many cirri that form a flattened crest-like covering**. A total of 12–13 eye-spots are also found along the dorsal fin of the male,

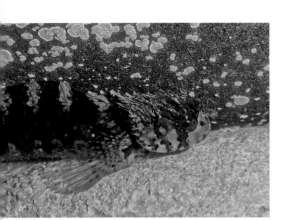

while bars are present in females.

SIZE: Length to 6″ (15 cm).

HABITAT: In rock crevices and rocky tidepools; low intertidal zone to depths of 200′ (60 m).

RANGE: Aleutian Islands, Alaska, to San Miguel Island, southern California.

NOTES: The mosshead warbonnet is a striking fish to discover at the lowest of tides, and its distinctive headdress makes it easy to identify. It is sometimes found hiding in shells or rock crevices with only its head showing. Spawning occurs from late winter to early spring. It is a known predator of nudibranchs.

....

Black Prickleback

Xiphister atropurpureus (Kittlitz, 1858)

OTHER NAMES: Black blenny; formerly classified as *Epigeichthys atropurpureus*.
DESCRIPTION: Color varies from black to reddish-brown overall. **Two dark bands with light edges radiate backward from the eyes.** A conspicuous **white vertical band is present at base of tail fin.** The body is elongated and the dorsal fin joins with the tail and anal fins.

SIZE: Length to 12″ (30.5 cm).
HABITAT: Under rocks, on cobble and in tidepools; low intertidal zone to depths of 25′ (7.6 m).
RANGE: Kodiak Island, Alaska, to Baja California, México.
NOTES: The omnivorous diet of the black prickleback is largely a result of its size. It feeds mostly on algae when young; however, that changes as it ages. Various algae and small crustaceans are the main food items for medium-sized fish. As the fish grows, other fish become one of its main foods. Females lay their eggs in a clump beneath a rock and the male guards them by wrapping its body around them.

....

Crescent Gunnel

Pholis laeta (Cope, 1873)

OTHER NAME: Bracketed blenny.
DESCRIPTION: Overall color varies widely from yellowish-green to nearly black. **A row of crescent-shaped markings highlight the back.** The body is elongated as with all gunnels.
SIZE: Length to 10″ (25 mm).

HABITAT: Beneath rocks and algae, and in tidepools; low intertidal zone to depths of 240′ (73 m).

RANGE: Bering Sea and Aleutian Islands, Alaska, to northern California.

NOTES: This wriggling fish feeds on a variety of small bivalves and nips off the cirri (feeding appendages) of barnacles. It wraps its body around its eggs to protect them from predators until they hatch. The crescent gunnel is a common species that has been known to live as long as 6 years. Mergansers are likely important predators.

Saddleback Gunnel

Pholis ornata (Girard, 1854)

OTHER NAME: Saddled blenny.

DESCRIPTION: Overall color varies from green to brown. **A repeated U-shaped arch pattern is present along upper body.** The body is elongated with extended dorsal and anal fins.

SIZE: Length to 13″ (30 cm).

HABITAT: Beneath rocks or in tidepools containing eelgrass; low intertidal zone to depths of 120′ (36 m).

RANGE: Southern British Columbia to southern California; Korea.

NOTES: The gunnels are a group of fish also frequently referred to as blennies. "Blenny" is a European term for several families of fish that include gunnels, pricklebacks and others. The eggs of the saddleback gunnel are laid in late winter to the first hint of spring and guarded by both parents.

SIMILAR SPECIES: Crescent gunnel is similar looking, with crescent-shaped marks along its upper body.

Sea hair, *Ulva intestinalis*

Seaweeds

PHYLA CHLOROPHYTA,
OCHROPHYTA, RHODOPHYTA

S eaweeds or marine algae use pigments such as chlorophyll to trap energy from the sun and store it as chemical energy in the bonds of a simple sugar (glucose). These plants are an important part of both the intertidal and subtidal ecosystems. Their presence provides food and shelter, as well as oxygen, to the wide variety of invertebrates and vertebrates found here. Seaweeds and phytoplankton are the base of many food webs to which countless species are linked. Seaweeds are classified into 3 separate groups (phyla) according to the types of pigments present: green algae (phylum Chlorophyta), brown algae (phylum Ochrophyta) and red algae (phylum Rhodophyta).

Cultures from all over the world have gathered and eaten seaweeds, probably for thousands of years. At least 70 species have been harvested from the Pacific Ocean.

Green Algae
PHYLUM CHLOROPHYTA

Green algae contain chlorophylls a (a primary photosynthetic pigment in plants that release oxygen) and b (an accessory pigment also found in vascular plants). In this way they are very similar to green land plants. The green algae are found in shallow waters where chlorophyll is most efficient. Green algae store their sugars as starch.

Sea Hair

Ulva intestinalis Linnaeus, 1753

OTHER NAMES: Cornrow sea lettuce, green string lettuce, tubeweed, tube weed, hair weed, link confetti, maiden hair sea lettuce, sea felt; formerly classified as *Enteromorpha intestinalis*.
DESCRIPTION: Color ranges from bright yellowish-green to yellowish when reproductive, or white when sun bleached.

The **elongated, unbranched hollow blades** are one layer of cells thick and arise from a tiny holdfast.

SIZE: Length normally to 8″ (20 cm); occasionally to 3.3′ (1 m).

HABITAT: On rocks; high to mid-intertidal zone and at freshwater seeps. Also an epiphyte on other species of algae (attached to the organism with no harm to it), often in tidepools.

RANGE: Cosmopolitan (temperate coastal regions); Aleutian Islands, Alaska, to México; Russia; Japan; Korea; Chile; Mediterranean; Atlantic; North Sea; Baltic; Australia.

NOTES: Upon close inspection, the fine tubes of sea hair may resemble hairs. This seaweed has been used in stews: a small amount flavors a large volume of stew. This species has recently been placed back in the genus *Ulva*, where it was originally placed by Linnaeus.

SIMILAR SPECIES: Flat-tube sea lettuce *Ulva linza* is tubular only at the base and is 2 layers thick.

....

Common Sea Lettuce

Ulva lactuca Linnaeus, 1753

OTHER NAMES: Green laver, sea lettuce, window seaweed, mistakenly *Ulva fenestrata*.

DESCRIPTION: Color ranges from **light green to darker. The thin blade bears a smooth surface** that may be split into broad lobes, **often with ruffled edge.** Several small holes may be present on blades.

SIZE: Length to 7″ (18 cm).

HABITAT: On rocks, other algae species or floating on mudflats; high to low intertidal zone.

RANGE: Bering Sea to Chile; Newfoundland to Florida; Japan; Russia.

NOTES: This alga is very tolerant of a great range of temperatures. It is often seen out of water, somewhat dried out, when the tide is low. Under fertile conditions, it will cover large areas. Similar species of sea lettuce have traditionally been eaten by Hawaiians in a variety of ways—mixed with other seaweeds and served with sushi, made into light soup and made into stews.

....

Corkscrew Sea Lettuce

Ulva taeniata (Setchell) Setchell & N.L. Gardner, 1920

OTHER NAME: Formerly classified as *Ulva fasciata* var. *taeniata*.

DESCRIPTION: Bright green **blades are elongated and ruffled with a spiral twist**. Blades can be either unbranched or branched.

SIZE: Length to 20″ (50 cm); width to 1.5″ (4 cm).

HABITAT: On rocks from mid- to low intertidal zone.

RANGE: Southern British Columbia to Baja California, México; Peru; New Zealand; Australia.

NOTES: This common green alga is very thin, only 2 cells thick. When viewed underwater, its corkscrew pattern is especially visible.

Tangle Weed

Acrosiphonia coalita (Ruprecht) Scagel, Garbary, Golden & M.W. Hawkes, 1986

OTHER NAMES:
Gametophyte (gamete producing) stage: green rope; formerly *Spongomorpha coalita*; **Sporophyte (spore producing) stage**: formerly *Chlorochytrium inclusum*.

DESCRIPTION: Occurs in 2 separate stages. **Gametophyte stage: bright green with many filaments, which become entangled to resemble rope.** These coarse filaments posess numerous hooklike lateral branches. **Sporophyte Stage:** tiny greenish spots on red algae.

SIZE: Length to 12″ (30 cm).

HABITAT: On exposed rocks or epiphytically on other algae; mid- to low intertidal zone.

RANGE: Aleutian Islands, Alaska, to San Luis Obispo County, California.

NOTES: The rope-like strands of tangle weed occur only in the gametophyte (sexual) stage of its life cycle. A one-celled spore (saprophyte) produced at this stage lives in the crustose stage of a few species of red algae, including papillate seaweed. Tangle weed is sometimes found as an epiphyte, attached to another species of algae without harming it. The sporophyte (asexual) stage is very difficult to find: it is unicellular and present only in the tissue of various red algae species.

Sea Moss

Cladophora spp. (Kützing, 1843)

OTHER NAMES: Green dome seaweed, green tuft.

DESCRIPTION: Color varies from bright green to yellowish-green. Individual strands are **filamentous in shape and many times branched, growing in low mats.**

SIZE: Length to 2″ (5 cm).

HABITAT: On rocks and in tidepools; mid- to low intertidal zone.

RANGE: Alaska to Baja California, México.

NOTES: The structure of sea moss enables it to hold large volumes of water, preventing it from drying out when the tide recedes. There are a few different species of sea moss, all growing low to the ground and forming moss-like mats or tufts.

Sea Pearls

Derbesia marina (Lyngbye) Solier, 1846

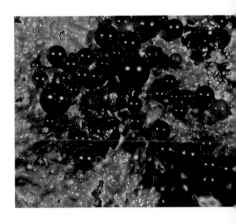

OTHER NAMES: Globose Stage: Green sea grape; formerly classified as *Halicystis ovalis*. **Filamentous (spore-producing) stage:** Green sea felt.

DESCRIPTION: Occurs in 2 separate stages. **Globose Stage:** Light to **dark green or black spherical globules** on a short stalk. **Filamentous Stage:** Thalli are irregularly branched, elongated filaments.

SIZE: Globose Stage: Diameter to 0.4″ (10 mm). **Filamentous Stage:** Length to 1.5″ (4 cm)

HABITAT: On rocks, encrusting coralline algae, and sponges, in exposed and sheltered situations; low intertidal zone to depths of 66′ (20 m).

RANGE: Aleutian Islands, Alaska, to La Jolla, California; Japan; Korea; Russia; Philippines; Chile; Peru; Southern Australia; North Atlantic.

NOTES: Only after careful laboratory study were the 2 distinct stages of this species determined to belong to the same marine alga. The globose stage, often referred to as the "Halicystis" stage, is the sexual stage that produces gametes, while the filamentous stage reproduces by cell division.

Sea Staghorn

Codium fragile

(Suringar) Hariot, 1889

OTHER NAMES: Dead man's fingers, felty fingers, green sea velvet, sponge seaweed.
DESCRIPTION: Color ranges from dark green to blackish-green. Thallus comprised of **many spongy elongated cylindrical branches** that rise from a basal disc.
SIZE: Length to 16″ (40 cm).
HABITAT: On rocks and shells; low intertidal zone to shallow subtidal depths.
RANGE: Green Island, Prince William Sound, Alaska, to Baja California, México; Japan Sea; northeastern United States (introduced).
NOTES: This seaweed resembles a sponge, but there are no green marine sponges found on the Pacific coast. The sea staghorn is very rich in vitamins and minerals, so it is often used in soups although it is hard to clean. It has invaded the New England coast, where it has caused some problems with the shellfish industry. Young plants often start growing on oysters, mussels and scallops, increasing the drag and causing the molluscs to be taken out to sea during storms. A small red alga, staghorn fringe *Ceramium codicola* lives exclusively on sea staghorn.

Spongy Cushion

Codium setchellii N.L. Gardner, 1919

OTHER NAMES: Green cushion weed, green spongy cushion.
DESCRIPTION: Overall color ranges from dark green to black. **Irregular spheres form smooth, flat cushions.** Texture changes from firm to spongy as the alga ages.
SIZE: Length to 10″ (25 cm); width to 0.6″ (15 mm).
HABITAT: On rocks of exposed shorelines; low intertidal zone.

RANGE: Sitka, Alaska, to Baja California, México.

NOTES: This common, distinctive seaweed is sometimes covered by sand for extended periods.

Brown Algae
PHYLUM OCHROPHYTA

Brown algae contain chlorophyll, but the green color is hidden by gold and brown pigments, which look light green to dark black because of their varying proportions. Several large brown algae are often referred to as kelp.

....

Fungal Crust Seaweed
Ralfsia fungiformis
(Gunnerus) Setchell & N.L. Gardner, 1924

OTHER NAMES: Sea fungus, fungiform tar spot alga, tar spot alga, tar spot seaweed, tar spot; formerly classified as *deusta*.

DESCRIPTION: The lobes are olive-brown overall often with a yellowish edge. The overlapping **crustose thalli are free along the margins, growing in circular form with obvious concentric and radial growth lines**. Numerous tiny, rootlike rhizoids hold this alga loosely to its substrate.

SIZE: Thallus to 2.4″ (6 cm) across, and 0.05″ (1 mm) thick.

HABITAT: On rocks and in tidepools; high to mid-intertidal zone.

RANGE: Aleutian Islands, Alaska, to Humboldt County, California; Arctic; North Atlantic; Korea; Japan; Siberia.

NOTES: Scientists in Washington state have shown that this species grows by only 0.5″ (13 mm) in diameter annually. The scientific name *fungiformis* was chosen to describe its resemblance to a type of encrusting fungus. This is a colder water species of the Northern Hemisphere.

Sea Cauliflower

Leathesia marina (Lyngbye) Decaisne, 1842

OTHER NAMES: Brain seaweed, cauliflower seaweed, golden spongy cushion, sea potato; formerly classified as *Leathesia difformis*, *Leathesia nana*, *Tremulla difformis*.

DESCRIPTION: The thallus is yellow to yellowish-brown. The **thallus is roughly spherical, convoluted, hollow and spongy.** The surface texture is slippery in nature.

SIZE: Diameter to 5″ (12 cm).

HABITAT: On rocks, in tidepools and on several species of algae (epiphytic); high to low intertidal zone.

RANGE: Bering Sea to Baja California, México; Chile; Europe; Sweden.

NOTES: When this species was first described by the famous botanist Carolus Linnaeus, it was thought to be a jelly fungus because of its unusual shape. The sea cauliflower is solid when young but becomes hollow as it matures.

....

Convoluted Sea Fungus

Petrospongium rugosum
(Okamura) Setchell & N.L. Gardner, 1924

OTHER NAME: Formerly classified as *Cylindrocarpus rugosus*.

DESCRIPTION: Color varies from chestnut brown to dark brown. Entire plant is gelatinous and **roughly circular with irregular convoluted ridges** on the upper surface.

SIZE: Diameter to 3″ (8 cm).

HABITAT: On rocks; high intertidal zone.

RANGE: Vancouver Island, British Columbia, to Baja California, México; Japan.

NOTES: This distinctive alga somewhat resembles a hollow fungus. Patches of it can be found where conditions are favorable, often in late autumn.

Flat Acid Leaf

Desmarestia ligulata

(Stackhouse) J.V. Lamouroux, 1813

OTHER NAMES: Acid seaweed, flattened acid kelp, wide desmarestia; formerly classified as *Fucus ligatulus.*
DESCRIPTION: Color from yellowish-brown to dark brown. **Thallus** is flat with numerous branches covered in fine hairs. All members of this genus secrete sulfuric acid, which damages tissue. Flat blades are attached to a central stipe (stalk).
SIZE: Length normally to 31″ (80 cm); occasionally to 26′ (8 m).
HABITAT: On rock; low intertidal zone to shallow subtidal depths.
RANGE: Unalaska Island, Alaska, to Baja California, México; western North Pacific; Iceland; eastern North Atlantic; Australia.
NOTES: This species secretes sulfuric acid when damaged, which can damage its own tissue as well as other seaweeds. This causes dramatic color changes. Flat acid leaf often becomes established in areas where the giant perennial kelp is hard hit by winter storms.

....

Stringy Acid Leaf

Desmarestia viridis

(O.F. Müller) J.V. Lamouroux, 1813

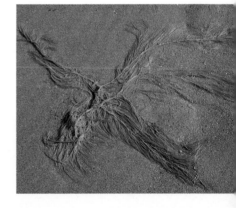

OTHER NAMES: Stringy acid hair; formerly classified as *Desmarestia media* var. *tenuis, Fucus viridis.*
DESCRIPTION: Color is generally light brown with greenish section. **A cylindrical stipe** arises from a discoid holdfast. All members of this genus secrete sulfuric acid, which damages tissue. Numerous very fine branches arise from the central axis with an opposite branching pattern. This is an extremely fragile species.
SIZE: Length normally to 24″ (60 cm); occasional to 47″ (120 cm).
HABITAT: On rock; low intertidal zone to depths of 148′ (45 m).
RANGE: Aleutian Islands, Alaska, to Baja California, México; Arctic Ocean; western North Pacific; North Atlantic; North Sea; New Zealand; Chile; Argentina; Antarctic and subantarctic islands.

NOTES: The sulfuric acid found in acid kelps (*Desmarestia* spp.) are stored inside vacuoles within the thalus. When there are low tides these vacuoles may be exposed to air and break down. This releases the acid that is so harmful to neighboring algae and the host alga alike. The stringy acid leaf is the most acidic of all the acid kelps.

Three-ribbed Kelp

Cymathere triplicata

(Postels & Ruprecht) J. Agardh, 1868

OTHER NAMES: Triple-rib kelp, triple rib kelp.
DESCRIPTION: Color varies from yellow-brown to red-brown. A **single elongated blade with 3 distinct ribs runs down the center** and originates from a holdfast.
SIZE: Length to 13′ (4 m); width to 7″ (18 cm).
HABITAT: On cobble, bedrock and boulders; low intertidal zone to shallow subtidal depths.
RANGE: Bering Sea and Aleutian Islands, Alaska, to northern Washington; Kurile Islands; Russia.
NOTES: This seaweed smells very much like fresh cucumber, especially when a blade is broken. The author has observed Sitka black-tailed deer (*Odocoileus hemionus sitkensis*) feeding on three-ribbed kelp at low tide. This deer is also reported to feed on the winged kelp under adverse conditions.

Sugar Kelp

Saccharina latissima

(Linnaeus) C.E. Lane, C. Mayes, Druehl & G.W. Saunders, 2006

OTHER NAMES: Oarweed, sea belt, poor man's weather glass, sugar wrack, sugar wrack kelp; formerly classified as *Laminaria agardhii*, *Laminaria saccharina*.
DESCRIPTION: The blade is a rich

yellowish-brown color. The thalus has a **short, stem-like stipe and noticeable wrinkled areas in the mid-blade** section.

SIZE: Length to 11′ (3.5 m); width to 10″ (25.4 cm).

HABITAT: On rocks, pilings, and ledges; low intertidal zone to depths of 98′ (30 m).

RANGE: Aleutian Islands, Alaska, to Santa Catalina Island, California; Japan; Arctic Ocean; Russia; Arctic to New Jersey; North Sea.

NOTES: This large, impressive kelp actively grows at an amazing rate. In cold northern waters, the entire blade will replace itself at least 5 times a year. Sugar kelp gets its name from the presence of mannite, a sugar alcohol, which gives it a sweet taste. This common alga is used as a stabilizing agent for some of our sweeter treats—candies, puddings and ice creams. It is only found at low tides or washed ashore from subtidal depths.

Split Kelp

Laminaria setchellii P.C. Silva, 1957

OTHER NAMES: Split blade kelp; formerly classified as *Laminaria andersonii*.

DESCRIPTION: Color ranges from rich brown to black. **Blade is deeply split, almost to the ends, and with a prominent stipe**.

SIZE: Blades to 32″ (80 cm) long, width to 10″ (25 cm); stipe to 32″ (80 cm) long, width to 0.8″ (20 mm).

HABITAT: On rocks of exposed shorelines; low intertidal zone to shallow subtidal depths.

RANGE: Eastern Gulf of Alaska to Baja California, México.

NOTES: The stipe of split kelp is stiff and makes the plant stand erect in exposed surf-swept stretches of the coast. Often this species is found in high enough concentrations to be called an "underwater forest." It adheres to the bottom with a very compact holdfast.

Sea Cabbage

Saccharina sessilis (C. Agardh) Kuntze, 1891

OTHER NAMES: Sea cabbage kelp; formerly classified as *Laminaria sessilis*.

DESCRIPTION: Color varies from brown to dark chocolate brown. Leather-like wrinkled

Smooth form.

Wrinkled form.

blades attached to rock with a sturdy holdfast. Blades become smooth and deeply split in surf-swept areas.

SIZE: Length normally to 20″ (50 cm); occasionally to 5′ (1.5 m).

HABITAT: On rocks; mid- to low intertidal zone

RANGE: Aleutian Islands, Alaska, to Monterey County, California.

NOTES: This variable species grows distinctively in different habitats. Rough waters give it a smooth form, while corrugated blades are found in quiet bays and similar habitats. The black Katy chiton feeds on sea cabbage. Sea urchins, however, do not feed on it, so it can become very abundant in areas where urchins are present.

....

Five-ribbed Kelp

Costaria costata

(C. Agardh) De A. Saunders, 1895

OTHER NAMES: Five-rib kelp, ribbed kelp, rib kelp, seersucker, seersucker kelp; formerly classified as *Costaria mertensii*, *Costaria turneri*, *Laminaria costata*.

DESCRIPTION: Color ranges from yellowish-brown to chocolate brown. A **single large blade** is supported with **5–7 prominent parallel ribs** attached to large stipe.

SIZE: Length to 10′ (3 m).

HABITAT: In rocky areas and occasionally on wood; low intertidal to shallow subtidal depths.

RANGE: Unalaska Island, Alaska, to southern California; Japan; Russia.

NOTES: Five-ribbed kelp is found in sheltered locations and also on the open coast, where it grows somewhat narrower. Tattered and sometimes discolored blades are commonly seen in early summer. Sea urchins feed readily on this kelp.

....

Old Growth Kelp

Pterygophora californica

Ruprecht, 1852

OTHER NAMES: Walking kelp, pompom kelp, wing-bearing kelp, palm kelp, woody-stemmed kelp.

DESCRIPTION: This dark brown alga has yellowish stipe. The **flattened, long, woody unbranched stipe** bears a single large blade at the tip. Near the holdfast are a series of **5–10 pairs of long, narrow sporophylls**.

SIZE: Stipe to 6.5′ (2 m) long, blades to 3′ (1 m) long.

HABITAT: On rocks and cobble in surf-swept or high-current sites; low intertidal zone to depths of 66′ (20 m).

RANGE: Cook Inlet, Alaska, to Baja California, México.

NOTES: Old growth kelp has been known to live to 20 years, with new blades growing each year. Its age can be calculated by counting the growth rings of its woody stipe. Remarkably, this species has the ability to "walk" along the bottom if attached to cobble or small boulders in strong surf.

....

Winged Kelp

Alaria marginata Postels & Ruprecht, 1840

OTHER NAMES: Angel wing kelp, broad-winged kelp, edible kelp, ribbon kelp, ribbed kelp.

DESCRIPTION: Color ranges from olive brown to dark brown. **A prominent linear blade is present at the tip of the rounded stipe.** A series of **20–40 short, wide sporophylls**

are present at the lower section of the stipe when mleep mature. These sporophylls often form a cluster at the base of the alga.

SIZE: Blade to 10′ (3 m) long, 8″ (20 cm) wide.

HABITAT: In rocky areas, often in areas exposed to high surf; mid-intertidal zone to depths of 26′ (8 m).

RANGE: Kodiak Island, Alaska, to Point Conception, California.

NOTES: Winged kelp is dried and used in cooking soups and stews, as a substitute for kombu (the Oriental species *Laminaria japonica*). It is also deep fried and eaten like potato chips, and the midrib can be eaten fresh in salads, or added to spaghetti sauce. This is truly a versatile seaweed!

Feather Boa Kelp

Egregia menziesii

(Turner) Areschoug, 1876

OTHER NAMES: Feather-boa kelp, feather boa, Venus's girdle; formerly classified as *Egregia laevigata*, *Egregia planifolia*.

DESCRIPTION: Color varies from olive green to dark brown. The flattened stipe and its **irregular flat branches** are **covered with broad to linear blades**. **Spherical floats are often located sparsely** along entire branch. This species is held securely to rock by a massive holdfast.

SIZE: Length to 35′ (10 m).

HABITAT: In rocky exposed areas; mid-intertidal zone to depths of 65′ (20 m).

RANGE: Haida Gwaii (Queen Charlotte Islands), British Columbia, to Punta Eugenio, Baja California Sur, México.

NOTES: Coastal farmers have used this species as a fertilizer for many years. If you look closely, the very specialized seaweed limpet can sometimes be found feeding on this seaweed's blades.

Sea Palm

Postelsia palmaeformis Ruprecht, 1852

OTHER NAMES: Palm kelp, sea palm kelp.

DESCRIPTION: Color ranges from greenish to golden brown or olive brown. The main stipe is round, upright (resembles a miniature palm tree) and supports as many as 100 flattened, deeply grooved blades at the tip.

SIZE: Height to 24″ (60 cm), blades to 9″ (24 cm) long.

HABITAT: On rocks, California mussels and similar firm surfaces in areas exposed to heavy surf; mid- to low intertidal zone

RANGE: Hope Island, British Columbia, to San Luis Obispo County, California.

NOTES: This distinctive species is very robust and it takes a daily pounding of heavy surf, bouncing back like an elastic band with every wave. The sea palm is an annual, producing spores that germinate close to the parent plant. The shield limpet can often be found clinging to the stipe or holdfast.

Netted Blade

Dictyoneurum californicum

Ruprecht, 1852

OTHER NAME: Net-of-cords kelp.

DESCRIPTION: Color varies from yellowish-brown to dark brown. Two flattened, equal stipes grow from a shoe-like holdfast. The **long, narrow blades** are tapered on both ends and **display reticulate veins** and no midrib.

SIZE: Length to 6.5′ (2 m).

HABITAT: On rocks; extreme low intertidal zone to depths of 33′ (10 m).

RANGE: Vancouver Island, British Columbia, to Point Conception and the Channel Islands, California.

NOTES: A lover of surf, netted blade prefers exposed coastal areas. Clumps of 25–100 blades are often found grouped together. Starting in mid-summer, darker reproductive structures grow between net-like veins. The base of this alga often harbors a wide array of invertebrates.

Bull Kelp

Nereocystis luetkeana

(K.Mertens) Postels & Ruprecht, 1840

OTHER NAMES: Bullwhip, bullwhip kelp, ribbon kelp.

DESCRIPTION: Thalli range in color from golden brown to dark brown. A sturdy holdfast bears a robust, **elongated stipe that terminates with a single float. Up to 20 blades are attached to the float**, which keeps the stipe afloat.

SIZE: Stipe to 82′ (25 m) long, occasionally to 118′ (36 m) long; float to 6.75″ (17 cm) in diameter; blades to 15′ (4.5 m) long, to 6″ (15 cm) wide.

HABITAT: On rocks; shallow subtidal to depths of 65′ (20 m); also commonly found washed up along beaches after storms.

RANGE: Aleutian Islands, Alaska, to San Luis Obispo County, California.

NOTES: Bull kelp is one of the largest kelps in the world. Studies in Washington state have shown that this species grows 5.5″ (14 cm) per day. Historically, various peoples including the Tlingits of Alaska have used this kelp to make fishing line. The stipe is often used to make pickles. Bull kelp has also been used in the production of dolls and ornamental musical instruments!

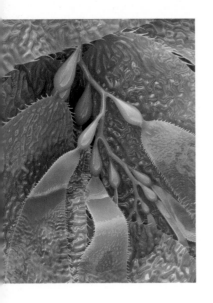

Giant Perennial Kelp

Macrocystis pyrifera (Linnaeus) C. Agardh, 1820

OTHER NAMES: Giant kelp (now includes small perennial kelp); includes *Macrocystis integrifolia*.

DESCRIPTION: Color varies from light yellowish-brown to dark brown. The stipe bears numerous **narrow leaf-like blades, each with a small air bladder or float along its entire length**. The holdfast securing the stipe to a rock varies in its shape and was once the basis for identification.

SIZE: Length to 99′ (30 m); blades to 16″ (40 cm) long.

HABITAT: On rocks of exposed shorelines; low intertidal zone to depths of 50′ (15 m).

RANGE: Kodiak Island, Alaska, to Monterey,

California; Baja California, México; Peru; Chile; Argentina; Tasmania; New Zealand; subantarctic islands.

NOTES: Giant perennial kelp is considered by some researchers to be the fastest-growing organism in the world. In California it has been found to grow an amazing 14″ (35 cm) per day. This kelp is harvested commercially for algin, a hydrophylic colloid. Algin is an amazing substance that is used as an emulsifying, stabilizing and suspending agent in a wide range of commercial products including ice cream, chocolate milk, icings, salad dressings, toothpaste, film emulsions, paint, insecticides and oil-well drilling mud.

....

Pacific Rockweed

Fucus distichus Linnaeus, 1767

OTHER NAMES: Bladderwrack, bladder wrack, bubble kelp, common brown rockweed, popping wrack, popweed, rock weed, rockweed; formerly classified as *Fucus evanescens*, *Fucus furcatus*, *Fucus gardneri*.

DESCRIPTION: Color varies from olive green to yellowish-green. Thallus is made up of **flat blades that branch regularly and dichotomously, each with a conspicuous midrib.** The branch ends are often inflated. A single stipe originates from each holdfast.

SIZE: Length to 16″ (40 cm).

HABITAT: Attached to rocks, mid- to low intertidal zone.

RANGE: Bering Sea and Aleutian Islands, Alaska, to central California; Kamchatka.

NOTES: Pacific rockweed is a common species that can withstand both the freezing of winter and the desiccation of summer. Its swollen yellow tips or receptacles contain the gametes for reproduction. When the tide goes out, the receptacles shrink, squeezing out the gametes. When the tide returns, sperm cells are able to find and fertilize the eggs. In protected areas, this alga can live for 5 years.

SIMILAR SPECIES: Dwarf rockweed.

Spindle-shaped Rockweed

Silvetia compressa

(J. Agardh) E. Serrao, T.O. Cho, S.M. Boo & Brawley, 1999

OTHER NAMES: Silva's rockweed; formerly classified as *Pelvetia compressa*, *Pelvetia compressa*, *Pelvetia fastigiata*.

DESCRIPTION: Color varies from greenish-olive to yellowish-brown. **Narrow branches are oval to nearly flat (with no midrib)** and dichotomous and regular divisions. At maturity the tips bear warty, spindle-like receptacles. Several branches originate from each holdfast.

SIZE: Length normally to 16″ (40 cm), occasionally to 36″ (90 cm).

HABITAT: On rocks with an exposure to surf but somewhat protected; high to mid-intertidal zone.

RANGE: Horswell Channel, British Columbia, to Punta Baja, Baja California, México. (Uncommon north of California.)

NOTES: The size of a mature plant is a good indicator in identification. Small individuals lack the swollen tips present in dwarf rockweed, a smaller species. When the individual reaches maturity, swollen branch tips form, where reproductive bodies are released from tiny pores.

Dwarf Rockweed

Pelvetiopsis limitata (J. Agardh) E. Serrao, T.O. Cho, S.M. Boo & Brawley, 1999

OTHER NAMES: Little rockweed, small rockweed.

DESCRIPTION: Color varies from olive green to light tan. Thalli **are short, flattened branches that** divide evenly, similar to rockweed, but there is **no midrib**.

SIZE: Length to 3″ (8 cm).

HABITAT: On rocks of exposed shores; high intertidal zone.

RANGE: Hope Island, British Columbia, to Cambria, San Luis Obispo County, California.

NOTES: This seaweed grows at a higher intertidal level than Pacific rockweed and so is only submerged at the highest of tides, and usually on the tops of the rocks. It is therefore well adapted to spending long periods out of water.

....

Northern Bladder Chain

Stephanocystis geminata
(C. Agardh) Draisma, Ballesteros,
F. Rousseau & T. Thibaut, 2010

OTHER NAMES: Northern bladder chain kelp; formerly classified as *Cystoseira geminata*.
DESCRIPTION: Overall color is dark brown with yellowish pneumatocysts or floats. The **main branches of the thallus produce several side branches that alternate**. Additional secondary branchlets may also be present with spherical pneumatocysts with a pointed end.
SIZE: Length to 26′ (8 m).
HABITAT: In rocky areas; low intertidal zone to shallow subtidal depths.
RANGE: Bering Sea and Aleutian Islands, Alaska, to northern Oregon; Japan.
NOTES: The new growth of spring brings the return of the distinctive, bead-like spherical floats. Over the winter months, only the lower portions of this plant remain, making it more difficult to identify
SIMILAR SPECIES: Wireweed.

....

Giant Bladder Chain

Stephanocystis osmundacea
(Turner) Trevisan, 1843

OTHER NAMES: Bladder chain, bladder chain kelp; formerly classified as *Cystoseira osmundacea*.
DESCRIPTION: Color ranges from tan to blackish-brown. Alga consists of 2 different sections: the **lower branches are flattened and pinnate, appearing somewhat fern-like, while those higher up are rounded with tiny pneumatocysts forming continuous chains**.
SIZE: Length to 26′ (8 m).

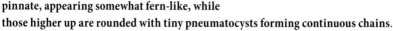

HABITAT: On rocks and in tidepools; low intertidal zone to depths of 33′ (10 m).
RANGE: Seaside, Oregon, to Ensenada, Baja California, México.
NOTES: The giant bladder chain is a large brown alga that can sometimes be found in tidepools in rocky habitats. This seaweed is a preferred habitat for spiral tube worms, which build calcareous tubes.

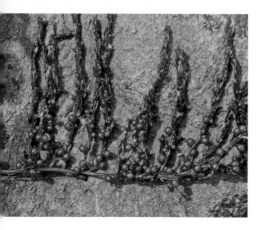

Wireweed

Sargassum muticum

(Yendo) Fensholt, 1955

OTHER NAMES: Japanese seaweed, Japanese weed, Japweed, sargassum; formerly classified as *Sargassum kjellmanianum muticum.*
DESCRIPTION: The stems and blades are golden brown. The **stipe bears many branches, small elongated blades and numerous single, tiny pneumatocysts or floats** attached individually to the stipe.

SIZE: Length to 6.5″ (2 m).
HABITAT: In protected rocky areas; low intertidal zone to depths of 20′ (6 m).
RANGE: Southeast Alaska to Baja California, México; Japan; southern England; France; Netherlands; Spain.
NOTES: Wireweed was accidentally introduced from Japan along with imported oysters in the 1930s. Since then it has spread along the Pacific coastline. This seaweed is often found washed up on the beach after drifting to shore. The green sea urchin has been noted as an important grazer on this introduced alga.

Red Algae
PHYLUM RHODOPHYTA

Red algae contain chlorophyll, but red and blue pigments are also present, giving these algae a reddish tinge. The life cycle of red algae usually involves three stages, rather than two as in other algae.

Red Fringe

Smithora naiadum

(C.L. Anderson) Hollenberg, 1959

OTHER NAME: Seagrass laver.
DESCRIPTION: Color ranges from purplish-red to deep purple. The thallus is made up of **very thin blades that grow epiphytically on eelgrasses and surfgrasses** from a cushion-like holdfast.
SIZE: Length to 2″ (5 cm).
HABITAT: Grows on eelgrass and surfgrass as an epiphyte; low intertidal zone to shallow subtidal depths.
RANGE: Kodiak Island, Alaska, to Isla Magdalena, Baja California Sur, México.
NOTES: Red fringe is a distinctive seaweed that is only one cell thick. It is attached to eelgrass or surfgrass as an epiphyte by a short, narrow portion of the blade. This delicate seaweed is found most often in late summer and fall, when it is abundant in many tidepools.

Staghorn Fringe

Ceramium codicola J. Agardh, 1894

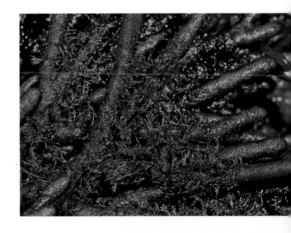

OTHER NAME: Staghorn felt.
DESCRIPTION: Thalli are dull reddish-brown, and are **thin, fringing tufts attached to the upper branches of sea staghorn** as an epithyte.
SIZE: Length to 1″ (2.5 cm).
HABITAT: On sea staghorn as an epiphyte; mid-intertidal zone to shallow subtidal depths.
RANGE: Sitka, Alaska, to IsIa San Benito, Baja California, México.
NOTES: Since staghorn fringe grows only on sea staghorn as an epiphyte, it is an easy species to identify. It attaches to its host with many bulbous and penetrating rhizoids.

Laver

Porphyra spp. C. Agardh, 1824

OTHER NAMES: Purple laver, red laver, dulse, nori, wild nori.

DESCRIPTION: Color varies from purple to green. The thallus is **a thin, single broad blade, often irregular in shape, with ruffled margins**. Often found in dense clusters.

SIZE: Length to 60″ (150 cm).

HABITAT: On rocks; high intertidal zone to upper subtidal zones. Can be epiphytic (attached to a plant with no harm to that organism) within these zones.

RANGE: Bering Sea and Aleutian Islands, Alaska, to Baja California, México.

NOTES: Laver is rubbery and gelatinous in texture, once out of the water. It is edible, and most species are considered to be very tasty as well as having large amounts of vitamins A and C. In Japan, this seaweed is called nori and has been collected and used as food for 1,000 years. Today laver is big business in Japan, worth $1 billion annually.

....

Rubber Threads

Nemalion elminthoides (Velley) Batters, 1902

OTHER NAMES: Sea noodles; formerly classified as *Nemalion helminthoides*.

DESCRIPTION: Color ranges from golden brown to reddish-brown with a **smooth, soft rubbery texture. The thallus is generally unbranched** but some branching may be present. Several plants often grow together in a cluster.

SIZE: Length normally to 8″ (20 cm); occasionally to 18″ (45 cm).

HABITAT: On rocks of exposed shorelines; high to mid-intertidal zone.

RANGE: Aleutian Islands, Alaska, to Baja California, México; Japan; North Atlantic; Australia; New Zealand.

NOTES: The obvious gametophytic (gamete producing)

stage of this alga is present in late spring to early summer, and it bears a close resemblance to an earthworm. This species is often found in clusters in the springtime. The sporophytic (spore producing) stage is visible only under a microscope.

....

Hairy Seaweed

Cumagloia andersonii

(Farlow) Setchell & N.L. Gardner, 1917

OTHER NAME: Formerly classified as *Nemalion andersonii*.
DESCRIPTION: Color varies from brown to reddish-purple. The cords are **tough, gelatinous and elongated with numerous fibers attached to the main cord** along the entire length. A single main stem or more arise from a small discoid holdfast. The cords of young specimens are typically cylindrical but as they age the cords become flattened.
SIZE: Length to 3′ (90 cm).
HABITAT: On rocks; high intertidal zone.
RANGE: Cold Bay, Alaska, to Baja California, México.
NOTES: This annual species grows back on the same rocks year after year. This large gamete-producing stage reaches its maximum size in August. After that time, it alternates with a microscopic stage that produces spores.

....

Bleached Brunette

Cryptosiphonia woodii

(J. Agardh) J. Agardh, 1876

OTHER NAMES: Dark branching-tube seaweed; formerly classified as *Pikea woodii*.
DESCRIPTION: Color varies greatly from olive brown to blackish-purple; **golden when branches are fertile, late in the season.** This alga is coarse overall, with **abundant cylindrical branches that are slender** with an irregular arrangement.
SIZE: Length to 10″ (25 cm).

HABITAT: On rocks; mid-intertidal zone.
RANGE: Unalaska Island, Alaska, to San Pedro, Los Angeles County, California.
NOTES: Bleached brunette is often one of the first seaweeds to colonize new areas. It grows in clusters and is commonly found in both exposed and protected sites.

....

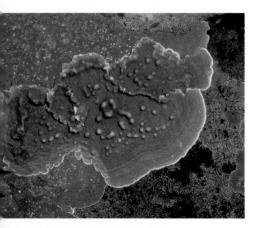

Encrusting Coralline Algae

Lithothamnion spp. and others
Heydrich, 1897

OTHER NAMES: Encrusting coral, mauve coralline algae, rock crust.
DESCRIPTION: Color varies from **light pink to purplish-pink. Thin, crust-like shapes resemble lichens.**
SIZE: Thickness to 0.1″ (2 mm).
HABITAT: On rocks; low intertidal zone to shallow subtidal depths.
RANGE: Alaska to Baja California, México.

NOTES: Rocks in tidepools and the shells of various gastropods are often covered with these algae. Several invertebrates feed on them, including whitecap limpet and lined chiton. It has been revealed that there are at least 5 different genera included in this group. The other genera include: *Clathromorphum*, *Melobesia*, *Mesophyllum* and *Pseudolithophyllum*.

....

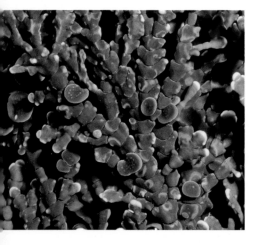

Stalked Coralline Disk

Callilithophytum parcum
(Setchell & Foslie) P.W. Gabrielson, W.H. Adey, G.P. Johnson & Hernandez-Kantun, 2015

OTHER NAMES: Formerly classified as *Lithothamnium parcum*, *Polyporolithon parcum*.
DESCRIPTION: Color varies from lavender to purplish. The **disc-shaped body** is smooth and slightly convex. Species is attached to a host plant by a **central stalk**.
SIZE: Diameter to 0.75″ (20 mm).

HABITAT: On coraline algae; low intertidal zone to shallow subtidal depths.
RANGE: Haida Gwaii (Queen Charlotte Islands), British Columbia, to San Louis Obispo County, California.
NOTES: This alga grows on a wide variety of articulated coralline algae, including tidepool coralline alga. It grows as single plants that do not crowd together.

Stone Hair

Lithothrix aspergillum

J.E. Gray, 1867

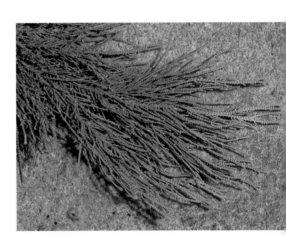

OTHER NAME: Formerly classified as *Amphiroa aspergillum*.
DESCRIPTION: Overall color is lavender-pink. **Articulated coralline alga with elongated branches** that are often densely branched into **tufts stemming from a crustose base**.
SIZE: Length to 5″ (13 cm); width to a mere 0.1″ (1 mm) in diameter.
HABITAT: In sandy areas on rocks; mid-intertidal zone to depths of 43′ (13 m).
RANGE: Cook Inlet, Alaska, to Isla Magdalena, Baja California Sur, México; South Africa.
NOTES: Stone hair is a delicate-looking seaweed with fine fronds. Its individual segments are short and minute, making it easy to identify. This elegant species attaches to both rocks and animals.

Tidepool Coralline Algae

Corallina officinalis var. *chilensis*

(Decaisne) Kützing, 1858

OTHER NAMES: Common coral seaweed, common coralline alga, coral seaweed, pink feather coralline, tall coralline alga, graceful coral seaweed; formerly classified as *Corallina chilensis*.
DESCRIPTION: The fronds are

white to pink or purple. The alga is **calcareous** with jointed segments and many flattened, pinnate or **feather-like branches** of equal size. **Segments on the central axis** are slightly flattened and **elongated**.

SIZE: Length to 6″ (15 cm).

HABITAT: On rock and in tidepools; mid-intertidal zone to water 33′ (10 m) deep.

RANGE: Prince William Sound, Alaska, to Baja California, México; Chile; Japan; Russia; Okhotsk Sea.

NOTES: This common articulated seaweed can often be seen in tidepools. Until the early 18th century it was used as a vermifuge (a substance that expels parasites from the body). An encrusting base adheres tightly to rock, from which the branches grow. Remarkably, this and several similar algae contain a very high percentage of calcium carbonate, the same material that makes up clam and snail shells.

....

Coral-leaf Algae

Bossiella spp. P.C. Silva, 1957

OTHER NAME: Coral leaf.

DESCRIPTION: A pink to purple calcareous seaweed with **jointed segments** that may have **both cylindrical and flattened sections**. They often have a "wingnut" shape. The **conceptacles occur on the flat sides of the segments** when present.

SIZE: Length to 8″ (20 cm).

HABITAT: On rocks and in tidepools; high to low intertidal zone to subtidal depths.

RANGE: Bering Sea, Alaska, to Baja California, México.

NOTES: There are 5 species of *Bossiella* present in the Pacific Northwest. This group is very similar to the genus *Calliarthron*. The conceptacles must be present to determine the genus.

....

Coarse Bead-coral Algae

Calliarthron tuberculosum (Postels & Ruprecht) E.Y. Dawson, 1964

OTHER NAMES: Formerly classified as *Corallina tuberculosa*, *Calliarthron regenerans*, *Calliarthron setchelliae*.

DESCRIPTION: A pink to purple calcareous seaweed with **jointed segments** that often have **both cylindrical and flattened sections**. Branching is irregular. The **conceptacles occur on the edges of the segments and occasionally the flat portions**. Branches grow from the main stem at more than a 60-degree angle. The "beads" or segments are generally coarse.

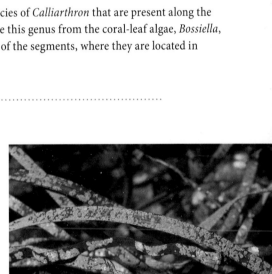

SIZE: Height to 8″ (20 cm).

HABITAT: On rocks, often in tidepools; low intertidal zone to subtidal depths.

RANGE: Alaska to Isla Cedros, Baja California, México.

NOTES: Coarse bead-coral alga is one species of *Calliarthron* that are present along the coast of the Pacific Northwest. To separate this genus from the coral-leaf algae, *Bossiella*, look for the conceptacles on the flat sides of the segments, where they are located in *Calliarthron* species.

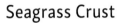

Seagrass Crust

Melobesia mediocris

(Foslie) Setchell & L.R. Mason, 1943

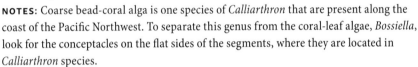

OTHER NAMES: Circular pink alga, surfgrass coralline seaweed; formerly classified as *Lithophyllum zostericola mediocris*.

DESCRIPTION: This alga is pinkish in color, and grows in **thin, circular patches** that may change in shape as they grow larger.

SIZE: To 0.2″ (5 mm) in diameter.

HABITAT: On the blades of eelgrasses and surfgrasses; low intertidal zone to shallow subtidal depths.

RANGE: Haida Gwaii (Queen Charlotte Islands), British Columbia, to Baja California, México; Costa Rica; Peru.

NOTES: This red alga is one of the easier species to identify. It is the only epiphyte that grows on eelgrasses and surfgrasses.

Nail Brush Seaweed

Endocladia muricata

(Endlichter) J. Agardh, 1847

OTHER NAMES: Brillo-pad alga, brillo-pad seaweed, nail brush, nailbrush, sea moss, wire brush alga; formerly *Gigartina muricata*.
DESCRIPTION: Color ranges widely from pinkish to nearly black. This species **grows in small, tight, bushy tufts, each with a wiry branch** stemming from a small, discoidal holdfast. The branching is basically dichotomous or two equal-sized cylindrical branches arise from each fork.
SIZE: Length to 3″ (8 cm).
HABITAT: On exposed rocks; high intertidal zone.
RANGE: Amchitka Island (Aleutian Islands), Alaska, to Punta Santo Tomas, Baja California, México.
NOTES: The nail brush seaweed dries out when the tide recedes. This alga is easily destroyed if it is walked upon because it is erect and so dry. Care should be taken when this species is on the same rocks you are on.

Broad Iodine Seaweed

Prionitis sternbergii (C. Agardh) J. Agardh, 1851

OTHER NAMES: Iodine seaweed, Lyall's iodine seaweed; formerly classified as *Prionitis lyallii*.
DESCRIPTION: Color varies greatly from brown to bright brick-red. Primary blades are lance-like, often with several smaller **secondary and tertiary blades stemming from primary blade margins**.
SIZE: Length normally to 14″ (35 cm); occasionally to 30″ (75 cm).
HABITAT: On rocks in tidepools; mid-intertidal zone to shallow subtidal depths. Coarse sand often covers the rock this species attaches to.
RANGE: Southern British Columbia to Punta María, Baja California, México.
NOTES: This seaweed smells like bleach as its common name indicates. It is often found in sandy areas.

Red Sea-leaf

Erythrophyllum delesserioides

J. Agardh, 1872

DESCRIPTION: Blades are **red with a prominent mid-rib** extending through the entire blade. **Lateral veins arise from the midrib in an alternating pattern**.

SIZE: Length normally to 20″ (50 cm); occasionally to 40″ (1 m).

HABITAT: On rocks; low intertidal zone to shallow subtidal depths.

RANGE: Kayak Island, eastern Gulf of Alaska, to Shell Beach, San Luis Obispo County, California.

NOTES: Red sea-leaf is found on exposed coasts and in situations such as surge channels where rough water predominates. Its blades are torn away more and more as the summer progresses until only the midrib and side veins remain. Late in the season, short nipple-like papillae, which are used for reproduction, cover most of this plant.

....

Succulent Seaweed

Sarcodiotheca gaudichaudii

(Montagne) P.W. Gabrielson, 1982

OTHER NAME: Formerly classified as *Agardhiella gaudichaudii*.

DESCRIPTION: Color varies from red to reddish-brown. **Branches slender, cylindrical, fleshy and irregular with many branchlets that taper to pointed tips.**

SIZE: Length to 18″ (45 cm).

HABITAT: On rocks near sand; low intertidal zone to depths of 100′ (30 m).

RANGE: Ketchikan, Alaska, to Baja California, México; Galapagos Islands; Peru; Chile.

NOTES: This common species often grows in clumps. It's interesting to note that this species favors areas with sand nearby even though it attaches to rock.

Peppered Spaghetti

Gracilaria pacifica I.A. Abbott, 1985

OTHER NAME: California limu.
DESCRIPTION: Color ranges widely from yellowish or pinkish to pale reddish or black. **Branches are slender,** sparsely branched and **spaghetti-like,** often **with small dark bump-like reproductive structures** attached.
SIZE: Length to 20″ (50 cm).
HABITAT: On rocks in areas of mud; mid-intertidal zone to shallow subtidal depths.
RANGE: Prince William Sound, Alaska, to Baja California, México; Atlantic coast.
NOTES: Peppered spaghetti is an edible seaweed that has also been commercially harvested as a source of agar, a substance used as a thickening agent. This distinctive species is sometimes found stranded on the shore in large numbers.

Flat-tipped Forked Seaweed

Ahnfeltiopsis linearis
(C. Agardh) P.C. Silva & DeCew, 1992

OTHER NAMES: Formerly classified as *Gymnogongrus Iinearis,* *Sphaerococcus linearis.*
DESCRIPTION: Thalli range in color from light brown to deep brownish-purple. **Branches are firm to horny with repeated branching and flattened tips.** Algae arise from a crust-like base to form dense tufts with up to 150 erect branches.
SIZE: Length to 7″ (18 cm).
HABITAT: On rocks that are often covered in sand; mid- to low intertidal zone.
RANGE: Southern British Columbia to Point Conception, California.
NOTES: This red alga is remarkably able to survive and thrive at sites where it may be seasonally buried in sand up to 3′ (90 cm) deep.

Flat-tipped Wire Algae

Mastocarpus jardinii

(J. Agardh) J.A. West, 1984

OTHER NAMES: Bushy turkish washcloth, narrow Turkish washcloth; **Gametophyte stage** formerly classified as *Gigartina agardhii*; **Sporophyte stage** formerly classified as *Petrocelis franciscana*.

DESCRIPTION:

Gametophyte (blade) stage: The color changes from reddish-brown to dark brown when out of water for extended periods of time. The thallus consists of small clumps of narrow and **wiry blades with flattened ends** and several even divisions. **Groups of nipple-like papillae are present on the blade surface.**

Sporophyte (crust) stage: Crust like, resembling the Sea Tar stage of Papillate Seaweed.

SIZE: Gametophyte stage: Length normally to 4″ (10 cm), occasionally to 6″ (15 cm).

Sporophyte stage: to 0.01″ 2.5 mm) thick

HABITAT: On rocks; high to mid-intertidal zone.

RANGE: Haida Gwaii (Queen Charlotte Islands), British Columbia, to Santa Barbara County, California.

NOTES: Like several other seaweeds, the flat-tipped wire alga displays distinct stages in its life history. The gametophyte stage is the sexual stage and most obvious while the sporophyte (asexual) stage is crust-like in nature. This sporophyte stage is often referred to as the *Petrocelis* stage since it was originally identified as a separate species, *Petrocelis franciscana*.

....

Turkish Towel

Chondracanthus exasperatus (Harvey & Bailey) Hughey, 1996

OTHER NAME: Formerly classified as *Gigartina exasperata*.

DESCRIPTION: The thalli are dark red to purple and may be iridescent when wet (young). Normally 2 or 3 blades present and a short stipe. Blade surface is covered with tiny rasp-like projections.

SIZE: Length normally to 20″ (50 cm), occasionally to 39″ (1 m) or more.

HABITAT: On rock; low intertidal zone to shallow subtidal depths.

RANGE: Southeast Alaska, to Baja California, México.
NOTES: This species is a source of carrageenan, a stabilizer for a wide range of products including cottage cheese and printer's ink, and has been experimentally farmed to produce this substance.

Papillate Seaweed/Sea Tar

Mastocarpus papillatus (C. Agardh) Kützing, 1843

OTHER NAMES: **Gametophyte stage:** Crisp leather, Turkish washcloth; formerly classified as *Gigartina papillata, Gigartina cristata.* **Sporophyte stage:** Tar spot, sea film; formerly classified as *Petrocelis franciscana.*

Both the sea tar and blade stages are shown here.

DESCRIPTION:
Gametophyte (blade) stage:
Color ranges from yellow-brown to dark purple or even black. Blades are flat, **palm-like in shape, with several branches**, irregularly branched. **Blades later develop small growths or projections.**
Sporophyte (crust) stage: Color ranges from dark red-brown to black. A smooth crust that grows on rock surfaces.
SIZE: **Gametophyte stage:** Length to 6″ (15 cm). **Sporophyte stage:** Diameter to 5″ (13 cm) across.

HABITAT: On rocks; high to mid-intertidal zone.

RANGE: Bering Sea and Aleutian Islands, Alaska, to Punta Baja, Baja California, México.

NOTES: This highly variable species had scientists mystified for years. It was originally thought that the two distinct stages were separate species. Only recently was it discovered that both stages are part of the same life cycle. The crust stage reproduces asexually to produce spores, which develop into the blade stage. Blades are either male or female and reproduce sexually. Studies have shown that the crustose stage of this alga grows at an extremely slow rate, about 0.5″ (13 mm) per year, and that larger specimens could reach the incredible age of 90 years old.

Iridescent Seaweed

Mazzaella splendens (Setchell & N.L. Gardner) Fredericq, 1994

OTHER NAMES: Rainbow leaf, rainbow seaweed; formerly classified as *Iridaea cordata* var. *splendens*, *Iridaea splendens*.

DESCRIPTION: Blades vary in color from green to bluish-purple, and appear **iridescent in sunlight**. Blades **shape varies from elongate to broadly ovate** and may also have a split, wedge shape, heart shape or lobed shape.

SIZE: Length to 4′ (1.2 m).

HABITAT: On rocks; mid-intertidal zone to shallow subtidal depths.

RANGE: Southeast Alaska to northern Baja California, México.

NOTES: This striking species is memorable for its dazzling iridescence, which is especially vivid when touched with sunlight underwater. Various snails feed on it, which is why several holes are sometimes found on the blades.

Sea Sacs

Halosaccion glandiforme

(S.G. Gmelin) Ruprecht, 1850

OTHER NAMES: Dead man's fingers, salt sacs, sea nipples, sea sacks.

DESCRIPTION: Color ranges widely from yellowish-brown (growth in sunshine) to reddish-purple (growth in shade). The thallus is **elongated, hollow and filled with seawater and air at the outer tip**.

SIZE: Length to 12″ (30 cm); width to 1.5″ (4 cm) in diameter.

HABITAT: On rocks and other algae; high to low intertidal zone.

RANGE: Bering Sea and Aleutian Islands, Alaska, to Point Conception, California; Russia.

NOTES: Sea sacs are an edible that can be eaten raw or added to soups. They are high in caloric value. Be sure to check any area for contamination before harvesting any seaweeds for the table.

Sea Belly

Neogastroclonium subarticulatum

(Turner) L. Le Gall, Dalen & G.W. Saunders, 2008

OTHER NAME: Formerly classified as *Gastroclonium coulteri*.

DESCRIPTION: Color varies from reddish-brown to yellowish-green. The cylindrical thallus branches bear **even branchlets with regular, slight constrictions**. The tips are rounded and normally hollow.

SIZE: Length to 12″ (30 cm).

HABITAT: On rocks, algae and worm tubes; mid-intertidal zone to depths of 46′ (14 m).

RANGE: Sitka, Alaska, to Punta Abreojos, Baja California, México.

NOTES: The Japanese have gone to great lengths to "cultivate" sea belly and other red algae for their consumption. They have actually blasted the turf off rock to promote growth for human use. This species often forms extensive mats at low tide.

Red Fan

Neoptilota asplenioides

(Esper) Scagel et al., 1989

OTHER NAMES: Red sea fern, sea fern; formerly classified as *Fucus asplenioides*, *Plumaria asplenioides*, *Ptilota asplenioides*.
DESCRIPTION: Color of this alga is bright red. Thallus with branches in pairs and a fern-like or fan-like shape. The **paired branches differ in appearance with one being fertile (with frills), the other sterile (without frills)**.
SIZE: Length to 12″ (30 cm).
HABITAT: On rocks of exposed shorelines; high to low intertidal zone.
RANGE: Bering Sea and Aleutian Islands, Alaska, to northern Washington; Japan; Siberia.
NOTES: This beautiful species is sometimes collected and dried for decoration, but it is not abundant so this practice is not encouraged. Like several other seaweeds, red fan requires additional study to learn more about its natural history.

Winged Fronds

Cumathamnion decipiens

(J. Agardh) M.J. Wynne & G.W. Saunders, 2012

OTHER NAMES: Baron delessert, winged rib.
DESCRIPTION: Color ranges widely from yellowish to pink or deep purple. Thallus consists of **delicate blades with a prominent midrib and repeated alternate branching**, with a thin delicate blade attached.
SIZE: Length normally to 10″ (25 cm); occasionally to 20″ (50 cm).
HABITAT: On rocks; low intertidal zone to depths of 60′ (18 m).
RANGE: Kodiak archipelago, Alaska, to San Luis Obispo County, California.
NOTES: This splendid seaweed has been found to photosynthesize at its maximum when in indirect sunlight, while harsh direct sunlight may in fact damage it. Winged fronds contain red water-soluble pigments called phycobilins, which are uncommon in algae. The elegant movement of the delicate blades drifting in quiet waters is truly beautiful to observe.

Veined Blade Algae

Hymenena spp. Greville, 1830

OTHER NAME: Black-lined red seaweeds.

DESCRIPTION: Color ranges from rose to brownish-red. Thallus is comprised of numerous **fan-shaped blades with very fine veins that may be divided dichotomously or palmately.**

SIZE: Length to 12″ (30 cm).

HABITAT: On rocks; low intertidal zone to shallow subtidal depths.

RANGE: Prince William Sound, Alaska, to Baja California, México; Russia; Okhotsk Sea.

NOTES: Veined blade algae, *Hymenena* spp., are very similar looking to hidden rib seaweeds, *Cryptopleura* spp. For identification a microscope is necessary. To make things even more difficult the algae must be in reproductive mode for identification of species.

Fringed Hidden Rib

Cryptopleura ruprechtiana
(J. Agardh) Kylin, 1924

OTHER NAMES: Hidden rib, ruche, ruffled red seaweed; formerly classified as *Botryoglossum farlowianum, Botryoglossum ruprechtianum, Nitophyllum ruprechtianum.*

DESCRIPTION: Color ranges from bright rose-red to brownish-red. Thallus comprised of **flat, fan-shaped blades with frilled edges**. A midrib is visible at the base, which gives rise to a network of fine veins.

SIZE: Length to 19″ (50 cm).

HABITAT: On rocks; low intertidal zone to depths of 98′ (30 m).

RANGE: Southeast Alaska to Punta Maria, Baja California, México.

NOTES: This distinctive alga is commonly encountered and widespread. It forms large patches in the low intertidal zone. Fringed hidden rib holds male and female gametes on separate plants.

Black Tassel

Pterosiphonia bipinnata

(Postels & Ruprecht) Falkenberg, 1901

OTHER NAMES: Formerly classified as *Polysiphonia bipinnata*, *Pterosiphonia robusta*.

DESCRIPTION: Color varies from bright red to brownish-red. **Branches are very fine, cylindrical and distichous** (arranged in 2 rows on opposite sides of the axis). **Branches at the tips of the fronds grow in a single plane** and the branch diameter is uniform over the plant.

SIZE: Length to 5″ (12 cm).

HABITAT: On rocks and epiphytic on other alga; mid-intertidal zone to shallow subtidal depths.

RANGE: Bering Sea and Aleutian Islands, Alaska, to San Pedro, California; Japan; Kamchatka.

NOTES: Black tassel occurs in both exposed and sheltered sites in the spring. It is often found dried out in the sun for long periods, which causes its outer layers to turn light pink. The species also grows as an epiphyte on other seaweeds (attached to them without harming them).

Diamond Cartilage Seaweed ⓘ

Chondria dasyphylla

(Woodward) C. Agardh, 1817

OTHER NAME: Diamond cartilage weed.

DESCRIPTION: Overall color ranges from straw-colored to brownish-purple. The **main branch is slender with numerous slender, pyramidal branchlets that are irregular and** alternate.

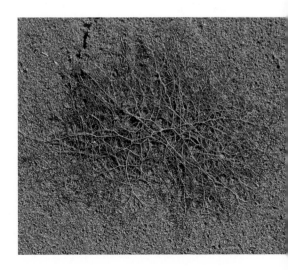

SIZE: Length to 8″ (20 cm).
HABITAT: On bedrock, rocks, shells and tidepools; mid-interitdal zone to depths of 65′ (20 m).
RANGE: British Columbia to Agua Verde, México; N. Atlantic; England; Japan; Taiwan.
NOTES: The diamond cartilage seaweed favors wave-sheltered sites. This species is introduced from the Atlantic coast. Artists who have tried to mount this species on paper have found that it tends to stain the paper.

....

Black Pine Seaweed

Neorhodomela larix (Turner) Masuda, 1982

OTHER NAMES: Black pine; formerly classified as *Fucus larix, Rhodomela larix*.
DESCRIPTION: Color of the entire organism is black to dark-brown. **The branches and side branchlets are uniform in size, coarse, very crowded and rather stiff**. The length of the side branchlets are all about the same—0.5″ (13 mm) or less.
SIZE: Length to 8″ (20 cm).
HABITAT: On rocks; mid- to low intertidal zone
RANGE: Aleutian Islands, Alaska, to Baja California, México; Japan, Siberia.
NOTES: This species thrives on rock in sandy, exposed situations such as the outer coast and in exposed rocky tidepools. Here it can grow into mats of many individuals. It is also more tolerant of sediment than other seaweeds. This alga has been found to contain bromophenols, which is believed to deter some herbivores.

Common pickleweed,
Salicornia depressa

Flowering Plants

PHYLUM ANTHOPHYTA

(OR MAGNOLIOPHYTA)

The flowering plants found in the intertidal zone lack the bright colors of flowering plants elsewhere, but they provide an important habitat for a wide array of both invertebrates and vertebrates (fish).

Common Pickleweed

Salicornia depressa Standley

OTHER NAMES: American glasswort, glasswort, perennial saltwort, Pacific samphire, pickleweed, salt horn, saltwort, samphire, sea asparagus; incorrectly annual sea asparagus; formerly classified as *Salicornia ambigua*, *Salicornia maritima*, *Salicornia pacifica*, *Salicornia virginica*.

DESCRIPTION: Color is green overall. The branches are **fleshy and succulent with jointed stems** and leaves reduced to minute scales. A **perennial** with minute flowers extending to the tips of the branches.

SIZE: Height to 12″ (30 cm) and stems that may trail to 39″ (1 m).

HABITAT: On sheltered shores at the high-tide mark and especially common in saltwater marshes and tide flats.

RANGE: Alaska to México; Atlantic coast.

NOTES: This perennial is the most common pickleweed that occurs in the Pacific Northwest. Pickleweeds have been used as food in cultures throughout the world for many generations. They are often pickled (hence their name), as well as being eaten as a fresh (and salty) veggie.

Scouler's Surfgrass

Phyllospadix scouleri W.J. Hooker, 1838

OTHER NAME: Basket grass.

DESCRIPTION: The **leaves are emerald-green**. The leaves are narrow with **3 veins that are**

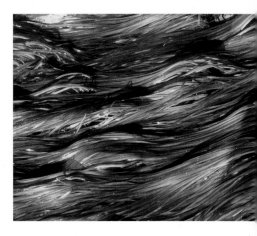

visible along the length of each leaf that are normally unbranched. The rhizome is irregular and holdfast-like that resembles a tuber that **attaches to rocks**.

SIZE: Length of leaves to 6.6′ (2 m); width to 0.2″ (5 mm).

HABITAT: On rocks of exposed shores; low intertidal zone to depths of 5′ (1.5 m).

RANGE: Sitka Sound, Alaska, to Baja California, México.

NOTES: Scouler's surfgrass is very common on rocky shores that are exposed to the full force of the surf. This common plant is found in just about all open coast sites. It provides food and shelter to many other plant and animal species. The sweet rhizomes of both surfgrass and eelgrass were traditionally eaten fresh or dried for the winter by both the Salish and Haida.

SIMILAR SPECIES: Serrulated surfgrass has tiny marginal serrations on its leaves.

Serrulated Surfgrass

Phyllospadix serrulatus

Ruprecht ex Ascherson, 1868

OTHER NAMES: Toothed surf-grass; toothed surfgrass; formerly included with *P. scouleri*.

DESCRIPTION: The plants are emerald-green. The leaves are **broad, and may be branched, with 5–7 veins that are visible** along the length of each leaf. The edge of the leaves normally have serrated margins that can be felt or observed under close scrutiny. The rhizome is short, with two roots that **attach to rocks**.

SIZE: Length to 39″ (1 m); width to 0.3″ (8 mm).

HABITAT: On rocks of exposed shorelines; low intertidal zone.

RANGE: Chirikof Island, Alaska, to Cape Arago, Oregon.

NOTES: Serrulated surfgrass resembles eelgrass with its broad leaves. This surfgrass, however, grows on the exposed coast where it attaches to rock.

SIMILAR SPECIES: Common eelgrass; Torrey's surfgrass.

Torrey's Surfgrass

Phyllospadix torreyi S. Watson, 1879

DESCRIPTION: The leaves are emerald-green, **very narrow, wiry,** branched, and are close to oval or circular in cross-section. The rhizome is irregular and resembles a tuber **that attaches to rocks.**
SIZE: Length of leaves to 10′ (3 m); width to 0.6″ (15 mm).
HABITAT: On rocks and in rocky pools of exposed shores; low intertidal zone to shallow subtidal depths.
RANGE: Alaska to Baja California, México.
NOTES: Torrey's surfgrass is common on rocky shores of the exposed coast but finds more sheltered sites to locate itself. Its slender, rounded leaves are distinctive.
SIMILAR SPECIES: Scouler's surfgrass.

Common Eelgrass

Zostera marina Linnaeus, 1753

OTHER NAMES: Common eel grass, eel grass, eelgrass.
DESCRIPTION: The **dull green leaves are flat and wide.** The plant is anchored in **muddy substrates** with slender rhizomes with numerous roots.
SIZE: Length of leaves to 4′ (1.2 m); width to 0.5″ (12 mm).
HABITAT: On muddy substrates of **protected shorelines;** low intertidal zone to depths of 20′ (6 m).
RANGE: Chukchi Sea, Alaska, to Baja California, México; Korea; Japan; Russia.
NOTES: Like common surfgrass, this is a species on which many other plants and animals depend for food and shelter. People have harvested the seeds of this species as they harvest wheat.
SIMILAR SPECIES: Japanese eelgrass.

Japanese Eelgrass ⓘ

Zostera japonica Ascherson & Graebner, 1907

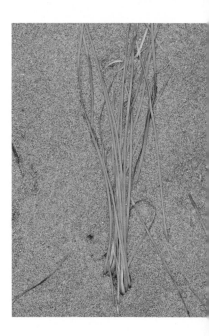

OTHER NAMES: Dwarf eelgrass; formerly classified as *Zostera nana*, *Zostera nolti*.

DESCRIPTION: The **dull green leaves are flat, fine, narrow and short**. The plant is anchored in **muddy substrates** with slender rhizomes with numerous roots.

SIZE: Length of leaves to 12″ (30 cm); width to 0.1″ (3 mm).

HABITAT: On muddy substrates; mid-intertidal zone.

RANGE: British Columbia to Oregon.

NOTES: Introduced from Japan this species survives winters as a seed, which then germinates in spring. It is much smaller in overall size and tends to colonize areas fairly quickly.

Seaside Plantain

Plantago maritima (Linnaeus, 1753)

OTHER NAMES: Goose-tongue seashore plantain, sea plantain; occasionally misspelled *Plantigo maritima*.

DESCRIPTION: The leaves are light green to brown, the stem is reddish-brown, and the flowers are greenish, changing to golden brown. L**eaves are long, narrow and tapered to a point at the tips**, and they grow from a taproot. One or more flowering stems are present, each producing numerous, **tiny flowers in crowded spikes**.

SIZE: Height to 10″ (25 cm).

HABITAT: On moist beaches, in crevices of large boulders, sandy or gravel beaches, and salt marshes; spray zone.

RANGE: Alaska to California; Arctic to Virginia; Eurasia; Patagonia; Galapagos Islands.

NOTES: This species produces its tiny flowers from June to October. Various native peoples of North America ate the young, salty leaves of the seaside plantain.

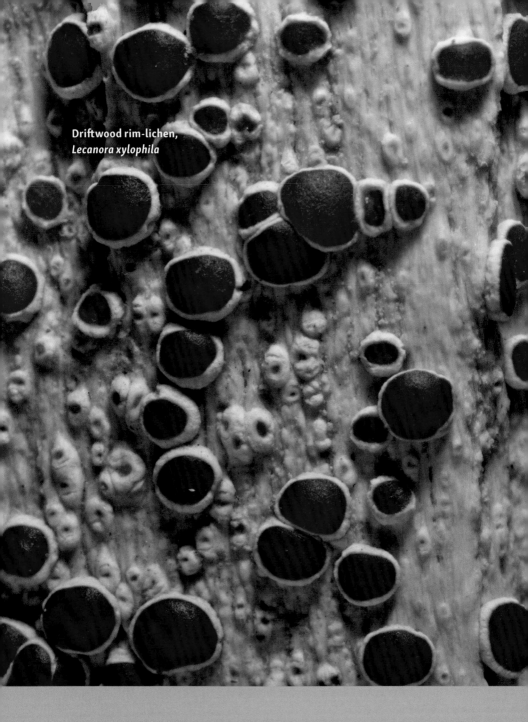

Driftwood rim-lichen,
Lecanora xylophila

Seashore Lichens

PHYLUM ASCOMYCOTINA

The phylum Ascomycotina (sac fungi) includes both lichens and cup fungi (but not true fungi). Lichens are a unique working partnership between two organisms: an algae component that photosynthesizes, much as higher plants do, and a fungus, which provides protection. Lichens reproduce both asexually and sexually. There are two types of fruiting bodies in the sexual reproduction of maritime lichens: apothecia (disk-like structures) and perithecia (tiny flask-shaped structures embedded in the thallus, or body).

Waxy Firedot

Caloplaca luteominia luteominia
(Tuck.) Zahlbr

OTHER NAME: Formerly classified as *Caloplaca laeta*.
DESCRIPTION: The thallus is frequently within the rock and is not visible. Apothecia are orange.
SIZE: Patches to 0.75″ (20 mm) in diameter; often merging with others to cover larger areas.
HABITAT: On rocks, above salt spray zone.
RANGE: Vancouver Island to California.
NOTES: This species is crustose or crust-like, lacking any leaf-like structures. It has two color phases, the common one (as pictured) with orange apothecia, and a less common phase with crimson apothecia. The waxy firedot prefers exposed sites without bird droppings. It also occurs in the Coast Mountains to at least 2,640′ (800 m) elevation.

Seaside Coccotrema Lichen

Coccotrema maritimum Brodo

DESCRIPTION: Thallus is cream colored to pinkish-gray or yellowish-gray. The apothecia are embedded in **cephalodia**, gall-like **structures, that are pink to brownish** and have flat surfaces. No soredia are present.

SIZE: Forms large patches or continuous bands. Apothecia to 0.1″ (1.5 mm) in diameter.
HABITAT: On rock; salt spray intertidal zone.
RANGE: Alaska to Washington.
NOTES: The seaside coccotrema lichen is a northern species that often forms patches or a white band above the black seaside lichen. This distinctive species can form bands that extend for significant distances.

Northern Barnacle Lichen

Collemopsidium halodytes

(Nyl.) Grube & B.D. Ryan

OTHER NAMES: Formerly classified as *Arthopyrenia halodytes, Pyrenocollema halodytes*.
DESCRIPTION: Thallus varies from brown to pale orange and is often not visible as it is located within the rock or shell of the barnacle or limpet. Perithecia are **very small black spheres**.
SIZE: Perithecia to 0.01″ (0.3 mm) in diameter.
HABITAT: On siliceous and limestone rocks as well as the **shells of barnacles, limpets,** etc.; high intertidal zone.
RANGE: British Columbia to California; Atlantic coast; Europe; Mediterranean.
NOTES: The northern barnacle lichen is a marine crustose lichen that contains cyanobacteria rather than the "normal" lichen partner—a green alga. There are not many lichens able to withstand partial submersion in sea water; however, this is one of them.

Shore Shingle Lichen

Fuscopannaria maritima (P.M. Jørg.)

OTHER NAMES: Matted lichen, seaside mouse; formerly classified as *Pannaria maritima*.
DESCRIPTION: The crustose thallus varies from dark yellow-brown to olive-brown, and is composed of **squamules that have bluish-white edges and felt-like tips**.

SIZE: Lobes to 0.1″ (3 mm) wide; patches may cover extended areas.

HABITAT: On various types of rocks; salt-spray intertidal zone.

RANGE: Alaska to Oregon.

NOTES: This lichen often goes unnoticed because it prefers shaded sites and lacks the bright colors of other species. Most truly maritime lichens contain green algae; however, this species includes cyanobacteria instead of green algae. Its common name comes from the tiny scales that make up the thallus.

....

Driftwood Rim-lichen

Lecanora xylophila Hue

OTHER NAMES: Driftwood rim lichen, volcano lichen; formerly classified as *Lecanora eyerdamii, Lecanora grantii, Lecanora laevis, Lecanora rlparla*.

DESCRIPTION: **Thallus is white to yellowish-gray.** Thickness is quite variable and the thallus may cover large areas. **Apothecia are dark reddish-brown**, smooth and shiny with a margin color that is the same as the thallus.

SIZE: Thallus may extend over large areas. Apothecia to 0.1″ (3 mm).

HABITAT: On weathered wood that has been beached for some time; spray intertidal zone.

RANGE: Alaska to Oregon; Newfoundland to Long Island, New York; northern Europe (rare).

NOTES: This lichen often produces patches of profusely crowded apothecia, which can be brightly colored on old weathered wood.

....

Mealy Sunburst Lichen

Polycauliona candelaria (L.) Frödén, Arup & Søchting

OTHER NAMES: Flame lichen, shrubby orange lichen, shining orange lichen; formerly classified as *Teloschistes lychneus, Xanthoria lychnea, Xanthoria candelaria*.

DESCRIPTION: Thallus varies from **bright yellow to orange and is covered with short leaf-like growths** that form into cushion-like shapes. Soredia are present and apothecia are rare.

SIZE: Patches to 1.25″ (3 cm) in diameter; often merging with others to cover larger areas.
HABITAT: On rocks; salt spray intertidal zone.
RANGE: British Columbia to California; circumpolar.
NOTES: The mealy sunburst lichen is not restricted to seaside sites. It is found at elevations to 6,000′ (1,800 m), on various trees and occasionally on mosses. It is often found on rocks with bird droppings, as it benefits from the nutrients in the droppings.

Blue-gray Rosette Lichen

Physcia caesia (Hoffm.) Hampe ex Fürnr., 1839

OTHER NAMES: Gray rock lace, bluegray blister lichen.
DESCRIPTION: The upper surface of the **thallus varies from grayish-white to blue-gray with spots.** The lower surface of the thallus varies from white to pale brown, often with dark tips. The thallus is foliose (leaf-like) with lobes that are convex and very strongly attached to rock. Soralia, or wart-like structures, are present on the upper surfaces. Apothecia are rare.
SIZE: Rosettes to 3″ (8 cm) in diameter.
HABITAT: On granite or calcareous rocks in beach areas, above salt spray zone.
RANGE: Circumpolar in the northern hemisphere.
NOTES: The blue-gray rosette lichen is found in a number of habitats besides the beach. It is so adaptable it is even found in alpine regions. This lichen is closely associated with bird droppings.

Smooth Seaside Firedot

Polycauliona rosei (Hasse) Arup, Frödén & Søchting

OTHER NAMES: Rose's orange lichen; formerly classified as *Caloplaca rosei*.
DESCRIPTION: **Thallus** ranges from **yellow to orange-yellow**; lower body portion is orange.

The thallus is also **distinctly cracked**.
Apothecia are sparse.

SIZE: Patches to 1.5″ (4 cm) in diameter, often merging with others to cover larger areas.

HABITAT: On intertidal rocks, above the salt spray zone, just above black seaside lichen. Exposed sites are generally avoided.

RANGE: Haida Gwaii (Queen Charlotte Islands), British Columbia, to Baja California.

NOTES: The smooth seaside firedot can be found on a wide range of rock, including volcanic, slate, sandstone and granite. Those lichens found growing on rock with bird droppings are very well developed.

....

Black Seaside Lichen

Hydropunctaria maura

(Wahlenb.) C. Keller, Gueidan & Thüs

OTHER NAMES: Black lichen, blackish blind lichen, sea tar; formerly classified as *Verrucaria maura*.

DESCRIPTION: Thallus varies from dark brown to **black** and gelatinous when wet. The thin, smooth surface changes to cracked patches around the perithecia, which are buried in the thallus and not visible, but their presence can be detected with **slight pimple-like elevations on the surface**.

SIZE: Patches to 4″ (10 cm) in diameter, more commonly in near-continuous strips to 39″ (1 m) wide, along shoreline.

HABITAT: On rocks; high intertidal to lower salt spray zones.

RANGE: Bering Sea to Washington State; Newfoundland to Massachusetts; Greenland and Ellesmere Island.

NOTES: The black seaside lichen clings tightly to its rock. It is often easier to see from a distance than up close. This is a common lichen, also found on the Atlantic coast. The Sitka periwinkle and checkered periwinkle are believed to feed on this tar-like lichen.

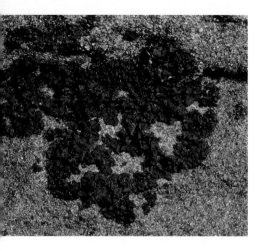

Seaside Tarspot Lichen

Verrucaria epimaura Brodo 1997

OTHER NAMES: Sea tar, black seaside lichen.
DESCRIPTION: Thallus is **dark black when wet**, yellowish-brown to black when dry, and **features a thick and lobed shape that is often circular**. Apothecia are absent.
SIZE: Patches to 1″ (2.5 cm) or more in diameter.
HABITAT: On rocks, especially siliceous rocks; high intertidal zone to the salt spray zone.
RANGE: Southeast Alaska to Vancouver Island, British Columbia.
NOTES: The seaside tarspot lichen was described as a new species of lichen in 1997. This species is found only along the coastline of the Pacific Northwest. Unlike some lichen species, which simply tolerate the salt spray, this species requires it. The seaside tarspot lichen is sometimes found growing on top of the closely related black seaside lichen.

Brown Woodscript Lichen

Xylographa opegraphella Nyl. 1857

OTHER NAME: Driftwood script lichen.
DESCRIPTION: Thallus is yellowish-white and frequently grows under the wood surface, viewed as a stain. The specialized **apothecia** (called lirellae) are **brown, elongated to ellipsoid and frequently with the grain of the wood**.
SIZE: Lirellae to 0.9″ (24 mm) in length.
HABITAT: On weathered wood; salt spray intertidal zone.
RANGE: Alaska to southern British Columbia; north Atlantic coasts; Europe.
NOTES: This lichen is easily passed by as its color closely matches the color of the wood substrate. It lives at sites with cooler temperatures. Its distinctive shape makes it an easy species for identification.

Illustrated Glossary

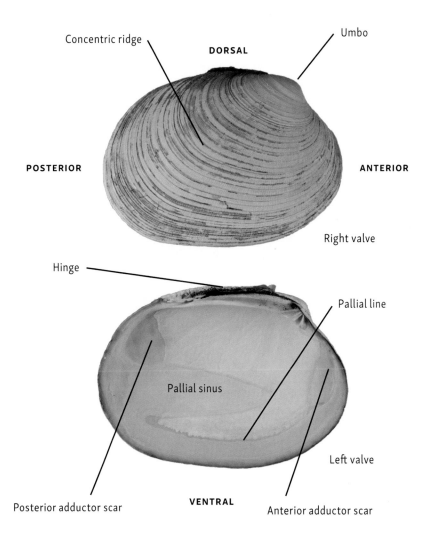

Concentric ridge

Umbo

DORSAL

POSTERIOR

ANTERIOR

Right valve

Hinge

Pallial line

Pallial sinus

Left valve

Posterior adductor scar

VENTRAL

Anterior adductor scar

BIVALVE: Thin-shelled littleneck, *Callithaca tenerrima*

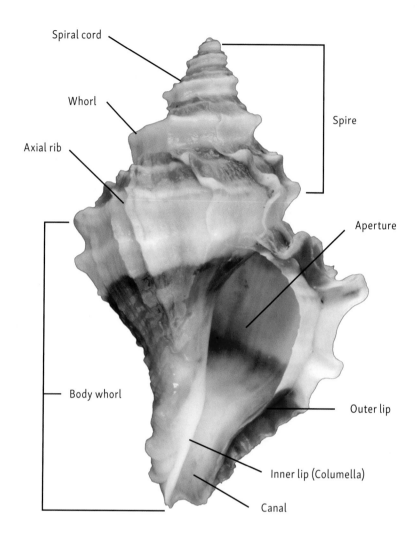

Spiral cord

Whorl

Axial rib

Spire

Aperture

Body whorl

Outer lip

Inner lip (Columella)

Canal

SNAIL: Frilled dogwinkle, *Nucella lamellosa*

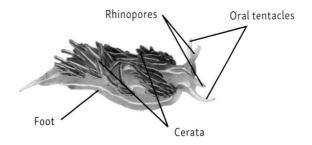

Rhinopores

Oral tentacles

Foot

Cerata

NUDIBRANCH: Opalescent nudibranch, *Hermissenda crassicornis*

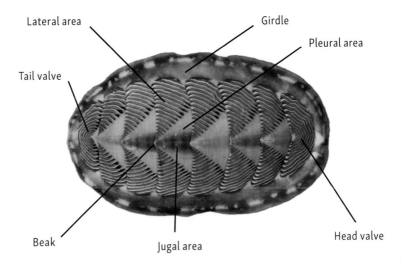

Lateral area

Girdle

Pleural area

Tail valve

Beak

Jugal area

Head valve

CHITON: Lined chiton, *Tonicella lineata*

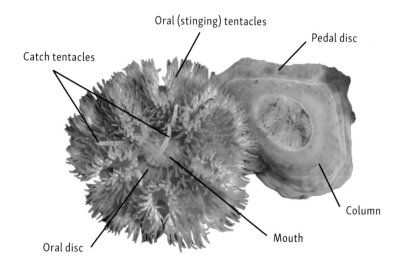

Catch tentacles

Oral (stinging) tentacles

Pedal disc

Oral disc

Mouth

Column

SEA ANEMONE: Short plumose anemone, *Metridium dianthus*

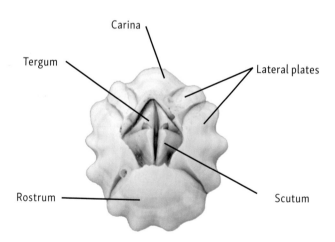

Carina

Tergum

Lateral plates

Rostrum

Scutum

BARNACLE: Common acorn barnacle, *Balanus glandula*

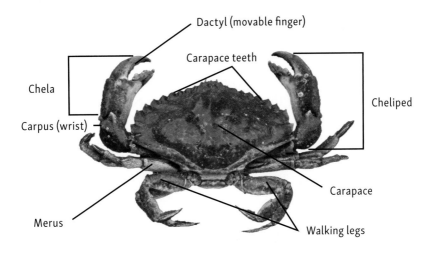

Dactyl (movable finger)

Carapace teeth

Chela

Cheliped

Carpus (wrist)

Carapace

Merus

Walking legs

CRAB: Red rock crab, *Cancer productus*

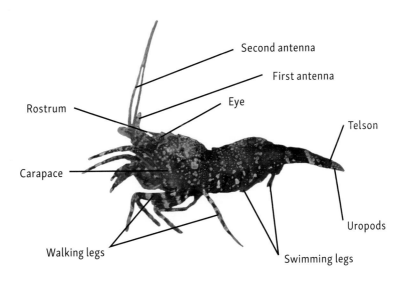

Second antenna

First antenna

Rostrum

Eye

Telson

Carapace

Uropods

Walking legs

Swimming legs

SHRIMP: Stout shrimp, *Heptacarpus brevirostris*

Glossary

ABORAL: The dorsal surface of an organism.

ACONTIA: Thin threads that contain nematocysts for use defensively by many anemones.

AELOID: A type of marine nudibranch with club-shaped cerata on the dorsal surface.

AESTHETES: Light-sensitive organs of a chiton.

ALGA (PLURAL ALGAE): Plants that live in an aquatic environment and lack a root system.

AMPHIPOD: One group of crustaceans with no carapace and normally a laterally compressed body.

ANNELID: A segmented worm; phylum Annelida.

ANTENNA (PLURAL ANTENNAE): A slender, sensory appendage that projects from the cephalic (head) area.

APERTURE: The opening into which the entire body of a snail can withdraw.

APEX: The top of a shell in a snail, limpet or other gastropod.

APICAL: Relating to the apex.

APOTHECIA: Disc-like fruiting bodies of lichens.

ATRIUM: A chamber of the heart.

BEAK: The projecting part of the hinge in bivalves.

BRYOZOAN: Moss animal.

BYSSAL THREADS/BYSSUS: Tough silk-like threads secreted by a gland in the foot of some bivalves to anchor their valves to a solid substrate.

CALLUS: A tongue-like covering of the umbilicus.

CAPITULUM: The head-like structure of a goose barnacle.

CARAPACE: The hard covering or exoskeleton that protects the upper portion of a shrimp or crab.

CARINA: A keel-shaped structure.

CARPUS: The wrist-like joint of crustaceans, such as shrimp; the third from last segment of a leg.

CATCH TENTACLE: A special tentacle of a sea anemone used for defense against other sea anemones.

CAUDAL: At or near the posterior part of the body.

CEPHALIC: Relating to the head.

CEPHALODIA: Gall-like structures on lichens that contain cyanobacteria.

CERAS (PLURAL CERATA): One of the elongated projections found on the back of aeolid nudibranchs used in gas exchange as well as extensions of the digestive gland.

CHAETAE: Bristles.

CHELA: A pincer-like organ on the terminal end of an arthropod, claw or pincer.

CHELIPED (PLURAL CHELIPEDS): The leg of an arthropod, such as crabs, that bears large pincers.

CHONDROPHORE: A spoon-shaped projection found near the hinge on one of the shells of a bivalve.

CILIA: Minute hair-like structures used for locomotion, food gathering, and other functions.

CIRRUS (PLURAL CIRRI): A tail-like extension, a penis equivalent, found on a flatworm.

CTENES: The comblike tufts of comb jellies.

COLUMELLA: The central axis of true snails.

COMMENSAL: The relationship between two different organisms in which one benefits and the other is not affected.

CONCEPTACLES: Hidden sunken cavities where the reproductive structures are located in various algae.

COSTAE: The raised ribs of gastropods.

CRUSTOSE: Crust-like in shape.

CUTICLE: The outer protective layer or part of an organism.

DACTYLUS (PLURAL DACTYLI): The segment of the crab's leg that is farthest from the body; claw(s).

DETRITUS: Debris that contains organic particles.

DEXTRAL: A right-handed spiral or clockwise coil.

DIATOM: Single-celled alga.

DICHOTOMOUS: Divided into two branches.

DORID: A type of marine nudibranch.

ELYTRA: Scales of an annelid worm.

EPIBIOTIC: Living on the surface of plants or living animals.

EPIPHYTE: A plant that lives on another plant but not as a parasite.

EXOSKELETON: An external skeleton, such as the shell of a crab.

EXCURRENT SIPHON: An opening in organisms that removes water from an organism.

EXUMBRELLA: The top of a jelly's bell.

FILTER FEEDER: An organism that strains particles of food from the water.

FLAGELLUM (PLURAL FLAGELLA): One of the whip-like extensions found on some cells, used for motility and feeding.

FOLIOSE: Leaf-like in shape.

GAMETOPHYTE: The sexual (gamete-forming) stage of algae.

GIRDLE: The muscular tissue that surrounds the eight valves of a chiton.

GLOBOSE: Globe-shaped.

GONADS: Reproductive organs.

GYNODIOECY: A sexual system in which females and hermaphrodites co-occur.

HOLDFAST: The root-like part of algae.

INCURRENT SIPHON: An opening in organisms that brings in water.

LIGAMENT: The tough, elastic part of the hinge that joins the two valves of a bivalve.

LIRELLA (PLURAL LIRELLAE): An elongated apothecium with a furrow along the center in lichens.

MADREPORITE: The sieve plate or a porous plate of a sea star that allows water to pass both in and out.

MANTLE: The soft flesh of a mollusc. Also, the sac-like hood that is present behind the eyes of an octopus.

MEDUSA: An organism that is umbrella-shaped. The final stage of a jelly.

MERUS: The segment of an arthropod's leg that is closest to its body; thigh equivalent.

MESOPLAX: A triangular accessory plate of certain bivalves.

MIDDEN: A pile of refuse.

MYOPORE: A calcareous projection from the shell of some bivalves.

NEMATOCYST: A cell that releases a stinging or entangling thread for the protection of jellies, sea anemones, and related organisms (phylum Cnidaria).

NEMERTEAN: A ribbon worm.

OCELLI: Eyespots on ribbon worms.

OPERCULUM: The calcareous or horn-like door that covers the aperture of a snail for protection when it has retreated inside its shell.

ORAL DISK: A disk with a central mouth for feeding, as found in sea anemones.

OSCULUM (PLURAL OSCULA): The large pore through which water exits from a sponge.

OSSICLE: A small calcareous element that is embedded in the outer body wall of echinoderms.

OSTIUM (PLURAL OSTIA): A minute incurrent pore through which water enters a sponge.

OTOCYST: A specialized organ involved in the balance and orientation of invertebrates.

OVOVIVIPAROUS: An animal that produces eggs that are hatched within the body, so that the young are born alive.

PALLIAL SINUS: The indentation at the hind end of the pallial line on the inner surface of the valves of bivalves.

PALMATE: Hand-like in shape.

PAPILLAE: The finger-like projections used in respiration on the dorsal side of nudibranchs.

PARAPODIA: The lateral extensions on the side of each segment of segmented worms.

PEDAL LACERATION: A form of asexual reproduction in sea anemones that consists of the pedal disc broadening, then moving away and leaving small particles of itself behind, which become new individuals.

PEDICELLARIAE: Pincer-like appendages found on sea stars and sea urchins.

PEDUNCLE: The stalk of a goose barnacle.

PELAGIC: Free-swimming in the ocean.

PERIOSTRACUM: The thin skin-like coat of organic material secreted by various molluscs on the outside of their shells.

PERITHECIUM (PLURAL PERITHECIA): A spherical, cylindrical or flask-shaped fruiting body in various lichens and fungi that contains sexual spore-bearing cells.

PHEROMONE: A chemical secreted by an animal that influences the behavior or physiology of others of the same species, often by attracting members of the opposite sex.

PHYSA: A swollen, bulb-like burrowing structure at the base of the column of an anemone.

PLANULA: Free-swimming larvae of many cnidarians.

PNEUMATOCYST: A floating structure that contains gas found on brown algae.

POLYCHAETE: Segmented worms that have paddle-like appendages, well-developed sense organs, and many setae.

POLYP: An elongated individual organism (in the phylum Cnidaria) with a mouth surrounded by tentacles at one end and attached to a substrate at the other end. Also an early stage of a jelly.

POLYPROPIONATES: Substances that are toxic to predators.

PROBOSCIS: The organ found at the "snout" of ribbon worms that can be extended. The anterior end of the digestive tract that can be found in some annelids; this organ can be everted. Also, a muscular tube found at the anterior end of the digestive tract in some snails used for feeding.

PROTANDROUS HERMAPHRODITE: An individual that changes from male to female after it grows to reach a minimum size.

PUSTULE: A raised spot or swelling; bump.

RADULA: A toothed, tongue-like ribbon in the mouth of molluscs used to rasp food from a hard surface.

RETICULATE: Net-like.

RHINOPHORE: One of a large pair of antennae-like sensory organs found on the head of nudibranchs.

RHOMBOIDAL: A parallelogram in which adjacent sides are of unequal lengths and angles that are non-right angled.

ROE: The eggs or ovaries of an invertebrate. Also, the eggs of fish.

ROSTRUM: An elongated, usually pointed structure found at the front of the carapace in various crustaceans.

SCUTUM (PLURAL SCUTA): One of two primary plates on the outer surface of a barnacle that opposes the tergum.

SESSILE: Lacking a stalk.

SETAE: Short bristles or stiff hairs found on various invertebrates.

SINISTRAL: A left-handed spiral or counter-clockwise coil.

SINUOUS: Curved.

SIPHONAL CANAL: An indentation or channel that accommodates the siphon of some gastropod shells.

SORALIA: Minute localized reproductive structures that form on the outer surface of some lichens.

SOREDIUM (PLURAL SOREDIA): A reproductive structure made of a cluster of algal cells on the thallus of a lichen.

SPICULE: A lime or glass rod that provides support for sponges.

SPOROPHYLLS: Spore-forming blades found at the base of some brown algae.

SPOROPHYTE: The asexual or vegetative stage of algae.

STIPE: The stalk of an alga.

STRIAE: Stretch marks.

SQUAMULE: A scale-like lobe on the thallus of a lichen.

SUBQUADRATE: Almost square, but with rounded corners.

SUTURE: The groove between the whorls of a gastropod.

TELSON: The last abdominal segment in crustaceans.

TENDRIL: A threadlike, leafless organ of some plants.

TENTACULAR CROWN: A cluster of tentacles of an annelid worm.

TERGUM (PLURAL TERGA): One of two primary plates on the outer surface of a barnacle that opposes the scutum.

TERMINAL: At the end.

TEST: The round internal skeleton of the sea urchin or sand dollar.

THALLUS (PLURAL THALLI): The main body of algae, lichens, and other organisms that lack roots. The holdfast or its equivalent is not included.

TUBERCLE: A nodule or small protuberance on the surface of a plant or animal.

TUBIFEROUS: Containing hollow chambers.

TUNIC: The tough outer covering of a tunicate that is made of cellulose.

TURRIFORM: Turret-like in shape.

UMBILICUS: The navel-like opening in the center of the columella at the base of true snails.

UMBO (OR UMBONE): The "beak" or prominent portion of the hinge on a bivalve.

UROPOD: The last pair of appendages in crustaceans.

VALVE: One of two calcareous coverings found on a bivalve; one of the eight shells covering the dorsal portion of a chiton.

VELIGER: The final larval stage of certain species of molluscs.

VELUM: A veil-like ring that hangs on the underside of a jelly.

VESICLES: Bladder in seaweeds; a membranous pouch in a plant or animal.

VIVIPAROUS: Producing living young.

ZOOECIUM (PLURAL ZOOECIA): Living chamber(s) constructed by a colony of zooids.

ZOOID: An individual bryozoan or moss animal within a colony.

Further Reading

General

Austin, W.C. 1985. *An Annotated Checklist of Marine Invertebrates in the Cold Temperate Northeast Pacific*, Vols. 1-3. Cowichan Bay, BC: Khoyatan Marine Laboratory.

Brodo, Irwin W., Slyvia Sharnoff, and Stephen Sharnoff. 2001. *Lichens of North America*. New Haven, CT: Yale University Press.

Carlton, J., ed. 2007. *The Light and Smith Manual. Intertidal Invertebrates from Central California to Oregon*. 4th edition, Completely Revised and Expanded. Berkeley, CA: University of California Press.

Cornwall, I.E. 1970. *Barnacles of British Columbia* (Handbook No. 7). Victoria, BC: British Columbia Provincial Museum.

Gotshall, Daniel W. 1994. *Guide to Marine Invertebrates—Alaska to Baja California*. Monterey, CA: Sea Challengers.

Harbo, R.M. 2011. *Whelks to Whales: Coastal Marine Life of the Pacific Northwest*. Madeira Park, BC: Harbour Publishing.

Jensen, Gregory C. 2014. *Crabs and Shrimps of the Pacific Coast: An E-Guide to West Coast Decapods, Alaska to Mexico*. Bremerton, WA: MolaMarine Publishing.

Hart, J.F.L. 1982. *Crabs and their Relatives of British Columbia* (Handbook No. 40). Victoria, BC: British Columbia Provincial Museum.

Kozloff, E.N. 1983. *Seashore Life of the Northern Pacific Coast: An Illustrated Guide to Northern California, Oregon, Washington and British Columbia*. Vancouver, BC: Douglas & McIntyre.

———. 1996. *Marine Invertebrates of the Pacific Northwest*. Seattle, WA: University of Washington Press.

Lamb, A., and P. Edgell. 1986. *Coastal Fishes of the Pacific Northwest*. Madeira Park, BC: Harbour Publishing.

Lamb, A., and B. Hanby. 2005. *Marine Life of the Pacific Northwest: A Photographic Encyclopedia of Invertebrates, Seaweeds and Selected Fishes*. Madeira Park, BC: Harbour Publishing.

Lamb, A., and P. Edgell. 2010. *Coastal Fishes of the Pacific Northwest*. Revised and expanded 2nd ed. Madeira Park, BC: Harbour Publishing.

Lambert, P. 1997. *Sea Cucumbers of British Columbia, Southeast Alaska and Puget Sound*. Royal British Columbia Museum Handbook. Vancouver, BC: UBC Press.

———. 2000. *Sea Stars of British Columbia, Southeast Alaska and Puget Sound*. Royal British Columbia Museum Handbook. Vancouver, BC: Royal BC Museum and UBC Press.

Lambert, P., and W.C. Austin. 2007. *Brittle Stars, Sea Urchins and Feather Stars of British Columbia, Southeast Alaska and Puget Sound*. Royal BC Museum Handbook, Victoria, BC.

Morris, R.H., et al. 1980. *Intertidal Invertebrates of California*. Stanford, CA: Stanford University Press.

O'Clair, R.M., and C.E. O'Clair. 1998. *Southeast Alaska's Rocky Shores: Animals*. Auke Bay, AK: Plant Press.

Ricketts, Edward F., and Jack Calvin. 1985. *Between Pacific Tides*. Stanford, CA: Stanford University Press.

Wrobel, D., and C. Mills. 1998. *Pacific Coast Pelagic Invertebrates: A Guide to the Common Gelatinous Animals*. Monterey, CA: Sea Challengers.

Algae

Abbott, I.A., and G.J. Hollenberg. 1976. *Marine Algae of California*. Stanford, CA: Stanford University Press.

Druehl, L.D., and B.E. Clarkston. 2016. *Pacific Seaweeds: A Guide to Common Seaweeds of the West Coast*. 2nd edition. Madeira Park, BC: Harbour Publishing.

Gabrielson, P.W., T.B. Widdowson, S.C. Lindstrom, M.W. Hawkes, and R.F. Scagel. 2000. *Keys to the Benthic Marine Algae and Seagrasses of British Columbia, Southeast Alaska, Washington and Oregon*. Phycological Contribution no. 5. Vancouver, BC: UBC Department of Botany.

Mondragon, J., and J. Mondragon. 2003. *Seaweeds of the Pacific Coast*. Monterey, CA: Sea Challengers.

O'Clair, R.M., and S.C. Lindstrom. 2000. North Pacific Seaweeds. Auke Bay, AK: Plant Press.

O'Clair, R.M., S.C. Lindstrom, and I.R. Brodo. 1996. Southeast Alaska's Rocky Shores: Seaweeds and Lichens. Auke Bay, AK: Plant Press.

Scagel, R.F., P.W. Gabrielson, D.J. Garbary, L. Golden, M.W. Hawkes, S.C. Lindstrom, J.C. Oliveira, and T.B. Widdowson. 1989. *A Synopsis of the Benthic Marine Algae of British Columbia, Southeast Alaska, Washington and Oregon*. Phycological Contribution no. 3. Vancouver, BC: UBC Department of Botany.

Molluscs

Abbott, R. Tucker. 1974. *American Seashells: The Marine Molluscs of the Atlantic and Pacific Coasts of North America*. Second Edition. New York: Van Nostrand Reinhold Company.

Behrens, David W., and Alicia Hermosillo. 2005. *Eastern Pacific Nudibranchs: A Guide to the Opisthobranchs from Alaska to Central America*. Monterey, CA: Sea Challengers.

Coan, E.V., P.V. Scott, and P.R. Bernard. 2000. *Bivalve Seashells of Western North America: Marine Bivalve Mollusks from Arctic Alaska to Baja California*. Santa Barbara, CA: Santa Barbara Museum of Natural History.

Foster, Nora R. 1991. *Intertidal Bivalves; A Guide to the Common Marine Bivalves of Alaska*. Fairbanks, AK: University of Alaska Press.

Griffith, Lela M. 1967. *The Intertidal Univalves of British Columbia* (Handbook No. 26). Victoria, BC: British Columbia Provincial Museum.

Harbo, R.M. 1997. *Shells & Shellfish of the Pacific Northwest: A Field Guide*. Madeira Park, BC: Harbour Publishing.

Morris, Percy A. 1966. *A Field Guide to Pacific Coast Shells: Including shells of Hawaii and the Gulf of California*. (The Peterson Field Guide Series) 2nd edition. Revised and Enlarged. Cambridge, MA: Houghton Mifflin Co., The Riverside Press.

Quayle, D.B. 1974. *The Intertidal Bivalves of British Columbia* (Handbook No. 17). Victoria, BC: British Columbia Provincial Museum.

Acknowledgments

I would like to thank the many people who assisted with this project in so many ways.

First, thank you to Harbour Publishing for creating this new edition and directing its production. And thanks to Peter Robson and Patricia Wolfe for their insightful editing.

Thanks to Andy Lamb (Thetis Island, BC), who graciously undertook many species identifications and confirmations.

I would also like to thank the following specialists who aided in identifying or confirming identifications, and in many instances added additional information: William Austin (sponges), Irwin M. Brodo (lichens), Sheila C. Byers (polychaete worms), Roger N. Clark (chitons), Matthew Dick (bryozoans), Doug Eernisse (chitons and limpets), Kristian Fauchald (polychaete worms), Daphne G. Fautin (sea anemones), Trevor Goward (lichens), Rick Harbo (molluscs), Leslie Harris (polychaete worms), Mike Hawkes (seaweeds), John Holle (flatworms), Gregory C. Jensen (decapods), Charles Lambert (tunicates), Gretchen Lambert (tunicates), Philip Lambert (echinoderms), John C. Ljubenkov (hydroids), Tara Macdonald (polychaete worms), Val Macdonald (polychaete worms), Catherine S. McFadden (soft corals), Bill Merilees (molluscs), Sandra Millen (nudibranchs), Claudia E. Mills (jellies), Pamela Roe (ribbon worms) and Hiroki Tomoe (polychaete worms).

In addition, my thanks go out to the following institutions for their help with site information and planning: Bamfield Marine Station; British Columbia Parks; Oregon Parks & Recreation Department; Olympic National Park, Washington; Seattle Aquarium; and Washington State Parks and Recreation Commission. Jeff Goddard (Oregon Institute of Marine Biology, Charleston, OR), Catherine Po (Vancouver Public Aquarium, Vancouver, BC) and Jim Salt (Victoria, BC) kindly gave me site suggestions and other useful information.

I would especially like to thank my son, Dusty Sept, for accompanying me on many of my field trips to the seashore. His keen interest, enthusiasm and sharp eyes are a welcome addition to each and every trip.

Index

Page numbers in **bold** refer to shell plates.